LONGER SCOTTISH POEMS

VOLUME TWO

ACKNOWLEDGEMENT

The Scottish Academic Press acknowledges the financial assistance of the Scottish Arts Council in the publication of this volume.

# LONGER SCOTTISH POEMS

Volume Two

1650–1830

*edited by*

Thomas Crawford
David Hewitt
Alexander Law

1987
SCOTTISH ACADEMIC PRESS
EDINBURGH

First published in Great Britain, 1987
by Scottish Academic Press Limited,
33 Montgomery Street, Edinburgh EH7 5JX





ISBN 0 7073 0329 x Cloth Bound
ISBN 0 7073 0510 1 Paper Bound

Typeset by Pindar (Scotland) Limited
Printed by Athenaeum Press Limited, Newcastle upon Tyne

# Contents

# Introduction

The first volume in this series covers the period 1375–1650. During the last hundred of those years five tendencies of great significance for the future of Scottish poetry may be observed. First, there were poems written in English, or in what looks like English on the printed page. William Drummond of Hawthornden (1585–1649), the most considerable Scots poet of the seventeenth century, wrote in a language which, though it would have sounded more Scottish on his lips than might be expected from its appearance, owes nothing to his medieval predecessors; and the same is true of such courtly poets as Sir Robert Ayton (1569–1638) and James Graham, Marquis of Montrose (1612–50). The writers of James VI's and Charles I's time began that custom of thirling the Scottish muse to the words, syntax and style of literary standard English, which in this volume is seen above all in the extracts from Mallet, Thomson, Beattie's *Minstrel*, Scott and Tennant, and which enabled Burns to profit from 'the *copia verborum*, the command of phraseology, which the knowledge and use of the English and Scottish dialects afforded him' (Robert Anderson to James Currie, 1799).

The second trend, also quite novel, is represented by *The Life and Death of the Piper of Kilbarchan or, The Epitaph of Habbie Simson* by Robert Sempill of Beltrees (1595?–1665?). It was important for its form, the six-line stanza rhyming AAABAB, having as a rule four strong stresses in the A lines and two in the B, known first as 'Standard Habbie' and later as the Burns stanza. More than any other verse form it became identified with the vernacular revival and therefore with a distinctively Scottish voice in poetry. Quite apart from being the progenitor of a long line of mock elegies on men and beasts, the poem on Habbie Simson is original in both matter and tone. It celebrates a local 'character', an outstanding representative of a small community whose customs and festivals are also part of the substance of the poem, rendered in a racy manner together with a 'note of pathos . . . stiffened against sentimentality by realistic detail'.[1] Thirdly, there were fresh attempts in the manner of the rustic brawl poem, a genre taking its subject matter from the life-styles of country people, though the poems were not written by plebeians. The best known early examples, *Christis Kirk on the Grene* and *Peblis to the Play* were confidently ascribed to a royal author, King James I (1394–1437): *Christis Kirk* was assigned to him by the transcriber of the Bannatyne MS (1568), the *Peblis* poem by the historian John Major (1521). Among the sixteenth-century continuations were Sir David Lyndsay's *Justing of Barbour and Watson* and Alexander Scott's *Justing and Debait*.

Fourthly, traditional ballads continued to be sung, orally transmitted and composed in ballad communities in the Borders, Aberdeenshire and other parts of Scotland.[2] Although some historians of literature still classify the ballads as 'medieval', many must have been composed in the seventeenth century or else have taken on their characteristic shape in that period. Fifthly, folk songs and popular lyrics continued to be made and sung. From the titles of the songs and tunes in *The Complaynt of Scotland* (1549) it is clear that by the mid-sixteenth century there already existed a Scottish popular song culture that borrowed extensively from the other side of the border, for many pieces mentioned in *The Complaynt* are English Tudor songs. The songs that were made and sung in Scotland during the seventeenth century, though many did not appear in print till after 1725, compensate to some extent for the dearth of longer poems in the fifty years that followed the Restoration.[3]

All five tendencies, those which were new as well as those carried forward from medieval times, reached fruition in the eighteenth century, and each acquired a quite different significance then as a vehicle for the rich experience of Scots at home and abroad. One reaction to the parliamentary union of 1707 was to try to beat the English at their own game — to achieve a European excellence in economic life, town and village planning, philosophy, speculative and applied science, historiography, and the new sociology.[4] Within literature proper this response to the challenge is seen in the work of the Scottish Augustans; perhaps it was the new Scottish passion for science that led so many of them to specialise in didactic verse, and it is surely significant that so many were medical men. One expatriate, John Arbuthnot (1667–1735), a mathematician who was also Queen Anne's personal physician and a member of the Scriblerus Club along with Pope, Swift, Gay, Congreve and others, produced a long tendentious work in heroic couplets on the theme of *Know Thyself*; a second, John Armstrong (1709–79), employed blank verse in the typically didactic *Art of Preserving Health* (1744); a third, William Falconer, brought the experience of seamanship — yet another exacting profession in which Scots have been prominent — to *The Shipwreck* (1762). James Grainger (?1721–66), another physician, reflected the Scottish involvement in the West Indies not only in his prose *Essay on the more common West India Diseases* (1764), but also in the blank verse of *The Sugar Cane: a Poem* (1764), which Dr Johnson praised in the *London Chronicle* when it first appeared, as a store of facts for 'all to whom Sugar contributes usefulness or pleasure'. We make no apology for our neglect of Grainger, but Robert Blair (1699–1746), who stayed at home as minister of Athelstaneford near Haddington, did write poetry of merit. Those who wish to sample his grim moralism should read the extracts from *The Grave* in the *Oxford Book of Eighteenth Century Verse* (pp. 304–6).

Blair is like the other Anglo-Scots in that his most interesting traits look forward to romanticism; more especially, it is his fondness for ghosts and superstitions that is 'non-Augustan'. The fact that *The Grave* is in blank verse reminds us that at the level of form, the Scots had a liking for metres other than the heroic couplet, and it is surely suggestive that so many Scots were concerned in the revival of the Spenserian stanza — Thomson, William Wilkie (1721–72), Beattie and William Julius Mickle (1735–88), for example. The Spenserian stanza is nothing if not leisurely and expansive; its 'linked sweetness long drawn out' has points in common with the prose poetry of Macpherson's Ossian, so different from the controlled balance of Dryden and Pope:

> I bade my white sails to rise, before the roar of Cona's wind. Three hundred youths looked, from their waves, on Fingal's bossy shield. High on the mast it hung, and marked the dark-blue sea — But when the night came down, I struck, at times, the warning boss: I struck, and looked on high, for fiery-haired Ul-erin.
>
> Nor wanting was the star of heaven: it travelled red between the clouds: I pursued the lovely beam, on the faint-gleaming deep. — With morning, Erin rose in mist. We came into the bay of Moi-lena, where its blue waters tumbled, in the bosom of echoing woods. — Here Cormac, in his secret hall, avoided the strength of Colc-ulla. Nor he alone avoids the foe: the blue eye of Ros-crana is there: Ros-crana, white-handed maid, the daughter of the king!
>
> (*Temora*, Book IV)

Northrop Frye has put the difference between the Augustan and the pre-romantic with his customary persuasiveness, as a contrast between literature as product and literature as process:

> Where the emphasis is on the communicated product, the qualities of consciousness take the lead: a regular metre, clarity of syntax, epigram and wit, repetition of sense in antithesis and balance rather than of sound. Swift speaks with admiration of Pope's ability to get more 'sense' into one couplet than he can into six: concentration of sense for him is clearly a major criterion of poetry. Where the emphasis is on the original process, the qualities of subconscious association take the lead, and the poetry becomes hypnotically repetitive, oracular, incantatory, dreamlike and in the original sense of the word charming. The response to it includes a subconscious factor, the surrendering to a spell. In Ossian, who carries this tendency further than anyone else, the aim is not concentration of sense but diffusion of sense . . .[5]

Macpherson's literature-as-process was the vehicle for a contemporary yearning for grandeur, even the grandiose, and for emotional liberation, and also for the creation of what John MacQueen has seen as a Tolkien-like imaginary but self-consistent world, a sort of dream-society with no relation to anything which really happened in either Scotland or Ireland.[6]

We have excluded Macpherson with some regret on the ground that what he wrote was not, properly speaking, verse, though his importance in the history of European taste was immense. We have, however, printed a canto of Beattie's *Minstrel*. The emotions which Macpherson and Beattie express are those appropriate to the movements which historians have labelled 'sentimentalism' and 'primitivism', and they are connected with ideas to be found in such Scottish philosophers as Francis Hutcheson (1694–1746) and even David Hume ('Reason is, and ought only to be, the slave of the passions'), not to speak of Rousseau. Thomson, as well as having strong links with Newtonian science, is often close to sentimentalism (e.g. his treatment of birds, the hare, sheep, and luxury's 'unreal wants' in *Winter: a Poem*, ll. 230–41, 390–5); but his main contribution to pre-romanticism was to transmit a Scottish attitude to landscape — particularly a winter landscape — into the mainstream of British and indeed European poetry. At the beginning of the next century Walter Scott summed up and transcended all this pre-romantic poetry in English. There is some similarity, in tendency at least, between his more mesmeric octosyllabics and the Ossianic poetry-as-process, and it appears as if he sometimes began a verse romance without knowing exactly how it would end. Yet the final result, however attained, always shows a definite narrative structure; and it was left to Byron in *Don Juan* and to Hogg in the neglected prose fantasia *The Three Perils of Man* to explore literature-as-process to the full.

We do not have space to examine in detail the contention that the linguistic division in Scottish writing from 1650 to 1830 mirrors a disastrous split in the Scottish psyche amounting almost to national schizophrenia.[7] Such a view, puckishly labelled the 'Caledonian antisyzygy', has rarely been questioned during the past forty years. It can be argued that the hundred years from Francis Hutcheson's ethical writings and Ramsay's *Gentle Shepherd* to the last novels of Scott and the first nay-sayings and yea-sayings of Carlyle were Scotland's greatest century. Is it not at least conceivable that these achievements took place not in spite of the split but because of it? Is division not perhaps a law of nature, seen equally in the evolution of galaxies and planetary systems and in the growth of individual minds and souls? 'Without contraries is no progression.'

No one can deny that the poetry of the vernacular revival — the poetry in Scots — is artistically better than the poems of the Scottish Augustans. Beattie's familiar epistle to Alexander Ross *is* superior to *The Minstrel*. But the attack on the Anglo-Scottish writing of this century has not confined itself to poetry. However uncertain the Scots felt about English, however great their inferiority complex (and inferiority complexes, too, can lead to success), no one who has actually read them can say that the philosopher Hume, the novelist Smollett, the biographer Boswell or the social philosophers Adam Ferguson and John Millar of Glasgow wrote bad prose; no one who has compared the Anglo-Scottish poets in this anthology with representative southern verse of the century can claim that they are noticeably inferior. Thomson's language is not 'worse' than Goldsmith's, nor Beattie's than Shenstone's.

The story of the vernacular revival has often been told; the details need not be repeated here.[8] From the outset, revival in both Scots and English was often cast in an antiquarian mould, and ballad imitation proceeded in sequence from Lady Wardlaw, Mallet and Hamilton of Bangour through to Scott and Hogg. But the substance poured into that matrix was predominantly contemporary — the living speech of the people, in all its many forms. Through its special historical position lowland Scotland was able in this century to develop a unique poetic medium for expressing the ideas and everyday experiences of ordinary men and women which the standard language and dialects of the south were incapable of equalling. Even poetry-as-process achieved more satisfying expression here than in the English of Ossian, Scott or Byron, because of the colloquial vigour of the vernacular and the expansive fluidity of the Habbie stanza, from

Ramsay's exchange of verse letters with Hamilton of Gilbertfield down to *Holy Willie's Prayer*, the Burns epistles, and *Death and Dr Hornbook*:

Sae I gat paper in a blink,
An' down gaed stumpie in the ink:
Quoth I, 'Before I sleep a wink,
        I vow I'll close it;
An' if ye winna mak it clink,
        By Jove I'll prose it!'

Sae I've begun to scrawl, but whether
In rhyme, or prose, or baith thegither,
Or some hotch-potch that's rightly neither,
        Let time mak proof;
But I shall scribble down some blether
        Just clean aff-loof.
                (Burns, *Second Epistle to Lapraik*, ll. 31–42)

The best poems of the vernacular revival are surely unsurpassed for their spontaneity anywhere in the English-speaking world.

In the longer poems represented in this collection, the values of the revival are most obviously revealed in those narratives which use the *Christis Kirk* tradition and the 'donnybrook' overtones of the rustic brawl: again and again the emphasis is on realism, comedy, genre pictures and restricted local scenes (Ramsay's additions to *Christis Kirk*, *The Christmass Bawing of Monimusk*, *Hallow-Fair*, *Leith Races*, Keith's *Farmer's Ha'*, Mayne's *Siller Gun*, Burns's *Love and Liberty*, *The Holy Fair* and *Halloween*). The most philosophic criticism of life occurs where satire prevails (*The Twa Dogs*, *The Holy Fair*). The finest vernacular poems do not rely solely on native Scots traditions, but are interfused with attitudes drawn from the Augustans, the sentimentalists and general Enlightenment culture. Poems featuring rural communities draw on the centuries-old European conventions of pastoral (*The Gentle Shepherd*, Ross's *Helenore*, *The Farmer's Ingle*, *The Twa Dogs*, *The Cotter's Saturday Night*), and gain an extra dimension from both echoes and implied criticism of those conventions. The social life of the city is treated as well as that of the clachan or the country town: in Allan Ramsay's mock elegies on low-life Edinburgh characters, or Fergusson's *Auld Reikie*, which owes so much to creative imitation of John Gay, English Augustan modes are used to lubricate the native realism. Even folk and popular songs, those slightest and apparently most ephemeral pieces, play their part in larger works. The expanded version of *The Gentle Shepherd* was a ballad opera, containing twenty-one songs written to popular tunes; Burns's anti-pastoral *Love and Liberty* (*The Jolly Beggars*) works the principal narrative stanza forms of the vernacular revival into a superb comic, satiric and libertarian synthesis with the song tradition, to which the Augustan *English* Newgate-pastoral, Gay's *Beggar's Opera*, also makes a contribution.

All currents in this century lead to the two giants, Burns and Scott, from whom new currents flow to irrigate both English and European literature. The most original parts of *To a Mouse* and *The Cotter's Saturday Night* point forward to the Wordsworth of the *Lyrical Ballads*. From Burns and from the popular ballad the Scottish values of community are transmitted to Scott, influence his treatment of poor and outcast characters in his novels, and are then passed on in a variety of ways to the nineteenth-century novel in England, Europe and America. Even the poems we have included primarily for their historical interest are worthy in their own right, and we hope that old favourites and familiar poems alike will give hours of pleasure both in and furth of Scotland.

## NOTES TO THE INTRODUCTION

1. K. Buthlay, '*Habbie Simson*', in *Bards and Makars* (Glasgow, 1977), 214–20.
2. See D. Buchan, *The Ballad and the Folk* (London, 1972).
3. See T. Crawford, *Love, Labour and Liberty* (Cheadle, 1976) and *Society and the Lyric* (Edinburgh, 1979).
4. See A. C. Chitnis, *The Scottish Enlightenment: a social history* (London, 1976).
5. 'Towards defining an age of sensibility', *English Literary History*, 23 (1956), 147–8.
6. Introduction to *Poems of Ossian* (Edinburgh, 1971).
7. See D. Daiches, *The Paradox of Scottish Culture* (London, 1964).
8. See e.g. M. Lindsay, *History of Scottish Literature* (London, 1977) and J. Butt and G. Carnall, 'Scottish Poetry' in *The Mid-Eighteenth Century*, being vol. VIII of *The Oxford History of English Literature* (Oxford, 1979).

# Note on Further Reading

In addition to the works by Buchan, Crawford, Chitnis, Daiches, Lindsay, and Butt and Carnall mentioned in the notes to this introduction, the reader is recommended to consult a good general history of the period, such as William Ferguson's *Scotland: 1689 to the Present* (1968) being vol. IV of *The Edinburgh History of Scotland*, and T. C. Smout's *A History of the Scottish People* (London, 1969), whose emphasis is primarily social. *Scottish Poetry: a critical survey*, edited by James Kinsley (London, 1955) is valuable for the two articles covering the period — A. M. Oliver, 'The Scottish Augustans' (pp. 119–49) and D. Daiches, 'Eighteenth-Century Vernacular Poetry' (pp. 150–84). John Speirs, *The Scots Literary Tradition* (London, 1940: 1962) and Kurt Wittig, *The Scottish Tradition in Literature* (Edinburgh and London, 1958: 1972) can still stimulate, but the best account of the vernacular revival remains M. P. McDiarmid's in vol. I of The Scottish Text Society's edition of Robert Fergusson (Edinburgh, 1954). A. M. Kinghorn's 'Biographical and Critical Introduction' in vol. IV of the S.T.S. edition of Allan Ramsay (1970) is invaluable, and no serious student should neglect the following treatments of the *Christis Kirk* tradition: James Kinsley, 'The Rustic Inmates of the Hamlet', *A Review of English Literature*, 1 (1960), and Allan H. Maclaine, 'The Christis Kirk Tradition: its evolution in Scots poetry to Burns', *Studies in Scottish Literature*, 2, nos. 1, 2, 3 and 4 (1964). Of the Scottish Augustans not represented in this anthology, the following are featured in the *Oxford Book of Eighteenth Century Verse*: Armstrong, Blair, Falconer, Grainger, and Mickle.

# Note on the Text

We have drawn up a set of rules for ourselves and interpreted them flexibly, even as regards the definition of 'longer poems'. Thus we have set our faces against lyrics and epistles however long — but included Cleland's *Hallow my Fancie* and Beattie's *To Alexander Ross*; and we have drawn the divide at 100 lines, but made an exception of *William and Margaret* (68 lines), and again *To Alexander Ross* (96). So far as possible we have aimed to print complete poems, or at least whole cantos: the exceptions here are Ross's *Helenore* and Keith's *Farmer's Ha'*, where we have given substantial extracts. The introductory epistles to the various cantos of *Marmion*, of which we print two, can almost stand in their own right as separate poems.

The source of the texts is clearly stated, either in the introductory paragraphs to each author or in the notes. We have set our faces against eclecticism: our first principle has been to select what seems the best single text on literary grounds, and publish that with as few substantive emendations as possible. For Ramsay, Fergusson and Ross we have gone to the Scottish Text Society's editions, and we must express our thanks to the Society for its permission to use them. For Burns and Scott we have not reproduced modern editions, but chosen early printings or manuscripts. Accidentals have been modernised, but not as radically as we could wish. Since the spelling of Scots in the eighteenth century was chaotic, reflecting the general linguistic uncertainty, with the same author often varying his practice from poem to poem and even in the course of the same work, there are attractive arguments for drawing up a standard orthography on the lines suggested by David Purves (*Scottish Literary Journal*, Supplement 9, Spring 1979, pp. 62–76) and applying it to every text from Ramsay to Hogg. But there is no agreement on such an orthography; its imposition might sometimes obscure real and subtle distinctions in the poems; the S.T.S. texts, conservative in the extreme, are what we have become accustomed to in Ramsay and Fergusson; and nineteenth-century editors of Burns long ago established a set of conventions which have been continued in the twentieth-century editions consulted by thousands of ordinary readers and devoted Burnsians. To go too violently against current practice would cause offence to many readers. Similar considerations hold good for the poems written in English: for example, to respect vernacular texts' alternation between *ed*, *'d* and *t* for the preterite of weak verbs but change every Scots Augustan *'d* to *ed* would create an imbalance in the anthology as a whole.

As a general rule, we have respected the spelling and punctuation of our chosen texts, while neglecting many features that reflect eighteenth-century printing practices but are not themselves meaningful. We have been fairly ruthless with initial capitals, except in proper names and abstractions which are clearly felt to be personifications and have therefore the same weight as proper names; and we have employed single quotation marks in the first instance in every case. Our instincts have been radical but our practice has been conservative so far as matters of substance are concerned.

# William Cleland
## 1661?–1689

Little is known about Cleland's birth and upbringing, but the name appears in the matriculation rolls of Edinburgh University in 1676 and 1678. He was a zealous presbyterian and took part in the battle of Drumclog in 1679, when he was about eighteen years of age, and he was a captain in the army defeated by Claverhouse at Bothwell Bridge in the same year. He sought refuge in Holland, where he remained, except for one brief visit to Scotland, until the Revolution of 1688. When his friend the Earl of Angus raised a regiment on the side of the government, Cleland became its lieutenant-colonel. That regiment was the Cameronians. Cleland brilliantly and successfully defended Dunkeld against the Highland army that had formerly been Claverhouse's, and, like Claverhouse, he died in the hour of victory.

A volume of Cleland's verse was published in 1697: most of it reflects his political and religious interests. The text we reproduce, from Watson's *Choice Collection* of 1706, bears the following note: 'It was thought fit to insert the following verses, because the one half of them (*viz.* from this mark *** to the end) were writ by Lieutenant Colonel Clealand of my Lord Angus's Regiment, when he was a student in the College of Edinburgh, and 18 years of age'. The mark is placed opposite line 81.

*Editions:*

*A Collection of Several Poems and Verses . . . By Mr William Cleland . . .* (1697).

*A Choice Collection of Comic and Serious Scots Poems*, ed. James Watson (Edinburgh, 1706); ed. Harriet Harvey Wood, Scottish Text Society (Edinburgh, 1977).

*Biography:*

*Dictionary of National Biography.*

## HALLOW MY FANCIE, WHITHER WILT THOU GO?

In melancholick Fancie,
   Out of my self,
In the Vulcan dancie,
All the world surveying,
No where staying,
   Just like a Fairie Elf:
Out o'er the tops of highest mountains skipping,
Out o'er the hills, the trees and vallies tripping,
Out o'er the ocean seas, without an oar or shipping.
   Hallow[n] my Fancie, whither wilt thou go?

Amidst the misty vapours,
   Fain would I know,
What doth cause the tapours:
Why the clouds benight us,
And afright us,
   While we travel here below!
Fain would I know, what makes the roaring thunder,
And what these lightnings be that rent the clouds asunder
And what these comets are, on which we gaze and wonder!
   Hallow my Fancie, whither wilt thou go?

Fain would I know the reason,
   Why the little ant,
All the summer season,
Layeth up provision,
On condition,
   To know no winter's want:
And how these huse-wives, that are so good and painful,
Do unto their husbands prove so good and gainful:
And why the lazie drons, to them do prove disdainful.
   Hallow my Fancie, whither wilt thou go?

Ships, ships, I will descrie you,
   Amidst the main,
I will come and try you,
What you are protecting,
And projecting,
   What's your end and aim.
One goes abroad for merchandise and treading,
Another stays to keep his country from invading,
A third is coming home with rich and wealth of loading.
   Hallow my Fancie, whither wilt thou go?

13 *tapours*: tapers, lights    37 *treading*: trading

When I look before me,
   There I do behold,
There's none that sees or knows me;
All the world's a gadding,
Running madding,
   None doth his station hold.
He that is below, envieth him that riseth,
And he that is above, him that's below despiseth,
So ev'ry man his plot and counter-plot deviseth.
Hallow my Fancie, whither wilt thou go?

Look, look, what busling
   Here I do espy;
Each another jusling,
Ev'ry one turmoiling,
Th' other spoiling,
   As I did pass them by.
One sitteth musing in a dumpish passion,
Another hangs his head, because he's out of fashion,
A third is fully bent on sport and recreation:
Hallow my Fancie, whither wilt thou go?

Amidst the foamie ocean,
   Fain would I know,
What doth cause the motion,
And returning,
In its journeying,
   And doth so seldom swerve!
And how these little fishes, that swim beneath salt water
Do never blind their eye, me thinks, it is a matter,
An inch above the reach of old Erra Pater![n]
Hallow my Fancie, whither wilt thou go?

Fain would I be resolved,
   How things are done!
And where the bull was calved,
Of bloody Phalaris![n]
And where the taylor is,
   That works to th' man in th' moon!
Fain would I know how Cupid aims so rightly!
And how these little fairies do dance and leap so lightly!
And where fair Cynthia[n] makes her ambles nightly!
Hallow my Fancie, whither wilt thou go?

***

In conceit like Phaëton,[n]
I'll mount Phœbus chair:
Having ne'er a hat on,
All my hair's a burning,
In my journeying,
Hurrying through the air.
Fain would I hear his fiery horses neighing!
And see how they on foamy bitts are playing!
All the stars and planets I will be surveying!
Hallow my Fancie, whither wilt thou go?

O from what ground of nature,
Doth the pelican,[n]
That self devouring creature,
Prove so froward,
And untoward,
Her vitals for to strain!
And why the subtile fox, while in death's wounds is lying
Doth not lament his pangs by howling and by crying!
And why the milk-white swan[n] doth sing when she's a dying!
Hallow my Fancie, whither wilt thou go?

Fain would I conclude this,
At least make essay,
What similitude is,
Why fowls of a feather
Flock and fly together,
And lambs know beasts of prey![n]
How natur's alchymists,[n] these small laborious creatures!
Acknowledge still a prince in ordering their matters,
And suffer none to live, who slothing lose their features!
Hallow my Fancie, whither wilt thou go?

I'm rapt with admiration,
When I do ruminate,
Men of an occupation,
How each one calls him brother,
Yet each invieth other,
And yet still intimate!
Yea, I admire to see, some natures farther sundred,
Than antipodes to us. Is it not to be wondred,
In myriads ye'll find, of one mind scarce an hundred!
Hallow my Fancie, whither wilt thou go?

What multitude of notions
Doth perturb my pate,
Considering the motions.
How th' heav'ns are preserved
And this world served,
In moisture, light and heat!
If one spirit sits the outmost circle turning,[n]
Or one turns another continuing in journeying,
If rapid circles motion be that which they call burning!
Hallow my Fancie, whither wilt thou go?

Fain also would I prove this,
By considering,
What that, which you call love, is:
Whether it be a folly,
Or a melancholy,
Or some heroick thing!
Fain I'd have it prov'd, by one whom love hath wounded
And fully upon one his desire hath founded,
Whom nothing else could please tho' the world were rounded!
Hallow my Fancie, whither wilt thou go?

To know this world's center,
Height, depth, breadth, and length,
Fain would I adventure,
To search the hid attractions,
Of magnetick actions,
And adamantick strength![n]
Fain would I know, if in some lofty mountain,
Where the moon sojourns, if there be trees or fountain,
If there be beasts of prey, or yet be fields to hunt in!
Hallow my Fancie, whither wilt thou go?

Fain would I have it tried,
By experiment,
By none can be denied;
If in this bulk of nature,
There be voids less or greater,
Or all remains compleat!
Fain would I know, if beasts have any reason!
If falcons killing eagles do commit a treason!
If fear of winter's want makes swallows fly the season!
Hallow my Fancie, whither wilt thou go?

Hallow my Fancie, hallow,
  Stay, stay at home with me,
I can thee no longer follow,
For thou hast betray'd me
And bewray'd me;
  It is too much for thee.
Stay, stay at home with me, leave off thy lofty soaring,
Stay thou at home with me, and on thy books be poring,
For he that goes abroad, lays little up in storing:
Thou'rt welcome home my Fancie, welcome home to me.

# Lady Wardlaw
## 1677–1727

Lady Wardlaw was born Elizabeth Halkett, daughter of Sir Charles Halkett of Pitfirran, in Fife, and married Sir Henry Wardlaw of Pitreavie in 1696. Little is known of her life, but she wrote a number of songs as well as *Hardyknute*. That poem first appeared anonymously in a folio version published by James Watson, Edinburgh, in 1719, and it is this version we have used here. Allan Ramsay later added thirteen stanzas of his own, and with that addition the poem appeared in his *Ever Green* in 1724, and his *Tea-Table Miscellany* in 1726.

As a little boy, Walter Scott, when he lived with his grandfather and aunt at Sandyknowe near Kelso, learned *Hardyknute* by heart: 'The ballad of Hardyknute I was early master of to the great annoyance of almost our only visitor, the worthy clergyman of the parish, Dr Duncan, who had not patience to have a sober chat interrupted by my shouting forth this ditty. Methinks I now see his tall thin emaciated figure, his legs cased in clasped gambadoes, and his face of a length that would have rivalled the Knight of Lamancha's, and hear him exclaiming, "One may as well speak in the mouth of a cannon as where that child is".' (*Scott on Himself*, ed. David Hewitt, Edinburgh, 1981, pp. 13–14). Scott said later: 'It was the first poem I ever learnt — the last I shall ever forget' (J. G. Lockhart, *Life of Scott*, ch. 2), which illustrates fittingly the exciting effect this fake ballad had even seventy years after its first appearance. It has all the traditional attributes of the heroic ballad — the pride in military and athletic skills, the comradeship of men, the respect for women, patriotism, admiration for the chivalry even of an enemy, exciting confused battle, simplicity of expression. It may be 'irreconcilable with all chronology' (Scott, *Poetical Works*, 1833, IV, 17), but it goes with a swing and evokes picturesque images. The language includes words that have a Scottish sound, are roughly similar to known Scots words — e.g. twirtle, darr, glist, meed — but are not elsewhere found with the meanings that seem to be suggested. Fake as it is, this poem turned men's minds towards the traditional ballads of Scotland, and influenced the collecting of them that is a feature of the later eighteenth century. The modern reader may still find these lines vivid and exciting.

*Bibliography:*
*Dictionary of National Biography.*
Henry Grey Graham, *Scottish Men of Letters in the Eighteenth Century* (London, 1901).

## HARDYKNUTE, A FRAGMENT

Stately stept he east the wa,
   And stately stept he west,
Full seventy years he now had seen
   Wi' scarce seven years of rest.
He liv'd when Britons breach of faith
   Wrought Scotland mickle wae:
And ay his sword tauld to their cost
   He was their deadly fae.

High on a hill his castle stood
   With ha's and tow'rs a height,
And goodly chambers fair to see,
   Where he lodg'd mony a knight.
His dame sae peerless anes and fair
   For chast and beauty deem'd
Nae marrow had in all the land,
   Save Elenor the Queen.

Full thirteen sons to him she bare
   All men of valour stout;
In bloody fight with sword in hand
   Nine lost their lives but doubt:
Four yet remain, lang may they live
   To stand by liege and land,
High was their fame, high was their might
   And high was their command.

Great love they bare to Fairly fair,
   Their sister saft and dear,
Her girdle shaw'd her middle gimp
   And gowden glist her hair.
What waefou wae her beauty bred!
   Waefou to young and auld,
Waefou I trow to kyth and kin,
   As story ever tauld.

The King of Norse in summer tyde,
   Puff'd up with pow'r and might,
Landed in fair Scotland the isle,
   With mony a hardy knight:

6 *mickle wae*: great woe
14 *chast*: chastity
15 *marrow*: equal
20 *but*: without
27 *gimp*: slim

The tydings to our good Scots King
   Came, as he sat at dine,
With noble chiefs in brave aray
   Drinking the blood-red wine.

'To horse, to horse, my royal liege,
   Your faes stand on the strand,
Full twenty thousand glittering spears
   The King of Norse commands.'
'Bring me my steed, page, dapple-gray',
   Our good King rose and cry'd,
A trustier beast in all the land
   A Scots King never try'd.

'Go little page, tell Hardyknute,
   That lives on hill so hie,
To draw his sword the dread of faes,
   And haste and follow me.'
The little page flew swift as dart,
   Flung by his master's arm,
'Come down, come down, Lord Hardyknute
   And rid your King of harm.'

Then red red grew his dark-brown cheeks,
   Sae did his dark-brown brow,
His looks grew keen as they were wont
   In dangers great to do;
He's ta'en a horn as green as glass,
   And gi'en five sounds sae shrill
That trees in green wood shook thereat,
   Sae loud rang every hill.

His sons in manly sport and glee,
   Had past that summer's morn,
When lo, down in a grassy dale,
   They heard their father's horn.
'That horn', quo' they, 'ne'er sounds in peace,
   We've other sport to bide';
And soon they hy'd them up the hill,
   And soon were at his side.

'Late late yestreen I ween'd in peace
   To end my lengthened life,
My age might well excuse my arm
   Frae manly feats of strife;

71 *hy'd*: hastened

But now that Norse do's proudly boast
  Fair Scotland to inthrall,
It's ne'er be said of Hardyknute,
  He fear'd to fight or fall.

'Robin of Rothsay, bend thy bow,
  Thy arrows shoot sae leel,
Mony a comely countenance
  They've turn'd to deadly pale:
Brade Thomas, take you but your lance,
  You need nae weapons mair,
If you fight wi't as you did anes
  'Gainst Westmoreland's fierce heir.

'Malcom, light of foot as stag
  That runs in forest wild,
Get me my thousands three of men
  Well bred to sword and shield:
Bring me my horse and harnisine
  My blade of mettal clear.'
If faes but ken'd the hand it bare,
  They soon had fled for fear.

'Farewell my dame sae peerless good,'
  And took her by the hand,
'Fairer to me in age you seem,
  Than maids for beauty fam'd:
My youngest son shall here remain
  To guard these stately towers,
And shut the silver bolt that keeps
Sae fast your painted bowers.'

And first she wet her comely cheeks,
  And then her boddice green,
Her silken cords of twirtle twist,
  Well plett with silver sheen;
And apron set with mony a dice
  Of needle-wark sae rare,
Wove by nae hand, as ye may guess,
  Save that of Fairly fair.

And he has ridden o'er moor and moss,
  O'er hills and mony a glen,
When he came to a wounded knight
  Making a heavy mane;

82 *leel*: accurately
85 *brade*: broadly built
93 *harnisine*: harness
107 *twirtle*: ?twisted thread
108 *plett*: pleated
109 *dice*: square, check

'Here man I lye, here man I dye,
  By treacherie's false guiles,
Witless I was that e'er ga' faith
  To wicked woman's smiles.'

'Sir Knight gin you were in my power
  To lean on silken seat,
My lady's kindly care you'd prove,
  Who ne'er knew deadly hate;
Her self wou'd watch you a the day,
  Her maids a dead of night;
And Fairly fair your heart wou'd chear,
  As she stands in your sight.'

* * * * *

Syne he has gane far hynd out o'er
  Lord Chattan's land sae wide,
That lord a worthy wight was ay
  When faes his courage say'd:
Of Pictish race by mother's side,
  When Picts rul'd Caledon,
Lord Chattan claim'd the princely maid,
  When he sav'd Pictish crown.

* * * * *

When bows were bent and darts were thrown,
  For thrang scarce cou'd they flee,
The darts clove arrows as they met,
  The arrows dart the tree.
Lang did they rage and fight fow fierce,
  With little skaith to man,
But bloody, bloody was the field,
  Ere that lang day was done.

The King of Scots that sinle brook'd
  The war that look'd like play,
Drew his brade sword, and brake his bow,
  Sin bows seem'd but delay;
Quoth noble Rothsay, 'Mine I'll keep,
  I wat it's bleed a score.'
'Haste up my merry men' cry'd the King
  As he rode on before.

119 *ga'*: gave
129 *hynd*: hence
132 *say'd*: tested
138 *thrang*: press of bodies
141 *fow*: full
142 *skaith*: harm
145 *sinle*: seldom

The King of Norse he sought to find,
With him to mense the faught,
But on his forehead there did light
A sharp and fatal shaft;
As he his hand put up to feel
The wound, an arrow keen,
O waefou chance! there pinn'd his hand
In midst between his een.

'Revenge, revenge,' cry'd Rothsay's heir,
'Your mail-coat sha' na bide
The strength and sharpness of my dart';
Then sent it through his side:
Another arrow well he mark'd,
It pierc'd his neck in twa,
His hands then quat the silver reins,
As low as earth did fa.

Sair bleeds my liege, sair, sair he bleeds,
Again wi' might he drew
And gesture dread his sturdy bow,
Fast the braid arrow flew:
Wae to the knight he ettled at,
Lament now Queen Elgreed,
High dames too wail your darling's fall,
His youth and comely meed.

'Take aff, take aff his costly jupe'
(Of gold well was it twin'd,
Knit like the fowler's net through which
His steelly harness shin'd)
'Take, Norse, that gift frae me, and bid
Him venge the blood it bears;
Say, if he face my bended bow,
He sure nae weapon fears.'

Proud Norse with giant body tall,
Braid shoulders and arms strong,
Cry'd, 'Where is Hardyknute sae fam'd
And fear'd at Britain's throne:
Tho' Britons tremble at his name,
I soon shall make him wail,
That e'er my sword was made sae sharp,
Sae saft his coat of mail.'

154 *mense*: adorn
176 *meed*: ?appearance
177 *jupe*: tunic
173 *ettled*: aimed

That brag his stout heart cou'd na bide,
  It lent him youthfou might:
'I'm Hardyknute this day', he cry'd,
'To Scotland's King I heght,
To lay thee low as horse's hoof;
  My word I mean to keep.'
Syne with the first stroke o'er he strake
  He garr'd his body bleed.

Norse een like gray gosehawk's stood wild
  He sigh'd wi' shame and spite;
'Disgrac'd is now my far fam'd arm
  That left you power to strike:'
Then ga' his head a blow sae fell,
  It made him down to stoop,
As laigh as he to ladies us'd
  In courtly guise to lout.

Fow soon he rais'd his bent body,
  His bow he marvell'd sair,
Sin blows till then on him but darr'd
  As touch of Fairly fair:
Norse marvell'd too as sair as he
  To see his stately look;
Sae soon as e'er he strake a fae,
  Sae soon his life he took.

*　*　*　*　*

There on a lee where stands a cross
  Set up for monument,
Thousands fow fierce that summer's day
  Kill'd, keen war's black intent,
Let Scots, whilst Scots, praise Hardyknute,
  Let Norse the name ay dread
Ay how he faught, aft how he spar'd,
  Shall latest ages read.

*　*　*　*　*

Loud and chill blew westlin wind,
  Sair beat the heavy shower,
Mirk grew the night ere Hardyknute
  Wan near his stately tower,

193 *brag*: boast
196 *heght*: ?belong
200 *garr'd*: caused to
205 *fell*: cruel
208 *lout*: bow down
211 *darr'd*: glanced
217 *lee*: meadow
227 *mirk*: dark
228 *wan*: won

His tow'r that us'd wi' torches light
   To shine sae far at night,
Seem'd now as black as mourning weed,
   Nae marvel sair he sigh'd.

*   *   *   *   *

# Allan Ramsay
## 1684–1758

This remarkable man, born in Leadhills, came to Edinburgh about the year 1700. After apprenticeship he became a wig-maker, and seems to have continued in that trade until about 1719. He early showed an interest in writing, and was a founder member of a society of young men called the Easy Club, which existed to promote discussion and the writing of verse. Some of his earliest poems were written for this club, and his popularity soon spread when he published individual poems — *Christ's Kirk on the Green* is one — and his collected *Poems* by subscription in 1721 and 1728. By that time wig-making had given way to bookselling, and Ramsay in his shop in the Luckenbooths had become the prominent figure in Edinburgh he was to remain throughout his life.

Ramsay's originality is seen not only in his considerable production of poetry — much of it ephemeral — but in other ways that affected the social and cultural life of Edinburgh and Scotland. In 1725 he founded the first subscription lending library, certainly in Scotland and probably in the United Kingdom. In 1729 he and his friends established the first Scottish school for painting, the Academy of St Luke, where his distinguished son received part of his early training in the art. He had always been interested in the theatre — his play, *The Gentle Shepherd*, which is discussed below, had been very successful — and in 1736 he opened, and for a short time ran, a theatre in Edinburgh. This venture, to his disappointment, was abruptly ended by the influence of extremists in the Edinburgh Presbytery. Ramsay devoted himself to the older Scottish literature, and his collection of songs, *The Tea-Table Miscellany* (4 vols, 1723–37) gathered together a large number mainly of Scots songs that might otherwise have been forgotten. In this he enlisted the help of young writers, some of them like David Mallet and William Hamilton of Bangour then students at Edinburgh University. *The Ever Green* (2 vols, 1724) is a collection of the older Scots poems, and it is typical of Allan Ramsay that to the works of Henryson, Dunbar, and the other Makars he did not hesitate to add something of his own in the antique style. Such a poem is *The Vision*. Judgment of his editing in *The Tea-Table Miscellany* and *The Ever Green* has to bear in mind, on the one hand that he preserved and brought to a wide audience songs and poems that might have been lost, and on the other that he did not scruple to alter old words or add new ones more to his own taste, an attitude not in keeping with the standards of modern scholarship.

In *Christ's Kirk on the Green*, Ramsay took an old poem, believed in his day to have been written by King James I, and added first one canto and later another. The two additional cantos are reproduced here as they appeared in Ramsay's

*Poems* of 1721. The first canto had featured a country dance which developed into a riot, and Ramsay continues this theme with descriptions of the rough brawling and excitements of a rustic wedding. The attractive stanza used in the Bannatyne Manuscript (1568) ends as follows:

In thair new kirtillis of gray full gay
At chrystis kirk of the grene.

Like James Watson, in whose *Choice Collection*, 1706, the poem also appears, Ramsay gives here the simpler form of:

In new kirtles of gray
Fou gay that day

which was later used and modified by Skinner, Fergusson, Burns, and other vernacular poets. In *The Vision* Ramsay imitates, not always accurately, the older Scots poets he was popularising in *The Ever Green*, but the style, with all its faults, is well suited to the expression of patriotic sentiments. *The Monk and the Miller's Wife* is really an old tale found with variations in French and Italian poems of the Middle Ages, here given a Scottish setting and some astringent Scots humour. In 1720 Ramsay published *Patie and Roger: A Pastoral*, in which the two shepherds talk about their loves for Peggy and Jenny. This gave him the idea for a pastoral play, *The Gentle Shepherd*, published in 1725. There is some evidence to suggest that it was written for production by the boys of Haddington Grammar School, and they certainly performed it in Edinburgh in 1729, when it had been altered to become a ballad-opera. *The Gentle Shepherd*, set in Scotland at the time of the Restoration in 1660, is a comedy of love, despair and reconciliation, interspersed with comic scenes, and written in racy Scots. It was immensely popular in Scotland for at least a hundred years after its first appearance, especially in the ballad-opera version which is embellished with attractive songs set to traditional tunes.

Ramsay died in 1758 in the house which he built and which still stands on the Castlehill of Edinburgh. His work is at times brilliant, at times uneven, but always permeated with zeal for the arts in general and for the achievement of his native land in particular. Both Fergusson and Burns owe much to his example.

All texts are those of the Scottish Text Society, modernised in accordance with the general principles of the anthology.

*Editions:*

*The Works of Allan Ramsay*, vols I and II ed. Burns Martin and J. W. Oliver, vols III–VI ed. A. M. Kinghorn and A. Law, Scottish Text Society (Edinburgh, 1945–74).

*Poems by Allan Ramsay and Robert Fergusson*, ed. A. M. Kinghorn and A. Law (Edinburgh, 1974).

Both editions include biographies and critical assessments.

*Criticism:*

Burns Martin, *Allan Ramsay: a study of his Life and Works* (Cambridge, Mass., 1931).

Allan H. Maclaine, 'The Christis Kirk Tradition: its Evolution in Scots Poetry to Burns', *Studies in Scottish Literature*, 2, nos. 1, 2, 3 and 4 (1964).

Thomas Crawford, *Society and the Lyric: a study of the Song Culture of eighteenth-century Scotland* (Edinburgh, 1979), chapter 5.

*Cassettes:*

*Allan Ramsay — Poems and Songs*, ed. Alexander Law (Scotsoun, Glasgow, 1979).

*Allan Ramsay — Extracts from 'The Gentle Shepherd'*, ed. Alexander Law (Scotsoun, Glasgow, 1979).

# CHRIST'S KIRK ON THE GREEN

## CANTO II

But there had been mair blood and skaith,
   Sair harship and great spulie,
And mony a ane had gotten his death
   By this unsonsie tooly:
But that the bauld good-wife of Braith
   Arm'd wi' a great kail gully,
Came bellyflaught[n], and loot an aith,
   She'd gar them a' be hooly
            Fou fast that day.

Blyth to win aff sae wi' hale banes
   Tho mony had clowr'd pows;
And dragl'd sae 'mang muck and stanes,
   They look'd like wirry-kows:
Quoth some, who 'maist had tint their aynds,
   'Let's see how a' bowls rows[n]:
And quat this brulyiement at anes,
   Yon gully is nae mows,
            Forsooth this day'.

Quoth Hutchon, 'I am well content,
   I think we may do war;
Till this time toumond I'se indent
   Our claiths of dirt will sa'r:
Wi' nevels I'm amaist fawn faint,
   My chafts are dung a char;'
Then took his bonnet to the bent,
   And daddit aff the glar,
            Fou clean that day.

1 *skaith*: harm
2 *sair*: sore
*harship*: plunder
*spulie*: booty
4 *unsonsie*: unfortunate
*tooly*: fight
6 *kail*: colewort
*gully*: large knife
7 *loot*: let forth
*aith*: oath
8 *gar*: make
*be . . . fast*: desist immediately (R.)
10 *blyth*: happy
*hale*: whole
11 *clowr'd*: damaged
*pows*: heads
13 *wirry-kows*: scarecrows
14 *tint*: lost
*aynds*: breath
15 *rows*: roll
16 *quat*: stop
*brulyiement*: broil
17 *nae mows*: no joke
20 *war*: worse
21 *toumond*: twelvemonth
*I'se indent*: I'll promise
22 *sa'r*: smell
23 *nevels*: punches
24 *chafts*: jaws
*dung a char*: beaten sideways
25 *bent*: field
26 *daddit*: beat
*glar*: mud

Tam Taylor, wha in time of battle
  Lay as gin some had fell'd him;
Gat up now wi' an unco' rattle,
  As nane there durst a quell'd him:
Bauld Bess flew till him wi' a brattle,
  And spite of his teeth held him
Closs by the craig, and with her fatal
  Knife shored she would geld him,
        For peace that day.

Syne a' wi' ae consent shook hands,
  As they stood in a ring;
Some red their hair, some set their bands,
  Some did their sark tails wring:
Then for a hap to shaw their brands,
  They did there minstrel bring,
Where clever houghs like willi-wands,
  At ilka blythsome spring
        Lap high that day.

Claud Peky was na very blate,
  He stood nae lang a dreigh;
For by the wame he gripped Kate,
  And gar'd her gi'e a skreigh:
'Had aff', quoth she, 'ye filthy slate,
  Ye stink o' leeks, O figh!
Let gae my hands, I say, be quait';
  And wow gin she was skeigh,
        And mim that day.

Now settl'd gossies sat, and keen
  Did for fresh bickers birle[n];
While the young swankies on the green
  Took round a merry tirle:
Meg Wallet wi' her pinky een,
  Gart Lawrie's heart-strings dirle,
And fouk wad threep, that she did green
  For what wad gar her skirle
        And skreigh some day.

32 *brattle*: fury
34 *craig*: throat
35 *shored*: threatened
37 *ae*: one
39 *red*: adjusted
40 *sark*: shirt
41 *hap*: hop
*brands*: calves of legs
43 *houghs*: legs
*willi-wands*: willow wands
44 *ilka*: each
45 *lap*: leapt
46 *blate*: bashful
47 *a dreigh*: at a distance
48 *wame*: belly
49 *skreigh*: screech
50 *slate*: sloven
53 *skeigh*: skittish
54 *mim*: affectedly modest
55 *gossies*: gossips
57 *swankies*: clever lads
58 *tirle*: ?dance
60 *dirle*: tingle
61 *threep*: allege
*green*: long for
62 *skirle*: yell

The manly miller, haff and haff,
   Came out to shaw good will.
Flang by his mittens and his staff,
   Cry'd, 'Gi'e me *Paty's-Mill*';
He lap bawk-hight[n], and cry'd, 'Had aff',
   They rus'd him that had skill;
'He wad do't better', quoth a cawf,
   'Had he another gill
            Of usquebae'.

Furth started neist a pensy blade,
   And out a maiden took,
They said that he was Falkland bred[n],
   And danced by the book;
A souple taylor to his trade,
   And when their hands he shook,
Ga'e them what he got frae his dad,
   *Videlicet* the yuke,
            To claw that day.

Whan a' cry'd out he did sae weel,
   He Meg and Bess did call up;
The lasses bab'd about the reel,
   Gar'd a' their hurdies wallop,
And swat like pownies whan they speel
   Up braes, or when they gallop,
But a thrawn knublock hit his heel,
   And wives had him to haul up,
            Haff fell'd that day.

But mony a pauky look and tale
   Gaed round whan glowming hous'd them[n],
The ostler wife brought ben good ale,
   And blade the lasses rouze them;
'Up wi' them lads, and I'se be bail
   They'll loo ye an ye touze them':
Quoth Gawssie, 'this will never fail
   Wi' them that this gate woes them,
            On sic a day'.

64 *haff and haff*: half fuddled (R.)
67 *Paty's-Mill*: title of a tune
69 *rus'd*: praised
70 *cawf*: calf, fool
72 *usquebae*: whisky
73 *neist*: next
   *pensy*: conceited
77 *souple*: supple
80 *yuke*: the itch
84 *bab'd*: danced
85 *hurdies*: buttocks
86 *swat*: sweated
   *speel*: climb
88 *thrawn*: twisted, accursed
   *knublock*: knob
91 *pauky*: sly, comical
92 *glowming*: twilight
95 *I'se be bail*: I'll guarantee
96 *loo*: love
   *an*: if
   *touze*: tease, rumple
98 *gate*: way

Syne stools and furms were drawn aside,
  And up raise Willy Dadle,
A short hought man, but fou o' pride,
  He said the fidler play'd ill;
'Let's ha'e the pipes', quoth he, 'beside';
  Quoth a', 'That is nae said ill';
He fits the floor syne wi' the bride
  To *Cuttymun* and *Treeladle*[n],
          Thick, thick that day.

In the mean time in came the laird,
  And by some right did claim,
To kiss and dance wi' Masie Aird,
  A dink and dortie dame:
But O poor Mause was aff her guard,
  For back gate frae her wame,
Beckin she loot a fearfu' raird,
  That gart her think great shame,
          And blush that day.

Auld Steen led out Maggie Forsyth,
  He was her ain good-brither;
And ilka ane was unco' blyth,
  To see auld fouk sae clever.
Quoth Jock, wi' laughing like to rive,
  'What think ye o' my mither?
Were my dad dead, let me ne'er thrive
  But she wa'd get anither
          Goodman this day'.

Tam Lutter had a muckle dish,
  And betwisht ilka tune,
He laid his lugs in't like a fish,
  And suckt till it was done;
His bags were liquor'd to his wish,
  His face was like a moon[n]:
But he cou'd get nae place to pish
  In, but his ain twa shoon,
          For thrang that day.

100 *furms*: forms
102 *short hought*: short legged
105 *a'*: all
106 *fits*: foots
112 *dink*: neat
  *dortie*: conceited
114 *back ... wame*: from her back passage
115 *beckin*: curtseying
  *raird*: fart
119 *good-brither*: brother-in-law
122 *rive*: split
128 *betwisht*: between
131 *bags*: entrails
134 *shoon*: shoes
135 *thrang*: crowd

The latter-gae of haly rhime[n],
Sat up at the boord-head,
And a' he said was thought a crime
To contradict indeed:
For in clark-lear he was right prime,
And cou'd baith write and read[n],
And drank sae firm till ne'er a styme
He cou'd keek on a bead[n],
Or book that day.

When he was strute, twa sturdy chiels,
Be's oxter and be's coller,
Held up frae cowping o' the creels[n]
The liquid logic scholar.
When he came hame his wife did reel,
And rampage in her choler,
With that he brake the spining-wheel,
That cost a good rix-dollar[n],
And mair some say.

Near bed-time now ilk weary wight
Was gaunting for his rest;
For some were like to tyne their sight,
Wi' sleep and drinking strest.
But ithers that were stomach-tight,
Cry'd out, it was nae best
To leave a supper that was dight,
To Brownies[n], or a ghaist,
To eat or day.

On whomelt tubs lay twa lang dails,
On them stood mony a goan,
Some fill'd wi' brachan, some wi' kail,
And milk het frae the loan.
Of daintiths they had routh and wale,
Of which they were right fon;
But nathing wad gae down but ale
Wi' drunken Donald Don
The smith that day.

137 *boord*: board, table
140 *lear*: learning
142 *styme*: blink
143 *keek*: peep, see
145 *strute*: drunk
146 *oxter*: arm pit
155 *gaunting*: yawning
156 *tyne*: lose
157 *strest*: overcome
160 *dight*: made ready
161 *ghaist*: ghost
162 *or*: ere
163 *whomelt*: turned upside down
*dails*: deal planks
164 *goan*: wooden meat dishes
165 *brachan*: oatmeal gruel
*kail*: broth
166 *het*: hot
*loan*: village common
167 *daintiths*: delicacies
*routh*: plenty
*wale*: choice

Twa times aught bannocks in a heap,
And twa good junts of beef,
Wi' hind and fore spaul of a sheep,
Drew whitles frae ilk sheath:
Wi' gravie a their beards did dreep,
They kempit with their teeth;
A kebbuck syn that 'maist cou'd creep
Its lane pat on the sheaf[n],
In stous that day.

The bride was now laid in her bed,
Her left leg ho was flung[n];
And Geordie Gib was fidgen glad,
Because it hit Jean Gun:
She was his jo, and aft had said,
'Fy, Geordie, had your tongue,
Ye's ne'er get me to be your bride':
But chang'd her mind when bung,
This very day.

'Tehee', quoth Touzie, when she saw
The cathel coming ben,
It pypin het gae'd round them a',
The bride she made a fen,
To sit in wylicoat sae braw,
Upon her nether en;
Her lad like ony cock did craw,
That meets a clockin hen,
And blyth were they.

The souter, miller, smith and Dick,
Lawrie and Hutchon bauld,
Carles that keep nae very strict
Be hours, tho they were auld;

172 *aught*: eight
173 *junts*: joints
174 *spaul*: shoulder
175 *whitles*: knives
176 *dreep*: drip
177 *kempit*: combed
178 *kebbuck*: cheese
*syn*: then
*'maist*: almost
179 *its lane*: by itself
*pat*: put
*sheaf*: slice of bread
180 *stous*: slices
182 *ho*: stocking
185 *jo*: sweetheart
*aft*: oft
186 *had*: hold
188 *bung*: fuddled
191 *cathel*: hot drink of ale, sugar and eggs
192 *het*: hot
193 *fen*: shift, pretence
194 *wylicoat*: under petticoat
*braw*: fine
197 *clockin hen*: hen sitting on eggs
199 *souter*: shoemaker
201 *carles*: fellows
202 *be*: by (here redundant)

Nor cou'd they e'er leave aff that trick,
But whare good ale was sald,
They drank a' night, e'en tho auld Nick
Shou'd tempt their wives to scald
Them for't neist day.

Was ne'er in Scotland heard or seen
Sic banqueting and drinkin,
Sic revelling and battles keen,
Sic dancing, and sic jinkin,
And unko wark that fell at e'en,
Whan lasses were haff winkin,
They lost their feet and baith their een,
And maidenheads gae'd linkin
Aff a' that day.

204 *sald*: sold
206 *scald*: scold
207 *neist*: next
212 *unko*: strange

## CHRIST'S KIRK ON THE GREEN

### CANTO III

Now frae East Nook of Fife the daw'n
Speel'd westlines up the lift,
Carles wha heard the cock had craw'n,
Begoud to rax and rift:
And greedy wives wi' girning thrawn,
Cry'd 'Lasses up to thrift';
Dogs barked, and the lads frae hand
Bang'd to their breeks like drift,
Be break of day.

But some wha had been fow yestreen,
Sic as the latter-gae,
Air up had nae will to be seen,
Grudgin their groat[n] to pay.
But what aft fristed's no forgeen,
When fouk has nought to say;
Yet sweer were they to rake their een[n],
Sic dizzy heads had they,
And het that day.

1 *Nook*: corner (i.e. peninsula)
2 *speel'd*: climbed
*westlines*: westwards
*lift*: sky
3 *carles*: men
4 *begoud*: began
*rax*: stretch
*rift*: belch
5 *girning*: grumbling
*thrawn*: twisted in the face
6 *thrift*: work
8 *bang'd to*: threw on
*breeks*: trousers
*like drift*: hastily
10 *fow*: drunk
12 *air*: early
14 *fristed*: trusted
*forgeen*: forgiven
16 *sweer*: reluctant

Be that time it was fair foor days[n],
As fou's the house cou'd pang,
To see the young fouk or they raise,
Gossips came in ding dang,
And wi' a soss aboon the claiths[n],
Ilk ane their gifts down flang:
Twall toop horn-spoons down Maggy lays,
Baith muckle mow'd and lang,
For kale or whey.

Her aunt a pair of tangs fush in,
Right bauld she spake and spruce,
'Gin your goodman shall make a din,
And gabble like a goose,
Shorin whan fou to skelp yer skin,
Thir tangs may be of use;
Lay them enlang his pow or shin,
Wha wins syn may make roose,
Between you twa'.

Auld Bessie in her red coat braw,
Cam wi' her ain oe Nanny,
An odd like wife, they said that saw,
A moupin runckled granny,
She fley'd the kimmers ane and a',
Word gae'd she was na kanny[n];
Nor wad they let Lucky awa,
Till she was burnt wi' branny,
Like mony mae.

Steen fresh and fastin 'mang the rest
Came in to get his morning,
Speer'd gin the bride had tane the test,
And how she loo'd her corning?

20 *pang*: squeeze in
21 *or*: before
22 *ding dang*: in rapid succession
23 *soss*: thump
25 *twall*: twelve
*toop*: ram
26 *muckle mow'd*: with wide mouths
27 *kale*: broth
28 *tangs*: tongs
*fush*: brought
29 *bauld*: boldly
*spruce*: to the point
30 *gin*: if
32 *shorin*: threatening
*skelp*: smack
34 *enlang*: along
*pow*: head
35 *make roose*: be in command
38 *oe*: grandchild
39 *like*: kind of
40 *moupin*: mumbling her food
*runckled*: wrinkled
41 *fley'd*: frightened
*kimmers*: gossips
43 *Lucky*: the old woman
44 *branny*: brandy
45 *mae*: more
47 *morning*: glass of spirits before breakfast

She leugh as she had fun a nest,
  Said, 'Let a be ye'r scorning'.
Quoth Roger, 'Fegs I've done my best,
  To ge'er a charge of horning,
        As well's I may'.

Kind Kirsh was there, a kanty lass,
  Black-ey'd, black-hair'd, and bonny;
Right well red up and jimp she was,
  And wooers had fow mony:
I wat na how it came to pass,
  She cutled in wi' Jonnie,
And tumbling wi' him on the grass,
  Dung a' her cockernonny
        A jee that day.

But Mause begrutten was and bleer'd,
  Look'd thowless, dowf and sleepy;
Auld Maggy kend the wyt, and sneer'd,
  Caw'd her a poor daft heepy:
'It's a wise wife that kens her weird,
  What tho ye mount the creepy[n];
There a good lesson may be lear'd,
  And what the war will ye be
        To stand a day.

'Or bairns can read, they first maun spell,
  I learn'd this frae my mammy,
And coost a legen-girth[n] my sell,
  Lang or I married Tammie:
I'se warrand ye have a' heard tell,
  Of bonny Andrew Lammy,
Stifly in loove wi' me he fell,
  As soon as e'er he saw me:
        That was a day'.

50 *leugh*: laughed
*fun a nest*: found a nest (of eggs)
53 *ge'er*: give her
*charge of horning*: legal process requiring a debtor to pay
55 *kanty*: cheerful
57 *red up*: dressed
*jimp*: slender
58 *fow*: full, very
59 *wat*: know
60 *cutled in*: wheedled her way
62 *dung*: broke
*cockernonny*: hair style
63 *a jee*: awry
64 *begrutten*: all in tears
65 *thowless*: spiritless
*dowf*: melancholy
66 *wyt*: reason
67 *heepy*: hypochondriac
68 *weird*: fate
70 *lear'd*: learned
71 *war*: worse
73 *maun*: must

Hait drink, frush butter'd caiks and cheese,
  That held their hearts aboon,
Wi' clashes mingled aft wi' lies,
  Drave aff the hale forenoon:
But after dinner an ye please,
  To weary not o'er soon,
We down to e'ning edge wi' ease
  Shall loup, and see what's done
        I' the doup o' the day.

Now what the friends wad fain been at,
  They that were right true blue;
Was e'en to get their wysons wat,
  And fill young Roger fou[n]:
But the bauld billy took his maut,
  And was right stiff to bow;
He fairly ga'e them tit for tat,
  And scour'd aff healths anew,
        Clean out that day.

A creel[n] bout fow of muckle stains
  They clinked on his back,
To try the pith o's rigg and reins,
  They gart him cadge this pack.
Now as a sign he had tane pains,
  His young wife was na slack,
To rin and ease his shoulder bains,
  And sneg'd the raips fow snack,
        We'er knife that day.

Syne the blyth carles, tooth and nail,
  Fell keenly to the wark;
To ease the gantrees of the ale,
  And try wha was maist stark;
'Till boord and floor, and a' did sail,
  Wi' spilt ale i' the dark;
Gart Jock's fit slide, he like a fail,
  Play'd dad, and dang the bark
        Aff's shins that day.

82 *hait*: hot
*frush*: fresh
83 *held . . . aboon*: cheered their spirits
84 *clashes*: chat
85 *drave*: drove
*hale*: whole
89 *loup*: leap
90 *doup*: end
92 *true blue*: genuine
93 *wysons*: throats, gullets
95 *billy*: comrade, brother
*maut*: malt, drink
96 *stiff to bow*: hard to bend
98 *scour'd*: drank off
*anew*: enough
102 *rigg*: back
*reins*: loins
103 *cadge*: carry
107 *sneg'd*: cut
*raips*: ropes
*snack*: nimbly
111 *gantrees*: ale-barrel stand
112 *stark*: strong
113 *sail*: swim
115 *fail*: turf
116 *dad*: falling against something
*dang the bark*: stripped skin off his shins

The souter, miller, smith and Dick,
   *Et cet'ra*, closs sat cockin,
Till wasted was baith cash and tick,
   Sae ill were they to slocken;
Gane out to pish in gutters thick,
   Some fell, and some gae'd rockin,
Sawny hang sneering on his stick,
   To see bauld Hutchon bockin
               Rainbows that day.

The smith's wife her black deary sought,
   And fand him skin and birn[n]:
Quoth she, 'This day's wark's be dear bought'.
   He ban'd, and gae a girn;
Ca'd her a jade, and said she mucht
   Gae hame and scum her kirn;
'Whisht ladren, for gin ye say ought
   Mair, I'se wind ye a pirn[n]
               To reel some day'.

'Ye'll wind a pirn! Ye silly snool,
   Wae-worth ye'r drunken saul',
Quoth she, and lap out o'er a stool,
   And claught him be the spaul:
He shook her, and sware 'Muckle dool
   Ye's thole for his, ye scaul;
I'se rive frae aff ye'r hips the hool,
   And learn ye to be baul
               On sic a day'.

'Your tippanizing, scant o' grace',
   Quoth she, 'gars me gang duddy;
Our nibour Pate sin break o' day's
   Been thumpin at his studdy,

119 *closs*: close
*cockin*: drinking
121 *slocken*: quench
124 *Sawny*: Sandy, Alexander
125 *Hutchon*: Hugh
*bockin*: vomiting
129 *'s be*: will be
130 *ban'd*: cursed
*gae a girn*: groaned
131 *mucht*: might
132 *kirn*: churn
133 *whisht*: hush
*ladren*: sloven
136 *snool*: pitiful, grovelling slave
137 *wae-worth*: woe befall
138 *lap*: leapt
139 *claught*: grabbed
*spaul*: shoulder
140 *dool*: sorrow
141 *thole*: suffer
*scaul*: scold
142 *rive*: tear
*hool*: covering
143 *baul*: bold
145 *tippanizing*: drinking
146 *duddy*: ragged
148 *studdy*: anvil

An it be true that some fowk says,
  Ye'll girn yet in a woody';
Syne wi' her nails she rave his face,
  Made a' his black baird bloody,
    Wi' scarts that day.

A gilpy that had seen the faught,
  I wat he was nae lang,
Till he had gather'd seven or aught
  Wild hempies stout and strang;
They frae a barn a kaber raught,
  Ane mounted wi' a bang,
Betwisht twa's shouders, and sat straught
  Upon't, and rade the stang[n]
    On her that day.

The wives and gytlings a' span'd out
  O'er middings, and o'er dykes,
Wi' mony an unco skirl and shout,
  Like bumbees frae their bykes;
Thro thick and thin they scour'd about,
  Plashin thro dubs and sykes,
And sic a reird ran thro the rout,
  Gart a' the hale town tykes
    Yamph loud that day.

But d'ye see fou better bred
  Was mens-fou Maggy Murdy,
She her man like a lammy led
  Hame, wi' a well wail'd wordy:
Fast frae the company he fled,
  As he had tane the sturdy[n];
She fleech'd him fairly to his bed,
  Wi' ca'ing him her burdy,
    Kindly that day.

149 *an*: if
*that*: what
150 *girn*: snarl
*woody*: gallows
151 *syne*: then
*rave*: tore
152 *baird*: beard
153 *scarts*: scratches
154 *gilpy*: young rogue
*faught*: fought
156 *aught*: eight
157 *hempies*: rogues
158 *kaber*: rafter
*raught*: reached
159 *wi' a bang*: hastily
163 *gytlings*: young children
*span'd*: stretched, fanned
164 *middings*: middens
165 *unco*: outlandish
*skirl*: shriek
166 *bykes*: bees' nests
168 *dubs*: puddles
*sykes*: streams
169 *reird*: loud sound
*rout*: disorderly crowd
170 *gart*: made
*tykes*: dogs
171 *yamph*: bark
172 *fou*: how
173 *mens-fou*: mannerly
174 *lammy*: lamb
175 *wail'd*: chosen
177 *tane the sturdy*: become dizzy
178 *fleech'd*: coaxed

But Lawrie he took out his nap
   Upon a mow of pease,
And Robin spew'd in's ain wife's lap;
   He said it ga'e him ease.
Hutchon wi' a three lugged cap,
   His head bizzin wi' bees,
Hit Geordy a mislushios rap,
   And brake the brig o's neese
               Right sair that day.

Syne ilka thing gae'd arse o'er head,
   Chanlers, boord, stools and stowps,
Flew thro' the house wi' muckle speed,
   And there was little hopes,
But there had been some ill done deed,
   They gat sic thrawart cowps;
But a' the skaith that chanc'd indeed,
   Was only on their dowps,
               Wi' faws that day.

Sae whiles they toolied, whiles they drank,
   Till a' their sense was smor'd;
And in their maws there was nae mank,
   Upon the furms some snor'd:
Ithers frae aff the bunkers sank,
   Wi' een like collops scor'd:
Some ram'd their noddles wi' a clank,
   E'en like a thick scull'd lord,
               On posts that day.

The young good-man to bed did clim,
   His dear the door did lock in;
Crap down beyont him, and the rim
   O' 'er wame he clap't his dock on:
She fand her lad was not in trim,
   And be this same good token,
That ilka member, lith and limb,
   Was souple like a doken,
               'Bout him that day.

182 *mow*: heap
185 *three lugged cap*: wooden cup with three handles
187 *mislushios*: malicious
188 *brig*: bridge
*neese*: nose
191 *chanlers*: candlesticks
*stowps*: pitchers, flagons
195 *thrawart*: perverse
*cowps*: falls
196 *skaith*: harm
197 *dowps*: backsides
198 *faws*: falls
199 *whiles*: at times
*toolied*: fought
200 *smor'd*: smothered
201 *mank*: lack, want
203 *bunkers*: benches
204 *een*: eyes
*collops*: minced or sliced meat
205 *clank*: sharp, noisy blow
208 *good-man*: husband
211 *dock*: backside
214 *lith*: joint
215 *doken*: dock (the plant)

# THE VISION

Compylit in Latin be a most lernit Clerk * in Tyme of our Hairship and Oppression, anno 1300, and translatit in 1524.

1

Bedoun the bents of Banquo brae[n]
Milane I wandert waif and wae,
Musand our main mischaunce;
How be thay faes we ar undone,
That staw the sacred stane frae Scone,[n]
And leids us sic a daunce:
Quhyle Ingland's Edert taks our tours,
And Scotland ferst obeys,
Rude ruffians ransakk ryal bours,
And Baliol homage pays;
Throch feidom our freidom
Is blotit with this skore,
Quhat Romans or no mans
Pith culd eir do befoir.

2

The air grew ruch with bousteous thuds,
Bauld Boreas[n] branglit outthrow the cluds,
Maist lyke a drunken wicht;
The thunder crakt, and flauchts did rift
Frae the blak vissart of the lift:
The forrest schuke with fricht;
Nae birds abune thair wing extenn,
They ducht not byde the blast,
Ilk beist bedeen bangd to thair den,
Until the storm was past:

*Hairship*: plundering
1 *bedoun*: down
*bents*: open fields
*brae*: hill
2 *milane*: alone
*waif*: solitary
*wae*: sad
4 *thay*: these
*faes*: foes
5 *staw*: stole
7 *Edert*: Edward I, of England
8 *ferst*: perforce
9 *bours*: palaces
11 *throch*: through
*feidom*: evil fortune
12 *blotit*: effaced
*skore*: obliteration
13 *quhat*: what, which
14 *pith*: strength
*eir*: ever
15 *ruch*: noisy
*bousteous*: boisterous
*thuds*: blows
16 *bauld*: bold
*branglit*: shook, threatened
*outthrow*: through
17 *wicht*: man
18 *flauchts*: flashes
*rift*: break forth
19 *vissart*: visor
*lift*: sky
21 *abune*: above
22 *ducht*: dare
*byde*: suffer
23 *bedeen*: quickly
*bang'd*: hastened

Ilk creature in nature
That had a spunk of sence,
In neid then, with speid then,
Methocht cryt, in defence.

3

To se a morn in May sae ill,
I deimt Dame Nature was gane will,
To rair with rackles reil;
Quhairfor to put me out of pain,
And skonce my skap and shanks frae rain,
I bure me to a beil,
Up ane hich craig that lundgit alaft,
Out owre a canny cave,
A curious cruif of nature's craft,
Quhilk to me schelter gaif;
Ther vexit, perplexit,
I leint me doun to weip,
In brief ther, with grief ther
I dottard owre on sleip.

4

Heir Somnus[n] in his silent hand
Held all my sences at command,
Quhyle I forget my cair;
The myldest meid of mortall wichts
Quha pass in peace the private nichts,
That wauking finds it rare[n];
Sae in saft slumbers did I ly,
But not my wakryfe mynd,
Quhilk still stude watch, and couth espy
A man with aspeck kynd,
Richt auld lyke and bauld lyke,
With baird thre quarters skant,
Sae braif lyke and graif lyke,
He seemt to be a sanct.

26 *spunk*: spark
28 *cryt*: ?hid
29 *sae*: so
30 *deimt*: thought
*gane will*: gone astray
31 *rair*: roar
*rackles*: careless
*reil*: dance
33 *skonce*: protect
*skap*: head
34 *bure me*: betook me
*beil*: shelter
35 *hich*: high
*lundgit*: overhung
36 *out owre*: above
*canny*: ?safe, comfortable
37 *cruif*: shelter
38 *gaif*: gave
42 *dottard*: ?nodded
45 *forget*: forgot
46 *meid*: reward
*wichts*: men
50 *wakryfe*: wakeful
51 *stude watch*: kept guard
*couth*: could
52 *aspeck*: looks
53 *auld*: old
*bauld*: bold
54 *baird*: beard
*thre quarters skant*: ?longish and thin
55 *braif*: bold
*graif*: serious
56 *sanct*: saint

5

Grit darring dartit frae his ee,
A braid-sword schogled at his thie,
On his left arm a targe;
A shynand speir filld his richt hand,
Of stalwart mak, in bane and brawnd,
Of just proportions, large;
A various rain-bow colourt plaid
Owre his left spaul he threw,
Doun his braid back, frae his quhyt heid,
The silver wymplers grew;
Amaisit, I gaisit
To se, led at command,
A strampant and rampant
Ferss lyon in his hand.

6

Quhilk held a thistle in his paw,
And round his collar graift I saw
This poesie pat and plain,
*Nemo me impune lacess—*
*—et*[n]: —— In Scots, *Nane sall oppress*
*Me, unpunist with pain*;
Still schaking, I durst naithing say,
Till he with kynd accent
Sayd, 'Fere let nocht thy hairt affray,
I cum to hier thy plaint;
Thy graining and maining
Haith laitlie reikd myne eir,
Debar then affar then
All eiryness or feir.

7

'For I am ane of a hie station,
The Warden[n] of this auntient nation,

57 *grit darring*: great courage
58 *braid*: broad
*schogled*: dangled
*thie*: thigh
59 *targe*: shield
61 *mak*: build
*bane and brawnd*: bone and brawn
63 *various*: varying (in colour)
64 *spaul*: shoulder
65 *quhyt*: white
66 *wymplers*: curls
69 *strampant*: stamping
70 *ferss*: fierce
71 *quhilk*: which
72 *graift*: engraved
73 *pat*: apt
79 *fere*: fear
80 *hier*: hear
81 *graining*: groaning
*maining*: moaning
82 *laitlie reikd*: lately reached
83 *debar*: abolish
*affar*: afar, away
84 *eiryness*: fearsomeness
85 *hie*: high
86 *auntient*: ancient

And can nocht do the wrang';
I vissyt him then round about,
Syne with a resolution stout,
Speird, quhair he had bene sae lang?
Quod he, 'Althocht I sum forsuke,
Becaus they did me slicht,
To hills and glens I me betuke,
To them that luves my richt;
Quhase mynds yet inclynds yet
To damm the rappid spate,
Devysing and prysing
Freidom at ony rate.

8

'Our trechour peirs thair tyranns treit,
Quha jyb them, and thair substance eit,
And on thair honour stramp;
They, pure degenerate! bend thair baks,
The victor, Langshanks[n], proudly cracks
He has blawn out our lamp:
Quhyle trew men, sair complainand, tell,
With sobs, thair silent greif,
How Baliol[n] thair richts did sell,
With small howp of reliefe;
Regretand and fretand
Ay at his cursit plot,
Quha rammed and crammed
That bargin doun thair throt.

9

'Braif gentrie sweir, and burgers ban,
Revenge is muttert be ilk clan
Thats to their nation trew;
The cloysters cum to cun the evil,
Mailpayers wiss it to the devil,
With its contryving crew:

87 *the*: thee
88 *vissyt*: scrutinised
89 *syne*: then
90 *speird*: asked
92 *did me slicht*: slighted me
95 *quhase*: whose
97 *devysing*: planning, contriving
99 *trechour peirs*: traitor nobles
*tyranns treit*: consort with tyrants
100 *jyb*: mock
*eit*: eat
102 *pure*: poor
103 *cracks*: boasts
105 *sair*: sorely
107 *richts*: rights
108 *howp*: hope
113 *sweir*: swear
*ban*: curse
114 *ilk*: each
116 *cloysters*: monasteries, the Church
*cun*: learn
117 *mailpayers*: farmers who pay rent
*wiss*: wish

The hardy wald with hairty wills,
Upon dyre vengance fall;
The feckless fret owre heuchs and hills,
And Eccho answers all,
Repetand and greitand,
With mony a sair alace,
For blasting and casting
Our honour in disgrace.'

10

'Waes me!' quod I, 'our case is bad,
And mony of us are gane mad,
Sen this disgraceful paction.
We are felld and herryt now by forse;
And hardly help fort, that's yit warse,
We are sae forfairn with faction.
Then has not he gude cause to grumble,
That's forst to be a slaif;
Oppression dois the judgment jumble
And gars a wyse man raif.
May cheins then, and pains then
Infernal be thair hyre
Quha dang us, and flang us
Into this ugsum myre.'

11

Then he with bauld forbidding luke,
And staitly air did me rebuke,
For being of sprite sae mein:
Said he 'It's far beneath a Scot
To use weak curses quhen his lot
May sumtyms sour his splein,
He rather sould mair lyke a man,
Some braif design attempt;
Gif its nocht in his pith, what than,
Rest but a quhyle content,

119 *wald*: would
*hairty*: hearty
121 *feckless fret*: the feeble grumble
*heuchs*: steep slopes
123 *greitand*: weeping
124 *alace*: alas
129 *sen*: since
*paction*: treaty
130 *felld and herryt*: struck down and ruined
131 *yit warse*: yet worse
132 *forfairn*: exhausted
134 *forst*: forced
*slaif*: slave
136 *gars*: makes
*raif*: rave
137 *cheins*: chains
138 *hyre*: reward
139 *dang*: struck
*flang*: flung
140 *ugsum*: loathsome
141 *luke*: look
143 *sprite*: spirit
146 *splein*: spleen
149 *gif*: if
*pith*: power
150 *quhyle*: while

Nocht feirful, but cheirful,
And wait the will of fate,
Which mynds to desygns to
Renew your auntient state.

12

'I ken sum mair than ye do all
Of quhat sall afterwart befall,
In mair auspicious tymes;
For aften far abufe the mune,
We watching beings do convene,
Frae round eard's outmost climes,
Quhair evry Warden represents
Cleirly his nation's case,
Gif famyne, pest, or sword torments,
Or vilains hie in place,
Quha keip ay, and heip ay
Up to themselves grit store,
By rundging and spunging
The leil laborious pure.'

13

'Say then,' said I, 'at your hie sate,
Lernt ye ocht of auld Scotland's fate.
Gif eir schoil be her sell?'
With smyle celest, quod he, 'I can,
But it's nocht fit an mortal man
Sould ken all I can tell:
But part to the I may unfold,
And thou may saifly ken,
Quhen Scottish peirs slicht Saxon gold,[n]
And turn trew heartit men;
Quhen knaivry and slaivrie,
Ar equally dispysd,
And loyalte and royalte,
Universalie are prysd.

153 *mynds*: intends
155 *ken*: know
*mair*: more
158 *abufe*: above
160 *frae*: from
*eard*: earth
163 *pest*: plague
167 *rundging*: despoiling
*spunging*: robbing
168 *leil*: loyal
*pure*: poor
169 *hie*: high
*sate*: seat
170 *ocht*: anything
171 *eir*: ever
*schoil*: she'll
*sell*: self
172 *celest*: heavenly
176 *saifly*: safely
177 *peirs*: peers
*slicht*: scorn
182 *prysd*: prized

14

'Quhen all your trade is at a stand,
And cunyie clene forsaiks the Land,
Quhilk will be very sune,
Will preists without their stypands preich?
For nocht will lawyers causes streich?
Faith thats nae easy done.
All this and mair maun cum to pass,
To cleir your glamourit sicht;
And Scotland maun be made an ass
To set her jugment richt.
They'il jade hir and blad hir,
Untill scho brak hir tether,
Thocht auld schois yit bauld schois,
And teuch lyke barkit lether.

15

'But mony a corss sall braithles ly,
And wae sall mony a widow cry,
Or all rin richt again;
Owre Cheviot prancing proudly north,
The faes sall tak the feild neir Forthe,[n]
And think the day their ain:
But burns that day sall rin with blude
Of them that now oppress;
Thair carcasses be corby's fude,
By thousands on the gress.
A king then sall ring then,
Of wyse renoun and braif,
Quhase pusians and sapiens,
Sall richt restoir and saif.'

16

'The view of freidomis sweit,' quod I,
'O say, grit tennant of the skye,

184 *cunyie*: money
186 *stypands*: stipends
187 *nocht*: nothing
*causes*: cases before court
*streich*: stretch out
190 *glamourit*: deceived
193 *jade*: ill-treat
*blad*: spoil
195 *schois*: shoes
196 *teuch*: tough
*barkit*: tanned
197 *corss*: corpse
*braithles*: breathless
198 *wae*: woe
199 *or*: before
*rin*: run
200 *owre*: over
201 *faes*: foes
202 *ain*: own
203 *burns*: streams
205 *corbys fude*: food for carrion crow
206 *gress*: grass
207 *ring*: reign
209 *pusians*: puissance, power
*sapiens*: wisdom
210 *richt*: right (*n.*)
*saif*: save
211 *quod*: said

How neiris that happie tyme?'
'We ken things but be circumstans,
Nae mair', quod he, 'I may advance,
Leist I commit a cryme.'
'Quhat eir ye pleis, gae on,' quod I,
'I sall not fash ye moir,
Say how, and quhair ye met, and quhy,
As ye did hint befoir.'
With air then sae fair then,
That glanst like rayis of glory,
Sae godlyk and oddlyk
He thus resumit his storie.

17

'Frae the sun's rysing to his sett,
All the pryme rait of wardens met,
In solemn bricht array,
With vehicles of aither cleir,
Sic we put on quhen we appeir
To sauls rowit up in clay;
Thair in a wyde and splendit hall,
Reird up with shynand beims,
Quhais rufe-treis wer of rainbows all,
And paist with starrie gleims,
Quhilk prinked and twinkled
Brichtly beyont compair,
Much famed and named
A castill in the air.

18

'In midst of quhilk a tabill stude,
A spacious oval reid as blude,
Made of a fyre-flaucht,
Arround the dazeling walls were drawn,
With rays be a celestial hand,
Full mony a curious draucht.

217 *quhat eir ye pleis*: whatever you please
218 *fash*: trouble
223 *oddlyk*: ?strange
226 *pryme*: foremost
*rait*: rank
228 *vehicles*: ?garments
*aither*: ether
229 *sic*: such
230 *rowit*: rolled
232 *reird up*: erected
234 *paist*: ?supported
235 *prinked*: shone forth
238 *castill*: castle
239 *tabill*: table
241 *fyre-flaucht*: lightning or ?meteorite
244 *draucht*: outline drawing

Inferiour beings flew in haist,
Without gyd or derectour,
Millions of myles throch the wyld waste,
To bring in bowlis of nectar:
Then roundly and soundly
We drank lyk Roman gods[n];
Quhen Jove sae dois rove sae,
That Mars and Bacchus nods.

19

'Quhen Phebus' heid turns licht as cork,
And Neptune leans upon his fork,
And limpand Vulcan blethers:
Quhen Pluto glowrs as he were wyld,
And Cupid, luve's we wingit chyld,
Fals down and fyls his fethers.
Quhen Pan forgets to tune his reid,
And slings it cairless bye,
And Hermes wingd at heils and heid,
Can nowther stand nor lye:
Quhen staggirand and swaggirand,
They stoyter hame to sleip,
Quhyle centeries at enteries
Imortal watches keip.

20

'Thus we tuke in the high browin liquour,
And bangd about the nectar biquour;
But evir with his ods:
We neir in drink our judgments drensch,
Nor scour about to seik a wensch
Lyk these auld baudy gods,
But franklie at ilk uther ask,
Quhat's proper we suld know,
How ilk ane hes performt the task,
Assigned to him below.

251 *dois*: does
253 *heid*: head
*licht*: light
255 *limpand*: limping
*blethers*: talks foolishly
256 *glowrs*: glares
257 *we*: wee, little
258 *fyls*: dirties
259 *reid*: reed-pipe
261 *heils*: heels
262 *nowther*: neither
263 *swaggirand*: swaggering
264 *stoyter*: stumble
265 *centeries*: i.e. pun on sentries and centuries
266 *watches*: guard
267 *high browin*: well brewed
268 *bangd*: sent speedily
*biquour*: glass or pot
269 *his ods*: ?this difference
271 *scour*: roam
272 *baudy*: lecherous
275 *ilk ane*: each one

Our minds then sae kind then,
Are fixt upon our care,
Ay noting and ploting
Quhat tends to thair weilfair.

21

'Gothus and Vandall[n] baith lukt bluff,
Quhyle Gallus sneerd and tuke a snuff,
Quhilk made Allmane to stare;
Latinus bad him naithing feir,
But lend his hand to haly weir,
And of cowd crouns tak care;
Batavius with his paddock-face
Luking asquint, cryd, 'pisch,
Your monks ar void of sence or grace,
I had leur ficht for fisch;
Your schule-men ar fule-men,
Carvit out for dull debates,
Decoying and destroying
Baith monarchies and states.'

22

'Iberius with a gurlie nod
Cryd, 'Hogan[n], yes we ken your god,
It's herrings ye adore;'
Heptarchus, as he usd to be,
Can nocht with his ain thochts agre,
But varies bak and fore;
Ane quhyle he says, 'It is not richt
A monarch to resist,'
Neist braith all ryall powir will slicht,
And passive homage jest;
He hitches and fitches
Betwein the hic and hoc,
Ay jieand and flieand
Round lyk a wedder-cock.

278 *care*: concern
281 *bluff*: cheated
285 *haly weir*: holy war, crusade
286 *cowd crouns*: subservient kings
287 *paddock*: frog
290 *leur*: rather
*ficht*: fight
291 *schule-men*: medieval logic-chopping scholars
292 *carvit out*: shaped
295 *gurlie*: surly
301 *ane quhyle*: sometimes
303 *neist braith*: next breath
*slicht*: scorn
304 *jest*: despise
305 *hitches*: hesitates
*fitches*: moves
306 *hic and hoc*: this and that
307 *jieand*: see-sawing

23

'I still support my precedens
Abune them all, for sword and sens,
Thocht I haif layn richt now lown,
Quhylk was, becaus I bure a grudge
At sum fule Scotis, quha lykd to drudge
To princes no thair awin;
Sum thanis thair tennants pykit and squeist,
And pursit up all thair rent,
Syne wallopit to far courts, and bleist.
Till riggs and schaws war spent;
Syne byndging and whyndging,
Quhen thus redusit to howps,
They dander and wander
About, pure lickmadowps.

24

'But now it's tyme for me to draw
My shynand sword against club-law,
And gar my lyon roir;
He sall or lang gie sic a sound,
The ecchoe sall be hard arround
Europe, frae schore to schore;
Then lat them gadder all thair strenth,
And stryve to wirk my fall,
Tho numerous, yit at the lenth
I will owrecum them all,
And raise yit and blaze yit
My braifrie and renown,
By gracing and placing
Arright the Scottis crown.

25

'Quhen my braif Bruce[n] the same sall weir
Upon his ryal heid, full cleir

309 *precedens*: pre-eminence
311 *lown*: quiet
312 *bure*: bore
315 *pykit*: defrauded
*squeist*: squeezed
316 *pursit up*: pocketed
317 *wallopit*: hastened
*bleist*: blazed, shone
318 *riggs and schaws*: fields and woods
319 *byndging*: cringing
*whyndging*: complaining
320 *howps*: hopes
322 *pure lickmadowps*: (?simple) arselickers, courtiers
324 *club-law*: political and social anarchy
326 *or lang*: ere long
327 *hard*: heard
334 *braifrie*: bravery

The diadem will shyne;
Then sall your sair oppression ceis,
His intrest yours he will not fleice,
Or leif you eir inclyne:
Thocht millions to his purse be lent,
Ye'll neir the puirer be,
But rather richer, quhyle its spent
Within the Scottish se:
The field then sall yeild then
To honest husband's welth,
Gude laws then sall cause then
A sickly state haif helth.'

26

Quhyle thus he talkit, methocht ther came
A wondir fair etherial dame,
And to our Warden sayd,
'Grit Callidon I cum in serch
Of you, frae the hych starry arch,
The counsill wants your ayd;
Frae every quarter of the sky,
As swift as quhirl-wynd,
With spirits' speid the chiftains hy,
Sum grit thing is desygnd
Owre muntains be funtains,
And round ilk fairy ring,
I haif chaist ye, O haist ye,
They talk about your king.'

27

With that my hand methocht he schuke,
And wischt I happyness micht bruke,
To eild be nicht and day;
Syne quicker than an arrows flicht,
He mountit upwarts frae my sicht,
Straicht to the Milkie Way;
My mynd him followit throw the skyes,
Untill the brynie streme
For joy ran trinckling frae myne eyes,
And wakit me frae dreme;

340 *ceis*: cease
341 *fleice*: fleece
342 *leif . . . inclyne*: ever incline to leave you
343 *thocht*: though
344 *neir*: never
348 *husband*: farmer
350 *haif*: have
354 *Callidon*: Caledonia, Scotland
355 *hych*: high
359 *hy*: hasten
366 *bruke*: enjoy
367 *eild*: old age
372 *brynie streme*: tears

Then peiping, half sleiping,
Frae furth my rural beild,
It eisit me and pleisit me
To se and smell the feild.

28

For Flora[n] in hir clene array,
New washen with a showir of May,
    Lukit full sweit and fair;
Quhyle hir cleir husband frae aboif
Sched doun his rayis of genial luve,
    Hir sweits perfumt the air;
The winds war husht, the welkin cleird,
    The glumand clouds war fled,
And all as saft and gay appeird
    As ane Elysion sched;
      Quhilk heisit and bleisit
      My heart with sic a fyre,
      As raises these praises
      That do to heaven aspyre.
                *Quod* AR. SCOT.[n]

386 *glumand*: lowering
388 *Elision sched*: ?Elysian field
389 *heisit*: lifted up

## THE GENTLE SHEPHERD

### ACT I. SCENE I.

*Beneath the south side of a craigy beild,*
*Where crystal springs the halesome waters yield,*
*Twa youthful shepherds on the gowans lay,*
*Tenting their flocks ae bonny morn of May.*
*Poor Roger granes till hollow echoes ring;*
*But blyther Patie likes to laugh and sing.*

### PATIE AND ROGER

*Pat.* This sunny morning, Roger, chears my blood,
And puts all nature in a jovial mood.

1 *craigy*: rocky
*beild*: shelter
2 *halesome*: healthy, wholesome
3 *gowans*: daisies
4 *tenting*: tending
*ae*: one
5 *granes*: groans

How heartsome 'tis to see the rising plants?
To hear the birds chirm o'er their pleasing rants?
How halesome 'tis to snuff the cauler air,
And all the sweets it bears when void of care?
What ails thee, Roger, then? what gars thee grane?
Tell me the cause of thy ill season'd pain.

*Rog*. I'm born, O Patie! to a thrawart fate;
I'm born to strive with hardships sad and great.
Tempest may cease to jaw the rowan flood,
Corbies and tods to grein for lambkins blood;
But I, opprest with never ending grief,
Maun ay despair of lighting on relief.

*Pat*. The bees shall loath the flower, and quit the hive,
The saughs on boggie-ground shall cease to thrive,
Ere scornful queans, or loss of warldly gear,
Shall spill my rest, or ever force a tear.

*Rog*. Sae might I say; but 'tis no easy done
By ane whase saul is sadly out of tune.
You have sae saft a voice, and slid a tongue,
You are the darling of baith auld and young.
If I but ettle at a sang, or speak,
They dit their lugs, syne up their leglens cleek;
And jeer me hameward frae the loan or bught,
While I'm confus'd with mony a vexing thought:
Yet I am tall, and as well built as thee,
Nor mair unlikely to a lass's eye.
For ilka sheep ye have, I'll number ten,
And should, as ane may think, come farer ben.

*Pat*. But ablins, nibour, ye have not a heart,
And downa eithly wi' your cunzie part.
If that be true, what signifies your gear?
A mind that's scrimpit never wants some care.

10 *chirm*: chirp and sing
*rants*: songs
11 *cauler*: fresh
13 *gars*: makes
15 *thrawart*: perverse
17 *jaw*: dash
*rowan*: rolling
18 *corbies*: carrion crows
*tods*: foxes
*grein*: long for
22 *saughs*: willows
23 *queans*: young women
24 *spill*: spoil
27 *slid*: smooth
29 *ettle*: attempt
30 *dit*: stop up
*lugs*: ears
*syne*: then
*leglens*: milk pails
*cleek*: catch
31 *loan*: strip of pasture
*bught*: shelter for sheep
35 *ilka*: each
36 *come farer ben*: be more prosperous
37 *ablins*: perhaps
38 *downa*: cannot
*eithly*: easily
*cunzie*: money
40 *scrimpit*: sparing, niggardly
*wants*: lacks

*Rog.* My byar tumbled, nine braw nowt were smoor'd,
Three elf-shot[n] were; yet I these ills endur'd:
In winter last, my cares were very sma',
Tho' scores of wathers perish'd in the snaw.

*Pat.* Were your bein rooms as thinly stock'd as mine,
Less you wad lose, and less you wad repine.
He that has just enough, can soundly sleep;
The o'ercome only fashes fowk to keep.

*Rog.* May plenty flow upon thee for a cross,
That thou may'st thole the pangs of mony a loss.
O mayst thou doat on some fair paughty wench,
That ne'er will lout thy lowan drouth to quench,
'Till bris'd beneath the burden, thou cry dool,
And awn that ane may fret that is nae fool.

*Pat.* Sax good fat lambs I sald them ilka clute
At the West-port[n], and bought a winsome flute,
Of plum-tree made, with iv'ry virles round,
A dainty whistle with a pleasant sound:
I'll be mair canty wi't, and ne'er cry dool,
Than you with all your cash, ye dowie fool.

*Rog.* Na, Patie, na! I'm nae sic churlish beast,
Some other thing lyes heavier at my breast:
I dream'd a dreary dream this hinder night,
That gars my flesh a' creep yet with the fright.

*Pat.* Now to a friend how silly's this pretence,
To ane wha you and a' your secrets kens:
Daft are your dreams, as daftly wad ye hide
Your well seen love, and dorty Jenny's pride.
Take courage, Roger, me your sorrows tell,
And safely think nane kens them but your sell.

41 *byar*: cow shed
*braw*: fine
*nowt*: cows
*smoor'd*: smothered
44 *wathers*: castrated rams
45 *bein*: comfortable
48 *o'ercome*: surplus
*fashes*: troubles
*fowk*: people
50 *thole*: suffer
51 *paughty*: haughty
52 *lout*: stoop
*lowan*: burning
*drouth*: thirst
53 *bris'd*: pressed
*dool*: grief
54 *awn*: own
55 *clute*: hoof
57 *virles*: ferrules, rings
59 *canty*: cheerful
60 *dowie*: miserable
61 *sic*: such
63 *hinder*: last
67 *daft*: foolish
68 *dorty*: conceited

*Rog*. Indeed now, Patie, ye have guess'd o'er true,
And there is nathing I'll keep up frae you.
Me dorty Jenny looks upon a-squint;
To speak but till her I dare hardly mint:
In ilka place she jeers me air and late,
And gars me look bumbaz'd, and unko blate:
But yesterday I met her 'yont a know,
She fled as frae a shelly coat[n] or kow.
She Bauldy loes, Bauldy that drives the car;
But gecks at me, and says I smell of tar.

*Pat*. But Bauldy loes not her, right well I wat;
He sighs for Neps — sae that may stand for that.

*Rog*. I wish I cou'dna loo her — but in vain,
I still maun doat, and thole her proud disdain.
My Bawty is a cur I dearly like,
Even while he fawn'd, she strak the poor dumb tyke:
If I had fill'd a nook within her breast,
She wad have shawn mair kindness to my beast.
When I begin to tune my stock and horn[n],
With a' her face she shaws a caulrife scorn.
Last night I play'd, ye never heard sic spite,
*O'er Bogie* was the spring, and her delyte;
Yet tauntingly she at her cousin speer'd,
Gif she cou'd tell what tune I play'd, and sneer'd.
Flocks, wander where ye like, I dinna care,
I'll break my reed, and never whistle mair.

*Pat*. E'en do sae, Roger, wha can help misluck,
Saebeins she be sic a thrawin-gabet chuck?
Yonder's a craig, since ye have tint all hope,
Gae till't your ways, and take the lover's lowp.

*Rog*. I needna mak sic speed my blood to spill,
I'll warrant death come soon enough a will.

74 *till*: to
*mint*: aim
75 *jeers*: mocks
*air*: early
76 *bumbaz'd*: like an idiot
*unko blate*: very bashful
77 *know*: hill
78 *kow*: goblin
79 *Bauldy*: abbrev. of Archibald
*loes*: loves
*car*: sledge
80 *gecks*: mocks
81 *wat*: know
82 *Neps*: abbrev. of Elizabeth
86 *strak*: struck
90 *caulrife*: chilly
92 *spring*: tune
93 *speer'd*: asked
95 *dinna*: don't
97 *misluck*: misfortune
98 *saebeins*: since
*thrawin-gabet*: with crabbed tongue
*chuck*: hen
99 *craig*: rock
*tint*: lost
100 *gae till't*: go to it
*lowp*: leap
102 *a will*: of its own accord

*Pat*. Daft gowk! leave off that silly whindging way;
Seem careless, there's my hand ye'll win the day.
Hear how I serv'd my lass I love as well
As ye do Jenny, and with heart as leel:
Last morning I was gay and early out,
Upon a dike I lean'd glowring about,
I saw my Meg come linkan o'er the lee;
I saw my Meg, but Meggy saw na me:
For yet the sun was wading thro' the mist,
And she was closs upon me ere she wist;
Her coats were kiltit, and did sweetly shaw
Her straight bare legs that whiter were than snaw;
Her cockernony snooded up fou sleek,
Her haffet-locks hang waving on her cheek;
Her cheek sae ruddy, and her een sae clear;
And O! her mouth's like ony hinny pear.
Neat, neat she was, in bustine waste-coat clean,
As she came skiffing o'er the dewy green.
Blythsome, I cry'd, my bonny Meg, come here,
I ferly wherefore ye're sae soon asteer;
But I can guess, ye're gawn to gather dew[n]:
She scour'd awa, and said, 'What's that to you?'
'Then fare ye well, Meg Dorts, and e'en's ye like,'
I careless cry'd, and lap in o'er the dike.
I trow, when that she saw, within a crack,
She came with a right thievless errand back;
Misca'd me first, — then bade me hound my dog
To wear up three waff ews stray'd on the bog.
I leugh, and sae did she; then with great haste
I clasp'd my arms about her neck and waste,
About her yielding waste, and took a fouth
Of sweetest kisses frae her glowing mouth.
While hard and fast I held her in my grips,
My very saul came lowping to my lips.

103 *gowk*: fool
*whindging*: complaining
106 *leel*: loyal
107 *gay and*: very
108 *dike*: wall
*glowring*: gazing
109 *linkan*: tripping
*lee*: pasture
112 *wist*: knew
113 *coats*: skirts
*kiltit*: tucked up
115 *cockernony*: gathering up of hair
*snooded*: fastened with a band
116 *haffet-locks*: locks on the cheeks
118 *hinny*: honey
119 *bustine*: fustian
120 *skiffing*: lightly speeding
122 *ferly*: wonder
*asteer*: astir
124 *scour'd*: hurried
126 *lap*: leaped
127 *trow*: believe
*within a crack*: immediately
128 *thievless*: pointless
130 *wear up*: stop
*waff*: wandering
131 *leugh*: laughed
133 *fouth*: abundance
136 *saul*: soul
*lowping*: leaping

Sair, sair she flet wi' me tween ilka smack;
But well I kent she meant nae as she spake.
Dear Roger, when your jo puts on her gloom,
Do you sae too, and never fash your thumb.
Seem to forsake her, soon she'll change her mood;
Gae woo anither, and she'll gang clean wood.

*Rog.* Kind Patie, now fair fa' your honest heart,
Ye're ay sae cadgy, and have sic an art
To hearten ane: For now as clean's a leek,
Ye've cherish'd me since ye began to speak.
Sae for your pains, I'll make ye a propine,
My mother (rest her saul) she made it fine,
A tartan plaid, spun of good hawslock woo,
Scarlet and green the sets, the borders blew,
With sprangs like gowd and siller, cross'd with black;
I never had it yet upon my back.
Well are ye wordy o't, wha have sae kind
Red up[n] my revel'd doubts, and clear'd my mind.

*Pat.* Well hald ye there; — and since ye've frankly made
A present to me of your braw new plaid,
My flute's be your's, and she too that's sae nice
Shall come a will, gif ye'll tak my advice.

*Rog.* As ye advise, I'll promise to observ't;
But ye maun keep the flute, ye best deserv't.
Now tak it out, and gie's a bonny spring,
For I'm in tift to hear you play and sing.

*Pat.* But first we'll take a turn up to the height,
And see gif all our flocks be feeding right.
Be that time bannocks, and a shave of cheese,
Will make a breakfast that a laird might please;
Might please the daintiest gabs, were they sae wise,
To season meat with health instead of spice.
When we have tane the grace-drink[n] at this well,
I'll whistle fine, and sing t' ye like my sell.

137 *sair*: sorely
*flet*: scolded
*smack*: kiss
139 *jo*: sweetheart
140 *fash your thumb*: trouble yourself
142 *wood*: mad
143 *fair fa'*: good luck to
144 *cadgy*: cheerful
147 *propine*: gift
149 *hawslock woo'*: best wool from the sheep's neck
150 *sets*: squares in the main pattern
151 *sprangs*: stripes
*gowd*: gold
*siller*: silver
153 *wordy*: worthy
154 *red*: cleared
*revel'd*: confused
155 *hald*: hold
157 *nice*: fastidious
158 *a will*: of her own accord
162 *tift*: good form
164 *gif*: if
167 *gabs*: mouths
169 *tane*: taken

## THE MONK AND THE MILLER'S WIFE

### A TALE

Now lend your lugs, ye benders fine,
Wha ken the benefit of wine;
And you wha laughing scud brown ale,
Leave jinks a wee, and hear a tale.

An honest miller wond in Fife,
That had a young and wanton wife,
Wha sometimes thol'd the parish priest
To mak her man a twa-horn'd beast:
He paid right mony visits till her;
And to keep in with Hab the miller,
He endeavour'd aft to mak him happy,
Where e'er he kend the ale was nappy.
Sic condescension in a pastor,
Knit Halbert's love to him the faster;
And by his converse, troth 'tis true,
Hab learn'd to preach when he was fou.
Thus all the three were wonder pleas'd,
The wife well serv'd, the men well eas'd.
This ground his corns, and that did cherish
Himsell with dining round the parish.
Bess the good-wife thought it nae skaith,
Since she was able to serve them baith.

When equal is the night and day,
And Ceres[n] gives the schools the play,
A youth sprung frae a gentle pater,
Bred at Saint Andro's *Alma Mater*[n],
Ae day gawn hameward, it fell late,
And him benighted by the gate:
To ly without, pit-mirk did shore him;
He coudna see his thumb before him:
But, clack, — clack, — clack, he heard a mill,
Whilk led him be the lugs theretill.

1 *lugs*: ears
*benders*: drinkers
3 *scud*: quaff
4 *jinks*: games
*wee*: little while
5 *wond*: lived
7 *thol'd*: allowed
8 *twa-horn'd beast*: cuckold
12 *nappy*: strong
15 *converse*: conversation
21 *skaith*: harm
27 *ae*: one
*gawn*: going
28 *gate*: way
29 *pit-mirk*: darkness
*shore*: threaten
32 *theretill*: to it

To tak the threed of tale alang,
This mill to Halbert did belang.
Not less this note your notice claims.
The scholar's name was Master James.

Now, smiling Muse, the prelude past,
Smoothly relate a tale shall last
As lang as Alps and Grampian Hills,
As lang as wind or water-mills.

In enter'd James, Hab saw and kend him,
And offer'd kindly to befriend him
With sic good chear as he cou'd make,
Baith for his ain and father's sake.
The scholar thought himsell right sped,
And gave him thanks in terms well bred.
Quoth Hab: 'I canna leave my mill
As yet; — but step ye west the kill
A bow-shot, and ye'll find my hame:
Gae warm ye, and crack with our dame,
Till I set aff the mill; syne we
Shall tak what Bessy has to gi'e.'
James, in return, what's handsome said,
O'er lang to tell; and aff he gade.
Out of the house some light did shine,
Which led him till't as with a line:
Arriv'd, he knock'd; for doors were steekit;
Straight throw a window Bessy keekit,
And cries: 'Wha's that gie's fowk a fright
At sic untimous time of night?'
James with good humour, maist discreetly,
Tald her his circumstance completely.
'I dinna ken ye', quoth the wife,
'And up and down the thieves are rife:
Within my lane, I'm but a woman;
Sae I'll unbar my door to nae man.
But since 'tis very like, my dow,
That all ye're telling may be true,
Hae there's a key, gang in your way
At the neist door, there's braw ait strae;

33 *threed*: thread
41 *kend*: knew
48 *kill*: kiln for drying corn
49 *hame*: home
50 *crack*: chat
51 *syne*: then
54 *gade*: went
56 *till*: to
57 *steekit*: shut
58 *keekit*: peeped
59 *fowk*: folk, people
60 *untimous*: untimely
65 *my lane*: by myself
66 *sae*: so
67 *dow*: dove
70 *neist*: next
*ait strae*: oat straw

Streek down upon't, my lad, and learn,
They're no ill lodg'd that get a barn.'
Thus after meikle clitter-clatter,
James fand he coudna mend the matter;
And since it might not better be,
With resignation took the key,
Unlockt the barn, — clam up the mou,
Where there was an opening near the hou,
Throw whilk he saw a glent of light,
That gave diversion to his sight:
By this he quickly cou'd discern
A thin wa' separate house and barn,
And throw this rive was in the wa',
All done within the house he saw:
He saw (what ought not to be seen,
And scarce gave credit to his een)
The parish priest of reverend fame
In active courtship with the dame. —
To lengthen out description here,
Wou'd but offend the modest ear,
And beet the lewder youthfu' flame,
That we by satyre strive to tame.
Suppose the wicked action o'er,
And James continuing still to glowre;
Wha saw the wife, as fast as able,
Spread a clean servite on the table,
And syne, frae the ha' ingle, bring ben
A pyping het young roasted hen,
And twa good bottles stout and clear,
Ane of strong ale, and ane of beer.

But wicked luck, just as the priest
Shot in his fork in chucky's breast,
Th' unwelcome miller ga'e a roar,
Cry'd, 'Bessy, haste ye open the door'. —
With that the haly letcher fled,
And darn'd himsell behind a bed;
While Bessy huddl'd a' things by,
That nought the cuckold might espy;
Syne loot him in; — but out of tune,
Speer'd why he left the mill sae soon,

71 *streek*: stretch
77 *clam*: climbed
*mou*: heap of corn straw
78 *hou*: roof-tree
83 *rive*: hole
86 *een*: eyes
91 *beet*: kindle
94 *glowre*: gaze
96 *servite*: table napkin
97 *ingle*: fire
*ben*: in
98 *het*: hot
102 *chucky*: chicken
106 *darn'd*: hid
107 *by*: away
109 *loot*: let
110 *speer'd*: enquired

'I come', said he, 'as manners claims,
To crack and wait on Master James,
Whilk I shou'd do, tho' ne'er sae bissy:
I sent him here, goodwife, where is he?'
'Ye sent him here!' quoth Bessy, grumbling;
'Kend I this James! A chiel came rumbling:
But how was I assur'd, when dark,
That he had been nae thievish spark,
Or some rude wencher, gotten a dose,
That a weak wife cou'd ill oppose?'
'And what came of him? Speak nae langer,'
Crys Halbert in a Highland anger.
'I sent him to the barn,' quoth she.
'Gae quickly bring him in,' quoth he.

James was brought in; — the wife was bawked;
The priest stood close; — the miller cracked:—
Then ask'd his sunkan gloomy spouse,
What supper had she in the house,
That might be suitable to gi'e,
Ane of their lodger's qualitie?
Quoth she, 'Ye may well ken, goodman,
Your feast comes frae the pottage-pan:
The stov'd or roasted we afford,
Are aft great strangers on our board.'
'Pottage,' quoth Hab, 'ye senseless tawpie!
Think ye this youth's a gilly-gawpy;
And that his gentle stamock's master
To worry up a pint of plaister,
Like our mill knaves that lift the laiding,
Whase kytes can streek out like raw plaiding.
Swith roast a hen, or fry some chickens,
And send for ale frae Maggy Pickens.'
'Hout I,' quoth she, 'ye may well ken,
'Tis ill brought butt that's no there ben;
When but last owk, nae farder gane,
The laird got a' to pay his kain.'

113 *bissy*: busy
116 *chiel*: fellow
118 *spark*: young blade
119 *dose*: venereal disease
125 *bawked*: frustrated
127 *sunkan*: ill-tempered
132 *pottage-pan*: broth pot
133 *stov'd*: potatoes simmered with butter etc.
135 *tawpie*: foolish wench
136 *gilly-gawpy*: fool
138 *worry*: choke on
*plaister*: plaster
139 *laiding*: heavy loads
140 *kytes*: stomachs
*streek*: stretch
*plaiding*: loose coarse cloth
141 *swith*: quickly
144 *butt . . . ben*: outer and inner apartments of a house
145 *owk*: week
*farder*: farther
146 *kain*: rent paid in kind

Then James, wha had as good a guess
Of what was in the house as Bess,
With pawky smile, this plea to end,
To please himsell, and ease his friend,
First open'd with a slee oration
His wond'rous skill in conjuration.
Said he, 'By this fell art I'm able
To whop aff any great man's table
What e'er I like, to make a mail of,
Either in part, or yet the haill off;
And if ye please, I'll shaw my art. —'
Crys Halbert, 'Faith, with a' my heart!'
Bess sain'd herself, — cry'd 'Lord be here!'
And near hand fell a swoon for fear.
James leugh, and bade her nathing dread,
Syne to his conjuring went with speed;
And first he draws a circle round,
Then utters mony a magick sound,
Of words part Latin, Greek and Dutch,
Enow to fright a very witch:
That done, he says, 'Now, now 'tis come,
And in the boal beside the lum:
Now set the board; goodwife, gae ben,
Bring frae yon boal a roasted hen.'
She wadna gang, but Haby ventur'd;
And soon as he the ambrie enter'd,
It smell'd sae well, he short time sought it,
And, wondring, 'tween his hands he brought it.
He view'd it round, and thrice he smell'd it,
Syne with a gentle touch he felt it.
Thus ilka sense he did conveen,
Lest glamour had beguil'd his een:
They all, in an united body,
Declar'd it a fine fat how-towdy.
'Nae mair about it,' quoth the Miller,
'The fowl looks well, and we'll fa' till her.'
'Sae be't,' says James; and in a doup,
They snapt her up baith stoup and roup.

149 *pawky*: crafty
151 *slee*: sly, clever
154 *whop*: whip
155 *mail*: meal
156 *haill*: whole
157 *shaw*: show
159 *sain'd*: blessed
160 *near hand*: almost
161 *leugh*: laughed
166 *enow*: enough
168 *boal*: cupboard in wall
*lum*: chimney
172 *ambrie*: large cupboard
177 *conveen*: bring to bear
178 *glamour*: magic
180 *how-towdy*: a young hen
183 *doup*: moment
184 *stoup and roup*: completely

'Neist, O!' crys Halbert, 'cou'd your skill,
But help us to a waught of ale,
I'd be oblig'd t' ye a' my life,
And offer to the Deel my wife,
To see if he'll discreeter make her,
But that I'm fleed he winna take her.'
Said James, 'Ye offer very fair;
The bargain's hadden, say nae mair.'

Then thrice he shook a willow wand,
With kittle words thrice gave command;
That done, with look baith learn'd and grave,
Said, 'Now ye'll get what ye wad have;
Twa bottles of as nappy liquor,
As ever ream'd in horn or bicquor,
Behind the ark that hads your meal,
Ye'll find twa standing corkit well.'
He said, and fast the miller flew,
And frae their nest the bottles drew;
Then first the scholar's health he toasted,
Whase art had gart him feed on roasted;
His father's neist, — and a' the rest
Of his good friends that wish'd him best,
Which were o'er langsome at the time,
On a short tale to put in rhime.

Thus while the miller and the youth,
Were blythly slock'ning of their drowth,
Bess fretting scarcely held frae greeting,
The priest enclos'd stood vex'd and sweating.

'O wow!' said Hab, 'if ane might speer,
Dear Master James, wha brought our chear?
Sic laits appear to us sae awfu',
We hardly think your learning lawfu'.'

'To bring your doubts to a conclusion,'
Says James, 'ken I'm a Rosiecrucian[n],
Ane of the set that never carries
On traffick with black deels or fairies:

186 *waught*: large draught
188 *deel*: devil
190 *fleed*: afraid
192 *hadden*: fixed
194 *kittle*: mysterious
197 *nappy*: sparkling
198 *ream'd*: foamed
*bicquor*: wooden drinking vessel with lugs
199 *ark*: large chest
*hads*: holds
204 *gart*: made
207 *langsome*: tedious
210 *slock'ning*: quenching
*drowth*: thirst
211 *greeting*: weeping
215 *laits*: manners

There's mony a sp'rit that's no a deel,
That constantly around us wheel.
There was a sage call'd Albumazor[n],
Whase wit was gleg as ony razor.
Frae this great man we learn'd the skill,
To bring these gentry to our will;
And they appear when we've a mind,
In ony shape of humane kind:
Now, if you'll drap your foolish fear,
I'll gar my Pacolet[n] appear.'

Hab fidg'd and leugh, his elbuck clew,
Baith fear'd and fond a sp'rit to view:
At last his courage wan the day,
He to the scholar's will gave way.

Bessy be this began to smell
A rat, but kept her mind to'r sell:
She pray'd like howdy in her drink,
But mean time tipt young James a wink.
James frae his eye an answer sent,
Which made the wife right well content.
Then turn'd to Hab, and thus advis'd,
'What e'er ye see, be nought surpriz'd;
But for your saul move not your tongue,
And ready stand with a great rung;
Syne as the sp'rit gangs marching out,
Be sure to lend him a sound rout.
I bidna this be way of mocking;
For nought delytes him mair than knocking.'

Hab got a kent, — stood by the hallan;
And straight the wild mischievous callan,
Cries, 'Radamanthus Husky Mingo,
Monk-horner, Hipock, Jinko, Jingo[n],
Appear in likeness of a priest,
No like a deel in shape of beast,
With gaping chafts to fleg us a'.
Wauk forth; the door stands to the wa'.'

224 *gleg*: sharp
229 *drap*: drop
230 *gar*: make
231 *fidg'd*: fidgeted
*leugh*: laughed
*elbuck*: elbow
*clew*: scratched
232 *fear'd*: afraid
233 *wan*: won
237 *howdy*: midwife
244 *rung*: bludgeon
246 *rout*: blow
247 *bidna*: don't ask
249 *kent*: shepherd's staff
*hallan*: partition
250 *callan*: youth
255 *chafts*: jaws
*fleg*: frighten

Then frae the hole where he was pent,
The priest approach'd right well content,
With silent pace strade o'er the floor,
Till he was drawing near the door;
Then, to escape the cudgel, ran;
But was not miss'd by the goodman,
Wha lent him on the neck a lounder,
That gart him o'er the threshold founder.
Darkness soon hid him frae their sight;
Ben flew the miller in a fright:
'I trow,' quoth he, 'I laid well on;
But wow he's like our ain Mess John!'

257 *pent*: hidden
263 *lounder*: sound blow
267 *trow*: believe
268 *Mess John*: parish priest

# James Thomson
## 1700–1748

The son of the minister of Ednam in Roxburghshire, two miles N.E. of Kelso, Thomson was educated at the College of Edinburgh (as that university was then called), supposedly for the church. He left for London by boat in 1725 to seek his literary fortune, and by July had become tutor to the son of the Earl of Haddington, a Scots lord living near the capital. In May of the following year he moved to 'Mr Watts' Academy in Little Tower-street, in quality of tutor to a young gentleman there'. Here he came into contact with the most advanced scientific ideas of the time, for Isaac Watts' academy taught 'mechanical and experimental philosophy'; one of its 'professors', James Stirling, was the correspondent of Newton and of many noted European mathematicians; and it even employed a mathematical instrument-maker to make the apparatus for the experiments. From November 1730 to early in 1732 Thomson was travelling tutor to Charles Richard Talbot, whose father later became the Lord Chancellor, and in 1733 was appointed to a sinecure in the Court of Chancery at a salary of £300 a year, but lost it on the Lord Chancellor's death in 1737. From then onwards he lived quietly and comfortably at Richmond on the earnings of his pen, supplemented by a pension of £100 a year from the Prince of Wales.

Three poems by him appeared in *The Edinburgh Miscellany* (1720), one of which, *Of a Country Life*, looks forward to *The Seasons*; and the first version of *Winter*, printed below, was published in April 1726, through the good offices of his fellow Scot, David Mallet. The tradition that he wrote *Winter: a Poem* in the Borders before he ever left for England, on a hill near the village of Widehope which rejoiced in the name of Parnassus, is almost certainly false (*Hist. Berwick Naturalists' Club*, 1916, xxii, 402); but it nevertheless points to the important truth that the scenes that inspired him were originally Scottish. *Summer* came out in February 1727, and in late April a poem *To the Memory of Isaac Newton* (a month after Newton's death), which went through four editions within the year. *Spring* was published in 1728, and in 1730 the entire *Seasons*, including *Autumn*, in a lavishly illustrated quarto. His first tragedy *Sophonisba* was produced at Drury Lane at about the same time, and his next plays *Agamemnon* (1738) and *Edward and Eleonora* (1739) were disguised attacks on the administration from a committed whig standpoint. His whig ideas appear most fully in *Liberty* (1735–6), where Liberty herself tells how her fortunes rose and fell throughout history in Greece, Rome and Britain. The modern idea of 'Britain' was in many ways a Scottish invention, and Thomson played a leading part in its creation — for example in *Alfred: a Masque*, written jointly with Mallet, and containing *Rule Britannia*, all of which is almost certainly by

Thomson. In 1748 he published *The Castle of Indolence*, a witty Spenserian imitation; his last play, *Coriolanus*, was staged posthumously in 1749.

In his boyhood Thomson must have spoken broad Scots and it is interesting that the prose letters he wrote before he left Edinburgh contain a number of specifically Scots-English idioms. Nor is the Miltonic diction of *The Seasons* non-Scottish; it fits in very well with Dunbar's and Gavin Douglas's employment of Latin words and aureate styles for special purposes, just as his urge to make poetry out of Newtonian ideas and the contemporary scientific vocabulary points forward to John Davidson and Hugh MacDiarmid. His best landscapes relate to memories of Border scenes; his intense sense of colour and light reminds one of Dunbar and Walter Scott; and his winter descriptions have points in common with both Gavin Douglas and Burns.

Thomson kept adding to *The Seasons* as time went on. The original *Winter* had only 405 lines, but by 1746 it had swollen to 1069 lines. Perhaps the best comment is Dr Johnson's: 'They are, I think, improved in general; yet I know not whether they have not lost part of what Sir William Temple calls their "race"; a word which, applied to wine in its primitive sense, means the flavour of the soil'. (*Lives of the Poets*, Everyman edn., II. 292). In *Winter*, the original soil is indubitably Scottish.

*Edition:*

*Poems*, ed. J. Logie Robertson (1908, repr. 1951). Oxford Standard Authors.

*Biography:*

Douglas Grant, *James Thomson, Poet of 'The Seasons'* (London, 1951).

*Criticism:*

Marjorie Hope Nicolson, *Newton Demands the Muse* (Princeton, 1946), chapter 5.

D. Nichol Smith, 'Thomson and Burns' in J. L. Clifford, ed., *Eighteenth Century English Literature* (New York, 1959), pp. 180–93.

Patricia M. Spacks, *The Varied God* (Berkeley, 1959).

Ralph Cohen, *The Art of Discrimination* (London, 1964); *The Unfolding of 'The Seasons'* (London, 1970).

# WINTER: A POEM

See! Winter comes, to rule the varied year,
Sullen, and sad; with all his rising train,
Vapours, and clouds, and storms: be these my theme,
These, that exalt the soul to solemn thought,
And heavenly musing. Welcome kindred glooms!
Wish'd, wint'ry, horrors, hail! — With frequent foot,
Pleas'd, have I, in my cheerful morn of life,
When, nurs'd by careless solitude, I liv'd,
And sung of Nature with unceasing joy,
Pleas'd, have I wander'd thro' your rough domains;
Trod the pure,virgin, snows, my self as pure:
Heard the winds roar, and the big torrent burst:
Or seen the deep, fermenting, tempest brew'd,
In the red, evening, sky. — Thus pass'd the time,
Till, thro' the opening chambers of the south,
Look'd out the joyous Spring, look'd out, and smil'd.

Thee too, inspirer of the toiling swain!
Fair Autumn, yellow rob'd! I'll sing of thee,
Of thy last, temper'd days and sunny calms;
When all the golden hours are on the wing,
Attending thy retreat, and round thy wain,
Slow-rolling, onward to the southern sky.

Behold! the well-pois'd hornet, hovering, hangs,
With quivering pinions in the genial blaze;
Flys off, in airy circles: then returns,
And hums, and dances to the beating ray.
Nor shall the man, that, musing, walks alone,
And, heedless, strays within his radiant lists
Go unchastis'd away. — Sometimes, a fleece
Of clouds, wide-scattering, with a lucid veil,
Soft, shadow o'er th' unruffled face of heaven;
And, thro' their dewy sluices, shed the sun,
With temper'd influence down. Then is the time
For those, whom Wisdom, and whom Nature charm,
To steal themselves from the degenerate croud,
And soar above this little scene of things:
To tread low-thoughted vice beneath their feet:
To lay their passions in a gentle calm,
And woo lone Quiet, in her silent walks.

2 *sad*: sombre
24 *genial*: pleasantly warm
28 *lists*: borders
21 *wain*: chariot

Now, solitary, and in pensive guise,
Oft let me wander o'er the russet mead,
Or thro' the pining grove; where scarce is heard
One dying strain, to chear the woodman's toil:
Sad Philomel,[n] perchance, pours forth her plaint,
Far, thro' the withering copse. Mean while, the leaves
That, late, the forest clad with lively green,
Nipt by the drizzly night, and sallow-hu'd,
Fall, wavering, thro' the air; or shower amain
Urg'd by the breeze, that sobs amid the boughs.
Then list'ning hares forsake the rusling woods,
And, starting at the frequent noise, escape
To the rough stubble, and the rushy fen.
Then woodcocks, o'er the fluctuating main,
That glimmers to the glimpses of the moon,
Stretch their long voyage to the woodland glade:
Where, wheeling with uncertain flight, they mock
The nimble fowler's aim. — Now Nature droops;
Languish the living herbs, with pale decay:
And all the various family of flowers
Their sunny robes resign. The falling fruits,
Thro' the still night, forsake the parent-bough,
That, in the first, grey, glances of the dawn,
Looks wild, and wonders at the wintry waste.

The year, yet pleasing, but declining fast,
Soft, o'er the secret soul, in gentle gales,
A philosophic melancholy breathes,
And bears the swelling thought aloft to heaven.
Then forming fancy rouses to conceive,
What never mingled with the vulgar's dream:
Then wake the tender pang, the pitying tear,
The sigh for suffering worth, the wish preferred
For humankind, the joy to see them bless'd,
And all the social offspring of the heart!

Oh! bear me then to high, embowering, shades;
To twilight groves, and visionary vales;
To weeping grottos, and to hoary caves;
Where angel-forms are seen, and voices heard,
Sigh'd in low whispers, that abstract the soul,
From outward sense, far into worlds remote.

48 *amain*: with full force

55 *stretch . . . voyage*: direct their course

69 *vulgar*: common people

71 *preferred*: put forward

Now, when the western sun withdraws the day,
And humid Evening, gliding o'er the sky,
In her chill progress, checks the straggling beams,
And robs them of their gather'd, vapoury, prey,
Where marshes stagnate, and where rivers wind,
Cluster the rolling fogs, and swim along
The dusky-mantled lawn: then slow descend,
Once more to mingle with their watry friends.
The vivid stars shine out, in radiant files;
And boundless Ether glows, till the fair moon
Shows her broad visage, in the crimson'd east;
Now, stooping, seems to kiss the passing cloud:
Now, o'er the pure cerulean, rides sublime.
Wide the pale deluge floats, with silver waves,
O'er the sky'd mountain, to the low-laid vale;
From the white rocks, with dim reflexion, gleams,
And faintly glitters thro' the waving shades.

All night, abundant dews, unnoted, fall,
And, at return of morning, silver o'er
The face of Mother-Earth; from every branch
Depending, tremble the translucent gems,
And, quivering, seem to fall away, yet cling
And sparkle in the sun, whose rising eye,
With fogs bedim'd, portends a beauteous day.

Now, giddy youth, whom headlong passions fire,
Rouse the wild game, and stain the guiltless grove,
With violence, and death; yet call it sport,
To scatter ruin thro' the realms of Love,
And Peace, that thinks no ill: but these, the Muse;
Whose charity, unlimited, extends
As wide as Nature works, disdains to sing,
Returning to her nobler theme in view —

For, see! where Winter comes, himself, confest,
Striding the gloomy blast. First rains obscure
Drive thro' the mingling skies, with tempest foul;
Beat on the mountain's brow, and shake the woods,
That, sounding, wave below. The dreary plain
Lies overwhelm'd, and lost. The bellying clouds
Combine, and deepening into night, shut up
The day's fair face. The wanderers of heaven,
Each to his home, retire; save those that love

89 *ether*: medium filling the upper regions of space
92 *cerulean*: deep blue (sky)
100 *Depending*: hanging
112 *confest*: visible in his own person
119 *wanderers of heaven*: birds

To take their pastime in the troubled air,
And, skimming, flutter round the dimply flood.
The cattle, from th' untasted fields, return,
And ask, with meaning low, their wonted stalls;
Or ruminate in the contiguous shade:
Thither, the household, feathery, people[n] croud,
The crested cock, with all his female train,
Pensive and wet. Mean while, the cottage-swain,
Hangs o'er th' enlivening blaze, and, taleful, there,
Recounts his simple frolic: much he talks,
And much he laughs, nor recks the storm that blows
Without, and rattles on his humble roof.

At last, the muddy deluge pours along,
Resistless, roaring; dreadful down it comes
From the chapt mountain, and the mossy wild,
Tumbling thro' rocks abrupt, and sounding far:
Then o'er the sanded valley, floating, spreads,
Calm, sluggish, silent; till again constrain'd,
Betwixt two meeting hills, it bursts a way,
Where rocks, and woods o'erhang the turbid stream.
There gathering triple force, rapid, and deep,
It boils, and wheels, and foams, and thunders thro'.

Nature! great parent! whose directing hand
Rolls round the seasons of the changeful year,
How mighty! how majestick are thy works!
With what a pleasing dread they swell the soul,
That sees, astonish'd! and, astonish'd sings!
You too, ye Winds! that now begin to blow,
With boisterous sweep, I raise my voice to you.
Where are your stores, ye viewless Beings! say?
Where your aerial magazines reserv'd,
Against the day of tempest perilous?
In what untravel'd country of the air,
Hush'd in still silence, sleep you, when 'tis calm?

Late, in the louring sky, red, fiery, streaks
Begin to flush about; the reeling clouds
Stagger with dizzy aim, as doubting yet
Which master to obey: while rising, slow,
Sad, in the leaden-colour'd east, the moon
Wears a bleak circle[n] round her sully'd orb.
Then issues forth the storm, with loud control,
And the thin fabrick of the pillar'd air[n]

135 *chapt*: crevassed    161 *control*: command

O'erturns, at once. Prone, on th' uncertain main,
Descends th' etherial force, and plows its waves,
With dreadful rift: from the mid-deep, appears,
Surge after surge, the rising, wat'ry, war.
Whitening, the angry billows rowl immense,
And roar their terrors, thro' the shuddering soul
Of feeble man, amidst their fury caught,
And, dash'd upon his fate: then, o'er the cliff,
Where dwells the sea-mew, unconfin'd, they fly
And, hurrying, swallow up the steril shore.

The mountain growls; and all its sturdy sons
Stoop to the bottom of the rocks they shade:
Lone, on its midnight-side, and all aghast,
The dark, way-faring, stranger, breathless, toils,
And climbs against the blast —
Low, waves the rooted forest, vex'd, and sheds
What of its leafy honours yet remains.
Thus, struggling thro' the dissipated grove,
The whirling tempest raves along the plain;
And, on the cottage thatcht, or lordly dome,
Keen-fastening, shakes 'em to the solid base.
Sleep, frighted, flies; the hollow chimney howls,
The windows rattle, and the hinges creak.

Then, too, they say, thro' all the burthen'd air,
Long groans are heard, shrill sounds, and distant sighs,
That, murmur'd by the demon of the night,
Warn the devoted wretch of woe, and death!
Wild Uproar lords it wide: the clouds commixt,
With stars, swift-gliding, sweep along the sky.
All Nature reels. — But hark! the Almighty speaks:
Instant, the chidden storm begins to pant,
And dies, at once, into a noiseless calm.

As yet, 'tis Midnight's reign; the weary clouds,
Slow-meeting, mingle into solid gloom:
Now, while the drousy world lies lost in sleep,
Let me associate with the low-brow'd night,
And Contemplation, her sedate compeer;
Let me shake off th' intrusive cares of day,
And lay the meddling senses all aside.

173 *sturdy sons*: trees
175 *midnight-side*: side of extreme darkness
180 *dissipated*: wasted
182 *dome*: house (from lat., *domus*)
198 *low-brow'd*: dark and forbidding (like overhanging cliffs)

And now, ye lying vanities of life!
You ever-tempting, ever-cheating train!
Where are you now? and what is your amount?
Vexation, disappointment, and remorse.
Sad, sickening, thought! and yet, deluded man,
A scene of wild, disjointed, visions past,
And broken slumbers, rises, still resolv'd,
With new-flush'd hopes, to run your giddy round.

Father of light, and life! Thou Good supreme!
O! teach me what is Good! teach me thy self!
Save me from folly, vanity and vice,
From every low pursuit! and feed my soul,
With knowledge, conscious peace, and vertue pure,
Sacred, substantial, never-fading bliss!

Lo! from the livid east, or piercing north,
Thick clouds ascend, in whose capacious womb,
A vapoury deluge lies, to snow congeal'd:
Heavy, they roll their fleecy world along;
And the sky saddens with th' impending storm.
Thro' the hush'd air, the whitening shower descends,
At first, thin-wavering; till, at last, the flakes
Fall broad, and wide, and fast, dimming the day,
With a continual flow. See! sudden, hoar'd,
The woods beneath the stainless burden bow,
Blackning, along the mazy stream it melts;
Earth's universal face, deep-hid, and chill
Is all one, dazzling, waste. The labourer-ox
Stands cover'd o'er with snow, and then demands
The fruit of all his toil. The fowls of heaven,
Tam'd by the cruel season, croud around
The winnowing store, and claim the little boon,
That Providence allows. The foodless wilds
Pour forth their brown inhabitants; the hare,
Tho' timorous of heart, and hard beset
By Death, in various forms, dark snares, and dogs,
And more unpitying men, the garden seeks,
Urg'd on by fearless want. The bleating kind
Eye the bleak heavens, and next, the glistening earth,
With looks of dumb despair; then sad, dispers'd,
Dig, for the wither'd herb, thro' heaps of snow.

232 *winnowing store*: grain kept in the barn to be winnowed during the winter

Now, shepherds, to your helpless charge be kind;
Baffle the raging year, and fill their penns
With food, at will: lodge them below the blast,
And watch them strict; for from the bellowing east,
In this dire season, oft the whirlwind's wing
Sweeps up the burthen of whole wintry plains,
In one fierce blast, and o'er th' unhappy flocks,
Lodg'd in the hollow of two neighbouring hills,
The billowy tempest whelms; till, upwards urg'd,
The valley to a shining mountain swells,
That curls its wreaths amid the freezing sky.[n]

Now, all amid the rigours of the year,
In the wild depth of winter, while without
The ceaseless winds blow keen, be my retreat
A rural, shelter'd, solitary scene;
Where ruddy fire, and beaming tapers join
To chase the chearless gloom: there let me sit,
And hold high converse with the mighty dead,
Sages of ancient time, as gods rever'd,
As gods beneficent, who blest mankind,
With arts, and arms, and humaniz'd a world.
Rous'd at th' inspiring thought — I throw aside
The long-liv'd volume, and, deep-musing, hail
The sacred shades, that, slowly-rising, pass
Before my wondering eyes — First, Socrates,
Truth's early champion, martyr for his god:
Solon,[n] the next, who built his commonweal,
On equity's firm base: Lycurgus,[n] then,
Severely good, and him of rugged Rome,
Numa,[n] who soften'd her rapacious Sons.
Cimon[n] sweet-soul'd, and Aristides[n] just.
Unconquer'd Cato,[n] virtuous in extreme;
With that attemper'd heroe,[n] mild, and firm,
Who wept the brother, while the tyrant bled.
Scipio,[n] the humane warriour, gently brave,
Fair Learning's friend, who early sought the shade,
To dwell, with Innocence, and Truth, retir'd.
And, equal to the best, the Theban,[n] he
Who, single, rais'd his country into fame.
Thousands behind, the boast of Greece and Rome,
Whom vertue owns, the tribute of a verse
Demand, but who can count the stars of heaven?
Who sing their influence on this lower world?

264 *long-liv'd volume*: Plutarch's *Lives*

But see who yonder comes! nor comes alone,
With sober state, and of majestic mien,
The sister-muses in his train — 'tis he!
Maro![n] the best of poets, and of men!
Great Homer too appears, of daring wing!
Parent of song! and, equal, by his side,
The British Muse,[n] join'd hand in hand, they walk,
Darkling, nor miss their way to fame's ascent.

Society divine! Immortal minds!
Still visit thus my nights, for you reserv'd,
And mount my soaring soul to deeds like yours.
Silence! thou lonely Power! the door be thine:
See, on the hallow'd hour, that none intrude,
Save Lycidas,[n] the friend, with sense refin'd,
Learning digested well, exalted faith,
Unstudy'd wit, and humour ever gay.

Clear frost succeeds, and thro' the blew serene,
For sight too fine, th' ætherial nitre[n] flies,
To bake the glebe, and bind the slip'ry flood.
This of the wintry season is the prime;
Pure are the days, and lustrous are the nights,
Brighten'd with starry worlds, till then unseen.
Mean while, the orient, darkly red, breathes forth
An icy gale, that, in its mid career,
Arrests the bickering stream. The nightly sky,
And all her glowing constellations pour
Their rigid influence[n] down: it freezes on
Till morn, late-rising, o'er the drooping world,
Lifts her pale eye, unjoyous: then appears
The various labour of the silent night,
The pendant icicle, the frost-work fair,
Where thousand figures rise, the crusted snow,
Tho' white, made whiter, by the fining north.
On blithsome frolics bent, the youthful swains,
While every work of man is laid at rest,
Rush o'er the watry plains, and, shuddering, view
The fearful deeps below: or with the gun,
And faithful spaniel, range the ravag'd fields,
And, adding to the ruins of the year,
Distress the feathery, or the footed game.

But hark! the nightly winds, with hollow voice,
Blow, blustering, from the south — the frost subdu'd,

292 *Darkling*: blind    317 *fining*: refining

Gradual, resolves into a weeping thaw.
Spotted, the mountains shine: loose sleet descends,
And floods the country round: the rivers swell,
Impatient for the day. — Those sullen seas,
That wash th' ungenial pole, will rest no more,
Beneath the shackles of the mighty north;
But, rousing all their waves, resistless heave, —
And hark! — the length'ning roar, continuous, runs
Athwart the rifted main; at once, it bursts,
And piles a thousand mountains to the clouds!
Ill fares the bark, the wretches' last resort,
That, lost amid the floating fragments, moors
Beneath the shelter of an icy isle;
While night o'erwhelms the sea, and horror looks
More horrible. Can human hearts endure
Th' assembled mischiefs, that besiege them round:
Unlist'ning hunger, fainting weariness,
The roar of winds, and waves, the crush of ice,
Now, ceasing, now, renew'd, with louder rage,
And bellowing round the main: nations remote,
Shook from their midnight-slumbers, deem they hear
Portentous thunder, in the troubled sky.
More to embroil the deep, Leviathan,
And his unwieldy train, in horrid sport,
Tempest the loosen'd brine; while, thro' the gloom,
Far, from the dire, unhospitable shore,
The lyon's rage, the wolf's sad howl is heard,
And all the fell society of night.
Yet, Providence, that ever-waking eye
Looks down, with pity, on the fruitless toil
Of mortals, lost to hope, and lights them safe,
Thro' all this dreary labyrinth of fate.

'Tis done! — Dread Winter has subdu'd the year,
And reigns, tremenduous, o'er the desart plains!
How dead the vegetable kingdom lies!
How dumb the tuneful! Horror wide extends
His solitary empire. — Now, fond Man!
Behold thy pictur'd life: pass some few years,
Thy flow'ring Spring, thy short-liv'd Summer's strength,
Thy sober Autumn, fading into age,
And pale, concluding, Winter shuts thy scene,
And shrouds thee in the grave — Where now, are fled
Those dreams of greatness? those unsolid hopes
Of happiness? those longings after fame?

331 *ungenial*: cold, sterile     349 *Leviathan*: the whale

Those restless cares? those busy, bustling days?
Those nights of secret guilt? those veering thoughts,
Flutt'ring 'twixt good, and ill, that shar'd thy life?
All, now, are vanish'd! Vertue, sole, survives,
Immortal, mankind's never-failing friend,
His guide to happiness on high — and see!
'Tis come, the glorious morn! the second birth
Of Heaven, and Earth! — awakening Nature hears
Th' almighty trumpet's voice, and starts to life,
Renew'd, unfading. Now, th' eternal scheme,
That dark perplexity, that mystic maze,
Which sight cou'd never trace, nor heart conceive,
To Reason's eye, refin'd, clears up apace.
Angels, and men, astonish'd, pause — and dread
To travel thro' the depths of providence,
Untry'd, unbounded. Ye vain learned! see,
And, prostrate in the dust, adore that power,
And goodness, oft arraign'd. See now the cause,
Why conscious worth, oppress'd, in secret long
Mourn'd, unregarded: Why the good man's share
In life, was gall and bitterness of soul:
Why the lone widow, and her orphans, pin'd,
In starving solitude; while luxury,
In palaces, lay prompting her low thought,
To form unreal wants: why heaven-born Faith,
And Charity, prime grace! wore the red marks
Of Persecution's scourge: why licens'd pain,
That cruel spoiler, that embosom'd foe,
Imbitter'd all our bliss. Ye good distrest!
Ye noble few! that, here, unbending, stand
Beneath life's pressures — yet a little while,
And all your woes are past. Time swiftly fleets,
And wish'd Eternity, approaching, brings
Life undecaying, love without allay,
Pure flowing joy, and happiness sincere.

389 *conscious*: internally aware of spiritual merit

# David Mallet
## 1702?-1765

Born in Crieff with the decent Perthshire name of Malloch, this writer changed it to Mallet when he went to live in London. According to Johnson (*Lives of the English Poets*), Mallet acted for a time as janitor at the High School of Edinburgh, probably when he was attending Edinburgh University. He became acquainted with Allan Ramsay and was one of a group of bright young men who helped with *The Tea-Table Miscellany*. He became tutor to the sons of the Duke of Montrose, and his subsequent career as essayist, poet, and dramatist was in London.

For many years it was thought that the original version of *William and Margaret* was that in Aaron Hill's *Plain Dealer* of 24 July, 1724, and it was difficult to reconcile this belief with Allan Ramsay's reference to the poem in a farewell address to Mallet in 1723, when he left Edinburgh for London. Now, however, Gordon Sleigh and D. F. Foxon have proved beyond doubt that the poem was written by Mallet and first published in Edinburgh, probably by Ramsay, in 1723. Mallet has thus at last been cleared of the charge of plagiarism which some of his contemporaries were ready to level at him: they held he had published as his own a poem either traditional or composed by another man. *William and Margaret* was widely known, as much in England as in Scotland; like *Hardyknute*, it was instrumental in reviving interest in the older ballads; and it will be noted that Ramsay was concerned in the publication of both of these influential poems. It was often sung — e.g. one early broadside has the note 'this ballad will sing to the tunes of Montrose's *Lilt*, Rothes's *Lament*, or the *Isle of Kell*', and it was printed with music in *Orpheus Caledonius* (London, 1725 and 1733), as well as in Johnson's *Scots Musical Museum* at the end of the century. The many minor variants in broadside and song-book texts suggest that this literary ballad-imitation was so popular as to be known by heart by editors and printers — that is, that there was an 'oral' factor in its transmission. Our text is from Dinsdale's edition, cited below, which followed *The Works of David Mallet*, 3 vols, 1759, and is modernised in accordance with the principles of this anthology.

*Edition:*
*The Works of David Mallet*, ed. F. T. Dinsdale (London, 1857).
Dinsdale's work also contains biographical and critical material.

*Biography:*
Samuel Johnson, *Lives of the English Poets*.

*Criticism:*

G. Sleigh, 'The authorship of William and Margaret', *The Library*, 5th series, 8 (1953), 121.

D. F. Foxon, *English Verse 1701–50* (Cambridge, 1975), item M59, vol. I, 444.

## WILLIAM AND MARGARET

'Twas at the silent, solemn hour,
When night and morning meet;
In glided Margaret's grimly ghost,
And stood at William's feet.

Her face was like an April morn,
Clad in a wintry cloud:
And clay-cold was her lily-hand,
That held her sable shroud.

So shall the fairest face appear,
When youth and years are flown:
Such is the robe that kings must wear,
When death has reft their crown.

Her bloom was like the springing flower,
That sips the silver dew;
The rose was budded in her cheek,
Just opening to the view.

But love had, like the canker-worm,
Consum'd her early prime:
The rose grew pale, and left her cheek;
She died before her time.

'Awake!' she cried, 'thy true love calls,
Come from her midnight grave;
Now let thy pity hear the maid,
Thy love refus'd to save.

'This is the dumb and dreary hour,
When injur'd ghosts complain;
When yawning graves give up their dead,
To haunt the faithless swain.

'Bethink thee, William, of thy fault,
Thy pledge and broken oath:
And give me back my maiden-vow,
And give me back my troth.

'Why did you promise love to me,
And not that promise keep?
Why did you swear my eyes were bright,
Yet leave those eyes to weep?

'How could you say my face was fair,
And yet that face forsake?
How could you win my virgin heart,
Yet leave that heart to break?

'Why did you say my lip was sweet,
And made the scarlet pale?
And why did I, young witless maid!
Believe the flattering tale?

'That face, alas! no more is fair;
Those lips no longer red:
Dark are my eyes, now clos'd in death,
And every charm is fled.

'The hungry worm my sister is;
This winding-sheet I wear:
And cold and weary lasts our night,
Till that last morn appear.

'But, hark! the cock has warn'd me hence;
A long and late adieu!
Come see, false man, how low she lies,
Who died for love of you.'

The lark sung loud; the morning smil'd,
With beams of rosy red:
Pale William quak'd in every limb,
And raving left his bed.

He hied him to the fatal place
Where Margaret's body lay:
And stretch'd him on the grass-green turf
That wrap'd her breathless clay.

And thrice he call'd on Margaret's name,
And thrice he wept full sore:
Then laid his cheek to her cold grave,
And word spoke never more!

# William Hamilton of Bangour

## 1704–1754

William Hamilton is generally given the name of his West Lothian estate to distinguish him from his older contemporary, Lieutenant William Hamilton of Gilbertfield, who exchanged lively verse epistles with Allan Ramsay and wrote a popular version of Hary's *Wallace*.

William Hamilton, the second son of James Hamilton of Bangour, was born and brought up a gentleman with a gentleman's interest in letters. He may have attended Edinburgh University: he certainly was acquainted with Allan Ramsay for his poem *The Braes of Yarrow*, with some others of his verses, appeared in Ramsay's *Tea-Table Miscellany*, and his poem *To the Countess of Eglintoun, with The Gentle Shepherd*, was prefixed to the second (1726) edition of Ramsay's pastoral play. Hamilton lived most of his life in or near Edinburgh, and his works include, besides the translations from the classics that one would expect from a gentleman scholar, some delightful verses describing the Edinburgh social scene, such as *To H. H. in the Assembly*, and *Interview of Miss Dalrymple and Miss Suttie between the Pillars at the Edinburgh Assembly: in imitation of Homer's Iliad, Book VI*. Hamilton was familiar with the highest society in the land.

He was on the Jacobite side in the Forty-five. He probably took no active part, since his wife was ill and died in October 1745, but he went into hiding and ultimately escaped to France. He was able to return in 1747 under the Act of Indemnity, and succeeded his older brother at Bangour in 1750. He became ill, however, went abroad for his health, and died at Lyons in 1754.

*The Braes of Yarrow* is, as its sub-title suggests, 'in imitation of the ancient Scottish manner', and follows a long ballad tradition of tragic fights by the Yarrow. Scott in his *Minstrelsy of the Scottish Border* claims that Hamilton's poem was probably suggested by the old ballad *The Dowie Dens of Yarrow*. Hamilton departs from the more usual stanza in common metre and produces an effect of pathos by the lengthening of the line and the repetitive use of affecting phrases. Lines like: 'Lang maun she weep, lang maun she, maun she weep' are breath-catching and turn this 'imitation' into memorable poetry.

*Edition:*

*The Poems and Songs of William Hamilton of Bangour*, ed. James Paterson (Edinburgh, 1850).

*Biography:*

Nelson S. Bushnell, *William Hamilton of Bangour, Poet and Jacobite* (Aberdeen, 1957).

## THE BRAES OF YARROW

### To Lady Jane Home

IN IMITATION OF THE ANCIENT SCOTTISH MANNER

*A.* 'Busk ye, busk ye, my bonnie, bonnie bride!
Busk ye, busk ye, my winsome marrow;
Busk ye, busk ye, my bonnie, bonnie bride,
And think nae mair on the Braes of Yarrow.'

*B.* 'Where gat ye that bonnie, bonnie bride?
Where gat ye that winsome marrow?'
*A.* 'I gat her where I dare na weil be seen.
Puing the birks[n] on the Braes of Yarrow.

'Weep not, weep not, my bonnie, bonnie bride!
Weep not, weep not, my winsome marrow;
Nor let thy heart lament to leive
Puing the birks on the Braes of Yarrow.'

*B.* 'Why does she weep, thy bonnie, bonnie bride?
Why does she weep, thy winsome marrow?
And why dare ye nae mair weil be seen
Puing the birks on the Braes of Yarrow?'

*A.* 'Lang maun she weep, lang maun she, maun she weep,
Lang maun she weep with dule and sorrow;
And lang maun I nae mair weil be seen
Puing the birks on the Braes of Yarrow.

For she has tint her luver, luver dear,
Her luver dear, the cause of sorrow;
And I hae slain the comeliest swain
That e'er pu'd birks on the Braes of Yarrow.

Why runs thy stream, O Yarrow, Yarrow, red?
Why on thy braes heard the voice of sorrow?
And why yon melancholeous weids
Hung on the bonnie birks of Yarrow?

1 *busk*: make ready
4 *braes*: hills
10 *marrow*: partner
17 *maun*: must
21 *tint*: lost

What yonder floats on the rueful, rueful flude?
What yonder floats? O dule and sorrow!
'Tis he, the comely swain I slew
Upon the duleful Braes of Yarrow.

Wash, O wash his wounds, his wounds in tears,
His wounds in tears, with dule and sorrow;
And wrap his limbs in mourning weids,
And lay him on the Braes of Yarrow.

Then build, then build, ye sisters, sisters sad,
Ye sisters sad, his tomb with sorrow,
And weep around, in waeful wise,
His hapless fate on the Braes of Yarrow.

Curse ye, curse ye, his useless, useless shield,
My arm that wrought the deed of sorrow,
The fatal spear that pierc'd his breast,
His comely breast, on the Braes of Yarrow.

Did I not warn thee not to lue,
And warn from fight? but to my sorrow,
O'er rashly bald, a stronger arm
Thou met'st, and fell on the Braes of Yarrow.

Sweet smells the birk, green grows, green grows the grass,
Yellow on Yarrow's bank the gowan;
Fair hangs the apple frae the rock,
Sweet the wave of Yarrow flowan.

Flows Yarrow sweet? as sweet, as sweet flows Tweed,
As green its grass, its gowan yellow;
As sweet smells on its braes the birk,
The apple frae the rock as mellow.

Fair was thy luve, fair, fair indeed thy luve,
In flow'ry bands thou him didst fetter;
Tho' he was fair and weil beluv'd again,
Than me, he never lued thee better.

Busk ye, then busk, my bonnie, bonnie bride!
Busk ye, busk ye, my winsome marrow;
Busk ye, and lue me on the banks of Tweed,
And think nae mair on the Braes of Yarrow.'

34 *dule*: grief
45 *lue*: love
47 *bald*: bold
50 *gowan*: daisy

*C.* 'How can I busk a bonnie, bonnie bride?
How can I busk a winsome marrow?
How lue him on the banks of Tweed,
That slew my luve on the Braes of Yarrow?

O Yarrow fields, may never, never rain,
No dew thy tender blossoms cover,
For there was basely slain my luve,
My luve, as he had not been a lover.

The boy put on his robes, his robes of green,
His purple vest, 'twas my awn seuing;
Ah! wretched me! I little, little ken'd
He was in these to meet his ruin.

The boy took out his milk-white, milk-white steed,
Unheedful of my dule and sorrow;
But ere the tofall of the night
He lay a corpse on the Braes of Yarrow.

Much I rejoic'd that waeful, waeful day,
I sang, my voice the woods returning;
But lang ere night the spear was flown
That slew my luve, and left me mourning.

What can my barbarous, barbarous father do,
But with his cruel rage pursue me?
My luver's blood is on thy spear,
How can'st thou, barbarous man, then woo me?

My happy sisters may be, may be proud,
With cruel, and ungentle scoffin,
May bid me seek on Yarrow Braes
My luver nailed in his coffin.

My brother Douglas may upbraid,
And strive with threat'ning words to muve me:
My luver's blood is on thy spear,
How can'st thou ever bid me luve thee?

Yes, yes, prepare the bed, the bed of luve,
With bridal sheets my body cover;
Unbar, ye bridal maids, the door,
Let in the expected husband luver.

79 *tofall of the night*: evening

But who the expected husband, husband is?
His hands, methinks, are bath'd in slaughter;
Ah me! what ghastly spectre's yon,
Comes, in his pale shroud, bleeding after?

Pale as he is, here lay him, lay him down,
O lay his cold head on my pillow;
Take aff, take aff these bridal weids,
And crown my careful head with willow.

Pale tho' thou art, yet best, yet best beluv'd,
O could my warmth to life restore thee!
Yet lie all night between my briests,
No youth lay ever there before thee.

Pale, pale indeed, O lovely, lovely youth!
Forgive, forgive so foul a slaughter;
And lie all night between my briests,
No youth shall ever lie there after'.

*A.* 'Return, return, O mournful, mournful bride,
Return and dry thy useless sorrow;
Thy luver heeds nought of thy sighs,
He lies a corpse on the Braes of Yarrow.'

# Alexander Ross
## 1699–1784

Alexander Ross was the son of a farmer in the Deeside parish of Kincardine-O'Neil, Aberdeenshire. From the local school, he proceeded to Marischal College, Aberdeen, from which he graduated M.A. in 1718. For a while he was tutor to the family of Sir William Forbes of Craigievar, and in 1732 or 1733 he was invited to become schoolmaster at Lochlee at the head of Glenesk, Angus, and he remained there for the rest of his life.

Lochlee is now a desolate spot in a sparsely inhabited glen some twenty miles from the nearest village, Edzell. In the eighteenth century it was more populous than now, and less remote, for Deeside was accessible on foot or horseback over the hill paths. In Ross's imagination this area forms a geographic entity that he exploits in *Helenore*. Admittedly, the name 'Flaviana' suggests a pastoral never-never land, and the directions taken by Nory on her journeys are inconsistent with each other. But the terrain is solid. The conditions encountered by Nory as she searches for Lindy are exactly those that might be encountered now on the hillsides and moors between Glenesk and Deeside:

> Sae up she rises, and about she spies,
> An' lo! beneath, a bony burnie lies,
> Out-throw the mist atweesh her an' the sun,
> That shin'd an' glanc'd in ilka pool an' lyn.
> A hail half mile she had at least to gang,
> Thro' birns, an' pits, an' scrabs, an' heather lang:
> Yet putt an' row, wi' mony a weary twine,
> She wins at last to where the pools did shine. (564–71)

The rural economy and the conditions of life as presented by Ross are also derived from circumstances as he knew them. The agricultural system was based on the rearing of animals and until 1745 was at risk from Highland caterans who plundered the lowlands for a living. The language of the poem is based on the sounds, vocabulary and grammar of local speech and Ross's characters tend to cast their thoughts in the form of proverbs thus giving the dialogue pith and pungency as in Colen's words — 'But mischief frae a midge's wing may spring' (2732). His work reflects the attitudes and outlook of the peasantry with whom he lived. The description of the birth of Nory (94–107) might be compared with Burns's description of Halloween. Ross is unselfconscious and presents superstitious practices as though they were entirely proper and expected, whereas Burns, both in his characters and in his own handling of them, treats of a condition of half-belief, of people doing things 'in case' or 'just to see', yet rationally withholding their assent.

*Helenore* was inspired by, and is modelled on, *The Gentle Shepherd*, yet Ross handles the strands of a more complex plot with assurance, and with greater regard to probability, than does Ramsay. Within the ampler narrative, other genres figure — for example, the squire's description of the wife his father wishes him to marry draws on the *mal marié(e)* tradition of popular song which goes back to the middle ages. (Ross was himself an accomplished writer of songs one of which appears in *Helenore*.)

Alexander Ross has been neglected by literary critics and historians perhaps because *Helenore* is the longest Scottish poem of the eighteenth century and is written in a dialect to which most readers are unused. It is hoped, however, that the following extracts will show that neglect to be unjust.

*Edition:*

*The Scottish Works of Alexander Ross*, ed. Margaret Wattie, Scottish Text Society, 3rd series, 9 (Edinburgh, 1938).

*Criticism:*

David Hewitt, 'The Ballad World and Alexander Ross' in *Literature of the North*, ed. David Hewitt and Michael Spiller (Aberdeen, 1983).

## HELENORE OR THE FORTUNATE SHEPHERDESS

The heroine of the poem, Helenore or Nory, is the daughter of Jean and Colen and was long the sweetheart of Lindy, son of Ralph. All live on Flaviana's Braes. The story is summarised by Colen:

'An' the tale is this:

Frae this aback, an' that nae monie days,
A band of kettrin[n] hamphis'd a' our braes;
Ca'd aff our store at twelve hours o' the day,
Nor had we maughts to turn again the prey;
Sair bargain made our hirds to hadd again,
But what needs mair? A' was but wark in vain.
The herds came hame, an' made a reefu' rair,
An' a' the braes rang loud wi' dool an' care.
My lassie, that it seems your honor's seen,
Frae kindness that ye shown her o' this green,
Like ane hairbrain'd, into the glens taks gate,
Whan now the night was gloomy, merk an' late.
Wi' our surprise she's nae mist till the morn,
An' now her mither blaws on me the horn,
An' I maun aff, an' seek her right or wrang,
An' monie a bootless fit did for her gang;
An' at the last I fell amo' my faes,
The cruel kettrin of Sevitia's braes.
An' that lad there, ye see wi' yellow hair
Did wi' me of the worst of chances share:
Into their hands we baith together fell,
An' they did guide's, I 'shure you, sharp an' snell:
Band's hard a' night, an' toil'd us hard a' day,
An' for our pains but sma' allowance gae.
The maiden o' the house saw our mishap,
An' out o' sight gae's monie a bit an' drap;
An' shortly to the lad sick liking took
That butt him she nae saught nor ease cud brook.
Nae ither boot she had but tell her care
Came frae the lad that had the yellow hair.

3065 *kettrin*: caterans, Highland robbers
*hamphis'd*: surrounded
3066 *store*: livestock
3067 *maughts*: might, power
3068 *hadd*: continue
3070 *reefu' rair*: loud roar, cry
3071 *dool*: sorrow
3074 *taks gate*: sets off
3075 *merk*: dark
3076 *mist*: missed
3077 *blaws . . . horn*: calls me up, warns me
3078 *maun*: must
3079 *fit*: foot
3085 *guide's*: treat, use us
*shure*: assure
*snell*: sharp
3086 *band's*: bound us
3089 *bit an' drap*: bit to eat and drop to drink
3091 *butt*: without
*saught*: peace
*cud*: could
3092 *boot*: remedy, cure

An' o' the night engag'd to let us gae,
Sae be the lad her for his ain wad hae,
An' tak her hame, syne join afore the priest.
A' this was promis'd, but by way of jest.
Sae on a night, as we did all agree,
She steals the key, an' sae she setts us free;
Aff a' together we three linking came.
But to get red, the lad contrives a sham,
To send her back for something he forgot;
Sae aff we scour'd, an' thought she'd slipt the knot.
But by your favour she is nae so blate;
She follows on, an' wi' my lassie met,
That at some gentle place had hab'ry ta'en —
I reed your honor does this better ken.'

The lad 'wi yellow hair' is, of course, Lindy. The 'maiden o' the house' is Bydby, and his 'honor' is a squire who befriends Nory (Helenore) when she is lost, and decides to marry her rather than the woman his father has chosen for him. Eventually the squire, Colen and Ralph persuade Lindy to take Bydby, and the squire gets Nory. The 'kettrins' arrive to recover Bydby, but are converted from their predatory ways by the marriages and the accompanying celebrations.

3100 *linking*: stepping out briskly
3101 *red*: rid, disentangled
3103 *scour'd*: removed (ourselves)
3104 *blate*: stupid, sheepish
3106 *hab'ry*: shelter
3107 *reed*: suppose

*Invocation and the birth of Nory*

Say, *Scota*[n], thou that anes upon a day
Gar'd Allan Ramsay's hungry hart strings play
The merriest sangs that ever yet were sung,
Pity anes mair, for I'm out-throw as clung.
'Twas that grim gossip, chandler-chafted want,
With threed-bair claithing, and an ambry scant,
Made him cry o' thee to blaw throw his pen
Wi' leed, that well might help him to come ben,
An' crack amo' the best of ilka sex,
An' shape his houghs to gentle bows and becks.
He wan thy heart, well wordy o't, poor man.
Take yet another gangrell by the hand;

1 *anes upon a day*: once upon a time
2 *gar'd*: made
4 *out-throw*: completely
*clung*: shrunk with hunger
5 *chandler-chafted*: lantern jawed
6 *ambry*: cupboard
8 *leed*: language
*ben*: into the inner (better) room in a two roomed house
9 *crack*: chat, talk
10 *houghs*: legs
*becks*: bows or curtsies
11 *wordy*: worthy
12 *gangrell*: vagrant

As gryt's my mister, an' my duds as bair,
And I as sib as he was, ilka hair.
Mak me but half as canny, there's no fear,
Tho' I be auld, but I'll yet gather gear.
O gin thou hadst not heard him first o'er well,
When he got maughts to write The Shepherd's Tale,
I meith ha had some chance of landing fair,
But O that sang, the mither of my care!
What wad I geen, that thou hadst put thy thumb
Upo' the well tauld tale, till I had come,
Then led my hand alongst it line for line!
O to my dieing day, how I wad shine,
An' as far yont it as syn Habbi$^{n}$ plaid,
Or Ga'in on Virgil matchless skill display'd!
An' mair I wadna wiss. But Ramsay bears
The gree himsel, an' the green laurels wears.
Well mat he brook them, for piece ye had spar'd
The task to me, Pate$^{n}$ meith na been a laird.
'Tis may be better, I's tak what ye gee:
Ye're nae toom-handed gin your heart be free;
But I's be willing as ye bid me write —
Blind horse, they say, ride hardy to the fight,
And by good hap may come awa but scorn:
They are na kempers a' that shear the corn.
Then Scota heard, and said: 'Your rough-spun ware
Sounds but right douff an' fowsome to my ear.
Do ye pretend to write like my ain bairn,
Or onie ane that wins beyont the Kairn?
Ye're far mistaen gin ye think sick a thought.
The Gentle Shepherd's nae sae easy wrought;
There's scenes an' acts, there's drift an' there's design,
An' a' maun like a new-ground whittle shine;
Sick wimpl'd wark would crack a pow like thine.'
'Kind mistris,' says I, 'gin this be your fear,
Charge nae mair shot than what the piece 'll bear.

13 *gryt*: great
*duds*: clothes
14 *sib*: related, akin
*ilka*: every
15 *canny*: skilful
16 *gear*: goods, property
17 *gin*: if
18 *maughts*: strength, power
*Shepherd's Tale*: i.e. Ramsay's *Gentle Shepherd*.
19 *meith*: might
21 *geen*: give
25 *yont*: beyond
*syn*: since, once
26 *Ga'in*: Gavin, i.e. Gavin Douglas, Bishop of Dunkeld (1475?–1522), translator of Virgil's *Æneid*
27 *wadna*: would not
*wiss*: want, wish
28 *gree*: prize, victory
29 *mat*: may
*brook*: enjoy
*piece*: although, had
31 *I's tak*: I'll take
32 *toom-handed*: empty handed
35 *hap*: chance
*but*: without
36 *kempers*: keen and vigorous workers, who try to outdo their fellows, here at reaping
38 *douff*: dull, spiritless
*fowsome*: coarse
40 *wins*: lives
41. *sick*: such
44 *whittle*: knife, dirk
45 *wimpl'd*: intricate, complicated
*pow*: head

Something but scenes or acts, that kittle game,
Yet what may please, bid me sit down an' frame.'
'Gae then,' she says, 'nor deave me with your dinn;
*Puff* — I inspire you, sae you may begin.
If ye o'er forthersome, turn tapsie turvy,
Blame your ain haste, an' say not that I spur ye;
But sound and seelfu' as I bid you write,
An' ready hae your pen when I indite.
Speak my ain leed, 'tis gueed auld Scots I mean;
Your Southren gnaps I count not worth a preen.
We've words a fouth, that we can ca' our ain,
Tho' frae them now my childer sair refrain,
An' are to my gueed auld proverb confeerin —
Neither gueed fish nor flesh, nor yet sa't herrin.
Gin this ye do, an' lyn your rime wi' sense,
But ye'll make friends of fremmet fouk, fa kens?
Wi' thir injunctions ye may set you down.'
'Mistris,' says I, 'I'm at your bidding boun.'

Sae I begins, my pen into my hand,
Just ready hearkning as she should command.
But then about her there was sic a dinn,
Some seeking this, some that, some out, some in,
That it's nae wonder, tho' I aft gae wrang,
An' for my ain, set down my neiper's sang;
For hundreds mair were learning at her school,
And some wrote fair, an' some like me wrote foul.

## CANTO I

When yet the leal an' ae-fauld shepherd life
Was nae oergane by faucit, sturt an' strife,
But here and there part o' that seelfu' race
Kept love an' lawty o' their honest face,
Piece long ere than, lowns had begun to spread,
An' riefing hereship was become a trade;

48 *kittle*: difficult
50 *deave*: deafen, bother
52 *fothersome*: rash, impetuous
54 *seelfu'*: happy
56 *gueed*: good
57 *gnaps*: affected speech
*preen*: pin
58 *fouth*: plenty
59 *childer*: children (of muse, i.e. poets)
60 *confeerin*: conforming
61 in giving up 'auld Scots' the children are speaking neither one thing nor another
62 *lyn*: line (with a lining)
63 *fremmet*: foreign, strange
*fouk*: folk
*fa*: who; in northern Scots initial 'wh' comes out as 'f', always in pronouns and often in other words
64 *thir*: these
71 *neiper*: neighbour
74 *leal*: loyal, faithful
*ae-fauld*: simple
75 *faucit*: falsehood
*sturt*: contention, trouble
77 *lawty*: loyalty
78 *piece . . . than*: and long before
*lowns*: (= louns) rogues, scoundrels
79 *riefing*: reaving, robbing

Yet of the honest sort, that did nae ken
Naething but that was downright fair an' plain,
A sonsie pair of lad an' lass was found,
Wha honest love wi' halie wedlock crown'd.
For joining hands they just were feer for feer,
An' liv'd to other, as A to B as near.
For bonyness an' other good out-throw,
They were as right as ever trade the dew.
The lad was Colen, and the lass was Jean;
An' how soon as the jimp three raiths was gane,
The dentyest wean bony Jean fuish hame
To flesh or blood that ever had a claim.
The name the wean gat was Helenore,
That her ain grandame brooked lang before.
Gryt was the care an' tut'ry[n] that was ha'en,
Baith night an' day about the bony wean.
The jizzen-bed wi' rantree leaves was sain'd,
An' sick like craft as the auld grandys kend;
Jean's paps wi' sa't and water washen clean,
For fear her milk gat wrang fan it was green;
Then the first hippen to the green was flung,
And unko words thereat baith said an' sung;
A burning coal with the hett tangs was ta'en
Frae out the ingle mids, well brunt an' clean,
An' thro' the corsy-belly letten fa',
For fear the wean should be ta'en awa'.
Dowing an' growing was the dayly prayer,
An' Nory tented was wi' unko care.
The oddest fike an' fisle that e'er was seen,
Was by the mither an' twa grandys ta'en;
An' the twa bobbys were baith fidging fain,
That they had gotten an oye o' their ain.
An' bony Nory answer'd a' their care,
For well she throove, and halesome was an' fair;
As clear an' calour as a water trout,
An' with her growth her beauty ay did sprout.

82 *sonsie*: bonny
84 *feer*: companion; *feer for feer*: equally matched
87 *trade*: trod
89 *jimp*: bare
*raiths*: quarters of a year
90 *wean*: child; pronounced here as a disyllable
*fuish*: fetched
93 *brooked*: enjoyed
94 *tutry*: care, protection
96 *jizzen-bed*: child-bed
*rantree*: rowan tree
*sain'd*: crossed, blessed
97 *grandys*: grandmothers
100 *hippen*: nappy
103 *ingle*: fire
*mids*: middle
104 *corsy-belly*: infant's first shirt
106 *dowing*: thriving
107 *tented*: looked after
108 *fike*: fuss, trouble
*fisle*: bustle
110 *bobbys*: grandfathers
*fidging fain*: restless with pleasure
111 *oye*: grandchild
114 *calour*: fresh

### *The hership o' the kettrins*

Now Flaviana was the country's name[n]
That ay this bony water-side did claim,
Frae yellow sands, that trindl'd down the same.
The fouks were wealthy, store was a' their stock;
With this, but little siller, did they trock.
Frae mang the stock his honour gat his fa',
An' got but little cunzie, or nane awa'.
The water fecklie on a level slede,
Wi' little dinn, but couthy, what it made.
On ilka side the trees grew thick an' strang,
An' a' the boughs wi' birds were in a sang;
On every side, a full bowshot an' mair,
The green was even, gowany an' fair;
With easy sklent, on every side the braes
To a good height, wi' scatter'd busses raise;
Wi' goats an' sheep aboon, an' cows below,
These bony braes all in a swarm did go.
No property these honest shepherds pled;
All kept alike, an' all in common fed.
But ah, misfortune! while they fear'd no ill,
A band of kettrins did their forrest fill;
On ilka side they took it in with care,
And i' the ca' nor cow nor ewe did spare;
The sakeless shepherds stroove with might an' main
To turn the dowie chase, but all in vain;
They had nae maughts for sick a toilsome task,
For bare-fac'd robb'ry had put off the mask.
Amo' the herds that plaid a maughty part,
Young Lindy kyth'd himsel wi' hand an' heart.
But mair nor master maws the field, an' sae
It far'd wi' him, poor man, that hapless day.
Three fallows bauld, like very lions strong,
Were a' his wrack, an' wrought him a' his wrang;
On him laid hands, whan he now dow na mair,
An' wi' teugh raips they band him hard an' sair,

*hership*: plundering
403 *country*: district
405 *trindl'd*: trickled
407 *trock*: trade, traffic
408 *fa'*: share, portion
409 *cunzie*: coin, money
*awa'*: at all
410 *fecklie*: mostly
*slede*: slide
415 *gowany*: covered with gowans, large daisies
416 *sklent*: slope
417 *busses*: bushes
418 *aboon*: above
425 *ca'*: driving
426 *sakeless*: innocent
*stroove*: strove
427 *dowie*: dismal, melancholy
431 *kyth'd*: showed
432 *maws*: mows
*nor*: than
435 *wrack*: destruction, injury
436 *dow*: was able to do
437 *teugh*: tough

An' left him there, till they shou'd cast about,
An' drive him hame before them i' the rout.
Ere they came back frae dighting o' the reer,
'Twas now as dark as it afore was clear;
They sought about, their seeking was in vain,
An' Lindy's left, poor man, to pine wi' pain.

The fouk at hame by this time hae their care,
An' that the gueeds are byding wonder sair.
To hillock heads an' knolls man, wife an' wean,
To spy about them gather now ilk ane;
Some o' them running here, some o' them there,
An' a' in outmost mazerment an' care.
Nory, poor 'oman, had some farther gane,
For Lindy fly'd, an' standin' was her lane,
Whan up there came twa shepherds out o' breath,
Rais'd like, an' blawing, an' as haw as death.
'Now,' Nory says, 'what's been the cause the day
The herds an' gueeds hae made sae lang a stay?'
'Of gueeds an' herds we need nae speak nae mair;
Dowie's this day,' an' gae the reefu' rair.
'They're a' made herships, an' for ought we ken,
The herds may a' be feckly ta'en or slain.'
At thir sad news poor Nory taks the gate,
What legs could lift, tho' it was dark an' late;
She ran an' skream'd, an' roove out at her hair,
An' to the glens the gainest gate can fare.
Ay as the lads came up, the news they spread;
I sanna tell you what effect it had;
For sick a ruther raise, tweesh riving hair,
Skreeding o' kurches, crying dool an' care,
Wi' thud for thud upon their bare breast bane,
To see't an' hear't wad rive a heart of stane.
Poor Nory rins till she dow rin nae mair,
An' syne fa's down; judge gin her heart was sair.
Out at her mow it just was like to bout
Intill her lap at every ither thaut.

438 *cast about*: arrange things
439 *rout*: lowing of cattle or general uproar
440 *dighting*: clearing up, mopping up
*reer*: rear
443 *pine*: suffer
445 *gueeds*: livestock
*byding*: staying, delaying
449 *mazerment*: amazement
451 *fly'd*: was frightened
*her lane*: herself
453 *rais'd*: excited
*haw*: pale
461 *what . . . lift*: as fast as she could go
462 *roove*: tore
463 *gainest gate*: quickest way
*can*: did
*fare*: go
465 *sanna*: shall not
466 *ruther*: noise, outcry
*skreeding*: tearing
467 *kurches*: kerchiefs, cloths used by women to cover their heads
468 *thud for thud*: thud after thud
469 *wad*: would
*rive*: split
472 *mow*: mouth
*bout*: spring, jump
473 *thaut*: sob

As lang as she had maughts to rin or gang,
'O Lindy! Lindy!' was her dowie sang;
'Well Lindy, bony Lindy, art thou dead?
I's never frae this hillock lift my head.
O dead, come also an' be kind to me,
An' frae this sad back-birn of sorrow free!'
Cry what she liked, Lindy cud na hear,
For she for that a quite wrang course did steer,
Twa miles at least, for he had follow'd on,
Till by the ruffians he was sae undone.

### *The wife the squire rejects*

'Ay, auntie, an' ye kent the bony aught!
'Tis true, she had of warld's gear a fraught.
But what was that to peace an' saught at hame,
An' mair nor that, to kirk an' merkat shame?
For had my father sought the warld round
Till he the very dightings o't had found,
A filthier hag could not come in his way
Than for my truncher what he had laid by:
An ugly, hulgie-backed, canker'd wasp,
Syne like to die for breath at ilka gasp;
Her teeth betweesh a yellow an' a black,
Some out, some in, an' a' of different mack;
Black, hairy wrats, about an inch between,
Outthrow her fiz, were like mustaches seen;
Her head lay back, an' her syde chafts sat out,
An' o'er her gab hang down a sneevling snout;
An' tak her a' together, rough an' right,
She wad na been by far four feet of height;
An' for her temper, maik she ne'er had nane:
She'd mak twa paps cast out on ae breast-bane.
But yet, say what I liked, nought wad do
But I maun gang this bony chap to woo.
My father he yeed wi' me at the first,
But a' the time my heart was like to birst,
To think to lead my life wi' sick an ape.
I'd rather mak my tesment in a raip.

479 *back-birn*: burden
481 *steer*: move
870 *aught*: creature
871 *fraught*: freight, load
872 *saught*: peace
875 *dightings*: refuse
877 *truncher*: trencher
878 *hulgie-backed*: hump-backed
881 *mack*: shape
882 *wrats*: warts
884 *chafts*: jaws
885 *gab*: mouth
*sneevling*: snivelling
887 i.e. she is much short of four feet
*maik*: match, equal
892 *yeed*: went
895 i.e. he would rather hang

But ugly as she was, there was na cure,
But I maun kiss her, 'cause I was the woo'r.
My father briskly loot me see the gate,
But I'll assure you I look'd unko blate;
An' very thrawart like I yeed in by.
"A young man look so blate!" he says, "O fy!"
Nor was it fairly, for her stinking breath
Was just enough to sconfise ane to death.
But frae my father monie a slaik she gat,
An' I, just like to spue, like blunty sat.
I canna say but she was wond'rous kind,
An' for her dresses, wow, but they were fine!
An' monie a bony thing was in our sight,
An' a' thing that we saw was snug an' tight;
Nae little wealth, I 'sure you, there we saw,
An' ilka thing was rich an' fine an' bra';
But for it a' I didna care a strae,
An' wad ha geen my neck to be awa'.'

*Nory's dream prefigures the change in her affections*

Neist day, whan morning thro the windows sprang,
Nory bangs up, an' crys, 'I've lain o'er lang.'
Betty, who was upo' the catch, replies,
'Lie still, sweet Nory, 'tis o'er soon to rise.'
As they are craking, aunty she comes ben,
An' smiling says, 'How sleept my bony hen?
Betty, hae ye about her ta'en gueed care?
Ye're but a restless bed-fellow, I fear.'
'Well hae I lien, sweet mistress,' Nory said;
'I never lay afore in sick a bed,
Sae saft an' warm, an' wi' sae bony claise;
I've lien indeed fu' well, at my ain ease.
Let you nor yours ne'er in sick takin be
As yon bra' laird, well mat he thram, fund me.
This bony bed has gar'd me ly o'er lang.
I maunna langer byde, but up an' gang.'

898 *gate*: way
899 *blate*: stupid, bashful
900 *thrawart*: perverse, stubborn
*in by*: near, close
903 *sconfise*: stifle
904 *slaik*: slobbering kiss
905 *blunty*: stupid, sullen person
1086 Nory, given her background, would naturally get up at sunrise
1087 *bangs*: starts
1088 *upo' the catch*: on the watch
1090 *craking*: cracking, chatting
1098 *takin*: plight
1099 *mat*: may
*thram*: thrive, prosper

'Huly,' she says, 'hae ye nae hasty care:
Ye need na rise these couple o' hours an' mair.
I's come again an' raise you time enough.
Our lads yet hanna budg'd to yoke the plough.'
Sae out she slips, an' snecks the door behind,
An' Bess an' Nory to their crack begin.
''Oman,' says Bess, 'I think we'll tak advice,
An' e'en ly still; my mither's unko wyse.
She's up, but canna ly for want o' breath,
An' says that early rising did her skaith.
O'er browden'd o' the warld she was ay;
'Tis best we guide our sells as lang's we may.
She says, tho' she were back at auld fifteen,
She's never do again as she has done.'
'But O!' says Nory, 'I am far frae hame,
An' this last night I had a dreary dream.
My heart's yet beatin wi' the very fright,
An' fan I'm waking, thinks I see the sight.

'I thought that we were washing at our sheep
Intill a pool, an' O! but it was deep.
I thought a lad therein was like to drown;
His feet yeed frae him, an' his head yeed down;
Flaught-bred into the pool my sell I keest,
Weening to keep his head aboon at least:
But ere I wist, I clean was at the float;
I sanna tell you what a gloff I got:
My eyn grew blind, the lad I cudna see,
But ane I kent na took a claught of me,
An' fuish me out, an' laid me down to dreep.
Sae burden'd was I, I coud hardly creep.
Gryte was the care this stranger took o' me,
An' O! I thought him bony, blyth an' free.
Dry claise, I thought, he gae me to put on,
Better by far an' bra'er than my own.
An' fan I had come something to my sell,
Ayont the pool I spy'd the lad that fell,
Drouket, an' looking unko ourlach-like.
A lass about him made a wond'rous fike,

1102 *huly*: softly
1106 *snecks*: latches
1110 *but*: i.e. but that's because she
1112 *browden'd*: attached to
1113 *guide*: save, spare
1114 *tho . . . fifteen*: if she were fifteen again
1121 *intill*: in
1124 *flaught-bred*: with outstretched hands *keest*: cast
1125 *weening*: imagining
1126 *wist*: knew *at the float*: floating
1127 *gloff*: fright, shock
1129 *claught*: grasp
1138 *drouket*: drenched *ourlach*: miserable
1139 *fike*: trouble

Drying an' dighting at him up an' down.
I kent her no, but stripped was her gown.
But O the skair that I got i' the pool!
I thought my heart had couped frae its hool.
An' sae I wakn'd, glamping here an' there;
I wat ye meith ha found me i' my care.'
Says Bess, ' 'Tis true your fump'ring wakn'd me;
I putted o' you for to set you free.'

As they are cracking, aunty she comes ben,
An' says, 'How are ye now, my bony hen?
'Tis now fair day, an' ye an' Bess may rise.
See, lass, there's for you a new pair o' stays;
An' there's a gown some longer nor your ain.
Bess, put a' on her well, an' syne come ben.'

### *Bydby and the fairies*

Whan she a mile or twa had farther gane,
She grows right eery to be sae her lane,
An' mair an' mair she frae the hills hads down,
Wissing that she meith light upon some town;
But she's as weak as very water grown,
An' tarrows at the browst that she had brown;
An' haflings wisses she had never seen
The bony lad she loo'd atweesh the eyn;
For now a' hopes of seeing him are lost,
That likly seeking him her life wou'd cost;
An' will an' wilsome was she, an' her breast
Wi' wae was bowden, even like to birst.
Nae sust'nance got, that of meal's corn grew,
An' only at the cauld wild berries gnew;
But frae that food nae pith came till her banes,
An' she was fu' an' hungry baith at anes.

Now she began to think within hersell
Upon a tale she heard a weerd-wife tell,
That thro' the cuintray telling fortunes yeed,
An' at babees an' placks came wond'rous speed:

1144 *glamping*: clutching herself or groping in the darkness
1146 *fump'ring*: whimpering
1147 *putted o'*: pushed at
1749 *eery*: frightened (with fears of the supernatural)
1750 *hads*: holds
1751 *town*: farm dwelling
1753 *tarrows at*: shrinks from
*browst*: brewing
*brown*: brewed
*haflings*: half
1758 *will*: astray
*wilsome*: lost
1759 *bowden*: swollen
1761 *gnew*: gnawed
1765 *weerd-wife*: woman who tells fortunes
1767 *babees*: halfpennies
*plack*: small Scottish coin, 4 pence Scots or $\frac{1}{3}$ of an old English penny

Whan she her loof had looked back an' fore,
An' drew her finger langlins ilka score,
Upo' her face look'd the auld hag forfairn,
An' says, 'Ye will hard fortun'd be, my bairn;
Frae fouk a-fiedlert, nae frae fouk at hame,
Will come the antercast ye'll hae to blame;
Gin ye be wysse, beware of unko men;
I dread, for sick ye'll anes be bare the ben;
Sae come ye speed, or miss ye o' your mark,
Ae thing I see, ye'll hae right kittle wark.'[n]
Then says my lass, 'Had I but been sae wysse
As hae laid up auld mummy's gueed advice,
Frae this mischance I meith hae kept me free.
But wha can frae what's laid afore them flee?'
Thus making at her main she lewders on,
Thro' scrabs an' craigs, wi' mony a heavie groan;
Wi' bleeding legs an' sair misguided shoon,
An' Lindy's coat ay feltring her aboon;
Till on a heigh brae-head she lands at last,
That pitlens down to a how burnie past;
Clear was the burnie, an' the busses green,
But rough an' steep the brae that lay between;
Her burning drowth inclin'd her to be there,
But want of maughts an' distance eek'd her care.
Now by this time the evening's fa'ing down,
Hill heads were red, an' hows were eery grown;
Yet wi' what pith she had she takes the gate,
An' wan the burn; but now it's growin late.
The birds about were making merry cheer;
She thought their musick sang, 'Ye're welcome here.'
Wi' the cauld stream she quencht her lowan drowth,
Syne o' the eaten berrys eat a fouth,
That black an' ripe upo' the bushes grew,
An' were new water'd with the evening dew;
Then sat she down aneth a birken shade
That clos'd aboon her, an' hang o'er her head.
Couthy an' warm an' gow'ny was the green,
Instead o' night, had it the daylight been:

1768 *loof*: palm of the hand
1769 *langlins*: along
1770 *forfairn*: forlorn
1772 *a-fiedlert*: afield
1773 *antercast*: misfortune
1774 *wysse*: prudent, sensible
*unko*: unknown, strange
1779 *auld mummy*: grandmother
1782 *main*: moan
*lewders*: plods
1783 *scrabs*: scrub
1784 *misguided*: spoilt
1785 *feltring*: encumbering
1786 *lands*: arrives
1787 *pitlens*: steeply
*how*: hollow
1790 *drowth*: thirst
1791 *eek'd*: increased
1798 *lowan*: burning
1799 *eaten*: juniper
*fouth*: plenty

But grim an' ghastly an' pick black, wi' fright,
A' things appear'd upo' the dead of night.
For fear she curr'd, like makine i' the seat,
An' dunt for dunt her heart began to beat.
Amidst this horror, sleep did on her steal,
An' for a wee her flightering breast did heal;
An' thus, whiles slouming, whiles starting wi' her fright,
She maks a shift to wear awa' the night.
As she hauf sleeping and hauf waking lay,
An unco din she hears of fouk and play.
The sough they made gar'd her lift up her eyn,
And O the gath'ring that was on the green
Of little foukies[n], clad in green and blue!
Kneefer and trigger never trade the dew;
In many a reel they scamper'd here and there,
Whiles on the yerd, and whiles up in the air.
The pipers play'd like ony touting horn;
Sic sight she never saw since she was born.
As she's behading all this mirthful glee,
Or e'er she wist, they're dancing in the tree
Aboon her head, as nimble as the bees
That swarm in search of honey round the trees.
Fear's like to fell her, reed that they sud fa',
And smore her dead, afore she wan awa';
Syne in a clap, as thick's the motty sin,
They hamphis'd her with unco fike and din;
Some cry'd, 'Tak ye the head, I'se tak a foot;
We'll lear her upon this tree-head to sit,
And spy about her!' Others said, 'Out fy!
Let be, she'll keep the King of Elfin's ky.'
Another said, 'O gin she had but milk!
Then sud she gae frae head to foot in silk,
With castings rare, and a gueed nourice-fee,
To nurse the King of Elfin's heir Fizzee.'
Syne ere she wist, like house aboon her head,
Great candles burning, and braw tables spread;
Braw dishes reeking, and just at her hand,
Trig green coats sairing, a' upon command.

1806 *pick*: pitch
1808 *curr'd*: crouched down
*makine*: hare
1811 *flightering*: fluttering
*heal*: hide
1812 *slouming*: dozing
1816 *sough*: rustling sound, noise
*gar'd.*: made
1819 *kneefer*: more alert
1821 *yerd*: ground
1824 *behading*: beholding
1828 *reed*: suppose
1829 *smore*: smother
*wan*: got
1830 *motty sin*: sunbeam picking up particles of dust
1831 *hamphis'd*: surrounded
1833 *lear*: teach
1838 *castings*: cast-off clothes
*nourice-fee*: nurse's fee
1842 *reeking*: smoking
1843 *sairing*: serving

To cut they fa', and she among the leave;
The sight was bonny, and her mou did crave;
The mair she ate, the mair her hunger grew;
Eat what she like, and she coud ne'er be fu';
The knible Elves about her ate ding-dang;
Syne to the play they up, and danc'd and flang;
Drink in braw cups was caw'd about gelore;
Some fell asleep, and loud began to snore;
Syne in a clap, the Fairies a' sat down,
And fell to crack about the table round:
Ane at another speer'd 'Fat tricks played ye,
When in a riddle ye sail'd o'er the sea?'
Quoth it: 'I steal'd the King of Sweden's knife,
Just at his dinner, sitting by his wife,
Whan frae his hand he newlins laid it down;
He blam'd the steward, said he had been the lown:
The sakeless man deny'd, syne yeed to look,
And, lifting of the tableclaith the nook,
I gae't a tit, and tumbl'd o'er the bree.
Tam got the wyte, and I gae the tehee.
I think I never saw a better sport,
But dool fell'd Tam, for sadly he paid for't.'
'But,' quoth another, 'I play'd a better prank:
I gar'd a witch fa' headlins in a stank,
As she was riding on a windlestrae;
The carling gloff'd, and cry'd out "Will-awae!"'
Another said: 'I couped Mungo's ale
Clean heels o'er head, fan it was ripe and stale,
Just whan the tapster the first chapin drew;
Then bad her lick the paill, and aff I flew.
Had ye but seen how blate the lassie looked,
Whan she was blam'd, how she the drink miscooked!'
Says a gnib elf: 'As an auld carle was sitting
Among his bags, and loosing ilka knitting
To air his rousty coin, I loot a claught,
And took a hundred dollars at a fraught.
Whan with the sight the carle had pleas'd himsell,
Then he began the glancing heap to tell.

1844 *cut . . . fa'*: 'they fall to'
*leave*: rest
1848 *knible*: nimble
1850 *caw'd about*: circulated
1859 *lown*: rascal
1861 *nook*: corner
1862 *tit*: tug
*bree*: broth
1863 *wyte*: blame
1867 *stank*: ditch
1868 *windlestrae*: stalk of dry grass
1869 *carling*: old woman
1872 *chapin*: quart
1875 *miscooked*: mismanaged
1876 *gnib*: quick, sharp
*carle*: old man
1877 *knitting*: fastening
1878 *loot*: aimed
*claught*: grab
1879 *fraught*: load
1881 *glancing*: shining

As soon's he miss'd it, he rampaged red-wood,
And lap and danc'd, and was in unco mood;
Ran out and in, and up and down; at last
His reeling eyn upon a raip he cast,
Knit till a bauk, that had hung up a cow:
He taks the hint, and there hings he, I trow.'
As she's behading ilka thing that past,
With a loud crack the house fell down at last.
The reemish put a knell unto her heart,
And frae her dream she waken'd wi' a start.

### *Nory and Bydby find a shieling*

Sae down they fare, an' rough, rough was the brae,
Wi' craigs an' scrabs a' scatter'd i' the way.
As they drew near, they heard an eldren dey
Singing fu' sweet at milking o' her ky.
In by they come, an' hails'd her cheerfully.
The wife looks up, some little in surprise,
An' leaning o' the boucht the maidens spies,
An' taks hersell, an' says, 'Wha have I here?
This day ye seem to be right soon asteer.'
Quo they: 'We hae ga'en will, an' out a' night,
An' spy'd this sheal, an' came to be set right.
Be but sae kind as tell us where we be,
An' ye's get thanks — 'tis a' we hae to gee.'
Quo she: 'Unto the sheal step ye o'er by,
An' warm yoursels, till I milk out my ky.
This morning's raw; gin ye've a' night been out,
That ye wad thole a warm I mak na doubt,
An' something mair, I's warrant. Ca' your wa',
The door it stands wide open to the wa'.
Hadd on a cow, till I come o'er the gate,
An' do the best you can to hadd you hett.'
The lasses bidding do, an' o'er they gaes,
An' of bleech'd birns pat on a canty bleeze.
Content they were at sick a lucky kyle,
An' fand they had na met wi' a beguile.

1882 *red-wood*: mad with rage
1890 *reemish*: crash
2282 *eldren*: elderly
*dey*: dairywoman
2286 *boucht*: sheep-fold
2288 *asteer*: astir
2289 *ga'en will*: lost the way
2290 *sheal*: sheiling
2297 *ca' your wa'*: go your way
2299 *hadd on*: put on
*cow*: stick
2300 *hadd you hett*: keep warm
2302 *bleach'd birns*: the burnt stems of heather, subsequently bleached by the elements
2303 *kyle*: chance
2304 *beguile*: disappointment

On skelfs a' round the wa's the cogs were set,
Ready to ream, an' for the cheese be het;
A hake was frae the rigging hinging fu'
Of quarter kebbocks, tightly made an' new.
Behind the door, a calour heather bed,
Flat o' the floor, of stanes an' fail was made.
An' lucky shortly follow'd o'er the gate
Wi' twa fu' leglins, froathing o'er an' het;
Syne ream'd her milk, an' set it o' the fire;
An' bade them eek the bleeze, an' nae to tyre;
That cruds, their weamfu', they sud get on haste,
As fresh an' gueed as ever they did taste.

2305 *skelfs*: shelves
*cogs*: wooden pails
2306 *ream*: skim
2307 *hake*: wooden rack (here for drying cheeses)
2308 *kebbocks*: cheeses
2310 *fail*: turf
2311 *lucky*: old woman
2312 *leglins*: milk pails
*cruds*: curds

# Adam Skirving
## 1719–1803

Adam Skirving was the farmer of Garleton, near Haddington, and had been brought up on his father's farm of Prestonmains, near the site of the Battle of Prestonpans. He was an athlete, a sportsman (he played golf at Gullane every Saturday) and a lover of poetry and the arts. He took no part in the rebellion, other than being robbed by victorious Highlanders on Seton sands as he describes, but is said to have written the famous song *Hey, Johnny Cope* as well as *Tranent Muir*. His eldest son, Archibald (1749–1819) was the well-known painter.

All accounts of Adam Skirving depict him as a larger-than-life figure, and perhaps the best indication of his legendary character is the story recounted by Thomas Carlyle (*Reminiscences of Thomas Carlyle*, ed. John Clubbe, Durham, N.C., 1974) where Carlyle refers to Lieutenant Smith who, according to Skirving, ran away from the battle: 'Smith was a Lieutenant of *Horse* (seemingly), used to Haddington Barracks, and familiar in society there. Returning after the Rebellion was over, he found this Ballad in everybody's mouth, and the Two Stanzas inconveniently twinkling up on him, wherever he shew'd face. After painful meditation he resolved on calling out Farmer Skirving (no hope of making him *recant* by milder methods, what he knew to be a fact); and sent a military Friend with his challenge . . . The military Friend found Skirving in his Farm-Yard . . . busy, with his men around him, "filling dung", i.e. forking it into carts for the ploughing field. Skirving paused, struck down his "graip" (big three pronged fork) and, resting his hands on the same . . . listened attentively to Smith's Messenger. Deliberately heard, & where necessary, questioned him, till the affair became quite clear; — where upon affair being clear in all points, Skirving, still leaning on his graip, made the following memorable answer: "God, I never saw Lieutenant Smith, I dinna ken whether I can fecht him or not: but if he come up here, I'll tak a look o' him; and if I think I can fecht him, I will; if not, I'll rin awa' as he did!" — and immediately resumed his forking, perhaps with new diligence for this Smith *parenthesis*, which had interrupted his men and him. Cartel Smith is no more heard of in history.'

There is an account of Skirving in Johnson's *Scots Musical Museum*, ed. W. Stenhouse and D. Laing (Edinburgh, 1853), Vol. IV.

*Bibliography:*
David Herd, *A Collection of Scots Songs* (Edinburgh, 1776).
A. Campbell, *The Poetry of Scotland* (Edinburgh, 1798).
James Johnson, *The Scots Musical Museum* (Edinburgh, 1853), Vols. I and IV.

## TRANENT MUIR

The Chevalier,[n] being void of fear,
Did march up Brisle brae,[n] man,
And thro' Tranent, e'er he did stent,
As fast as he could gae, man:
While General Cope did taunt and mock,
Wi' mony a loud huzza,[n] man;
But e'er next morn proclaim'd the cock,
We heard another craw, man.

The brave[n]-Lochaber men[n] came up
Wi' Keappock at their head, man,
A fearfu' toolie then began, —
The red-coats fled wi' speed, man;
The highland lads wi' keen claymores
Cut clean, nor turn'd about, man,
Till English loons, foot and dragoons
War fairly on the rout, man.

The brave Lochiel,[n] as I heard tell,
Led Camerons on in clouds, man;
(The morning fair, and clear the air,)
They loos'd wi' devilish thuds, man:
Down guns they threw, and swords they drew,
And soon did chace them aff, man;
On Seaton-Crafts[n] they buft their chafts,
And gart them rin like daft, man,

The bluff dragoons swore blood and 'oons,
They'd make the rebels run, man;
And yet they flee when them they see,
And winna fire a gun, man:
They turn'd their back, the foot they brake,
Such terror seiz'd them a', man;
Some wet their cheeks, some fyl'd their breeks,
And some for fear did fa', man.

The volunteers prick'd up their ears,
And vow gin they were crouse, man;
But when the bairns saw't turn to earn'st,
They were not worth a louse, man;

3 *stent*: stop
11 *toolie*: battle
15 *loons*: fellows (contemptuous)
20 *loos'd*: fired their guns
23 *buft*: bashed, struck
*chafts*: chops, jaws
25 *'oons*: God's wounds (abbrev.)
31 *fyl'd*: dirtied
*breeks*: trousers
34 *vow*: wow! (interj.)
*crouse*: confident

Maist feck gade hame; O fy for shame!
They'd better staid awa', man,
Than wi' cockade to make parade,
And do nae good at a', man.

Menteith the great,[n] when hersell shit,
Un'wares did ding him o'er, man.
Yet wad nae stand to bear a hand,
But aff fou fast did scour, man;
O'er Soutra hill,[n] e'er he stood still,
Before he tasted meat, man:
Troth he may brag o' his swift nag,
That bare him aff sae fleet, man,

And Simpson[n] keen, to clear the een
Of rebels far in wrang, man,
Did never strive wi' pistols five,
But gallop'd with the thrang, man:
He turned his back, and in a crack
Was cleanly out o' sight man;
And thought it best; it was nae jest
Wi' Highlanders to fight, man.

'Mangst a' the gang nane bade the bang
But twa, and ane was tane, man;
For Campbell[n] rade, but Myrie[n] staid,
And sair he paid the kain,[n] man;
Fell skelps he got, was war than shot
Frae the sharp-edg'd claymore, man;
Frae mony a spout came running out
His reeking-het red gore, man.

But Gard'ner[n] brave did still behave,
Like to a hero bright, man;
His courage true, like him were few
That still despised flight, man;
For king and laws, and country's cause,
In honour's bed he lay, man;
His life, but not his courage, fled,
While he had breath to draw, man.

37 *maist feck*: the greater number
*gade*: went
42 *ding*: drive, smash
49 *een*: eyes
52 *thrang*: throng
53 *crack*: instant
58 *tane*: taken
61 *skelps*: blows

And major Bowle, that worthy soul,
Was brought down to the ground, man;
His horse being shot, it was his lot
For to get mony a wound, man:
Lieutenant Smith, of Irish birth,
Frae whom he call'd for aid, man,
Being full of dread, lap o'er his head,
And wadna be gainsaid man.

He made sic haste, sae spur'd his beast,
'Twas little there he saw, man;
To Berwick rade, and safely said,
The Scots were rebels a', man:
But let that end, for well 'tis kend
His use and wont to lie, man;
The Teague is naught, he never faught
When he had room to flee man.

And Caddell drest, amang the rest,
With gun and good claymore, man,
On gelding grey he rode that way,
With pistols set before, man;
The cause was good, he'd spend his blood,
Before that he would yield, man;
But the night before he left the corps,
And never fac'd the field, man.

But gallant Roger, like a soger,
Stood and bravely fought, man;
I'm wae to tell, at last he fell,
But mae down wi' him brought, man:
At point o' death, wi' his last breath,
(Some standing round in ring, man,)
On's back lying flat he wav'd his hat.
And cry'd, God save the king, man.

Some highland rogues, like hungry dogs,
Neglecting to pursue, man,
About they fac'd and in great haste
Upon the booty flew, man;
And they, as gain, for all their pain,
Are deck'd wi' spoils o' war, man;
Fu' bald can tell how her nainsell[n]
Was ne'er sae pra before, man.

79 *lap*: leapt
87 *Teague*: derogatory term for an Irishman
97 *soger*: soldier
100 *mae*: more
111 *bald*: boldly, with certainty
112 *pra*: braw, fine

At the thorn-tree, which you may see
Be-west the meadow-mill, man,
There mony slain lay on the plain,
The clans pursuing still man.
Sic unco' hacks, and deadly whacks,
I never saw the like man;
Lost hands and heads cost them their deads,
That fell near Preston-dyke man.

That afternoon, when a' was done,
I gaed to see the fray man;
But had I wist what after past,
I'd better staid away man:
On Seaton sands,[n] wi' nimble hands,
They pick'd my pockets bare man;
But I wish ne'er to drie sic fear,
For a' the sum and mair, man.

114 *Be-west*: west of 117 *hacks*: slashes 127 *drie*: endure

# John Skinner
## 1721–1807

John Skinner was born in the parish of Birse on Deeside where his father was schoolmaster. He was brought up near Aberdeen and graduated from Marischal College, Aberdeen, in 1738. While teaching in Monymusk, some 20 miles N.W. of Aberdeen, he was converted to episcopacy. After a spell in Shetland he took holy orders and became episcopal minister at Longside near Peterhead in 1742.

In July 1746 his house was pillaged and his church burnt down by soldiers of Cumberland's army trying to root out Jacobitism. Skinner was never a Jacobite; he endeavoured to register himself as an episcopal minister under the Toleration Act of 1746 which involved, among other requirements, taking the oaths of allegiance and abjuration and praying for King George by name in church. In 1748, however, because the episcopal church refused to recognise George II as rightful king, an act of parliament effectively outlawed episcopacy, by disqualifying its clergy and proscribing public worship. The law was evaded by episcopalians and Skinner was reported to the legal authorities in 1753, tried and given six months imprisonment. By the seventies persecution ceased; after the death of Prince Charles Edward in 1788 the episcopalians reconciled themselves with the state and they were relieved of all penal enactments in 1804.

Skinner was author of *An Ecclesiastical History of Scotland* (1788). He was a pamphleteer and controversialist. He also possessed a considerable poetic ability, which he never fully utilised. He wrote verses in Latin; he wrote lampoons against his persecutors; he wrote odes and verse epistles in English and in Scots, including one to Burns. He is best known, however, as the author of *Tullochgorum*, which Burns described as 'the best Scotch Song ever Scotland saw', and of that other fine song *The Ewie wi' the Crookit Horn*.

*The Christmass Bawing of Monimusk* is inspired by *Christ's Kirk on the Green*, a poem Skinner is said to have had by heart at the age of twelve. It takes over incidents, names and phrases but is not merely derivative for Skinner is a master of alliteration. It exhibits great verbal energy, but while the alliteration allows him to avoid verbal repetition (almost inevitable in descriptions of battles) the cost is the introduction of many obscure and frequently archaic words. The *Bawing* maintains the tradition, revived by Ramsay, of recording Scottish rural life in an appropriate language, while turning the whole into a celebration of a community spirit.

*Editions:*
*A Miscellaneous Collection of Fugitive Pieces of Poetry* (Edinburgh, 1809).
*A Garland from the Vernacular and other Verses* (Aberdeen, 1921).

*Biography:*
W. Walker, *The Life and Times of John Skinner* (London, 1883).
*Dictionary of National Biography.*

## THE CHRISTMASS BAWING OF MONIMUSK

*Anno*, 1739
*In Imitation of 'Christ-Kirk o' the Green'*

1

Has never in a' this country been
  Sic shoudering and sic fawing,
As happent twa, three days senseen,
  Here at the Christmass Ba'ing:
At evening syne the fallows keen,
  Drank till the neist day's dawing,
Sae snell that some tint baith their een,
  And coudna pay their lawing
    For a' that day.

2

Like bumbees bizzing frae a bike,
  Whan hirds their riggins tirr,
The swankies lap thro' mire and slike,
  Wow! as their heads did birr:
They yowph'd the ba' frae dike to dike,
  Wi' unco' speed and virr,
Some baith their shouders up did fyke,
  For blythness some did flirr
    Their teeth that day.

3

Rob Roy, I wot, he was na dull,
  He first loot at the ba',
And wi' a rap clash'd Geordy's skull,
  Hard to the steeple wa':
Wha was aside but auld Tam Tull,
  His frien's mishap he saw,
Syne brein'd like ony baited bull,
  And wi' a thud dang twa
    To th' yird that day.

2 *fawing*: falling
3 *senseen*: since
6 *neist*: next
7 *snell*: keenly
*tint*: lost the use of
*een*: eyes
8 *lawing*: bill
10 *bumbees*: bumblebees
11 *hirds*: herds
*riggins*: roofs
*tirr*: tear, strip off
12 *swankies*: agile, strong men
*slike*: deposit of mud left by river
13 *did birr*: were in a state of confusion
14 *yowph'd*: struck, swiped
15 *virr*: vigour, energy
16 *fyke*: hitch, shrug
17 *flirr*: grind
20 *loot*: aimed
25 *brein'd*: bellowed
26 *dang*: knocked
27 *yird*: earth

4

The hurry-burry now began,
  Was right well worth the seeing,
Wi' bensils bauld tweish man and man,
  Some getting fa's, some gieing,
And a' the tricks o' foot and hand,
  That ever were in being:
Sometimes the ba' a yirdlins ran,
  Sometimes in air was fleeing
      Fou heigh that day.

5

The tanner was a primpit bit,
  And light like ony feather,
He thought it best to try a hit,
  Ere a' the thrang shoud gather:
He flew wi' neither fear nor wit,
  As fou' o' wind's a bladder,
Unluckily he tint the fit
  Aud tann'd his ain bum-leather
      Fell well that day.

6

Syne Francy Winsy steppit in,
  A sauchin slav'ry slype,
Ran forrat wi' a fearfu' din,
  And drew a swingeing swype,
But hieland Tammy thought nae sin
  T' come o'er him wi' a snype,
Levell'd his nose maist wi' his chin,
  And gart his swall'd een sype
      Sawt tears that day.

7

Bockin red bleed the fliep mair cawm,
  Ran to the house to mammie,
'Alas,' co' Katie when she saw him,
  'Wha did you this, my lammie?'
'A muckle man,' co' he, 'foul fa' him,

30 *bensils*: blows, struggling
*tweish*: between
37 *primpit*: correct, affected, formal
45 *fell*: very
47 *sauchin*: lacking in energy or spirit
*slav'ry*: slavering
*slype*: worthless, uncouth person
51 *snype*: smart blow
52 *maist*: almost
53 *swall'd*: swollen
*sype*: ooze, leak
55 *bockin*: spurting
*fliep*: stupid fellow
*mair cawm*: more calm

They ca' him hieland Tammie,
Rax'd me alang the chafts a whawm
As soon as ever he saw me,
And made me blae.'

8

'Waeworth his chandler chafts,' co' Kate,
'Deil rax his saul a whang,
Gin I had here the countra skate
Sae beins I shoud him bang.'
The gilpy glowr'd and leuk'd fell blate
To see'r in sic a sang,
He squeel'd to her like a young gyte,
But wadna mird to gang
Back a' that day.

9

Stout Steen gart mony a fallow stoyt
And flang them down like faill,
Said he'd nae care ae clypit doyt
Tho' a' should turn their taill,
But wi' a yark Gib made his queet,
As dwabill as a flail,
And o'er fell he, maist like to greet,
Just at the westmost gaill
O' th' kirk that day.

10

In came the inset dominie,[n]
Just riftin frae his dinner,
A young Mess John as ane cou'd see,
Was neither saint nor sinner:

61 *rax'd*: dealt
*chafts*: jaw
*whawm*: blow
63 *blae*: cry
64 *chandler chafts*: lantern jaws
65 *whang*: blow
66 *skate*: objectionable person (contemptuous)
67 *sae beins*: that being so
68 *gilpy*: young fellow
*blate*: sheepish, stupid
70 *gyte*: goat
71 *mird*: try
73 *gart*: made
*stoyt*: bounce, stagger
74 *faill*: turf used for building or roofing
75 *clypit*: clipped
*doyt*: small Dutch coin worth $\frac{1}{12}$ of an English penny
77 *yark*: hard knock or thump
*queet*: ankle
78 *dwabill*: pliant
80 *gaill*: end-wall
82 *inset*: substitute, locum
83 *riftin*: belching
84 *Mess John*: minister

A brattlin band unhappilie,
  Drave bý him wi' a binner,
And heels-o'er-gowdie cowpit he,
  And rave his guid horn penner
      In twa that day.

11

Leitch lent the ba' a lounrin lick,
  She flew fast lik a stane,
Syne lightit whare faes were maist thick,
  Gart ae gruff grunshy grane:
The cawrl whoppit up a stick,
  I wot he was na fain,
Leitch wi' 's fit gae him sic a kick,
  Till they a' thought him slain
      That very day.

12

Was nae ane there coud Cowley bide,
  The gryte gudman, nor nane,
He stenn'd bawk-height at ilka stride,
  And rampag'd thro' the green:
For the Kirk-yard was braid and wide,
  And o'er a knabliech stane,
He rumbled down a rammage glyde,
  And peel'd the gardie-bane
      O' him that day.

13

His cousin was a bierly swank,
  A stier young man heght Robb,
To mell wi' twa he wadna mank
  At staffy-nevel job:

86 *brattlin*: noisy, tumultuous
87 *binner*: noise
88 *heels-o'er-gowdie*: head over heels
*cowpit*: fell over
89 *rave*: broke
*penner*: box for holding pens
91 *lounrin lick*: heavy wallop
94 *grunshy*: big, stoutly built person
95 *cawrl*: fellow
*whoppit*: whipped
100 *bide*: stand, suffer
101 *gryte gudman*: huge farmer
*nor nane*: not anyone
102 *stenn'd*: leaped, bounded
*bawk-height*: as high as the rafters
105 *knabliech stane*: large, unevenly shaped stone
106 *rammage*: rough, uneven, broken
*glyde*: road or opening
107 *gardie-bane*: arm bone
109 *bierly*: well-built, powerful
110 *stier*: active
*heght*: called
111 *mell*: brawl, fight
*mank*: fail
112 *staffy-nevel*: a set-to with cudgels and fists

I wat na fow, but on a bank,
Whare thrangest was the mob,
The cousins bicker'd wi' a clank,
Gart ane anither sob
And gasp that day.

14

Tho' Rob was stout, his cousin dang
Him down wi' a gryte shudder,
Syne a' the drochlin hempy thrang
Gat o'er him wi' a fudder:
Gin he shou'd rise, an' hame o'er gang,
Lang was he in a swidder,
For bleed frae's mou and nize did bang,
And in braid burns did bludder
His face that day.

15

A huddrin hynd came wi' his pattle,
As he'd been at the pleugh,
Said there was nane in a the battle,
That broolzied bend aneugh:
But i' the mids' o' 's windy tattle,
A chiel came wi' a feugh,
Box'd him on 's arse wi' a bauld brattle,
Till a' the kendlins leuch
At him that day.

16

A stalwart stirk in tartain claise,
Sware mony a sturdy aith,
To bear the ba' thro' a' his faes,
And nae kepp muckle skaith:
Rob Roy heard the frieksome fraise,

113 *fow*: how
114 *thrangest*: thickest
115 *bicker'd*: fought
*clank*: resounding blow
120 *drochlin*: inclined to hang back
*hempy*: roguish
*thrang*: throng
121 *fudder*: sudden rush
123 *swidder*: state of indecision
124 *nize*: nose
125 *bludder*: make bloody
127 *huddrin*: awkward, clumsy
*hynd*: ploughman
*pattle*: plough staff
130 *broolzied*: fought
*bend*: bravely
132 *feugh*: smart, resounding blow
133 *brattle*: clashing noise
134 *kendlins*: young persons
*leuch*: laughed
139 *kepp*: suffer
*skaith*: harm, damage
140 *frieksome*: freakish
*fraise*: (= phrase), great talk

Well browden'd in his graith,
Gowph'd him alang his shins a blaise,
And gart him tyne his faith
And feet that day.

17

His neipor was a man o' might,
Was few there cou'd ha quell'd him,
He didna see the dreary sight,
Till some yap gilpy tell'd him:
To Robin syne he flew outright,
As he'd been gawing to geld him,
But suddenly frae some curst wight,
A clammyhowat fell'd him
Hawf dead that day.

18

The prior's man, a chiel as stark
Amaist as giant cou'd be,
Had kent afore o' this day's wark,
For certain that it wou'd be:
He ween'd to drive in o'er the park,
And ilkane thought it shou'd be:
What way it was he miss'd the mark,
I canna tell, but fou'd be
He fell that day.

19

Ere he wan out o' that foul lair,
That black mischance had gi'en him,
There tumbl'd a mischievous pair
O' mawtent lolls aboon him:
It wad ha made your heart fou sair,
Gin ye had only seen him,
An't had na been for Davy Mair,
The rascals had ondane him,
Belyve that day.

141 *browden'd*: adorned
*graith*: clothes
142 *gowph'd*: hit
*blaise*: blow
143 *tyne*: lose
145 *neipor*: neighbour
148 *yap*: eager
150 *gawing*: going
151 *wight*: fellow
152 *clammyhowat*: blow, drubbing
154 *stark*: strong, sturdy
158 *ween'd*: thought
161 *fou'd be*: meaning obscure, but perhaps 'however it was'
166 *mawtent lolls*: lazy idlers
171 *belyve*: quickly

20

But waes my heart for Petry Gibb,
The carlie's head was scawt,
It gat a fell uncanny skib,
That gart him yowl and claw't:
So he took gate to hodge to Tibb,
And spy at hame some fawt;
I thought he might ha' gotn a snib,
Sae thought ilk ane that saw 't
O' th' green that day.

21

The Taylor Hutchin he was there,
A curst illtrickit spark,
Saw Pate had caught a camshuch care
At this unsonsy wark:
He stood na lang to seek his lare,
But wi' a yawfou' yark,
Whare Pate's richt spawl by hap was bare,
He derfly dang the bark
Frae 's shin that day.

22

Poor Petry gae a weary winch,
He coudna do but bann;
The taylor baith his sides did pinch,
Wi' laughing out o' hand:
He jee'd na out o' that an inch,
Afore a menseless man,
Came a' at anes athort his hinch
A sowph, and gart him pran
His arse that day.

173 *scawt*: bald and scabby
174 *skib*: hard crack or smack
176 *took gate*: started off
*hodge*: hobble
177 *fawt*: injury
178 *snib*: cut
182 *illtrickit*: full of mischief
183 *camshuch care*: unlucky or perverse concern
184 *unsonsy*: treacherous
185 *lare*: meaning obscure but perhaps 'he did not stand and think' or 'he did not stick to the spot'
186 *yawfou' yark*: awful blow
187 *spawl*: limb
188 *derfly*: boldly, roughly
190 *winch*: kick
191 *bann*: curse
194 *jee'd*: budged, moved aside
195 *menseless*: boorish
196 *athort*: across
*hinch*: haunch
197 *sowph*: blow
*pran*: bruise

23

The town sutor like Laury lap
Three fit at ilka stenn,
He didna miss the ba' ae chap,
Ilk ane did him commenn:
But a lang trypal there was snap,
Came on him wi' a benn,
Gart him ere ever he wist cry clap
Upon his nether end,
And there he lay.

24

Sanny soon saw the sutor slain,
He was his ain hawf-brither;
I wat mysell he was fou' brain,
And how cou'd he be ither?
He ran to help wi' might and main,
Twa buckl'd wi'm the gether,
Wi' a firm gowph he fell'd the t'ane
But wi' a gowph the tither
Fell'd him that day.

25

The millart lad, a souple fallow,
Ran 's he had been red wood,
He fether'd fierce like ony swallow,
Cry'd hegh at ilka thud:
A stiblart gurk wi' phiz o' yellow
In youthit's sappy bud,
Nae twa there wadha gart him wallow,
Wi' fair play i' the mud
On 's back that day.

26

Tam Tull upon him kiest his ee,
Saw him sae mony foolzie,
He green'd again some prott to pree,
An' raise anither bruilzie:

199 *sutor*: shoemaker
*Laury*: the fox
200 *stenn*: leap
201 *chap*: stroke
202 *commenn*: command
203 *a*: one (pron. stressed, 'ae')
*trypal*: tall, thin person
*snap*: smart
204 *benn*: bound
210 *brain*: angry, furious
213 *the gether*: together
214 *gowph*: buffet
218 *red wood*: stark, staring mad
219 *fether'd*: flew
221 *stiblart gurk*: stout young fellow
222 *youthit*: youth

Up the kirk-yard he fast did jee,
I wat he was na hooly,
And a' the ablachs glowr'd to see
A bonny kind o' toolzie
Atween them twae.

27

The millart never notic'd Tam,
Sae browden'd he the ba',
He rumbl'd rudely like a ram,
Dang o'er whiles ane, whiles twa:
The traitor in afore him came,
Ere ever he him saw,
Rawght him a rap o' the forestamm,
But hadna time to draw
Anither sae.

28

Afore he cou'd step three inch back,
The millart drew a knife,
A curst-like gully and a snack,
Was made, fowk said, in Fife:
The lave their thumbs did blythely knack,
To see the sturty strife,
But Tam, I ken, wadha gien a plack,
T' ha been safe wi' his wife
At hame that day.

29

The parish-clerk came up the yard,
A man fou' meek o' mind,
Right jinsh he was and fell well fawr'd,
His claithing was fou' fine:

227 *foolzie*: trample
228 *green'd*: longed
*prott*: trick
*pree*: try
230 *jee*: move
231 *hooly*: slow, cautious
*ablachs*: good-for-nothings
233 *toolzie*: fight
236 *browden'd*: was intent on
241 *rawght*: dealt
*forestamm*: forehead
246 *snack*: quick in action
248 *lave*: rest
*knack*: snap or crack
249 *sturty*: causing trouble
250 *plack*: 4 pennies Scots, or ⅓ of an old English penny
255 *jinsh*: neat, spruce
*well fawr'd*: well favoured

Just whare their feet the dubs had glaar'd
   And brew'd them a' like brine,
Daft Davy Don wi' a derf dawrd,
   Beft o'er the grave divine
            On 's bum that day.

30

When a' were pitying sic mishap,
   And swarm'd about the clark,
Wi' whittles some his hat did scrap,
   Some dighted at his sark:
Will Winter gae the ba' a chap,
   He ween'd he did a wark,
While Sanny wi' a well-wyl'd wap,
   Yowph'd her in o'er the park
            A space and mae.

31

Wi' that Rob Roy gae a rair,
   A rierfou' rowt rais'd he,
Twas hard, they said, three mile and mair,
   Wha likes may crydit gie:
His paughty heart was fou' o' cair,
   And knell'd fell sair to see
The cleverest callant that was there,
   Play himsell sic a slee
            Begeck that day.

32

Jock Jalop shouted like a gun,
   As something had him ail'd,
'Fy sirs,' quo' he, 'the bonspale's win,
   And we the ba' have hail'd.'

257 *glaar'd*: muddied
258 *brew'd*: stained
259 *derf dawrd*: violent push
260 *beft*: knocked
264 *whittles*: knives
265 *dighted*: wiped clean
*sark*: shirt
268 *well-wyl'd*: well chosen
*wap*: stroke
272 *rierfou*: frenzied
*rowt*: roar
273 *hard*: heard
274 *crydit*: credit
275 *paughty*: stout
276 *knell'd*: throbbed
279 *begeck*: trick
282 *bonspale . . . hail'd*: match is won and we have taken the ball over the boundary or goal line

Some grien'd for ae hawf hour's mair fun,
'Cause fresh and nae sair fail'd,
Ithers did Sanny great thanks cunn,
And thro' their haffats trail'd
Their nails that day.

33

Syne a' consentit to be freins,
And lap like suckand fillies,
Some redd their hair, some main'd their banes,
Some bann'd the bangsom billies:
The pensy lads dosst down on stanes,
Whopt out their snishin-millies,
And a' were fain to tak' their einds
And club a pint o' Lillie's
Best ale that day.

34

In Monimuss was never seen
Sae mony well beft skins,
Of a' the ba'-men there was nane
But had twa bleedy shins:
Wi' streinzeit shoulders mony ane
Dree'd penance for their sins,
And what was warst, scowp'd hame, them lane,
Maybe to hungry inns
And cauld that day.

FINIS

*Ad lectorem peroratio*

Now, cankart carl, wha-e'er ye be,
Of lay or haly calling,
Gin ye shou'd ever chance to see
This auld Scots way o' scrawling,

284 *grien'd*: longed
286 *cunn*: express
287 *haffats*: hair, particularly over the temples
290 *lap*: leaped
291 *redd*: tidied
*main'd*: moaned
292 *bangsom*: quarrelsome
*billies*: fellows
293 *pensy*: sensible
*dosst*: threw themselves down
294 *whopt*: whipped
*snishin-millies*: snuff boxes
295 *einds*: breaths
299 *beft*: beaten
302 *streinzeit*: strained
304 *scowp'd*: hurried
305 *inns*: dwellings
*ad lecturem peroratio*: summing up to the reader
307 *cankart*: ill-natured

Ye'd better steik your gab awee,
  Nor plague me wi' your bawling,
In case ye find that I can gie
  Your censorship a mawling,
    Some orra day.

311 *steik*: shut
*gab*: mouth
*awee*: a bit
315 *orra*: other

# James Beattie
## 1735–1803

The son of a shopkeeper and small farmer in Laurencekirk, Kincardineshire, James Beattie graduated M.A. from Marischal College, Aberdeen, in 1753. After a spell of schoolmastering in Fordoun near Laurencekirk and at Aberdeen Grammar School, he was appointed to the chair of moral philosophy and rhetoric at Marischal College in 1760. Beattie's first volume of poetry was published in 1761 and he became widely known as an essayist. His *Essay on Truth* (1771), an unsympathetic and intellectually flaccid attempt to refute the scepticism of Hume, went through five editions in four years and was translated into French, German, Italian and Dutch. Perhaps the most popular *British* man of letters to come to the fore in the 1770s, he defended orthodoxy against what was termed 'sophistry' and gained the approval and friendship of Dr Johnson, not to speak of an honorary D.C.L. from Oxford. We include him for historical reasons: *The Minstrel* is almost as important as 'Ossian' for both English and European romanticism.

The first book of *The Minstrel* was published in 1771, the second in 1774. In it Beattie attempts 'to trace the progress of a poetical genius'; in other words, he is concerned with the education and growth of a poetic sensibility, as Wordsworth was on a far grander scale when he wrote *The Prelude*. Edwin is a hero of the contemporary cult of individuality and primitivism, and Beattie tries to embody in a portrait the thinking of men such as Thomas and Joseph Warton, Edward Young and Richard Hurd on the nature of the poet and poetry. They stressed individual poetic power and the need for 'a creative and glowing *imagination*' (Joseph Warton), unhampered by prescriptive rules. They believed the sublimer scenes of nature to be the source of the truest poetry and that genius was more likely to appear in primitive societies, or among the lower orders, because there the absence of formal education and social rules gave genius more freedom to express itself. Edwin is to be a 'poetical genius'; it is therefore appropriate that he should be born in 'a rude age', the son of a shepherd, that he should contemplate nature, and 'horrors', and that he should be destined to be a minstrel, who sang extempore and had no book learning. It is also appropriate that the poem should use the Spenserian stanza, whose 'Gothick structure and original' was associated with the rejection of classical precept, and felt to be the acme of spontaneity.

*The Minstrel* is not a great poem, but though much of it is decidedly insipid there are impressive passages (e.g. Book I stanzas 21, 34–5, 38–9, 53–4). Its achievement is to depict in verse a probable poet-figure that others could use and surpass. And it is, of course, written in English. Like so many of the *literati*, Beattie was troubled by the linguistic dichotomy of his century, generally eschewing the vernacular. He even published a list of Scotticisms so that aspiring writers might avoid them! Yet his one completely successful poem is his only known work in Scots, the epistle *To Mr Alexander Ross*, in which he defends the language of the north-east as a vehicle for poetry.

*Editions:*
*Poetical Works*, ed. A. Dyce (London, 1831).

*Biography:*
Sir William Forbes, *Account of the Life and Writings of James Beattie*, 2 vols (Edinburgh, 1806).

*Criticism:*
E. H. King, *James Beattie* (Boston, 1977).
James Kinsley, 'The Music of the Heart', *Renaissance and Modern Studies* 8 (1964), 5–52.
Joan H. Pittock, 'James Beattie: A Friend to All', in *Literature of the North*, ed. David Hewitt and Michael Spiller (Aberdeen, 1983).

# TO MR ALEXANDER ROSS AT LOCHLEE, AUTHOR OF THE FORTUNATE SHEPHERDESS, AND OTHER POEMS, IN THE BROAD SCOTCH DIALECT

O Ross, thou wale of hearty cocks,
Sae crouse and canty wi' thy jokes!
Thy hamely auldwarld muse provokes
    Me, for a while,
To ape our guid plain countra folks
    In verse and stile.

Sure never carle was haff sae gabby,
E'er since the winsome days of Habby.[n]
O mayst thou ne'er gang clung or shabby,
    Nor miss thy snaker!
Or I'll call fortune, nasty drabby,
    And say, pox take her.

O may the roupe ne'er roust thy weason!
May thrist thy thrapple never gizzen!
But bottled ale, in mony a dozen,
    Ay lade thy gantry!
And fowth o' vivers, a' in season,
    Plenish thy pantry!

Lang may thy stevin fill wi' glee
The glens and mountains of Lochlee,
Which were right gowsty but for thee,
    Whase sangs enamour
Ilk lass, and teach wi' melody
    The rocks to yamour.

Ye shak your head; but, o' my fegs,
Ye've set auld *Scota* on her legs.
Lang had she lyen, wi' beffs and flegs
    Bumbaz'd and dizzie.
Her fiddle wanted strings and pegs.
    Wae's me! poor hizzie!

1 *wale*: choice, best
2 *crouse*: cheerful
*canty*: lively
7 *carle*: man
*gabby*: eloquent
9 *clung*: hungry
10 *snaker*: glass of brandy
11 *drabby*: diminutive of drab, strumpet
13 *roupe*: hoarseness
*roust*: rust
*weason*: gullet, throat
14 *thrapple*: throat
*gizzen*: dry up
16 *lade*: load
17 *fowth*: plenty
*vivers*: victuals
19 *stevin*: voice
21 *gowsty*: dreary, desolate
24 *yamour*: cry out
25 *o' my fegs*: on my faith
26 *Scota*: Alexander Ross's muse
27 *beffs*: blows
*flegs*: severe blows
28 *bumbaz'd*: confounded
30 *hizzie*: hussy

Since Allan's death, naebody car'd
For anes to speer how Scota far'd;
Nor plack nor thristled turner war'd,
To quench her drouth;
For, frae the cottar to the laird,
We a' rin south.

The southland chiels indeed hae mettle,
And brawly at a sang can ettle;
Yet we right couthily might settle
On this side Forth.
The devil pay them wi' a pettle,
That slight the north.

Our countra leed is far frae barren,
It's even right pithy and auldfarren.
Oursells are neiper-like, I warran,
For sense and smergh,
In kittle times, whan faes are yarring,
We're no thought ergh.

O bonny are our greensward hows,
Where through the birks the burny rows,
And the bee bums, and the ox lows,
And saft winds rusle,
And shepherd-lads on sunny knows,
Blaw the blythe fusle.

It's true, we norlans manna fa'
To eat sae nice, or gang sae bra',
As they that come from far-awa';
Yet sma's our skaith:
We've peace (and that's well worth it a')
And meat and claith.

31 *Allan*: Allan Ramsay
32 *speer*: ask
33 *plack*: 4 pennies Scots, $\frac{1}{3}$ of an old English penny
*thristled*: thistled
*turner*: 2 pennies Scots, $\frac{1}{6}$ of an old English penny; these coins ceased to be legal tender after the Union in 1707
*war'd*: spent
34 *drouth*: thirst
37 *chiels*: fellows
38 *ettle*: try, aim
39 *couthily*: kindly, pleasantly
41 *pettle*: ploughstaff
43 *leed*: speech, language
44 *auldfarran*: old-fashioned
45 *neiper-like*: neighbourly
*warran*: warrant, guarantee
46 *smergh*: pith, vigour
47 *kittle*: difficult
*yarring*: snarling
48 *ergh*: backward
49 *hows*: hollows
50 *rows*: rolls
54 *fusle*: whistle
55 *norlans*: people in the north
*manna*: must not
58 *skaith*: harm

Our fine newfangle sparks, I grant ye,
Gie poor auld Scotland mony a taunty;
They're grown sae ugertfu' and vaunty,
        And capernoited,
They guide her like a canker'd aunty,
        That's deaf and doited.

Sae comes of ignorance, I trow;
It's this that crooks their ill-fa'rd mou'
With jokes sae course, they gar fouk spue
        For downright skonner.
For Scotland wants na sons enew
        To do her honour.

I here might gie a screed of names,
Dawties of Heliconian Dames!
The foremost place Gawin Douglas[n] claims,
        That canty priest.
And wha can match the first King James[n]
        For sang or jest?

Montgomery[n] grave, and Ramsay gay,
Dunbar, Scot, Hawthornden[n], and mae
Than I can tell; for o' my fae,
        I maun brak aff;
'Twould take a live-lang summer-day
        To name the haff.

The saucy chiels — I think they ca' them
Criticks — the muckle sorrow claw them,
(For mense nor manners ne'er could awe them
        Frae their presumption)
They need na try thy jokes to fathom,
        They want rumgumption.

But ilka Mearns and Angus bairn
Thy tales and sangs by heart shall learn;
And chiels shall come frae yont the Cairn-
        amounth[n], right vousty,
If Ross will be so kind as share in
        Their pint at Drousty[n].

62 *taunty*: ?diminutive of 'taunt'
63 *ugertfu*: proud
64 *capernoited*: crabbed
65 *guide*: use
*doited*: foolish, senile
67 *trow*: trust
*ill-fa'rd*: ill-favoured, ugly
69 *fouk*: folk
70 *skonner*: disgust
73 *screed*: a long speech or piece of writing
74 *dawties*: darlings
*Heliconian Dames*: the muses
81 *fae*: faith
86 *claw*: scratch
87 *mense*: propriety
90 *rumgumption*: common sense
91 *Mearns*: lowland Kincardineshire, south of the Deeside hills
94 *vousty*: boastful, proud

# THE MINSTREL

or the

# PROGRESS OF GENIUS

## Preface

The design was, to trace the progress of a poetical genius, born in a rude age, from the first dawning of fancy and reason, till that period at which he may be supposed capable of appearing in the world as *a minstrel*, that is, as an itinerant poet and musician; — a character which, according to the notions of our forefathers, was not only respectable, but sacred.

I have endeavoured to imitate Spenser in the measure of his verse, and in the harmony, simplicity, and variety, of his composition. Antique expressions I have avoided; admitting, however, some old words, where they seemed to suit the subject: but I hope none will be found that are now obsolete, or in any degree not intelligible to a reader of English poetry.

To those, who may be disposed to ask, what could induce me to write in so difficult a measure, I can only answer, that it pleases my ear, and seems, from its gothick structure and original, to bear some relation to the subject and spirit of the poem. It admits both simplicity and magnificence of sound and of language, beyond any other stanza that I am acquainted with. It allows the sententiousness of the couplet, as well as the more complex modulation of blank verse. What some criticks have remarked, of its uniformity growing at last tiresome to the ear, will be found to hold true, only when the poetry is faulty in other respects.

## THE FIRST BOOK

1

Ah! who can tell how hard it is to climb
The steep where fame's proud temple shines afar;
Ah! who can tell how many a soul sublime
Has felt the influence of malignant star,
And waged with fortune an eternal war;
Check'd by the scoff of pride, by envy's frown,
And poverty's unconquerable bar,
In life's low vale remote has pined alone,
Then dropt into the grave, unpitied and unknown![n]

2

And yet, the languor of inglorious days
Not equally oppressive is to all.
Him, who ne'er listen'd to the voice of praise,
The silence of neglect can ne'er appal.

There are, who, deaf to mad ambition's call,
Would shrink to hear th' obstreperous trump of fame;
Supremely blest, if to their portion fall
Health, competence, and peace. Nor higher aim
Had *He*, whose simple tale these artless lines proclaim.

3

The rolls of fame I will not now explore;
Nor need I here describe in learned lay,
How forth *the minstrel*[n] fared in days of yore,
Right glad of heart, though homely in array;
His waving locks and beard all hoary grey:
While from his bending shoulder, decent hung
His harp, the sole companion of his way,
Which to the whistling wind responsive rung:
And ever as he went some merry lay he sung.

4

Fret not thyself, thou glittering child of pride,
That a poor villager inspires my strain;
With thee let pageantry and power abide:
The gentle muses haunt the sylvan reign;
Where through wild groves at eve the lonely swain
Enraptured roams, to gaze on nature's charms.
They hate the sensual, and scorn the vain,
The parasite their influence never warms,
Nor him whose sordid soul the love of gold alarms.

5

Though richest hues the peacock's plumes adorn,
Yet horror screams from his discordant throat.
Rise, sons of harmony! and hail the morn,
While warbling larks on russet pinions float:
Or seek at noon the woodland scene remote,
Where the grey linnets carol from the hill.
O let them ne'er, with artificial note,
To please a tyrant, strain the little bill,
But sing what heaven inspires, and wander where they will.

6

Liberal, not lavish, is kind nature's hand;
Nor was perfection made for man below.
Yet all her schemes with nicest art are plann'd,
Good counteracting ill, and gladness wo.

With gold and gems if Chilian mountains glow;
If bleak and barren Scotia's hills arise;
There plague and poison, lust and rapine grow;
Here peaceful are the vales, and pure the skies,
And freedom fires the soul, and sparkles in the eyes.

7

Then grieve not, thou, to whom th' indulgent muse
Vouchsafes a portion of celestial fire;
Nor blame the partial fates, if they refuse
Th' imperial banquet, and the rich attire.
Know thine own worth, and reverence the lyre.
Wilt thou debase the heart which God refined?
No; let thy heaven-taught soul to heaven aspire,
To fancy, freedom, harmony, resign'd;
Ambition's grovelling crew for ever left behind.

8

Canst thou forego the pure ethereal soul
In each fine sense so exquisitely keen,
On the dull couch of luxury[n] to loll,
Stung with disease, and stupefied with spleen;
Fain to implore the aid of flattery's screen,
Even from thyself thy loathsome heart to hide,
(The mansion then no more of joy serene),
Where fear, distrust, malevolence, abide,
And impotent desire, and disappointed pride?

9

O how canst thou renounce the boundless store
Of charms which nature to her votary yields!
The warbling woodland, the resounding shore,
The pomp of groves, and garniture of fields;
All that the genial ray of morning gilds,
And all that echoes to the song of even,
All that the mountain's sheltering bosom shields,
And all the dread magnificence of heaven,
O how canst thou renounce, and hope to be forgiven!

10

These charms shall work thy soul's eternal health,
And love, and gentleness, and joy, impart.
But these thou must renounce, if lust of wealth
E'er win its way to thy corrupted heart:

For, ah! it poisons like a scorpion's dart;
Prompting th' ungenerous wish, the selfish scheme,
The stern resolve unmoved by pity's smart,
The troublous day, and long distressful dream.
Return, my roving muse, resume thy purposed theme.

11

There lived in gothick days[n], as legends tell,
A shepherd-swain, a man of low degree;
Whose sires, perchance, in fairyland[n] might dwell,
Sicilian groves, or vales of Arcady;
But he, I ween, was of the north countrie[n]:
A nation famed for song, and beauty's charms;
Zealous, yet modest; innocent, though free;
Patient of toil; serene amidst alarms;
Inflexible in faith; invincible in arms.

12

The shepherd-swain of whom I mention made,
On Scotia's mountains fed his little flock;
The sickle, scythe, or plough, he never sway'd;
An honest heart was almost all his stock;
His drink the living water from the rock;
The milky dams supplied his board, and lent
Their kindly fleece to baffle winter's shock;
And he, though oft with dust and sweat besprent,
Did guide and guard their wanderings, wheresoe'er they went.

13

From labour health, from health contentment springs.[n]
Contentment opes the source of every joy.
He envied not, he never thought of, kings;
Nor from those appetites sustain'd annoy,
That chance may frustrate, or indulgence cloy:
Nor fate his calm and humble hopes beguiled;
He mourn'd no recreant friend, nor mistress coy,
For on his vows the blameless Phœbe smiled,
And her alone he loved, and loved her from a child.

14

No jealousy their dawn of love o'ercast,
Nor blasted were their wedded days with strife;
Each season look'd delightful, as it past,
To the fond husband, and the faithful wife.

Beyond the lowly vale of shepherd life
They never roam'd; secure beneath the storm
Which in ambition's lofty land is rife,
Where peace and love are canker'd by the worm
Of pride, each bud of joy industrious to deform.

15

The wight, whose tale these artless lines unfold,
Was all the offspring of this humble pair.
His birth no oracle or seer foretold:
No prodigy appear'd in earth or air,
Nor aught that might a strange event declare.
You guess each circumstance of *Edwin's* birth;
The parent's transport, and the parent's care;
The gossip's prayer for wealth, and wit, and worth;
And one long summer-day of indolence and mirth.

16

And yet poor Edwin was no vulgar boy;
Deep thought oft seem'd to fix his infant eye.
Dainties he heeded not, nor gaude, nor toy,
Save one short pipe of rudest minstrelsy.
Silent when glad; affectionate, though shy;
And now his look was most demurely sad;
And now he laugh'd aloud, yet none knew why.
The neighbours stared and sigh'd, yet bless'd the lad:
Some deem'd him wondrous wise, and some believed him mad.

17

But why should I his childish feats display?
Concourse, and noise, and toil, he ever fled;
Nor cared to mingle in the clamorous fray
Of squabbling imps; but to the forest sped;
Or roam'd at large the lonely mountain's head;
Or, where the maze of some bewilder'd stream
To deep untrodden groves his footsteps led,
There would he wander wild, till Phœbus' beam,[n]
Shot from the western cliff, released the weary team.[n]

18

Th' exploit of strength, dexterity, or speed,
To him nor vanity nor joy could bring.
His heart, from cruel sport estranged, would bleed
To work the wo of any living thing,

By trap, or net; by arrow, or by sling;
These he detested, those he scorn'd to wield:
He wish'd to be the guardian, not the king,
Tyrant far less, or traitor of the field.
And sure the sylvan reign unbloody joy might yield.

19

Lo! where the stripling, wrapt in wonder, roves
Beneath the precipice o'erhung with pine;
And sees, on high, amidst th' encircling groves,
From cliff to cliff the foaming torrents shine:
While waters, woods, and winds, in concert join,
And Echo swells the chorus to the skies.
Would Edwin this majestic scene resign
For aught the huntsman's puny craft supplies?
Ah! no: he better knows great nature's charms to prize.[n]

20

And oft he traced the uplands, to survey,
When o'er the sky advanced the kindling dawn,
The crimson cloud, blue main, and mountain grey,
And lake, dim-gleaming on the smoky lawn;
Far to the west the long long vale withdrawn,
Where twilight loves to linger for a while;
And now he faintly kens the bounding fawn,
And villager abroad at early toil.
But, lo! the sun appears! and heaven, earth, ocean, smile.

21

And oft the craggy cliff he loved to climb,
When all in mist the world below was lost.
What dreadful pleasure! there to stand sublime,
Like shipwreck'd mariner on desert coast,
And view th' enormous waste of vapour, tost
In billows, lengthening to th' horizon round,
Now scoop'd in gulfs, with mountains now emboss'd!
And hear the voice of mirth and song rebound,
Flocks, herds, and waterfalls, along the hoar profound![n]

22

In truth he was a strange and wayward wight,
Fond of each gentle, and each dreadful scene.[n]
In darkness, and in storm, he found delight:
Nor less, than when on ocean-wave serene

The southern sun diffused his dazzling shene.
Even sad vicissitude amused his soul:
And if a sigh would sometimes intervene,
And down his cheek a tear of pity roll,
A sigh, a tear, so sweet, he wish'd not to control.

23

'O ye wild groves, O where is now your bloom!'
(The muse interprets thus his tender thought.)
'Your flowers, your verdure, and your balmy gloom,
Of late so grateful in the hour of drought!
Why do the birds, that song and rapture brought
To all your bowers, their mansions now forsake?
Ah! why has fickle chance this ruin wrought?
For now the storm howls mournful through the brake,
And the dead foliage flies in many a shapeless flake.

24

'Where now the rill, melodious, pure, and cool,
And meads, with life, and mirth, and beauty crown'd!
Ah! see, th' unsightly slime, and sluggish pool,
Have all the solitary vale imbrown'd;
Fled each fair form, and mute each melting sound.
The raven croaks forlorn on naked spray.
And, hark! the river, bursting every mound,
Down the vale thunders; and with wasteful sway
Uproots the grove, and rolls the shatter'd rocks away.

25

'Yet such the destiny of all on earth:
So flourishes and fades majestic man.
Fair is the bud his vernal morn brings forth,
And fostering gales a while the nursling fan.
O smile, ye heavens, serene; ye mildews wan,
Ye blighting whirlwinds, spare his balmy prime,
Nor lessen of his life the little span.
Born on the swift, though silent, wings of time,
Old age comes on apace to ravage all the clime.

26

'And be it so. Let those deplore their doom,
Whose hope still grovels in this dark sojourn.
But lofty souls, who look beyond the tomb,
Can smile at fate, and wonder how they mourn.

Shall spring to these sad scenes no more return?
Is yonder wave the sun's eternal bed?
Soon shall the orient with new lustre burn,
And spring shall soon her vital influence shed,
Again attune the grove, again adorn the mead.

27

'Shall I be left forgotten in the dust,
When fate, relenting, lets the flower revive?
Shall nature's voice, to man alone unjust,
Bid him, though doom'd to perish, hope to live?
Is it for this fair virtue oft must strive
With disappointment, penury, and pain?
No: heaven's immortal spring shall yet arrive;
And man's majestic beauty bloom again,
Bright through th' eternal year of love's triumphant reign.'

28

This truth sublime his simple sire had taught.
In sooth, 'twas almost all the shepherd knew.
No subtle nor superfluous lore he sought,
Nor ever wish'd his Edwin to pursue.
'Let man's own sphere (said he) confine his view,
Be man's peculiar work his sole delight.'
And much, and oft, he warn'd him, to eschew
Falsehood and guile, and aye maintain the right,
By pleasure unseduced, unawed by lawless might.

29

'And, from the prayer of want, and plaint of wo,
O never, never turn away thine ear!
Forlorn, in this bleak wilderness below,
Ah! what were man, should heaven refuse to hear!
To others do (the law is not severe)
What to thyself thou wishest to be done.
Forgive thy foes; and love thy parents dear,
And friends, and native land; not those alone;
All human weal and wo learn thou to make thine own.'

30

See, in the rear of the warm sunny shower,
The visionary boy from shelter fly!
For now the storm of summer-rain is o'er,
And cool, and fresh, and fragrant is the sky.

And, lo! in the dark east, expanded high,
The rainbow brightens to the setting sun!
Fond fool, that deem'st the streaming glory nigh,
How vain the chace thine ardor has begun!
'Tis fled afar, ere half thy purposed race be run.

31

Yet couldst thou learn, that thus it fares with age,
When pleasure, wealth, or power the bosom warm,
This baffled hope might tame thy manhood's rage,
And disappointment of her sting disarm.
But why should foresight thy fond heart alarm?
Perish the lore that deadens young desire!
Pursue, poor imp, th' imaginary charm,
Indulge gay hope, and fancy's pleasing fire:
Fancy and hope too soon shall of themselves expire.

32

When the long-sounding curfew from afar
Loaded with loud lament the lonely gale,
Young Edwin, lighted by the evening star,
Lingering and listening wander'd down the vale.
There would he dream of graves, and corses pale;[n]
And ghosts that to the charnel-dungeon throng,
And drag a length of clanking chain, and wail,
Till silenced by the owl's terrific song,
Or blast that shrieks by fits the shuddering isles along.

33

Or, when the setting moon, in crimson dyed,
Hung o'er the dark and melancholy deep,
To haunted stream, remote from man, he hied,
Where fays of yore their revels wont to keep;
And there let fancy rove at large, till sleep
A vision[n] brought to his intranced sight.
And first, a wildly murmuring wind 'gan creep
Shrill to his ringing ear; then tapers bright,
With instantaneous gleam, illumed the vault of night.

34

Anon in view a portal's blazon'd arch
Arose; the trumpet bids the valves unfold;
And forth an host of little warriors march,
Grasping the diamond lance, and targe of gold.

299 *valves*: leaves of a double door

Their look was gentle, their demeanour bold,
And green their helms, and green their silk attire;
And here and there, right venerably old,
The long-robed minstrels wake the warbling wire,
And some with mellow breath the martial pipe inspire.

35

With merriment, and song, and timbrels clear,
A troop of dames from myrtle bowers advance;
The little warriors doff the targe and spear,
And loud enlivening strains provoke the dance.
They meet, they dart away, they wheel askance;
To right, to left, they thrid the flying maze;
Now bound aloft with vigorous spring, then glance
Rapid along: with many-colour'd rays
Of tapers, gems, and gold, the echoing forests blaze.

36

The dream is fled. Proud harbinger of day,
Who scar'dst the vision with thy clarion shrill,
Fell chanticleer! who oft hast reft away
My fancied good, and brought substantial ill!
O to thy cursed scream, discordant still,
Let harmony aye shut her gentle ear:
Thy boastful mirth let jealous rivals spill,
Insult thy crest, and glossy pinions tear,
And ever in thy dreams the ruthless fox appear.

37

Forbear, my muse. Let love attune thy line.
Revoke the spell. Thine Edwin frets not so,
For how should he at wicked chance repine,
Who feels from every change amusement flow?
Even now his eyes with smiles of rapture glow,
As on he wanders through the scenes of morn,
Where the fresh flowers in living lustre blow,
Where thousand pearls the dewy lawns adorn,
A thousand notes of joy in every breeze are born.

38

But who the melodies of morn can tell?
The wild brook babbling down the mountain side;
The lowing herd; the sheepfold's simple bell;
The pipe of early shepherd dim descried

In the lone valley; echoing far and wide
The clamorous horn along the cliffs above;
The hollow murmur of the ocean-tide;
The hum of bees, and linnet's lay of love,
And the full choir that wakes the universal grove.

39

The cottage-curs at early pilgrim bark;
Crown'd with her pail the tripping milkmaid sings;
The whistling plowman stalks afield; and, hark!
Down the rough slope the ponderous waggon rings;
Through rustling corn the hare astonish'd springs;
Slow tolls the village-clock the drowsy hour;
The partridge bursts away on whirring wings;
Deep mourns the turtle in sequester'd bower,
And shrill lark carols clear from her aërial tour.

40

O nature, how in every charm supreme!
Whose votaries feast on raptures ever new!
O for the voice and fire of seraphim,
To sing thy glories with devotion due!
Blest be the day I 'scaped the wrangling crew,
From Pyrrho's maze, and Epicurus' sty;[n]
And held high converse with the godlike few,
Who to th' enraptur'd heart, and ear, and eye,
Teach beauty, virtue, truth, and love, and melody.

41

Hence! ye, who snare and stupefy the mind,
Sophists, of beauty, virtue, joy, the bane!
Greedy and fell, though impotent and blind,
Who spread your filthy nets in truth's fair fane,
And ever ply your venom'd fangs amain!
Hence to dark Error's den,[n] whose rankling slime
First gave you form! hence! lest the muse should deign,
(Though loath on theme so mean to waste a rhyme),
With vengeance to pursue your sacrilegious crime.

42

But hail, ye mighty masters of the lay,[n]
Nature's true sons, the friends of man and truth!
Whose song, sublimely sweet, serenely gay,
Amused my childhood, and inform'd my youth.

O let your spirit still my bosom sooth,
Inspire my dreams, and my wild wanderings guide:
Your voice each rugged path of life can smooth;
For well I know, where-ever ye reside,
There harmony, and peace, and innocence abide.

43

Ah me! neglected on the lonesome plain,
As yet poor Edwin never knew your lore,
Save when against the winter's drenching rain,
And driving snow, the cottage shut the door.
Then, as instructed by tradition hoar,
Her legend when the beldame 'gan impart,
Or chant the old heroic ditty o'er,
Wonder and joy ran thrilling to his heart;
Much he the tale admired, but more the tuneful art.

44

Various and strange was the long-winded tale;
And halls, and knights, and feats of arms, display'd;
Or merry swains, who quaff the nut-brown ale,
And sing, enamour'd of the nut-brown maid;[n]
The moon-light revel of the fairy glade;
Or hags, that suckle an infernal brood,
And ply in caves th' unutterable trade,
'Midst fiends and spectres, quench the moon in blood,
Yell in the midnight storm, or ride th' infuriate flood.

45

But when to horror his amazement rose,
A gentler strain the beldame would rehearse,
A tale of rural life, a tale of woes,
The orphan-babes, and guardian uncle fierce.
O cruel! will no pang of pity pierce
That heart by lust of lucre sear'd to stone?
For sure, if aught of virtue last, or verse,
To latest times shall tender souls bemoan
Those hopeless orphan-babes by thy fell arts undone.

46

Behold, with berries smear'd, with brambles torn[n],
The babes now famish'd lay them down to die.
Amidst the howl of darksome woods forlorn,
Folded in one another's arms they lie;

Nor friend, nor stranger, hears their dying cry:
'For from the town the man returns no more.'
But thou, who heaven's just vengeance darest defy,
This deed with fruitless tears shalt soon deplore,
When death lays waste thy house, and flames consume thy store.

47

A stifled smile of stern vindictive joy
Brighten'd one moment Edwin's starting tear.
'But why should gold man's feeble mind decoy,
And innocence thus die by doom severe?'
O Edwin! while thy heart is yet sincere,
Th' assaults of discontent and doubt repel:
Dark even at noontide is our mortal sphere;
But let us hope; to doubt is to rebel;
Let us exult in hope, that all shall yet be well.

48

Nor be thy generous indignation check'd,
Nor check'd the tender tear to misery given;
From guilt's contagious power shall that protect,
This soften and refine the soul for heaven.
But dreadful is their doom, whom doubt has driven
To censure fate, and pious hope forego:
Like yonder blasted boughs by lightning riven,
Perfection, beauty, life, they never know,
But frown on all that pass, a monument of wo.

49

Shall he, whose birth, maturity, and age,
Scarce fill the circle of one summer day,
Shall the poor gnat with discontent and rage
Exclaim, that nature hastens to decay,
If but a cloud obstruct the solar ray,
If but a momentary shower descend!
Or shall frail man heaven's dread decree gainsay,
Which bade the series of events extend
Wide through unnumber'd worlds, and ages without end!

50

One part, one little part, we dimly scan
Through the dark medium of life's feverish dream;
Yet dare arraign the whole stupendous plan,
If but that little part incongruous seem,

Nor is that part perhaps what mortals deem;
Oft from apparent ill our blessings rise.
O then renounce that impious self-esteem,
That aims to trace the secrets of the skies:
For thou art but of dust; be humble, and be wise.

51

Thus heaven enlarged his soul in riper years.
For nature gave him strength and fire, to soar
On fancy's wing above this vale of tears;
Where dark cold-hearted sceptics, creeping, pore
Through microscope of metaphysic lore:
And much they grope for truth, but never hit.
For why? their powers, inadequate before,
This idle art makes more and more unfit;
Yet deem they darkness light, and their vain blunders wit.

52

Nor was this ancient dame a foe to mirth.
Her ballad, jest, and riddle's quaint device
Oft cheer'd the shepherds round their social hearth;
Whom levity or spleen could ne'er entice
To purchase chat or laughter, at the price
Of decency. Nor let it faith exceed,
That nature forms a rustic taste so nice.
Ah! had they been of court or city breed,
Such delicacy were right marvellous indeed.

53

Oft, when the winter-storm had ceased to rave,
He roam'd the snowy waste at even, to view
The cloud stupendous, from th' Atlantic wave
High-towering, sail along th' horizon blue:
Where 'midst the changeful scenery ever new
Fancy a thousand wondrous forms descries
More wildly great than ever pencil drew,
Rocks, torrents, gulfs, and shapes of giant size,
And glittering cliffs on cliffs, and fiery ramparts rise.

54

Thence musing onward to the sounding shore
The lone enthusiast oft would take his way,
Listening with pleasing dread to the deep roar
Of the wide-weltering waves. In black array

When sulphurous clouds roll'd on th' autumnal day,
Even then he hasten'd from the haunt of man,
Along the trembling wilderness to stray,
What time the lightning's fierce career began,
And o'er heaven's rending arch the rattling thunder ran.

55

Responsive to the sprightly pipe when all
In sprightly dance the village-youth were join'd,
Edwin, of melody aye held in thrall,
From the rude gambol far remote reclined,
Sooth'd with the soft notes warbling in the wind.
Ah then, all jollity seem'd noise and folly.
To the pure soul by fancy's fire refined,
Ah what is mirth but turbulence unholy,
When with the charm compared of heavenly melancholy!

56

Is there a heart that music cannot melt?
Alas! how is that rugged heart forlorn!
Is there, who ne'er those mystic transports felt
Of solitude and melancholy born?
He needs not woo the muse; he is her scorn.
The sophist's rope of cobweb he shall twine;
Mope o'er the schoolman's peevish page; or mourn,
And delve for life, in Mammon's dirty mine;
Sneak with the scoundrel fox, or grunt with glutton swine.

57

For Edwin fate a nobler doom had plann'd;
Song was his favourite and first pursuit.
The wild harp rang to his adventurous hand,
And languish'd to his breath the plaintive flute.
His infant muse, though artless, was not mute:
Of elegance as yet he took no care;
For this of time and culture is the fruit;
And Edwin gain'd at last this fruit so rare:
As in some future verse I purpose to declare.

58

Meanwhile, whate'er of beautiful, or new,
Sublime, or dreadful, in earth, sea, or sky,
By chance, or search, was offer'd to his view,
He scan'd with curious and romantic eye.

Whate'er of lore tradition could supply
From gothic tale, or song, or fable old,
Roused him, still keen to listen and to pry.
At last, though long by penury control'd,
And solitude, his soul her graces 'gan unfold.

59

Thus on the chill Lapponian's dreary land,[n]
For many a long month lost in snow profound,
When Sol from Cancer sends the season bland,
And in their northern cave the storms are bound;
From silent mountains, straight, with startling sound,
Torrents are hurl'd; green hills emerge; and lo,
The trees with foliage, cliffs with flowers are crown'd;
Pure rills through vales of verdure warbling go;
And wonder, love, and joy, the peasant's heart o'erflow.

60

Here pause, my gothic lyre, a little while.
The leisure hour is all that thou canst claim.
But on this verse if *Montagu*[n] should smile,
New strains erelong shall animate thy frame.
And her applause to me is more than fame;
For still with truth accords her taste refined.
At lucre or renown let others aim,
I only wish to please the gentle mind,
Whom nature's charms inspire, and love of humankind.

# Robert Fergusson

## 1750–1774

Robert Fergusson, born in the Cap and Feather Close off the High Street of Edinburgh, was the child of Aberdeenshire parents. He attended the High School of Edinburgh for three years, and was then presented to the Fergusson of Strathmartine bursary which took him for two years to the Grammar School of Dundee and thereafter to St Andrews University. He left in 1768 before taking a degree, probably because his father had died leaving the family in financial difficulties. The following year he spent some months on his uncle's farm in Aberdeenshire, and it seems likely that his family hoped his uncle would be able to help him to a congenial post. But Robert and his uncle quarrelled, these hopes were dashed, and he returned on foot to Edinburgh, glad to take up copying work in the Commissary Clerk's Office. This was a job far beneath the abilities of a trained university scholar, but it at least gave him a little to live on, and leisure to write poetry.

Walter Ruddiman's *Edinburgh Weekly Magazine* had been started in 1768, and Fergusson's first contributions to its poetry section were pieces in English on traditional lines, in February 1771. Less than a year later, on 2 January, 1772, he contributed *The Daft Days*, an exhilarating comic description in Scots of New Year's Day in Edinburgh. It was clear to Ruddiman's readers that a genuine poet had arrived, and for the next two years Scots poems followed every month, and sometimes oftener. In that short period of sustained poetic energy Fergusson also wrote and published what is in some ways his most characteristically Scots poem, *Auld Reikie*, an affectionate yet crisp and clear-eyed description of his native city. Most of his Scots poems in fact concern Edinburgh, the paving of its streets, fairs and celebrations, benefactors like George Heriot and George Watson, its Town Council. Yet Fergusson shows also a love of rural life — *The Farmer's Ingle* has a smack of truth that is certainly based on experience, probably on his uncle's farm. And his musical ear picked up with delight in *Leith Races* the Buchan accents of the salesmen and the Gaelic sounds of the Highland warriors in the City Guard. Fergusson was a fine singer and an amusing companion, and became a popular figure in the Cape Club, one of the most famous of Edinburgh's many social clubs, where songs and poems were contributed by members in a cheerful bohemian atmosphere. Towards the end of 1773, the Cape Club members heard that the young poet was ill and subsequently afflicted with religious melancholia. He made a temporary recovery, but after an accidental fall he had in the end to be removed, delirious, to the Edinburgh Bedlam, where he died in distressing circumstances at the beginning of his twenty-fifth year on 17 October, 1774, 'regretted', as his friend and benefactor Thomas Ruddiman wrote, 'by his friends, and lamented by the lovers of poetry, of wit, and of song'.

A collection of his poems appeared in 1773, and in the same year *Auld Reikie* was published separately. A larger collection followed in 1779, including the 1773 poems, and this is generally known as the first edition. A. B. Grosart's edition of 1851 collected most of the poems and gave much detail about Fergusson's life, but sources that Grosart quoted have been lost and his conclusions cannot now be checked. The most reliable text and the most complete critical analysis are to be found in M. P. McDiarmid's Scottish Text Society edition. This is the text that has been followed here, modernised according to the principles of this anthology.

*Editions:*

*The Works of Robert Fergusson; with Life of the Author and an Essay on his Genius and Writings* by A.B. G. [A. B. Grosart], 1851.

*The Poems of Robert Fergusson*, ed. M. P. McDiarmid, Scottish Text Society, 2 vols (Edinburgh and London, 1954–56).

*The Scots Poems of Allan Ramsay and Robert Fergusson*, edited by A. M. Kinghorn and Alexander Law (Edinburgh, 1974).

These editions include biographical details and criticism.

*Criticism:*

*Robert Fergusson 1750–1774*, ed. Sydney Goodsir Smith (Edinburgh, 1952).

Allan H. Maclaine, *Robert Fergusson* (New York, 1965).

David Daiches, *Robert Fergusson* (Edinburgh, 1982).

F. W. Freeman, *Robert Fergusson and the Scots Humanist Compromise* (Edinburgh, 1984).

*Cassettes:*

*Robert Fergusson (1): An Edinburgh Calendar* (Scotsoun, Glasgow, 1974).

*Robert Fergusson (2): People and Places* (Scotsoun, Glasgow, 1974).

*Robert Fergusson (3): The Farmer's Ingle and Other Poems* (Scotsoun, Glasgow, 1974).

# HALLOW-FAIR

At Hallowmas,[n] whan nights grow lang,
And starnies shine fu' clear,
Whan fock, the nippin cald to bang,
Their winter hap-warms wear,
Near Edinbrough a fair there hads,
I wat there's nane whase name is,
For strappin dames and sturdy lads,
And cap and stoup, mair famous
Than it that day.

Upo' the tap o' ilka lum
The sun began to keek,
And bad the trig made maidens come
A sightly joe to seek
At Hallow-fair, whare browsters rare
Keep gude ale on the gantries,
And dinna scrimp ye o' a skair
O' kebbucks frae their pantries,
Fu' saut that day.

Here country John in bonnet blue,
An' eke his Sunday's claise on,
Rins after Meg wi' rokelay new,
An' sappy kisses lays on;
She'll tauntin say, 'Ye silly coof!
Be o' your gab mair spairin;'
He'll tak the hint, and criesh her loof
Wi' what will buy her fairin,
To chow that day.

Here chapmen billies tak their stand,
An' shaw their bonny wallies;
Wow, but they lie fu' gleg aff hand
To trick the silly fallows:

2 *starnies*: stars
3 *bang*: overcome
4 *hap-warms*: warm clothes
5 *hads*: holds
6 *wat*: know
8 *cap*: cup
*stoup*: flagon
10 *ilka*: every
*lum*: chimney
11 *keek*: peep
12 *trig*: neat
13 *joe*: sweetheart
14 *browsters*: ale-wives
15 *gantries*: stands
16 *scrimp*: stint
*skair*: share
17 *kebbucks*: cheeses
18 *saut*: salt
20 *eke*: also
*claise*: clothes
21 *rokelay*: mantle
22 *sappy*: moist
23 *coof*: fool
24 *gab*: mouth
25 *criesh*: grease
*loof*: palm
26 *fairin*: present from the fair
*chow*: chew
28 *chapmen billies*: salesmen
29 *bonny wallies*: gewgaws
30 *gleg*: cleverly

Heh, Sirs! what cairds and tinklers come,
An' ne'er-do-weel horse-coupers,
An' spae-wives fenying to be dumb,
Wi' a' siclike landloupers,
To thrive that day.

Here Sawny[n] cries, frae Aberdeen;
'Come ye to me fa need:
The brawest shanks that e'er were seen
I'll sell ye cheap an' guid.
I wyt they are as protty hose
As come frae weyr or leem:
Here tak a rug, and shaw's your pose:
Forseeth, my ain's but teem
An' light this day.'

Ye wives, as ye gang thro' the fair,
O mak your bargains hooly!
O' a' thir wylie lowns beware,
Or fegs they will ye spulyie.
For fairn-year Meg Thamson got,
Frae thir mischievous villains,
A scaw'd bit o' a penny note,
That lost a score o' shillins
To her that day.

The dinlin drums alarm our ears,
The serjeant[n] screechs fu' loud,
'A' gentlemen and volunteers
That wish your country gude,
Come here to me, and I sall gie
Twa guineas and a crown,
A bowl o' punch, that like the sea
Will soum a lang dragoon
Wi' ease this day.'

Without the cuissers prance and nicker,
An' our the ley-rig scud;
In tents the carles bend the bicker,
An' rant an' roar like wud.

32 *cairds*: beggars
*tinklers*: tinsmiths
33 *ne'er-do-weel*: good for nothing
*horse-coupers*: horse dealers
34 *spae-wives*: fortune tellers
36 *siclike*: such
*landloupers*: vagabonds
43 *pose*: store of money
44 *teem*: empty
47 *hooly*: carefully
48 *lowns*: rascals
49 *fegs*: truly!
*spulyie*: cheat, rob
50 *fairn-year*: last year
52 *scaw'd*: worthless
55 *dinlin*: rattling
62 *soum*: swim
64 *cuissers*: stallions
*nicker*: whinny
65 *our*: over
*ley-rig*: grass field
*scud*: career
66 *bend the bicker*: drink up
67 *wud*: mad

Then there's sic yellowchin and din,
Wi' wives and wee-anes gablin,
That ane might true they were a-kin
To a' the tongues at Babylon,
Confus'd that day.

Whan Phœbus ligs in Thetis lap,[n]
Auld Reikie gies them shelter,
Whare cadgily they kiss the cap,
An' ca't round helter-skelter.
Jock Bell gaed furth to play his freaks,
Great cause he had to rue it,
For frae a stark Lochaber aix[n]
He gat a clamihewit,
Fu' sair that night.

'Ohon!' quo' he, 'I'd rather be
By sword or bagnet stickit,
Than hae my crown or body wi'
Sic deadly weapons nicket.'
Wi' that he gat anither straik
Mair weighty than before,
That gar'd his feckless body aik,
An' spew the reikin gore,
Fu' red that night.

He peching on the cawsey lay,
O' kicks and cuffs weel sair'd;
A highland aith[n] the serjeant gae,
'She maun pe see our guard.'
Out spak the weirlike corporal,
'Pring in ta drunken sot.'
They trail'd him ben, an' by my saul,
He paid his drunken groat[n]
For that neist day.

Good fock, as ye come frae the fair,
Bide yont frae this black squad;
There's nae sic savages elsewhere
Allow'd to wear cockade.

68 *yellowchin*: yelling
70 *true*: believe
73 *ligs*: lies
75 *cadgily*: cheerfully
*kiss the cap*: drink
76 *ca't*: send it
77 *freaks*: tricks
79 *stark*: stout
80 *clamihewit*: shocking blow
83 *bagnet*: bayonet
85 *nicket*: cut
86 *straik*: stroke
88 *feckless*: feeble
89 *reikin*: steaming
91 *peching*: panting
*cawsey*: street
92 *sair'd*: served
95 *weirlike*: warlike
97 *ben*: inside
101 *bide yont*: keep away from

Than the strong lion's hungry maw,
  Or tusk o' Russian bear,
Frae their wanruly fellin paw
  Mair cause ye hae to fear
      Your death that day.

A wee soup drink dis unco weel
  To had the heart aboon;
It's good as lang's a canny chiel
  Can stand steeve in his shoon.
But gin a birkie's owr weel sair'd,
  It gars him aften stammer
To pleys that bring him to the guard,
  An' eke the Council-chawmir,
      Wi' shame that day.

106 *wanruly*: unruly
109 *wee soup*: drop
*dis*: does
*unco*: very
110 *had*: hold
111 *canny chiel*: merry fellow
112 *steeve*: firm
*shoon*: shoes
113 *gin*: if
*birkie*: lad
*sair'd*: served
114 *stammer to*: blunder into
115 *pleys*: ploys, schemes
116 *chawmir*: chamber where the magistrate sat

## AULD REIKIE,

## A

## POEM

Auld Reikie, wale o' ilka town
That Scotland kens beneath the moon;
Where couthy chiels at e'ening meet
Their bizzing craigs and mous to weet;
And blythly gar auld care gae bye
Wi' blinkit and wi' bleering eye:
O'er lang frae thee the Muse has been
Sae frisky on the simmer's green,
Whan flowers and gowans wont to glent
In bonny blinks upo' the bent;
But now the leaves a yellow die
Peel'd frae the branches, quickly fly;
And now frae nouther bush nor brier
The spreckl'd mavis greets your ear;
Nor bonny blackbird skims and roves
To seek his love in yonder groves.

1 *wale*: best
*ilka*: every
3 *couthy*: sociable
*chiels*: fellows
4 *bizzing*: dry
*craigs*: throats
*mous*: mouths
5 *gar*: make
*gae*: go
6 *bleering*: only half-seeing
9 *gowans*: daisies
*glent*: gleam
10 *blinks*: moments of sunshine
*bent*: fields
11 *a*: all
13 *nouther*: neither
14 *mavis*: thrush

Then, Reikie, welcome! Thou canst charm
Unfleggit by the year's alarm;
Not Boreas[n] that sae snelly blows,
Dare here pap in his angry nose:
Thanks to our dads, whase biggin stands
A shelter to surrounding lands.

Now morn, with bonny purpie-smiles,
Kisses the air-cock o' St Giles[n];
Rakin their ein, the servant lasses
Early begin their lies and clashes;
Ilk tells her friend of saddest distress,
That still she brooks frae scouling mistress;
And wi' her joe in turnpike stair[n]
She'd rather snuff the stinking air,
As be subjected to her tongue,
When justly censur'd in the wrong.

On stair wi' tub, or pat in hand,
The barefoot housemaids looe to stand,
That antrin fock may ken how snell
Auld Reikie will at morning smell:
Then, with an inundation big as
The burn that 'neath the Nore Loch Brig[n] is,
They kindly shower Edina's roses,[n]
To quicken and regale our noses.
Now some for this, wi' satyr's leesh,
Ha'e gi'en auld Edinburgh a creesh:
But without souring nocht is sweet;
The morning smells that hail our street,
Prepare, and gently lead the way
To simmer canty, braw and gay:
Edina's sons mair eithly share,
Her spices and her dainties rare,
Then he that's never yet been call'd
Aff frae his plaidie or his fauld.

Now stairhead critics, senseless fools,
Censure their aim, and pride their rules,
In Luckenbooths[n], wi' glouring eye,
Their neighbours sma'est faults descry:

18 *unfleggit*: unfrightened
19 *snelly*: bitterly
20 *pap*: pop
21 *biggin*: building
23 *purpie*: purple
24 *air-cock*: weather-cock
25 *rakin*: rubbing
*ein*: eyes
26 *clashes*: gossiping
27 *ilk*: each
29 *joe*: sweetheart
33 *pat*: pot
35 *antrin*: chance-met
41 *leesh*: lash
42 *creesh*: beating
46 *canty*: cheerful
47 *eithly*: easily
50 *plaidie*: plaid
*fauld*: sheepfold
53 *glouring*: glaring

If ony loun should dander there,
Of aukward gate, and foreign air,
They trace his steps, till they can tell
His pedigree as weel's himsell.

Whan Phœbus[n] blinks wi' warmer ray
And schools at noonday get the play,
Then bus'ness, weighty bus'ness comes;
The trader glours; he doubts, he hums:
The lawyers[n] eke to Cross repair,
Their wigs to shaw, and toss an air;
While busy agent closely plies,
And a' his kittle cases tries.

Now night, that's cunyied chief for fun,
Is wi' her usual rites begun;
Thro' ilka gate the torches blaze,
And globes send out their blinking rays.
The usefu' cadie[n] plies in street,
To bide the profits o' his feet;
For by thir lads Auld Reikie's fock
Ken but a sample, o' the stock
O' thieves, that nightly wad oppress,
And make baith goods and gear the less.
Near him the lazy chairman[n] stands,
And wats na how to turn his hands,
Till some daft birky, ranting fu',
Has matters somewhere else to do;
The chairman willing, gi'es his light
To deeds o' darkness and o' night:

Its never sax pence for a lift
That gars thir lads wi' fu'ness rift;
For they wi' better gear are paid,
And whores and culls support their trade.

Near some lamp-post, wi' dowy face,
Wi' heavy ein, and sour grimace,
Stands she that beauty lang had kend,
Whoredom her trade, and vice her end.

55 *loun*: fellow
*dander*: stroll about
62 *glours*: looks stern
63 *eke*: also
64 *shaw*: show off
65 *agent*: solicitor
66 *kittle*: tricky
67 *cunyied*: known
72 *bide*: wait
73 *thir*: those
78 *wats na*: knows not
79 *birky*: lad
*rantin fu*: riotously drunk
84 *rift*: belch
85 *gear*: riches
86 *culls*: dupes
87 *dowy*: sad

But see wharenow she wuns her bread
By that which Nature ne'er decreed;
And sings sad music to the lugs,
'Mang burachs o' damn'd whores and rogues.
Whane'er we reputation loss
Fair chastity's transparent gloss!
Redemption seenil kens the name,
But a's black misery and shame.

Frae joyous tavern, reeling drunk,
Wi' fiery phizz, and ein half sunk,
Behad the bruiser, fae to a'
That in the reek o' gardies fa':
Close by his side, a feckless race
O' macaronies[n] shew their face,
And think they're free frae skaith or harm,
While pith befriends their leaders arm:
Yet fearfu' aften o' their maught,
They quatt the glory o' the faught
To this same warrior wha led
Thae heroes to bright honour's bed;
And aft the hack o' honour shines
In bruiser's face wi' broken lines:
Of them sad tales he tells anon,
Whan ramble and whan fighting's done;
And, like Hectorian, ne'er impairs
The brag and glory o' his sairs.

Whan feet in dirty gutters plash,
And fock to wale their fitstaps fash;
At night the macaroni drunk,
In pools or gutters aftimes sunk:
Hegh! what a fright he now appears,
Whan he his corpse dejected rears!
Look at that head, and think if there
The pomet slaister'd up his hair!
The cheeks observe, where now cou'd shine
The scancing glories o' carmine?

91 *wuns*: wins
93 *lugs*: ears
94 *burachs*: disorderly gatherings
97 *seenil*: seldom
100 *phizz*: face
101 *behad*: behold
*bruiser*: prize-fighter
*fae*: foe
102 *reek*: reach
*gardies*: arms
103 *feckless*: futile
105 *skaith*: hurt
106 *pith*: strength
107 *maught*: power
108 *faught*: fight
110 *thae*: those
111 *aft*: often
*hack*: cut, scar
115 *Hectorian*: a blusterer
116 *sairs*: wounds
118 *wale*: choose
*fitstaps*: footsteps
*fash*: take care
122 *corpse*: (living) body
*dejected*: fallen
124 *pomet*: pomade
*slaister'd*: greased
126 *scancing*: shining
128 *eidant*: busy

Ah, legs! in vain the silk-worm there
Display'd to view her eidant care;
For stink, instead of perfumes, grow,
And clarty odours fragrant flow.

Now some to porter, some to punch,
Some to their wife, and some their wench,
Retire, while noisy ten-hours drum[n]
Gars a' your trades gae dandring home.
Now mony a club, jocose and free,
Gie a' to merriment and glee,
Wi' sang and glass, they fley the pow'r
O' care that wad harrass the hour:
For wine and Bacchus still bear down
Our thrawart fortune's wildest frown:
It maks you stark, and bauld and brave,
Ev'n whan descending to the grave.

Now some, in Pandemonium's shade[n]
Resume the gormandizing trade;
Whare eager looks, and glancing ein,
Forespeak a heart and stamack keen.
Gang on, my lads; it's lang sin syne
We kent auld Epicurus line;[n]
Save you, the board wad cease to rise,
Bedight wi' daintiths to the skies;
And salamanders cease to swill
The comforts of a burning gill.

But chief, O Cape,[n] we crave thy aid,
To get our cares and poortith laid:
Sincerity, and genius true,
Of knights have ever been the due:
Mirth, music, porter deepest dy'd,
Are never here to worth deny'd;
And health, o' happiness the queen,
Blinks bonny, wi' her smile serene.

Tho' joy maist part Auld Reikie owns,
Eftsoons she kens sad sorrow's frowns;
What group is yon sae dismal grim,
Wi' horrid aspect, cleeding dim?
Says Death, 'They'r mine, a dowy crew,
To me they'll quickly pay their last adieu.'

130 *clarty*: filthy
134 *dandring*: wandering
135 *jocose*: jocular
137 *fley*: put to flight
140 *thrawart*: contrary
141 *stark*: firm
147 *sin syne*: since the time
150 *daintiths*: delicacies
154 *poortith*: poverty
162 *eftsoons*: at times
164 *cleeding*: clothing
165 *dowy*: melancholy

How come mankind, whan lacking woe,
In saulie's[n] face their heart to show,
As if they were a clock, to tell
That grief in them had rung her bell?
Then, what is man? why a' this phraze?
Life's spunk decay'd, nae mair can blaze.
Let sober grief alone declare
Our fond anxiety and care:
Nor let the undertakers be
The only waefu' friends we see.

Come on, my Muse, and then rehearse
The gloomiest theme in a' your verse:
In morning, whan ane keeks about,
Fu' blyth and free frae ail, nae doubt
He lippens not to be misled
Amang the regions of the dead:
But straight a painted corp he sees,
Lang streekit 'neath its canopies.
Soon, soon will this his mirth controul,
And send damnation to his soul:
Or when the dead-deal, (awful shape!)
Makes frighted mankind girn and gape,
Reflection then his reason sours,
For the niest dead-deal may be ours.
Whan sybil led the Trojan down[n]
To haggard Pluto's dreary town,
Shapes war nor thae, I freely ween
Cou'd never meet the soldier's ein.

If kail sae green, or herbs delight,
Edina's street attracts the sight;
Not Covent-garden, clad sae braw,
Mair fouth o' herbs can eithly shaw:
For mony a yeard is here sair sought,
That kail and cabbage may be bought;
And healthfu' sallad to regale,
Whan pamper'd wi' a heavy meal.
Glour up the street in simmer morn,
The birks sae green, and sweet brier-thorn,

171 *phraze*: ado
172 *spunk*: spark
179 *keeks*: peers
180 *ail*: ill
181 *lippens*: expects
184 *streekit*: stretched
187 *dead-deal*: board for measuring the dead
188 *girn*: grimace
190 *niest*: next
193 *war*: worse
*nor*: than
*ween*: think
195 *kail*: colewort, cabbage
197 *braw*: finely
198 *fouth*: plenty
*eithly*: easily
199 *yeard*: garden
*sair*: strenuously
203 *glour*: glance
204 *birks*: birches

Wi' sprangit flow'rs that scent the gale,
Ca' far awa' the morning smell,
Wi' which our ladies' flow'r-pat's fill'd,
And every noxious vapour kill'd.
O Nature! canty, blyth and free,
Whare is there keeking-glass like thee?
Is there on earth that can compare
Wi' Mary's shape, and Mary's air,
Save the empurpl'd speck, that grows
In the saft faulds of yonder rose?
How bonny seems the virgin breast,
Whan by the lillies here carest,
And leaves the mind in doubt to tell
Which maist in sweets and hue excel?

Gillespie's snuff[n] should prime the nose
Of her that to the market goes,
If they wad like to shun the smells
That buoy up frae markest cells;
Whare wames o' paunches sav'ry scent
To nostrils gi'e great discontent.
Now wha in Albion could expect
O' cleanliness sic great neglect?
Nae Hottentot that daily lairs
'Mang tripe, or ither clarty wares,
Hath ever yet conceiv'd, or seen
Beyond the line, sic scenes unclean.

On Sunday here, an alter'd scene
O' men and manners meets our ein:
Ane wad maist trow some people chose
To change their faces wi' their clo'es,
And fain wad gar ilk neighbour think
They thirst for goodness, as for drink:
But there's an unco dearth o' grace,
That has nae mansion but the face,
And never can obtain a part
In benmost corner of the heart.
Why should religion make us sad,
If good frae virtue's to be had?

205 *sprangit*: many coloured
206 *ca'*: drive
207 *flower-pat*: chamber-pot (euph.)
209 *canty*: cheerful
210 *keeking-glass*: mirror
222 *markest*: darkest
223 *wames*: stomachs
227 *lairs*: lies
228 *clarty*: dirty
230 *line*: equator
233 *maist trow*: almost believe
237 *unco*: strange
240 *benmost*: innermost

Na, rather gleefu' turn your face;
Forsake hypocrisy, grimace;
And never have it understood
You fleg mankind frae being good.

In afternoon, a' brawly buskit,
The joes and lasses loe to frisk it:
Some tak a great delight to place
The modest bongrace o'er the face;
Tho' you may see, if so inclin'd,
The turning o' the leg behind.
Now Comely-Garden,[n] and the Park,
Refresh them, after forenoon's wark;
Newhaven, Leith or Canon-mills,
Supply them in their Sunday's gills;
Whare writers aften spend their pence,
To stock their heads wi' drink and sense.

While dandring cits delight to stray
To Castlehill, or public way,
Whare they nae other purpose mean,
Than that fool cause o' being seen;
Let me to Arthur's Seat[n] pursue,
Whare bonny pastures meet the view;
And mony a wild-lorn scene accrues,
Befitting Willie Shakespeare's muse:
If fancy there would join the thrang,
The desart rocks and hills amang,
To echoes we should lilt and play,
And gie to mirth the lee-lang day.

Or shou'd some canker'd biting show'r
The day and a' her sweets deflour,
To Holyrood-house[n] let me stray,
And gie to musing a' the day;
Lamenting what auld Scotland knew
Bien days for ever frae her view:
O Hamilton, for shame! the Muse
Would pay to thee her couthy vows,
Gin ye wad tent the humble strain
And gie's our dignity again:

245 *fleg*: frighten
247 *brawly*: beautifully
*buskit*: dressed
248 *loe*: love
250 *bongrace*: large bonnet
256 *gills*: i.e., of spirits
257 *writers*: attorneys
276 *bien*: prosperous
278 *couthy*: friendly
279 *tent*: heed

For O, waes me! the thistle springs
In domicile of ancient kings,
Without a patriot to regrete
Our palace, and our ancient state.

Blest place![n] whare debtors daily run,
To rid themselves frae jail and dun;
Here, tho' sequester'd frae the din
That rings Auld Reikie's waas within,
Yet they may tread the sunny braes,
And brook Apollo's cheery rays;
Glour frae St Anthon's grassy hight,[n]
O'er vales in simmer claise bedight,
Nor ever hing their head, I ween,
Wi' jealous fear o' being seen.
May I, whanever duns come nigh,
And shake my garret wi' their cry,
Scour here wi' haste, protection get,
To screen mysell frae them and debt;
To breathe the bliss of open sky,
And Simon Fraser's[n] bolts defy.

Now gin a lown should ha'e his clase
In thread-bare autumn o' their days,
St Mary, brokers' guardian saint,
Will satisfy ilk ail and want;
For mony a hungry writer, there
Dives down at night, wi' cleading bare,
And quickly rises to the view
A gentleman, perfyte and new.
Ye rich fock, look no wi' disdain
Upo' this ancient brokage lane!
For naked poets are supplied,
With what you to their wants deny'd.

Peace to thy shade, thou wale o' men,
Drummond![n] relief to poortith's pain:
To thee the greatest bliss we owe;
And tribute's tear shall grateful flow:
The sick are cur'd, the hungry fed,
And dreams of comfort tend their bed:

288 *waas*: walls
289 *braes*: slopes
290 *brook*: enjoy
295 *duns*: debt-collectors
297 *scour*: hurry
301 *gin*: if
*lown*: fellow
*clase*: clothes
306 *cleading*: clothing
313 *wale*: best

As lang as Forth weets Lothian's shore,
As lang's on Fife her billows roar,
Sae lang shall ilk whase country's dear,
To thy remembrance gie a tear.
By thee Auld Reikie thrave, and grew
Delightfu' to her childer's view:
Nae mair shall Glasgow[n] striplings threap
Their city's beauty and its shape,
While our new city spreads around
Her bonny wings on fairy ground.

But provosts[n] now that ne'er afford
The smaest dignity to 'lord',
Ne'er care tho' every scheme gae wild
That Drummond's sacred hand has cull'd:
The spacious brig neglected lies,
Tho' plagu'd wi' pamphlets, dunn'd wi' cries;
They heed not tho' destruction come
To gulp us in her gaunting womb.
O shame! that safety canna claim
Protection from a provost's name,
But hidden danger lies behind
To torture and to fleg the mind;
I may as weel bid Arthur's Seat
To Berwick-Law make gleg retreat,
As think that either will or art
Shall get the gate to win their heart;
For politics are a' their mark,
Bribes latent, and corruption dark:
If they can eithly turn the pence,
Wi' city's good they will dispense;
Nor care tho' a' her sons were lair'd
Ten fathom i' the auld kirk-yard.

To sing yet meikle does remain,
Undecent for a modest strain;
And since the poet's daily bread is
The favour of the Muse or ladies,
He downa like to gie offence
To delicacy's bonny sense;
Therefore the stews remain unsung,
And bawds in silence drop their tongue.

319 *weets*: wets
323 *thrave*: thrived
325 *threap*: boast
333 *brig*: bridge
334 *dunn'd*: importuned
336 *gaunting*: yawning
342 *gleg*: smart
344 *gate*: way, road
349 *lair'd*: buried
355 *downa*: would not

Reikie, farewel! I ne'er cou'd part
Wi' thee but wi' a dowy heart;
Aft frae the Fifan coast[n] I've seen,
Thee tow'ring on thy summit green;
So glowr the saints when first is given
A fav'rite keek o' glore and heaven;
On earth nae mair they bend their ein,
But quick assume angelic mein;
So I on Fife wad glowr no more,
But gallop'd to Edina's shore.

364 *glore*: glory
366 *mein*: appearance

## MUTUAL COMPLAINT OF *PLAINSTANES* AND *CAUSEY*, IN THEIR MOTHER-TONGUE

Since Merlin[n] laid Auld Reikie's causey,
And made her o' his wark right saucy,
The spacious street and plainstanes
Were never kend to crack but anes,
Whilk happened on the hinder night,
Whan Fraser's ulie[n] tint its light,
Of Highland sentries[n] nane were waukin,
To hear thir cronies glibbly taukin;
For them this wonder might hae rotten,
And, like night robb'ry, been forgotten,
Had na' a cadie,[n] wi' his lanthorn,
Been gleg enough to hear them bant'rin,
Wha came to me neist morning early,
To gi'e me tidings o' this ferly.
Ye taunting lowns trow this nae joke,
For anes the ass of Balaam[n] spoke,
Better than lawyers do, forsooth,
For it spake naething but the truth:
Whether they follow its example,
You'll ken best whan you hear the sample.

### Plainstanes

My friend, thir hunder years and mair,
We've been forfoughen late and air,

*plainstanes*: pavement, sidewalk
*causey*: street
4 *crack*: gossip
*anes*: once
5 *whilk*: which
*hinder*: last
6 *ulie*: oil lamp
*tint*: lost
7 *waukin*: awake
8 *thir*: those
12 *gleg*: smart
13 *neist*: next
14 *ferly*: wonder
15 *lowns*: urchins
*trow*: believe
22 *forfoughen*: wearied
*air*: early

In sun-shine, and in weety weather,
Our thrawart lot we bure thegither.
I never growl'd, but was content
Whan ilk ane had an equal stent,
But now to flyte I'se e'en be bauld,
Whan I'm wi' sic a grievance thrall'd.
How haps it, say, that mealy bakers,
Hair-kaimers, crieshy gezy-makers,
Shou'd a' get leave to waste their powders
Upon my beaux and ladies' shoulders?
My travellers are fley'd to deid
Wi' creels wanchancy, heap'd wi' bread,
Frae whilk hing down uncanny nicksticks,[n]
That aften gie the maidens sic licks,
As make them blyth to skreen their faces
Wi' hats and muckle maun bon-graces,
And cheat the lads that fain wad see
The glances o' a pauky eie,
Or gie their loves a wylie wink,
That erst might lend their hearts a clink.
Speak, was I made to dree the laidin
Of Gallic chairman[n] heavy treadin,
Wha in my tender buke bore holes
Wi' waefu' tackets i' the soals
O' broags, whilk on my body tramp,
And wound like death at ilka clamp.

## Causey

Weil crackit friend — It aft hads true,
Wi' naething fock make maist ado:
Weel ken ye, tho' ye doughtna tell,
I pay the sairest kain mysell;
Owr me ilk day big waggons rumble,
And a' my fabric birze and jumble;
Owr me the muckle horses gallop,
Enought to rug my very saul up;

23 *weety*: wet
24 *thrawart*: bitter
*bure*: bore
26 *ilk ane*: each one
*stent*: portion
27 *flyte*: scold
*I'se*: I shall
28 *thrall'd*: oppressed
30 *hair-kaimers*: barbers
*crieshy*: greasy
*gezy-makers*: wig-makers
33 *fley'd to deid*: scared to death
34 *creels*: large baskets
*wanchancy*: dangerous
35 *uncanny*: outlandish
*nicksticks*: tally sticks
36 *sic licks*: such blows
38 *muckle maun bon-graces*: large bonnets of coarse straw
42 *lend . . . clink*: give . . . knock
43 *dree*: endure
*laidin*: load
45 *buke*: body
46 *tackets*: hobnails
*soals*: soles
47 *broags*: brogues
49 *crackit*: said
51 *doughtna*: dare not
52 *kain*: rent paid in kind
54 *birze*: squeeze
55 *muckle*: huge
56 *rug*: tear
*saul*: soul

And coachmen never trow they're sinning,
While down the street his wheels are spinning,
Like thee, do I not bide the brunt
Of Highland chairman's heavy dunt?
Yet I hae never thought o' breathing
Complaint, or making din for naething.

Plainstanes

Had sae, and lat me get a word in,
Your back's best fitted for the burden;
And I can eithly tell you why,
Ye're doughtier by far than I;
For whin-stanes,[n] howkit frae the craigs,
May thole the prancing feet of naigs,
Nor ever fear uncanny hotches
Frae clumsy carts or hackney-coaches,
While I, a weak and feckless creature,
Am moulded by a safter nature.
Wi' mason's chissel dighted neat,
To gar me look baith clean and feat,
I scarce can bear a sairer thump
Than comes frae sole of shoe or pump.
I grant, indeed, that, now and than,
Yield to a paten's pith I maun;
But patens, tho' they're aften plenty,
Are ay laid down wi' feet fou tenty,
And stroaks frae ladies, tho' they're teazing,
I freely maun avow are pleasing.
For what use was I made, I wonder,
It was na tamely to chap under
The weight of ilka codroch chiel,
That does my skin to targits peel;
But gin I guess aright, my trade is
To fend frae skaith the bonny ladies,
To keep the bairnies free frae harms
Whan airing in their nurses arms,
To be a safe and canny bield
For growing youth or drooping eild.

59 *bide*: endure
60 *dunt*: blow
65 *eithly*: easily
67 *howkit*: dug
*craigs*: crags
68 *thole*: put up with
*naigs*: horses
69 *hotches*: jolts
71 *feckless*: ineffective
73 *dighted*: shaped
74 *feat*: smart
78 *paten*: wooden shoe
*pith*: weight
80 *tenty*: careful
84 *chap*: break
85 *codroch*: foolish
86 *targits*: tatters
87 *gin*: if
88 *fend*: save
*skaith*: harm
91 *canny*: comfortable
*bield*: shelter
92 *eild*: old age

Take then frae me the heavy load
Of burden-bearers heavy shod,
Or, by my troth, the gude auld town shall
Hae this affair before their council.

### Causey

I dinna care a single jot,
Tho' summon'd by a shelly-coat,
Sae leally I'll propone defences,
As get ye flung for my expences;
Your libel[n] I'll impugn *verbatim*,
And hae a *magnum damnum datum*[n];
For tho' frae Arthur's-seat[n] I sprang,
And am in constitution strang,
Wad it no fret the hardest stane
Beneath the Luckenbooths[n] to grane?
Tho' magistrates the Cross[n] discard,
It makes na whan they leave the Guard,[n]
A lumbersome and stinkin bigging,
That rides the sairest on my rigging.
Poor me owr meikle do ye blame,
For tradesmen tramping on your wame,
Yet a' your advocates and braw fock
Come still to me 'twixt ane and twa clock,
And never yet were kend to range
At Charlie's Statue or Exchange.[n]
Then tak your beaux and macaronies,
Gie me trades-fock and country Johnies;
The deil's in't gin ye dinna sign
Your sentiments conjunct wi' mine.

### Plainstanes

Gin we twa cou'd be as auld-farrant
As gar the council gie a warrant,
Ilk lown rebellious to tak,
Wha walks not in the proper track,
And o' three shilling Scottish suck him;
Or in the water-hole sair douk him;
This might assist the poor's collection,
And gie baith parties satisfaction.

98 *shelly-coat*: sheriff's officer
99 *propone*: propose
100 *flung for*: landed with
106 *grane*: groan
108 *makes na*: does not matter
109 *bigging*: building
110 *sairest*: sorest
*rigging*: back
111 *meikle*: much
112 *wame*: belly
113 *braw fock*: fashionable people
115 *kend*: known
117 *macaronies*: foolish fops
121 *auld-farrant*: shrewd
122 *gar*: make
126 *douk*: duck

Causey

But first, I think it will be good
To bring it to the Robinhood,[n]
Whare we shall hae the question stated,
And keen and crabbitly debated,
Whether the provost and the baillies,[n]
For the town's good whase daily toil is,
Shou'd listen to our joint petitions,
And see obtemper'd the conditions.

Plainstanes

Content am I — But east the gate is
The sun, wha taks his leave of Thetis,[n]
And comes to wauken honest fock,
That gang to wark at sax o'clock;
It sets us to be dumb a while,
And let our words gie place to toil.

132 *crabbitly*: bitterly
136 *obtemper'd*: fulfilled
141 *sets*: suits

## THE FARMER'S INGLE

*Et multo in primis hilarans convivia Baccho,*
*Ante focum, si frigus erit.* VIRG. *Buc.*

Whan gloming grey out o'er the welkin keeks,
Whan Batie[n] ca's his owsen to the byre,
Whan Thrasher John, sair dung, his barn-door steeks,
And lusty lasses at the dighting tire:
What bangs fu' leal the e'enings coming cauld,
And gars snaw-tapit winter freeze in vain;
Gars dowie mortals look baith blyth and bauld,
Nor fley'd wi' a' the poortith o' the plain;
Begin, my Muse, and chant in hamely strain.

Frae the big stack, weel winnow't on the hill,
Wi' divets theekit frae the weet and drift,
Sods, peats, and heath'ry trufs the chimley fill,
And gar their thick'ning smeek salute the lift;

1 *keeks*: peers
2 *ca's*: drives
*owsen*: oxen
3 *dung*: exhausted
*steeks*: shuts
4 *dighting*: winnowing
5 *bangs*: overcomes
6 *gars*: causes
*snaw-tapit*: snow-covered
7 *dowie*: melancholy
*bauld*: bold
8 *fley'd*: frightened
*poortith*: poverty
11 *divets*: turfs
*theekit*: thatched
*drift*: blown snow
12 *chimley*: fireplace
13 *smeek*: smoke
*lift*: sky

The gudeman, new come hame, is blyth to find,
Whan he out o'er the halland flings his een,
That ilka turn is handled to his mind,[n]
That a' his housie looks sae cosh and clean;
For cleanly house looes he, tho' e'er sae mean.

Weel kens the gudewife that the pleughs require
A heartsome meltith, and refreshing synd
O' nappy liquor, o'er a bleezing fire:
Sair wark and poortith douna weel be join'd.
Wi' butter'd bannocks now the girdle reeks,
I' the far nook the bowie briskly reams;
The readied kail stand by the chimley cheeks,
And had the riggin het wi' welcome steams,
Whilk than the daintiest kitchen nicer seems.

Frae this lat gentler gabs a lesson lear;
Wad they to labouring lend an eidant hand,
They'd rax fell strang upo' the simplest fare,
Nor find their stamacks ever at a stand.
Fu' hale and healthy wad they pass the day,
At night in calmest slumbers dose fu' sound,
Nor doctor need their weary life to spae,
Nor drogs their noddle and their sense confound,
Till death slip sleely on, and gi'e the hindmost wound.

On sicken food has mony a doughty deed
By Caledonia's ancestors been done;
By this did mony wight fu' weirlike bleed
In brulzies frae the dawn to set o' sun:
'Twas this that brac'd their gardies, stiff and strang,
That bent the deidly yew in antient days,
Laid Denmark's daring sons[n] on yird alang,
Gar'd Scottish thristles bang the Roman bays;
For near our crest their heads they doughtna raise.

14 *gudeman*: head of the household
15 *halland*: wooden partition
17 *cosh*: comfortable
19 *pleughs*: ploughmen
20 *meltith*: meal
*synd*: drink
21 *nappy*: strong ale
22 *poortith*: poverty
*douna*: cannot
*weel*: comfortably
23 *girdle*: griddle
*reeks*: steams
24 *bowie*: barrel
*reams*: rises, foams
25 *kail*: broth
*cheeks*: sides (of fire)
26 *had*: hold, keep
*riggin*: roof
27 *kitchen*: fare
*nicer*: more delicate
28 *gabs*: mouths
29 *eidant*: careful
30 *rax*: grow
*fell*: very
34 *spae*: foretell
35 *drogs*: drugs
36 *sleely*: stealthily, easily
*hindmost*: final
37 *sicken*: such
39 *weirlike*: warlike
40 *brulzies*: fights
41 *gardies*: arms
43 *yird*: earth
45 *doughtna*: dared not

The couthy cracks begin whan supper's o'er,
The cheering bicker gars them glibly gash
O' simmer's showery blinks and winters sour,
Whase floods did erst their mailin's produce hash:
'Bout kirk and market eke their tales gae on,
How Jock woo'd Jenny here to be his bride,
And there how Marion, for a bastard son,
Upo' the cutty-stool[n] was forc'd to ride,
The waefu' scald o' our Mess John[n] to bide.

The fient a chiep's amang the bairnies now;
For a' their anger's wi' their hunger gane:
Ay maun the childer, wi' a fastin mou',
Grumble and greet, and make an unco mane,
In rangles round before the ingle's low:
Frae gudame's mouth auld warld tale they hear,
O' warlocks louping round the wirrikow,
O' gaists that win in glen and kirk-yard drear,
Whilk touzles a' their tap, and gars them shak wi' fear.

For weel she trows that fiends and fairies be
Sent frae the de'il to fleetch us to our ill;
That ky hae tint their milk wi' evil eie,
And corn been scowder'd on the glowing kill.
O mock na this, my friends! but rather mourn,
Ye in life's brawest spring wi' reason clear,
Wi' eild our idle fancies a' return,
And dim our dolefu' days wi' bairnly fear;
The mind's ay cradled whan the grave is near.

Yet thrift, industrious, bides her latest days,
Tho' age her sair dow'd front wi' runcles wave,
Yet frae the russet lap the spindle plays,
Her e'enin stent reels she as weel's the lave.

46 *couthy*: sociable
*cracks*: talk
47 *bicker*: drinking cup
*gash*: chatter
49 *mailin*: farm
*hash*: spoil
50 *eke*: also
54 *scald*: scolding
*bide*: endure
55 *fient a chiep*: devil a cheep
57 *childer*: children
58 *greet*: weep
*unco*: great
*mane*: moan
59 *rangles*: groups
*ingle's low*: fire's light
61 *warlocks*: male witches
*louping*: leaping
*wirrikow*: scarecrow, or the Devil
62 *win*: live
63 *touzles . . . tap*: makes their hair stand on end
64 *trows*: believes
65 *de'il*: devil
*fleetch*: trick
66 *ky*: cows
*tint*: lost
67 *scowder'd*: scorched
*kill*: kiln
69 *brawest*: finest
70 *eild*: age
74 *dow'd*: faded
*runcles*: wrinkles
76 *stent*: allocation
*lave*: the others

On some feast-day, the wee-things buskit braw
  Shall heeze her heart up wi' a silent joy,
Fu' cadgie that her head was up and saw
  Her ain spun cleething on a darling oy,
  Careless tho' death shou'd make the feast her foy.

In its auld lerroch yet the deas remains,
  Whare the gudeman aft streeks him at his ease,
A warm and canny lean for weary banes
  O' lab'rers doil'd upo' the wintry leas:
Round him will badrins and the colly come,
  To wag their tail, and cast a thankfu' eie
To him wha kindly flings them mony a crum
  O' kebbock whang'd, and dainty fadge to prie;
  This a' the boon they crave, and a' the fee.

Frae him the lads their morning counsel tak,
  What stacks he wants to thrash, what rigs to till;
How big a birn maun lie on bassie's back,
  For meal and multure to the thirling mill.[n]
Niest the gudewife her hireling damsels bids
  Glowr thro' the byre, and see the hawkies bound,
Take tent case crummy tak her wonted tids,
  And ca' the leglin's treasure on the ground,
  Whilk spills a kebbuck nice, or yellow pound.

Then a' the house for sleep begin to grien,
  Their joints to slack frae industry a while;
The leaden god[n] fa's heavy on their ein,
  And hafflins steeks them frae their daily toil:
The cruizy too can only blink and bleer,
  The restit ingle's done the maist it dow;
Tacksman and cottar eke to bed maun steer,
  Upo' the cod to clear their drumly pow,
  Till wauken'd by the dawning's ruddy glow.

77 *wee-things*: little ones
*buskit*: dressed
78 *heeze*: lift
79 *cadgie*: happy
80 *cleething*: clothing
*oy*: grandchild
81 *foy*: farewell
82 *lerroch*: place
*deas*: settle
83 *streeks*: stretches
84 *canny lean*: comfortable support
85 *doil'd*: exhausted
86 *badrins*: cat
89 *kebbock*: cheese
*whang'd*: sliced
*fadge*: flat loaf
*prie*: taste
92 *rigs*: fields
93 *birn*: burden
*bassie*: old horse (fam.)
94 *multure*: the miller's fee
96 *glowr*: look attentively
*hawkies*: cows
97 *tent*: care
*crummy*: cow with crooked horns
*tids*: tantrums
98 *ca'*: upset
*leglin*: milk pail
99 *spills*: spoils
*kebbuck*: cheese
100 *grien*: long
103 *hafflins*: partly
*steeks*: shuts
104 *cruizy*: oil lamp
*bleer*: flicker
105 *restit*: burnt out
*ingle*: fire
*dow*: can
106 *tacksman*: lessee
107 *cod*: pillow
*drumly*: weary

Peace to the husbandman and a' his tribe,
   Whase care fells a' our wants frae year to year;
Lang may his sock and couter turn the gleyb,
   And bauks o' corn bend down wi' laded ear.
May Scotia's simmers ay look gay and green,
   Her yellow har'sts frae scowry blasts decreed;
May a' her tenants sit fu' snug and bien,
   Frae the hard grip of ails and poortith freed,
   And a lang lasting train o' peaceful hours succeed.

111 *sock*: ploughshare
*couter*: coulter
*gleyb*: glebe
112 *bauks*: strips
*laded*: loaded
115 *bien*: comfortable
116 *poortith*: poverty

## THE GHAISTS: A KIRK-YARD ECLOGUE

*Did you not say, on good Ann's day,*
   *And vow and did protest, Sir,*
*That when Hanover should come o'er,*
   *We surely should be blest, Sir?*
An auld Sang made new again.

Whare the braid planes in dowy murmurs wave
Their antient taps out o'er the cald, clad grave,
Whare Geordie Girdwood, mony a lang-spun day,
Houkit for gentlest banes the humblest clay,
Twa sheeted ghaists[n], sae grizly and sae wan,
'Mang lanely tombs their douff discourse began.

### Watson

   Cauld blaws the nippin north wi' angry sough,
And showers his hailstanes frae the Castle cleugh
O'er the Greyfriars, whare, at mirkest hour,
Bogles and spectres wont to tak their tour,
Harlin' the pows and shanks to hidden cairns,
Amang the hamlocks wild, and sun-burnt fearns,
But nane the night save you and I hae come
Frae the dern mansions of the midnight tomb,

1 *braid*: broad
*dowy*: melancholy
2 *clad*: i.e. turfed
4 *houkit*: dug
5 *ghaists*: ghosts
6 *douff*: gloomy
7 *sough*: rushing sound
8 *cleugh*: rock
9 *mirkest*: darkest
10 *bogles*: goblins, ghosts
*tour*: turn (of walking)
11 *harlin*: dragging
*pows*: heads
*shanks*: legs
11 *cairns*: heaped stones marking graves
13 *the night*: tonight
14 *dern*: hidden

Now whan the dawning's near, whan cock maun craw,
And wi' his angry bougil gar's withdraw,
Ayont the kirk we'll stap, and there tak bield,
While the black hours our nightly freedom yield.

Herriot

I'm weel content; but binna cassen down,
Nor trow the cock will ca' ye hame o'er soon,
For tho' the eastern lift betakens day,
Changing her rokelay black for mantle grey,
Nae weirlike bird our knell of parting rings,
Nor sheds the caller moisture frae his wings.
Nature has chang'd her course; the birds o' day
Dosin' in silence on the bending spray,
While owlets round the craigs at noon-tide flee,
And bludey bawks sit singand on the tree.
Ah, Caledon! the land I yence held dear,
Sair mane mak I for thy destruction near;
And thou, Edina! anes my dear abode,
Whan royal Jamie sway'd the sovereign rod,
In thae blest days, weel did I think bestow'd,
To blaw thy poortith by wi' heaps o' gowd;
To mak thee sonsy seem wi' mony a gift,
And gar thy stately turrets speel the lift:
In vain did Danish Jones[n], wi' gimcrack pains,
In Gothic sculpture fret the pliant stanes:
In vain did he affix my statue here,
Brawly to busk[n] wi' flow'rs ilk coming year;
My tow'rs are sunk, my lands are barren now,
My fame, my honour, like my flow'rs maun dow.

Watson

Sure Major Weir[n], or some sic warlock wight,
Has flung beguilin' glamer o'er your sight;
Or else some kittle cantrup thrown, I ween,
Has bound in mirlygoes my ain twa ein,

16 *bougil*: crowing
*gar*: make
17 *ayont*: beyond
*bield*: shelter
19 *cassen*: cast
20 *trow*: believe
21 *lift*: sky
22 *rokelay*: cloak
23 *weirlike*: warlike
24 *caller*: cool
28 *bawks*: bats
29 *yence*: once
30 *mane*: moan
34 *poortith*: poverty
35 *sonsy*: attractive
36 *speel*: climb
40 *brawly*: bravely
*busk*: adorn
42 *dow*: fade
43 *wight*: fellow
44 *glamer*: magic
45 *kittle*: cunning
*cantrup*: spell
46 *mirlygoes*: fancies

If ever aught frae sense cou'd be believ'd
(And seenil hae my senses been deceiv'd),
This moment, o'er the tap of Adam's tomb[n],
Fu' easy can I see your chiefest dome:
Nae corbie fleein' there, nor croupin' craws,
Seem to forspeak the ruin of thy haws,
But a' your tow'rs in wonted order stand,
Steeve as the rocks that hem our native land.

Herriot

Think na I vent my well-a-day in vain,
Kent ye the cause, ye sure wad join my mane.
Black be the day that e'er to England's ground
Scotland was eikit by the Union's bond;
For mony a menyie of destructive ills
The country now maun brook frae *mortmain bills*,
That void our test'ments, and can freely gie
Sic will and scoup to the ordain'd trustee,
That he may tir our stateliest riggins bare,
Nor acres, houses, woods, nor fishins spare,
Till he can lend the stoitering state a lift
Wi' gowd in gowpins as a grassum gift[n];
In lieu o' whilk, we maun be weel content
To tyne the capital at three *per cent*.
A doughty sum indeed, whan now-a-days
They raise provisions as the stents they raise,
Yoke hard the poor, and lat the rich chiels be,
Pamper'd at ease by ither's industry.
Hale interest for my fund can scantly now
Cleed a' my callants' backs, and stap their mou'.
How maun their weyms wi' sairest hunger slack,
Their duds in targets flaff upo' their back,
Whan they are doom'd to keep a lasting Lent,
Starving for England's weel at *three per cent*.

48 *seenil*: seldom
51 *corbie*: raven
*croupin'*: crowing
52 *forspeak*: foretell
*haws*: halls
54 *steeve*: firm
55 *well-a-day*: lament
56 *kent*: knew
*mane*: moan
58 *eikit*: joined
59 *menyie*: crowd
62 *scoup*: scope
63 *tir*: strip
*riggins*: roofs
65 *stoitering*: staggering
66 *gowd*: gold
*gowpins*: handfuls
68 *tyne*: lose
70 *stents*: local assessments
71 *chiels*: people
73 *scantly*: barely
74 *cleed*: clothe
*callants*: boys
*stap*: stop
75 *weyms*: stomachs
76 *duds*: clothes
*targets*: tatters
*flaff*: flap
78 *weel*: wealth

### Watson

Auld Reikie than may bless the gowden times,
Whan honesty and poortith baith are crimes;
She little kend, whan you and I endow'd
Our hospitals for back-gaun burghers gude,
That e'er our siller or our lands shou'd bring
A gude bien living to a back-gaun king,
Wha, thanks to ministry! is grown sae wise,
He douna chew the bitter cud of vice;
For gin, frae Castlehill to Netherbow[n],
Wad honest houses baudy-houses grow,
The crown wad never spier the price o' sin,
Nor hinder younkers to the de'il to rin;
But gif some mortal grien for pious fame,
And leave the poor man's pray'r to sane his name,
His geer maun a' be scatter'd by the claws
O' ruthless, ravenous, and harpy laws.
Yet, shou'd I think, altho' the bill tak place,
The council winna lack sae meikle grace
As lat our heritage at wanworth gang,
Or the succeeding generations wrang
O' braw bien maintenance and walth o' lear,
Whilk else had drappit to their children's skair;
For mony a deep, and mony a rare engyne
Ha'e sprung frae Herriot's wark, and sprung frae mine.

### Herriot

I find, my friend, that ye but little ken,
There's einow on the earth a set o' men,
Wha, if they get their private pouches lin'd,
Gie na a winnelstrae for a' mankind;
They'll sell their country, flae their conscience bare,
To gar the weigh-bauk turn a single hair.
The government need only bait the line
Wi' the prevailing flee, the gowden coin,

82 *back-gaun*: needy
84 *bien*: comfortable
86 *douna*: dare not
87 *gin*: if
89 *spier*: ask
91 *grien*: long for
92 *sane*: bless
96 *meikle*: much
97 *wanworth*: low price
98 *wrang*: cheat
99 *braw bien*: fine, comfortable
*walth*: wealth
*lear*: learning
100 *drappit*: dropped
*skair*: share
101 *engyne*: intelligence
102 *wark*: endowment
104 *einow*: at present
106 *winnelstrae*: straw
107 *flae*: flay
108 *weigh-bauk*: scales
110 *flee*: fly

Then our executors, and wise trustees,
Will sell them fishes in forbidden seas,
Upo' their dwining country girn in sport,
Laugh in their sleeve, and get a place at court.

Watson

'Ere that day come, I'll 'mang our spirits pick
Some ghaist that trokes and conjures wi' Auld Nick,
To gar the wind wi' rougher rumbles blaw,
And weightier thuds than ever mortal saw:
Fire-flaught and hail, wi' tenfald fury's fires,
Shall lay yird-laigh Edina's airy spires:
Tweed shall rin rowtin' down his banks out o'er,
Till Scotland's out o' reach o' England's pow'r;
Upo' the briny Borean jaws to float,
And mourn in dowy saughs her dowy lot.

Herriot

Yonder's the tomb of wise Mackenzie[n] fam'd,
Whase laws rebellious bigotry reclaim'd,
Freed the hail land frae covenanting fools,
Wha erst ha'e fash'd us wi' unnumber'd dools;
Till night we'll tak the swaird aboon our pows,
And then, whan she her ebon chariot rows,
We'll travel to the vaut wi' stealing stap,
And wauk Mackenzie frae his quiet nap:
Tell him our ails, that he, wi' wonted skill,
May fleg the schemers o' the *mortmain-bill*.

113 *dwining*: decaying
*girn*: jeer
116 *trokes*: deals
*Auld Nick*: the devil
119 *fire-flaught*: lightning
120 *yird-laigh*: low on the earth
121 *rowtin'*: roaring
123 *Borean*: northern
*jaws*: waves
124 *saughs*: willows
127 *hail*: whole
128 *erst*: formerly
*dools*: sorrows
129 *swaird*: sward
130 *rows*: rolls, drives
131 *vaut*: vault
*stap*: step
134 *fleg*: frighten

## LEITH RACES

In July month[n], ae bonny morn,
Whan Nature's rokelay green
Was spread o'er ilka rigg o' corn
To charm our roving een;

1 *ae*: one
2 *rokelay*: mantle
3 *ilka*: every
*rigg*: ridge or row

Glouring about I saw a quean,
The fairest 'neath the lift;
Her een ware o' the siller sheen,
Her skin like snawy drift,
Sae white that day.

Quod she, 'I ferly unco sair,
That ye sud musand[n] gae,
Ye wha hae sung o' Hallow-fair,
Her winter's pranks and play:
Whan on Leith-Sands the racers rare,
Wi' Jocky louns are met,
Their orro pennies there to ware,
And drown themsel's in debt
Fu' deep that day.'

'An' wha are ye, my winsome dear,
That takes the gate sae early?
Whare do ye win, gin ane may spier,
For I right meikle ferly,
That sic braw buskit laughing lass
Thir bonny blinks shou'd gi'e,
An' loup like Hebe[n] o'er the grass,
As wanton and as free
Frae dule this day.'

'I dwall amang the caller springs
That weet the Land o' Cakes,[n]
And aften tune my canty strings
At bridals and late-wakes:[n]
They ca' me Mirth; I ne'er was kend
To grumble or look sour,
But blyth wad be a lift to lend,
Gif ye wad sey my pow'r
An' pith this day.'

5 *glouring*: gazing
*quean*: young woman
6 *lift*: sky
7 *siller*: silver
10 *quod*: said
*ferly*: marvel
*unco*: very
*sair*: grievously
15 *louns*: lads
16 *orro*: spare
*ware*: spend
20 *gate*: road
21 *win*: live
*gin*: if
*spier*: ask
23 *braw buskit*: well dressed
24 *blinks*: glances
25 *loup*: leap
26 *wanton*: frisky
27 *dule*: sorrow
28 *caller*: fresh
29 *weet*: moisten
30 *canty*: cheerful
32 *kend*: known
34 *blyth*: happy
*lift*: diversion
35 *sey*: try
36 *pith*: strength

'A bargain be't, and, by my feggs,
  Gif ye will be my mate,
Wi' you I'll screw the cheery pegs,[n]
  Ye shanna find me blate;
We'll reel an' ramble thro' the sands,
  And jeer wi' a' we meet;
Nor hip the daft and gleesome bands
  That fill Edina's street
      Sae thrang this day.'

Ere servant maids had wont to rise
  To seeth the breakfast kettle,
Ilk dame her brawest ribbons tries,
  To put her on her mettle,
Wi' wiles some silly chiel to trap,
  (And troth he's fain to get her,)
But she'll craw kniefly in his crap,[n]
  Whan, wow! he canna flit her
      Frae hame that day.

Now, mony a scaw'd and bare-ars'd lown
  Rise early to their wark,
Enough to fley a muckle town,
  Wi' dinsome squeel and bark.
'Here is the true an' faithfu' list
  O' noblemen and horses;
Their eild, their weight, their height, their grist,
  That rin for plates or purses
      Fu' fleet this day.'

To whisky plooks that brunt for wooks
  On town-guard soldiers' faces,
Their barber bauld his whittle crooks,
  An' scrapes them for the races:
Their stumps erst us'd to filipegs,
  Are dight in spaterdashes,
Whase barkent hides scarce fend their legs
  Frae weet, and weary plashes
      O' dirt that day.

37 *by my feggs*: truly
40 *shanna*: shall not
*blate*: backward
43 *hip*: miss
45 *thrang*: crowded
47 *seeth*: boil
50 *chiel*: fellow
51 *fain*: eager
52 *craw*: crow
*kniefly*: vigorously
*crap*: stomach
53 *flit*: remove
55 *scaw'd*: worthless
57 *fley*: frighten
*muckle*: large
58 *dinsome*: noisy
61 *eild*: age
*grist*: size
64 *plooks*: pimples
*brunt*: burned
*wooks*: weeks
66 *whittle*: knife, razor
68 *stumps*: legs
*erst*: formerly
*filipegs*: kilt
69 *dight*: dressed
*spaterdashes*: type of gaiters
70 *barkent*: tanned
71 *weet*: wet

'Come, hafe a care[n] (the captain cries),
On guns your bagnets thraw;
Now mind your manual exercise,
An' marsh down raw by raw.'
And as they march he'll glowr about,
'Tent a' their cuts and scars:
'Mang them fell mony a gausy snout
Has gusht in birth-day wars,[n]
Wi' blude that day.

Her nanesel maun be carefu' now,
Nor maun she pe misleard,
Sin baxter lads[n] hae seal'd a vow
To skelp and clout the guard:
I'm sure Auld Reikie kens o' nane
That wou'd be sorry at it,
Tho' they should dearly pay the kane,[n]
An' get their tails weel sautit[n]
And sair thir days.

The tinkler billies i' the Bow[n]
Are now less eidant clinking,
As lang's their pith or siller dow,
They're daffin', and they're drinking.
Bedown Leith-walk[n] what burrochs reel
Of ilka trade and station,
That gar their wives an' childer feel
Toom weyms for their libation
O' drink thir days.

The browster wives thegither harl
A' trash that they can fa' on;
They rake the grounds o' ilka barrel,
To profit by the lawen:

77 *glowr*: look fiercely
78 *tent*: note
79 *fell mony*: a great many
*gausy*: prominent
*snout*: nose
83 *misleard*: ill-bred
85 *skelp*: smite
*clout*: hit
86 *Auld Reikie*: Edinburgh
89 *sautit*: salted
90 *sair*: sore
*thir*: these
91 *tinkler*: tinsmith
*billies*: fellows
92 *eidant*: busy
93 *pith*: strength
*siller*: money
*dow*: allow
94 *daffin'*: making merry
95 *burrochs*: gatherings
98 *toom*: empty
*weyms*: stomachs
100 *browster wives*: ale-wives
*harl*: drag
102 *grounds*: dregs
103 *lawen*: tavern bill

For weel wat they a skin leal het
  For drinking needs nae hire;
At drumbly gear they take nae pet;
  Foul water slockens fire
      And drouth thir days.

They say, ill ale has been the deid
  O' mony a beirdly lown;
Then dinna gape like gleds wi' greed
  To sweel hail bickers down;
Gin Lord send mony ane the morn,
  They'll ban fu' sair the time
That e'er they toutit aff the horn[n]
  Which wambles thro' their weym
      Wi' pain that day.

The Buchan bodies[n] thro' the beech
  Their bunch of Findrums cry,[n]
An' skirl out baul', in Norland speech,
  'Gueed speldings, fa will buy.'
An', by my saul, they're nae wrang gear
  To gust a stirrah's mow;
Weel staw'd wi' them, he'll never spear
  The price o' being fu'
      Wi' drink that day.

Now wyly wights at rowly powl,[n]
  An' flingin' o' the dice,
Here brake the banes o' mony a soul
  Wi' fa's upo' the ice:
At first the gate seems fair an' straught,
  So they had fairly till her;
But wow! in spite o' a' their maught,
  They're rookit o' their siller
      An' goud that day.

104 *leal het*: thoroughly hot
105 *hire*: inducement
106 *drumbly*: impure
*gear*: stuff, matter
106 *pet*: offence
107 *slockens*: quenches
108 *drouth*: thirst
109 *deid*: death
110 *beirdly*: strong
*lown*: lad
111 *gleds*: kites
112 *sweel*: swill
*bickers*: drinking cups
114 *ban*: curse
116 *wambles*: moves uneasily
*weym*: stomach
118 *beech*: beach, seashore
123 *gust*: please
*stirrah*: fellow
*mow*: mouth
124 *staw'd*: stuffed
*spear*: ask
127 *wyly*: cunning
131 *gate*: way
132 *had*: hold
133 *maught*: skill
134 *rookit*: robbed
135 *goud*: gold

Around whare'er ye fling your een,
The haiks like wind are scourin';
Some chaises honest folk contain,
An' some hae mony a whore in;
Wi' rose and lilly, red and white,
They gie themselves sic fit airs,
Like Dian,[n] they will seem perfite;
But its nae goud that glitters
Wi' them thir days.

The Lyon[n] here, wi' open paw,
May cleek in mony hunder,
Wha geck at Scotland and her law,
His wyly talons under;
For ken, tho' Jamie's laws[n] are auld,
(Thanks to the wise recorder),
His Lyon yet roars loud and bawld,
To had the Whigs[n] in order
Sae prime this day.

To town-guard drum of clangor clear,
Baith men and steeds are raingit;
Some liveries red or yellow wear,
And some are tartan spraingit:
And now the red, the blue e'en-now
Bids fairest for the market;
But, 'ere the sport be done, I trow
Their skins are gayly yarkit
And peel'd thir days.

Siclike in Robinhood[n] debates,
Whan twa chiels hae a pingle;
E'en-now some couli gets his aits,
An' dirt wi' words they mingle,
Till up loups he, wi' diction fu',
There's lang and dreech contesting;
For now they're near the point in view;
Now ten miles frae the question
In hand that night.

137 *haiks*: hackney coaches
*scourin'*: speeding
141 *fit*: pretentious
142 *perfite*: perfect
146 *cleek in*: seize
*hunder*: hundreds
147 *geck*: mock
153 *prime*: drunk
155 *raingit*: lined up
157 *spraingit*: striped
161 *gayly*: much
*yarkit*: bruised
163 *siclike*: just as
164 *pingle*: quarrel
165 *couli*: low fellow
*gets his aits*: gets proper punishment
167 *loups*: leaps
*diction*: words, verbosity
168 *dreech*: dull

The races o'er, they hale the dools,[n]
Wi' drink o' a' kin-kind;
Great feck gae hirpling hame like fools,
The cripple lead the blind.
May ne'er the canker o' the drink
E'er make our spirits thrawart,
'Case we git wharewitha' to wink
Wi' een as blue's a blawart
Wi' straiks thir days!

173 *a kin-kind*: every kind
174 *feck*: number
177 *thrawart*: bad-tempered
179 *blawart*: bluebell
180 *straiks*: blows

## THE ELECTION

*Nunc est bibendum, et bendere* BICKERUM *magnum;*
*Cavete* TOWN-GUARDUM, *Dougal Geddum atque Campbellum*

Rejoice, ye Burghers, ane an' a',
Lang look't for's come at last;
Sair war your backs held to the wa'
Wi' poortith an' wi' fast:
Now ye may clap your wings an' craw,
And gayly busk ilk' feather,
For Deacon Cocks hae pass'd a law
To rax an' weet your leather
Wi' drink thir days.

'Haste, Epps,' quo' John, 'an' bring my gez,
Take tent ye dinna't spulyie:
Last night the barber ga't a friz,
An' straikit it wi' ulyie.
Hae done your paritch lassie Liz,
Gi'e me my sark an' gravat;
I'se be as braw's the Deacon is
Whan he taks affidavit
O' faith[n] the day.'

1 *ane an' a'*: one and all
2 *lang*: long
3 *sair*: sorely
*war*: were
4 *poortith*: poverty
6 *busk*: dress
8 *rax*: stretch
9 *thir*: those
10 *Epps*: Elizabeth (dim.)
*gez*: wig
11 *tent*: care
*spulyie*: spoil
12 *ga't a*: gave it a
*friz*: curl
13 *straikit*: smoothed
*ulyie*: oil
14 *paritch*: porridge
15 *sark*: shirt
*gravat*: scarf
16 *I'se*: I'll

'Whar's Johnny gaun', cries neebor Bess,
  'That he's sae gayly bodin
Wi' new kam'd wig, weel syndet face,
  Silk hose, for hamely hodin?'
'Our Johny's nae sma' drink you'll guess,
  He's trig as ony muir-cock,
An' forth to mak a Deacon, lass;
  He downa speak to poor fock
      Like us the day.'

The coat ben-by i' the kist-nook,
  That's been this towmonth swarmin,
Is brought yence mair thereout to look,
  To fleg awa the vermin:
Menyies o' moths an' flaes are shook,
  An' i' the floor they howder,
Till in a birn beneath the crook
  They're singit wi' a scowder
      To death that day.

The canty cobler quats his sta',
  His rozet an' his lingans;
His buik has dree'd a sair, sair fa'
  Frae meals o' bread an' ingans:
Now he's a pow o' wit an' law,
  An' taunts at soals an' heels;
To Walker's[n] he can rin awa,
  There whang his creams an' jeels
      Wi' life that day.

The lads in order tak their seat,
  (The de'il may claw the clungest)
They stegh an' connach sae the meat,
  Their teeth mak mair than tongue haste:
Their claes sae cleanly dight an' feat,

19 *gaun*: going
20 *bodin*: arrayed
21 *kam'd*: combed
*syndet*: washed
22 *for*: instead of
*hamely*: homely
*hodin*: natural homespun
24 *trig*: smart
*muir*: moor
26 *downa*: won't
28 *ben-by*: in inner room
*kist-nook*: corner of a chest
29 *towmonth*: year
30 *yence*: once
31 *fleg*: scare
32 *menyies*: crowds
*flaes*: fleas
33 *howder*: swarm
34 *birn*: heap
*crook*: hook hung over open fire
35 *scowder*: scorching
37 *canty*: merry
*quats*: quits
*sta'*: stall
38 *rozet*: resin
*lingans*: threads
39 *buik*: body
*dree'd*: suffered
40 *ingans*: onions
41 *pow*: head
44 *whang*: cut
*jeels*: jellies
47 *claw*: seize
*clungest*: hungriest
48 *stegh*: stuff
*connach*: devour
50 *dight*: prepared, brushed
*feat*: smart

An' eke their craw-black beavers,
Like masters' mows hae found the gate
To tassels teugh wi' slavers
Fu' lang that day.

The dinner done, for brandy strang
They cry, to weet their thrapple,
To gar the stamack bide the bang,
Nor wi' its laden grapple.
The grace is said — its no o'er lang;
The claret reams in bells;
Quod Deacon let the toast round gang,
'Come, here's our noble sel's
Weel met the day.'

'Weels me o' drink', quo' cooper Will,
'My barrel has been geyz'd ay,
An' has na gotten sic a fill
Sin fu' on handsel-Teysday[n]:
But makes-na, now it's got a sweel,
Ae gird I shanna cast lad,
Or else I wish the horned de'el
May Will wi' kittle cast dad
To hell the day.'

The Magistrates fu' wyly are,
Their lamps[n] are gayly blinking,
But they might as leive burn elsewhere,
Whan fock's blind fu' wi' drinking.
Our Deacon wadna ca' a chair,
The foul ane durst him na-say;
He took shanks-naig, but fient may care,
He arselins kiss'd the cawsey
Wi' bir that night.

51 *beavers*: hats of beaver fur
52 *mows*: mouths
*gate*: way
53 *tassels*: tussles
*teugh*: tough
*slavers*: spittle
56 *thrapple*: throat
57 *bide*: cope with
*bang*: attack
58 *laden*: load
60 *reams*: foams
*bells*: bubbles
64 *weels me o'*: blessings on
65 *geyz'd*: warped dry
68 *makes-na*: no matter
*sweel*: swill, soaking
69 *gird*: barrel-hoop
71 *kittle cast*: nice or difficult throw
*dad*: dash
73 *wyly*: cunning
75 *as leive*: rather, preferably
77 *ca'*: call
*chair*: sedan chair
78 *the foul ane*: devil a one, nobody
*na-say*: contradict
79 *took shanks-naig*: walked
*fient*: devil
80 *arselins*: on his backside
*cawsey*: street
81 *bir*: force

Weel loes me o' you, souter Jock,
  For tricks ye buit be trying,
Whan greapin for his ain bed-stock,
  He fa's whare Will's wife's lying,
Will coming hame wi' ither fock,
  He saw Jock there before him;
Wi' master laiglen, like a brock
  He did wi' stink maist smore him
      Fu' strang that night.

Then wi' a souple leathern whang
  He gart them fidge and girn ay,
'Faith, chiel, ye's no for naething gang
  Gin ye man reel my pirny.'[n]
Syne wi' a muckle alshin lang
  He brodit Maggie's hurdies;
An' 'cause he thought her i' the wrang,
  There pass'd nae bonny wordies
      'Mang them that night.

Now, had some laird his lady fand
  In sic unseemly courses,
It might hae loos'd the haly band,
  Wi' law-suits an' divorces:
But the niest day they a' shook hands,
  And ilka crack did sowder,
While Megg for drink her apron pawns,
  For a' the gude-man cow'd her
      Whan fu' last night.

Glowr round the cawsey, up an' down,
  What mobbing and what plotting!
Here politicians bribe a loun[n]
  Against his saul for voting.
The gowd that inlakes half a crown
  Thir blades lug out to try them,
They pouch the gowd, nor fash the town
  For weights an' scales to weigh them
      Exact that day.

82 *weel . . . you*: my blessings on you
*souter*: shoemaker
83 *buit*: must
84 *greapin*: groping
*stock*: fore part
88 *laiglen*: chamber pot
*brock*: badger
89 *smore*: smother
90 *strang*: strong
91 *whang*: thong, strap
92 *fidge*: jump
*girn*: groan
93 *chiel*: fellow
95 *alshin*: awl
96 *brodit*: prodded
*hurdies*: buttocks
102 *haly band*: holy bond
104 *niest*: next
105 *sowder*: solder
107 *gude-man*: master of the household
109 *glowr*: stare
112 *saul*: soul
113 *gowd*: gold
*inlakes*: is deficient in
114 *thir blades*: those impudent fellows
115 *pouch*: pocket (v.)
*fash*: trouble

Then Deacons at the counsel stent
  To get themsel's presentit:
For towmonths twa their saul is lent,
  For the town's gude indentit:
Lang's their debating thereanent;
  About protests[n] they're bauthrin,
While Sandy Fife,[n] to mak content,
  On bells plays *Clout the caudron*[n]
      To them that day.

Ye lowns that troke in doctor's stuff,
  You'll now hae unco slaisters;
Whan windy blaws their stamacks puff,
  They'll need baith pills an' plaisters;
For tho' ev'now they look right bluff,
  Sic drinks, 'ere hillocks meet,
Will hap some Deacons in a truff,
  Inrow'd in the lang leet[n]
      O' death yon night.

118 *stent*: hasten
120 *towmonths*: twelve months
121 *indentit*: covenanted, under an obligation
122 *thereanent*: about it
123 *bauthrin*: fussing
127 *troke*: deal
128 *slaisters*: mixtures
132 *'ere . . . meet*: soon
133 *hap*: cover
*truff*: turf
134 *inrow'd*: enrolled

# John Mayne
## 1759–1836

John Mayne, born and educated in Dumfries, became an apprentice in the printing office of Robert Jackson, proprietor of the *Dumfries Journal*. One of his fellows in that office was the young poet Charles Salmon, a friend of Robert Fergusson, and in 1773 Fergusson walked from Edinburgh to Dumfries to visit him. On that occasion John Mayne, then fourteen, met Fergusson; his later description of that visit, and the first draft of Fergusson's poem *Dumfries* as recorded by Mayne, are printed in a life of Fergusson. (D.C., 'Robert Fergusson' in *Lives of Scottish Poets*, by the Society of Ancient Scots, ed. Joseph Clinton Robertson, London, 1821–2, vol. 2 part 4, pp. 73–7. The description is quoted in the S.T.S. edition of Fergusson, I, p. 63.) Fergusson's poems clearly fascinated the young man and remained an influence on his own work. Mayne moved to Glasgow, probably to the Foulis Press, and in 1787 to London where he spent the rest of his life. He was one of the founders of *The Star and Evening Advertiser*, a newspaper with which he was connected until his death in 1836.

In 1777 Mayne witnessed the shooting-match by the seven incorporated trades of Dumfries for the 'siller gun', a tube ten inches long presented for this competition by King James VI, and the comedy of the occasion inspired the young man to write and print a dozen stanzas in the style of Fergusson's *King's Birthday in Edinburgh*. An enlarged version of three cantos appeared in Ruddiman's *Edinburgh Weekly Magazine* beginning on 19 June, 1780. A more expanded version was published by the Foulis Press in 1783, along with his poem *Hallow E'en*. These early versions bear the title *The Silver Gun*, but the adjective was changed to 'Siller' in the Glocester (*sic*) 1808, and subsequent English editions. The 1808 edition was of four, and that of 1836, five cantos.

In describing Scots folk festivals Mayne forms an interesting link between Fergusson and Burns. He took Fergusson's *Hallow-fair* as a model for his *Hallow E'en*, and Burns in his turn took ideas from Mayne's poem for his own *Hallow-een*. Mayne follows Fergusson's *King's Birthday* in *The Siller Gun* when he describes the marching men, the onlookers, the celebrations, and some of the aftermath, and he acknowledged his debt in the last verse of his 1780 text:

> But thae were scenes, alackanie!
> Fit only, *Fergusson*! for thee . . .

There is kindliness, humour, and acute observation in Mayne's description, though he lacks Fergusson's incisiveness and grasp of form. Mayne has some of Fergusson's high spirits, but cannot equal his skilful comic rhyming. It is doubtful if anyone would nowadays agree with Sir Walter Scott (*The Lady of the Lake*, Canto V, note to stanza 20), who thought that Mayne's poem surpassed Fergusson and 'comes near to those of Burns', but Mayne's work as a whole has been undervalued.

*Biography:*
*Dictionary of National Biography.*
W. McDowall, *History of the Burgh of Dumfries* (Edinburgh, 1867).

# THE SILLER GUN

## A POEM

*A sight so rare,*
*Makes Wisdom smile, and Folly stare.*
ANON.

### CANTO FIRST

For loyal feats, and trophies won,
Dumfries shall live till time be done!
Ae simmer's morning, wi' the sun,
The sev'n trades there,[n]
Forgather'd, for their siller gun[n]
To shoot ance mair.

To shoot ance mair in grand array,
And celebrate the King's birth-day,
Crouds, happy in the gentle sway
Of ane sae dear,
Were proud their fealty to display,
And marshal here.

O, George! the best o' kings and men!
For thee our daily pray'rs ascend!
Of ilka blessing Heav'n can send,
May'st thou ha'e store;
And may thy royal race extend
'Till time be o'er!

For weeks before this fête sae clever,
The fowk were in a perfect fever,
Scouring gun-barrels i' the river —
At marks practizing —
Marching wi' drums and fifes forever —
A' sodgerizing!

And turning coats, and mending breeks,
New-seating where the sark-tail keeks;
(Nae matter tho' the cloot that eeks
Is black or blue;)
And darning, with a thousand steeks,
The stockings too.

3 *ae*: one
15 *ilka*: every
20 *fowk*: people
25 *breeks*: breeches
26 *sark-tail*: shirt-tail
27 *cloot*: patch
*eeks*: joins
29 *steeks*: stitches

Between the last and this occasion,
Lang, unco lang, seem'd the vacation,
To him wha wooes sweet recreation
In nature's prime;
And him wha likes a day's potation
At ony time.

The lift was clear, the morn serene,
The sun just glinting owr the scene,
When James M‘Noe[n] began again
To beat to arms,
Rouzing the heart o' man and wean
Wi' war's alarms.

Frae far and near, the country lads
(Their joes ahint them on their yads,)
Flock'd in to see the show in squads;
And, what was dafter,
Their pawky mithers and their dads
Came trotting after.

And mony a beau and belle were there,
Doited wi' dozing on a chair;
For, lest they'd, sleeping, spoil their hair,
Or miss the sight,
The gowks, like bairns before a fair,
Sat up a' night!

Wi' hats as black as ony raven,
Fresh as the rose, their beards new-shaven,
And a' their Sunday's cleeding having
Sae trim and gay,
Forth came our trades, some ora saving
To wair that day.

Fair fa' ilk canny caidgy carl!
Weel may he bruik his new apparel!
And never dree the bitter snarl
O' scowling wife;
But, blest in pantry, barn, and barrel,
Be blithe thro' life!

37 *lift*: air, sky
41 *wean*: child
44 *joes*: sweethearts
*yads*: worked-out horses
45 *squads*: groups
47 *pawky*: artful, good-humoured
50 *doited*: stupefied
53 *gowks*: fools
57 *cleeding*: clothing
59 *ora*: surplus
60 *wair*: spend
61 *fair fa'*: good luck to
*caidgy*: cheerful
62 *bruik*: enjoy
63 *dree*: suffer

Heh, Sirs! what crouds were gather'd round,
To see them marching up and down!
Lasses and lads, sun-burnt and brown —
Women and weans,
Gentle and semple, mingling, crown
The gladsome scenes!

Meanwhile, before ilk deacon's dwalling,
His ain brigade was made to fall in;
And, while the muster-roll was calling,
Mull'd ale and wine
Were dealt about in mony a gallon,
And gardevine:

And cheese-and-bread, and bits o' ham,
Laid the foundation for a dram
O' whisky, gin frae Amsterdam,
Or cherry-brandy;
Whilk after, a' was fish that cam
To Jock or Sandy.

For weel ken they wha loo their chappin,
Drink makes the auldest swack and strappen;
Gars Care forget the ills that happen —
The blate, look spruce —
And e'en the thowless cock their tappin,
And craw fu' croose!

The muster owr, the diff'rent bands
File aff in parties to the Sands,
Where, midst loud laughs and clapping hands,
Gleed Geordy Smith[n]
Reviews them, and their line expands
Alang the Nith.[n]

And ne'er, for uniform or air,
Was sic a groupe review'd elsewhere!
The short, the tall; fat fowk, and spare;
Side coats, and dockit;[n]
Wigs, queus, and clubs, and curly hair;
Round hats, and cockit!

71 *gentle*: persons 'of the better sort'
*semple*: persons 'of the lower orders'
78 *gardevine*: wine bottle usually holding two quarts
84 *Sandy*: Alexander (abbrev.)
85 *loo*: love
*chappin*: quart, or drink in general
86 *swack*: supple
87 *gars*: makes
88 *blate*: diffident
*spruce*: lively
89 *thowless*: spiritless
*tappin*: head
90 *croose*: boldly
91 *owr*: over
94 *gleed*: squint-eyed
100 *side coats*: greatcoats
*dockit*: cut away
101 *queus*: pigtails
*clubs*: hair worn in a club-shaped knot or tail

As to their guns — thae fell engines,
Borrow'd or begg'd, were of a' kinds
For bloody war, or bad designs,
        Or shooting cushies —
Lang fowling-pieces, carabines,
        And blunder-busses!

Maist feck, tho' oil'd to make them glimmer,
Hadna been shot for mony a simmer;
And Fame, the story-telling limmer,
        Jocosely hints,
That some o' them had bits o' timmer,
        Instead o' flints.

Some guns, she threeps, within her ken,
Were spik'd, to let nae priming ben;
And, as in twenty there were ten
        Worm-eaten stocks,
Sae, here and there, a rozit-end
        Held on their locks!

And then, to show what diff'rence stands
'Tween him that gets, and gi'es commands,
Claymores that, erst, at Prestonpans,[n]
        Gart faes stand yon',
Were quiv'ring i' the feckless hands
        O' mony a drone!

'Ohon!' quo' George, and ga'e a graen,
'The age o' chivalry is gane!'
Syne, having owr and owr again
        The hale survey'd,
Their route, and a' things else, made plain,
        He snuff'd, and said:

'Now, Gentlemen! now mind the motion,
And dinna, this time, make a botion:
Shouther your arms! — O! had them tosh on,
        And not athraw!
Wheel wi' your right-hands to the ocean,
        And march awa!'

103 *thae*: those
106 *cushies*: wild pigeons
109 *feck*: of their number
111 *limmer*: bold wench
115 *threeps*: insists
*ken*: knowledge
116 *ben*: inside
119 *rozit-end*: piece of shoemaker's resined thread
123 *erst*: formerly
124 *yon*: far back
125 *feckless*: feeble
127 *graen*: groan
129 *syne*: then
130 *hale*: whole
134 *botion*: botch
135 *shouther*: shoulder
*tosh*: neat, straight
136 *athraw*: awry

Wi' that, the dinlin drums rebound,
Fifes, clarionets, and hautboys sound!
Thro' crouds on crouds, collected round,
The corporations
Trudge aff, whilst Echo's self was drown'd
With acclamations!

Their steps to martial airs agreeing,
And a' the Sev'n-Trades' colours fleeing,
Bent for the Craigs[n], O! weel worth seeing!
They hy'd awa';
Their bauld Convener proud o' being
The chief owr a'.

Attended by his body-guard,
He stepp'd in gracefu'ness unpair'd!
Straight as the poplar on the swaird,
And strong as Sampson,
Nae eie cou'd look without regard
On Robin Tamson.[n]

His craft, the blacksmith's, first ava,
Led the procession, twa and twa;
The squaremen follow'd i' the raw,
And syne the weavers,
The taylors, souters, skinners a',
And marrow-cleavers.

Their journeymen were a' sae gaucy,
Th' apprentices sae kir and saucy,
That, as they gaed alang the causey,
Sae tight and braw,
Th' applauding heart o' mony a lassie
Was stown awa.

Brisk as a bridegroom gawn to wed,
Ilk deacon march'd before his trade:
Foggies the zig-zag followers led,
But scarce had pow'r
To keep some, fitter for their bed,
Frae stoit'ring owr.

139 *dinlin*: vibrant, rolling
140 *hautboys*: oboes
146 *fleeing*: flying
148 *hy'd*: hurried
149 *bauld*: bold
153 *swaird*: sward, meadow
157 *ava*: of all
159 *squaremen*: carpenters
*raw*: raw, rank
161 *souters*: shoemakers
162 *marrow-cleavers*: butchers
163 *gaucy*: cheerful
164 *kir*: happy
165 *causey*: street
166 *tight*: well-made, virile
*braw*: brave, fine
168 *stown*: stolen
169 *gawn*: going
171 *foggies*: old soldiers
174 *stoit'ring*: lurching, keeling

For blithesome Sir John Barleycorn
Had sae allur'd them i' the morn,
That, what wi' drams, and mony a horn,
And reaming bicker,
The ferly is, withouten scorn,
They wauk'd sae sicker!

As thro' the town their banners fly,
Frae windows low, frae windows high,
A' that cou'd find a nook to spy,
Were leaning o'er;
The streets, stair-heads, and carts, forbye,
Were a' uproar!

To see his face whom she loo'd best,
Hab's wife was there amang the rest;
And, while wi' joy her sides she prest,
Like mony mae,
Her exultation was exprest
In words like thae:

'Wow! but it makes ane's heart lowp light
To see auld fowk sae cleanly dight!
E'en now our Habby seems as tight
As when, lang syne,
His looks were first the young delight
And pride o' mine!'

But on the meeker maiden's part,
Deep sighs alane her love impart!
Deep sighs, the language o' the heart,
Will aft reveal
A flame which a' the pow'rs of art
In vain conceal!

Frae rank to rank while thousands bustle,
In front, like waving corn, they hustle;
Where, deck'd wi' ribbons round its muzzle,
The Siller Gun,
A trinket like a penny whustle,
Gleam'd i' the sun!

175 *Sir John Barleycorn*: whisky
178 *reaming*: foaming
*bicker*: drinking-cup
179 *ferly*: wonder
180 *wauk'd*: wakened
*sicker*: steady
185 *forbye*: as well
188 *Hab*: Albert (abbrev.)
190 *mae*: more
192 *thae*: those
193 *lowp*: leap
194 *dight*: turned out, accoutred
196 *syne*: since, ago

Suspended frae a painted pole,
A glimpse o't sae inspir'd the whole,
That auld and young, wi' heart and soul,
Their heads were cocking,
Keen as ye've seen, at bridals droll,
Maids catch the stocking![n]

In honour o' this gaudy thing,
And eke in honour o' the King,
A fouth o' flow'rs the gard'ners bring,
And frame sweet posies
Of a' the relics o' the spring,
And simmer's roses!

Amang the flow'ry forms they weave,
There's Adam, to the life, and Eve:
She, wi' the apple in her neeve,
Enticing Adam;
While Satan's laughing in his sleeve,
At him and madam!

The lily white, the vi'let blue,
The heather-bells of azure hue;
And birken chaplets not a few,
And yellow broom —
Athwart the scented welkin threw
A rich perfume!

Perfume, congenial to the clime,
The sweetest, i' the sweetest time!
The merry bells, in jocund chime,
Rang thro' the air,
And minstrels play'd, in strains sublime,
To charm the fair!

And fairer than our Nithsdale Fair,
Or handsomer, there's nane elsewhere!
Pure as the streams that murmur there,
In them ye'll find
That Virtue and the Graces rare
Are a' enshrin'd!

218 *eke*: also
219 *fouth*: plenty, abundance
225 *neeve*: fist
231 *birken*: of birch
233 *welkin*: sky, air

Lang may the bonny bairns recline
On Plenty's bosom, saft and kind!
And, O! may I, ere life shall dwine
To its last scene,
Return, and a' my sorrows tine
At hame again!

251 *tine*: lose

# Charles Keith
## died 1807

Little is known about Charles Keith's life except that he lived as a young man in Montrose, and attended Marischal College, Aberdeen, where he graduated M.A. in 1779. He proceeded to study medicine in Edinburgh, and his training there was accepted by Marischal College for the degree of M.D. in 1784. According to *The Scots Magazine* (Vol. 69), Dr Charles Keith, physician at Harrogate, died at Durham, 8 April, 1807.

In November and December 1774, a number of poems by Keith appeared in Ruddiman's *Edinburgh Magazine*, beginning with *An Attempt towards a Pastoral Elegy to the Memory of Mr. Robert Fergusson, that youthful Prodigy of Song* in the issue of 3 November, and followed on 8 December by *Written extempore to a young Gentleman, on his getting a Cloak and Wig: in the Scots Dialect*, and on 30 December by *Farmer's Ha'*. This was published separately in 1776 by Chalmers of Aberdeen with the title, *Farmer's Ha': a Scots Poem. By a Student of Marischal College*, and a note saying: 'Some stanzas entitled the *Farmer's Ha'* were published in Mr Ruddiman's Magazine, in December 1774: but the Author thinking the plan too contracted, resolved to enlarge the poem, and present it to the public in the present form'. The 19 stanzas of the first version had been expanded to 65. We print most of the author's revised version of 1776.

*Farmer's Ha'* was inspired by Fergusson's *Farmer's Ingle* and Keith's Angus scene is not unlike Fergusson's recollections of an Aberdeenshire farmhouse; but Keith's merely interesting lines lack the glow of Fergusson's, and his skill in rhyming, promising in a young man, is an apprentice's compared with the master's. Burns, like Keith, knew Fergusson's poem, but there is no sign in *The Cotter's Saturday Night* that he had read *Farmer's Ha'*. The three poems have common themes — hard work in an unrelenting climate, friendliness when labour is done, respect for the independent man, and nostalgia for a way of life that was passing. These interests remain in the differing settings of Fergusson's small farm in the Garioch, Keith's larger establishment in the rich pasturage of Angus, with its separate hall for the farm-servants, and Burns's little cot-house, where the older lads and girls of the family have to go out to other farms to find work.

## FARMER'S HA'

In winter nights, whae'er has seen
The farmer's canty ha' conveen,
Finds a' thing there to please his een,
And heart enamour,
Nor langs to see the town, I ween,
That houff o' clamour.

Whan stately stacks are tightly theekit,
And the wide style is fairly steekit,
Nae birkie sure, save he war streekit
For his lang hame,[n]
But wad gi'e mair for ae short week o't
Than I can name.

Hire-women ay the glowmin hail,
For syne the lads come frae the flail,
Or else frae haddin the plough-tail,
That halesome wark;
Disease about they dinna trail,
Like city spark.

They a' drive to the ingle cheek,
Regardless o' a flan o' reek,
And well their meikle fingers beek,
To gi'e them tune,
Syne sutors al'son nimbly streek,
To mend their shoon.[n]

They pow and rax the lingel tails,
Into their brogs they ca' the nails,
Wi' hammers now, instead of flails,
They make great rackets,
And set about their heels wi' rails
O' clinkin tackets.

2 *canty*: cheerful
6 *houff*: haunt
7 *theekit*: thatched
8 *style*: gate
*steekit*: shut
9 *birkie*: lively fellow
*streekit*: laid out for burial
11 *ae*: one
13 *hire-women*: maid-servants
*glowmin*: evening
14 *syne*: then
15 *haddin*: holding
19 *ingle cheek*: fireside
20 *flan o' reek*: gust of wind blowing smoke down
21 *beek*: warm
23 *sutors al'son*: shoemaker's awl
*streek*: ply
24 *shoon*: shoes
25 *pow . . . tails*: pull and stretch the shoemaker's string
26 *brogs*: shoes
*ca'*: drive
30 *tackets*: hob-nails

And ay till this mis-thriven age,
The gudeman here sat like a sage,
Wi' mill in hand, and wise adage,
He spent the night;
But now he sits in chamber cage,[n]
A pridefu' wight.

The lasses wi' their unshod heels,
Are sitting at their spinning wheels,
And weel ilk blythsome kemper dreels,
And bows like wand;
The auld goodwife the pirney reels
Wi' tenty hand.

The carlin ay for spinnin bent,
Tells them right aft, they've fawn ahent,
And that the day is e'en far spent,
Reminds ilk hussey,
And crys, 'Ye'll nae make out your stent,
Save ye be busy.'

Tib braks, wi' haste, her foot-broad latch;
Meg lights the crusey wi' a match,
Auld luckie bids her mak dispatch,
And girdle heat,
For she maun yet put out a batch
O' bear and ait.

There's less wark for the girdle now,
Nor was in days of yore, I trow,
Gude scouder'd bannocks has nae gou'
To husbandmen;
For o'en wheat bread dits ilka mou'
That stays the ben.

The young gudewife and bairns a'
Right seenil now look near the ha',

31 *mis-thriven*: thriftless
32 *gudeman*: farmer
33 *mill*: snuff mill
35 *chamber cage*: separate part of hall
39 *kemper*: worker
*dreels*: works quickly
40 *bows*: bends
41 *pirney*: bobbin
42 *tenty*: careful
43 *carlin*: old woman
*bent*: intent
44 *fawn ahent*: fallen behind
47 *stent*: stint, task
49 *braks*: breaks
*foot-broad latch*: pedal for the foot
50 *crusey*: small oil lamp
51 *luckie*: old woman (fam.)
*mak*: make
52 *girdle*: griddle
54 *bear and ait*: cakes of barley and oatmeal
57 *scouder'd*: toasted
*gou'*: taste
59 *o'en*: oven
*dits*: pleases
60 *stays the ben*: stays in the inner, private, part of the house
62 *seenil*: seldom

For fear their underlins sud shaw
A cauld neglect:
But pride was never kent to draw
Love or respect.

The taylor lad, lang fam'd for fleas,[n]
Sits here and maks and mends the claes;
And vow! the swankies like to teaze
Him wi' their mocks,
The women cry, he's ill to please,
And crack their jokes.

But he's a slee and cunning lown,
And taunts again ilk jeering clown;
For tho' nae bred in borrows town,
He's wondrous gabby,
And fouth o' wit comes frae his crown,
Tho' he be shabby.

Auld farrant tales he skreeds awa',
And ca's their lear but clippings a',
And bids them gang to Thimble-ha',
Wi' needle speed,[n]
And learn wit without a flaw,
Frae the board head.

Auld luckie says they're in a creel,
And redds them up, I trow, fu' weel,
Cries, 'Lasses, occupy your wheel,
'And strait the pin;'
And bids the taylor haste and dreel
Wi' little din.

Quo' she, 'Ye've meikle need to sew,
'O times are sairly alter'd now!
'For two-pence was the wage, I trow,
'To ony Scot;
'But now-a-days ye crook your mou,
'To seek a groat.'

63 *underlins*: underlings
68 *claes*: clothes
*vow!*: wow! (interj.)
69 *swankies*: young lads
73 *slee*: sly
*lown*: fellow
74 *ilk*: each
75 *borrows town*: burgh
76 *gabby*: talkative
77 *fouth*: plenty
79 *farrant*: fashioned
*skreeds*: holds forth at length
80 *ca's*: calls
*lear*: learning
*clippings*: little bits
81 *Thimble-ha'*: tailor's workshop
85 *in a creel*: in confusion
86 *redds*: clears, tidies
89 *dreel*: work quickly
95 *crook your mou'*: draw lips together in scorn
96 *groat*: fourpence

The colly dog lies i' the nook,
The place whilk his auld father took,
And aft toward the door does look,
Wi' aspect crouse;
For unco' fouk he canno' brook
Within the house.

Here bawdrins sits, and cocks her head,
And smooths her coat o' nature's weed,
And purrs contentedly indeed,
And looks fu' lang,
To see gin fowk be takin heed
To her braw sang.

The auld gudewife, who kens her best,
Behads her wash her face and breast;
Syne honest luckie does protest
That rain we'll hae,
Or on-ding[n] o' some kind at least,
Afore't be day.

To her remarks lists ilka lass,
And what she says aft comes to pass,
Altho' she hae nae chymic mass
To weigh the air;
For pussy's granum's weather-glass
I do declare.

Nae sooner has auld luckie done,
Nor Meg cries, she'll wad baith her shoon,
That we sall hae weet very soon,
And weather rough;
For she saw round about the moon
A meickle brough.

Aft-times the canty lilt gaes round,
And ilka face wi' mirth is crown'd,
And whiles they sing in safter sound,
Sic as the swain
Of Yarrow,[n] or some lover drown'd
In ruthless main.

100 *crouse*: alert
101 *unco*: stranger
*fouk*: folk
103 *bawdrins*: the cat
107 *gin*: if
*braw*: fine
110 *behads*: sees
111 *luckie*: old woman
113 *on-ding*: downfall
115 *lists*: listens
117 *chymic mass*: barometer
119 *granum*: grandmother
122 *Nor*: than
*wad*: wager
*shoon*: shoes
123 *weet*: wet
126 *meickle brough*: great circle
127 *canty*: merry
130 *sic*: such

O royal tales gae brawly on,
And feats of fowk that's dead and gone;
The windy piper sounds his drone,
As well he can;
And aft they speak of their Mess John,
That haly man.

They banish hence a' care and dool,
For they were bred at mirthfu' school;
They count how lang it is to yule,
Wi' pleasure vast;
And tell wha' sat the cutty stool[n]
On sabbath last.

The chapman lad wi' gab sae free,
Comes in, and mixes i' the glee,
After he's trampet out the e'e
O' mony dub,
And gotten frae the blast to dree
A hearty drub.

He says he did Auld Reekie ca',
To bring them things to mak' them braw,
And got them free o' crack and flaw,
And patterns rare:
The proverb says, 'Fowls far awa'
Ha'e feathers fair.'

He tells them he's weel sorted now
O' a' thing gude, and cheap, and new;
His sleekit speeches pass for true
Wi' ane and a';
The pedlars ken fu' well the cue
O' Farmer's Ha'.

He hads his trinkets to the light,
And speirs what they're to buy the-night;
Syne a' the lasses loup bawk height
Wi' perfect joy,
Cause lads for them coff broach so bright,
Or shining toy.[n]

* * * * *

135 *windy piper*: bagpiper
137 *Mess John*: minister
139 *a'*: all
*dool*: grief
141 *yule*: New Year
143 *cutty stool*: stool of repentance
145 *chapman*: pedlar
*gab*: mouth, merry talk
148 *dub*: pool of water
149 *dree*: endure
150 *drub*: buffeting
151 *Auld Reekie*: Edinburgh
157 *sorted*: supplied
159 *sleekit*: plausible, deceitful
161 *cue*: humour, mood
165 *loup*: leap
*bawk height*: as high as the rafters
167 *coff*: buy

While I descrive this happy spot,
The supper manna' be forgot,
Now lasses round the ingle trot,
To make the brose,
And swankies they link aff the pot,
To hain their joes.

The dishes set on unspread table,
To answer nature's wants are able,
'Round caps and plates, the cutties sable
Are flung ding dang:
The lads and lasses to enable
Their wames to pang.

They a' thrang round the lang board now,
Whare there is meat for ilka mou'
Hiremen their hats and bonnets pu'
Upo' their face,
But gentle folks think shame to bow,
Or say a grace.

O here are joys uninterrup'
Far hence is pleasure's gangrene cup;
Clear blooded health tends ilka sup
O' simple diet;
But flies awa' frae keeping't up,
And midnight riot.

When supper's o'er, and thanks are gi'en,
Mirth dances round wi' canty mein,
In daffin', and in gabbin' keen
An hour they pass;
And ilka lad, wi' pawky een,
Looks at his lass.

But Morpheus begins to chap,
And bids them a' gae tak a nap;
And whan they've sleepit like a tap,
They rise to wark,
Like Phoebus out o' Thetis' lap,
As blyth's a lark.

355 *descrive*: describe
357 *ingle*: fireside
358 *brose*: the local type of porridge
359 *link aff*: lift off the chain set above the fire
360 *hain*: protect
*joes*: sweethearts
363 *cutties sable*: short black spoons
366 *wames*: bellies
*pang*: satisfy
369 *hiremen*: male farm-servants
380 *mein*: appearance
381 *daffin'*: fun, flirtation
383 *pawky*: knowing
385 *Morpheus*: god of sleep
*chap*: stroke (of a clock)
389 *Phoebus*: Apollo, god of light
*Thetis*: sea-goddess

# Robert Burns
## 1759–1796

One of the greatest of twentieth-century Scots scholars, David Nichol Smith, used to begin a standard lecture on Burns with a reference to the Burns cult that was quite without the shriller overtones of Hugh MacDiarmid's attacks on the annual folk festival on the 25th of January. Smith used to ask his audience to ponder quite seriously *why* a people who valued practicality so highly, a nation of engineers and entrepreneurs, of Clydeside fitters and emigrant pioneers, should choose a poet as their national hero. Burns undoubtedly appealed to his immediate contemporaries and their nineteenth-century successors because he could so easily be made to fit the stereotype of the inspired genius who owes nothing to birth, education or a refined *milieu*. The cult of the primitive which we have noted in Beattie and in Ossian, as well as the pastoral simplicity of Ramsay's *Gentle Shepherd*, seemed to find their real-life incarnation in Rab Mossgiel. Yet he was no heaven-taught ploughman, as the leading *littérateur* of contemporary Edinburgh, Henry Mackenzie, called him in his 1786 review of the Kilmarnock edition, but a well-educated — though a self-educated — man. Francis Jeffrey, the most influential periodical critic of the next generation, put it like this: 'His taste for reading was encouraged by his parents and many of his associates; and, before he had ever composed a single stanza, he was not only familiar with many prose writers, but far more intimately acquainted with Pope, Shakespeare and Thomson, than nine tenths of the youth that leave school for the university ... he could write in the dialect of England with far greater purity and propriety than nine tenths of those who are called well educated in that country'. (Review of Cromek's *Reliques of Robert Burns*, in *Edinburgh Review*, 13, January 1809, 249–76; reprinted Jeffrey, *Contributions to the Edinburgh Review*, II, London, 1844, 389–421).

Burns was heir not only to the vernacular tradition as extended by Ramsay and Fergusson, but also to the Augustan and sentimentalist traditions of eighteenth-century Scotland and England. His complex personality, so full of clashing opposites, caused him to respond remarkably to these varied influences. No one has put it better than Byron: 'What an antithetical mind! — tenderness, roughness — delicacy, coarseness — sentiment, sensuality — soaring and grovelling, dirt and deity — all mixed up in that one compound of inspired clay!' (*Journal*, 13 December, 1813). Here, perhaps, lies the answer to Nichol Smith's question: it was that same contradictoriness which made it possible for his works, and his myth, to find favour with so many different types of Scot.

Though as a boy he had read Hamilton of Gilbertfield's *Wallace* and some of Allan Ramsay's poems, and though he had derived a wide knowledge of traditional tales, proverbs, folk ballads and popular lyrics from his mother, her female servants and relatives, it was not until he met with the Scots poems of Fergusson that he became aware of the full possibilities of Scots as a creative medium. Fergusson's poetry was a catalyst, fusing with English influences and the extraordinary events of his own life to produce the great poems printed here. Ayrshire was a stronghold of last-ditch calvinism in the church disputes of the eighteenth century, and Burns found in vernacular measures and traditions the perfect instruments for his 'priest-skelpin' turns against the ministers and elders of the Auld Licht persuasion. By mid 1786 amorous entanglements had made it almost impossible for him to continue in and around Mauchline, and he seriously considered emigrating to Jamaica. But the huge success of his carefully chosen selection of 34 poems, the famous Kilmarnock edition of 31 July, led him to change his plans. November saw him in the capital, to arrange for an Edinburgh edition (published 17 April, 1787). He was the social sensation of the year. Tours of the Borders and the Highlands followed, and he spent much of the first three months of 1788 in Edinburgh. Later in 1788 he acknowledged his previous irregular marriage with Jean Armour, and combined his lease of Ellisland farm in Dumfriesshire with a minor job in the Excise from September 1789. In November 1791 he moved to Dumfries as a full-time exciseman. Burns performed his excise duties faithfully, although his outspoken support of the French Revolution caused some trouble with his superiors (the Excise Board investigated his loyalty between December 1792 and January 1793) and made him unpopular with the local establishment. He often got drunk, but his early death was not due to alcoholism but to a rheumatic heart condition aggravated by the treatment prescribed by his doctors — bathing in the Solway.

Burns's place in world literature rests mainly on the poems in the Kilmarnock edition; on certain works written at about the time of that volume but excluded from it, like *Holy Willie's Prayer*; on *Tam o' Shanter*; and on his songs. We print all five of the longer Kilmarnock poems: *The Vision*, which so daringly moves from a realistic picture of the poet in his 'clay biggin' to the celebration of local society and the Scottish nation as a whole; *The Holy Fair*, at once a piece in the rustic brawl tradition and a satire on religious hypocrisy; *The Twa Dogs*, an urbane comical satire which draws on the old beast-fable convention and some of the varieties of pastoral, but whose form and style are indebted to Fergusson's city poem, *Plainstanes and Causey*; *The Cotter's Saturday Night*, which attempts something grander and more profound than its immediate stimulus, Fergusson's *Farmer's Ingle*; and *Halloween*, where the *Christis Kirk* stanza and conventions are pressed into the service of a delicately humorous but slightly aloof antiquarian observation. The class of poems excluded from the Kilmarnock volume is represented below by *Love and Liberty (The Jolly Beggars)*, that most vigorous and joyous expression of what George Orwell called 'humanity's unofficial self', which can also be regarded as the supreme masterpiece of the entire rustic brawl genre. Like *Love and Liberty*, *Tam o' Shanter* makes telling use of mock-heroic techniques. Burns himself called it his 'standard performance in the poetical line'; it is certainly one of the three or four best medium length narrative poems composed in the British Isles, and one of the very finest comic poems (Chaucer not excepted). We have rejected only one of Burns's longer poems, *The Brigs of Ayr*, primarily for reasons of space.

Modelled directly on Fergusson's dialogue poems, it does not improve on them to any extent.

*Editions:*

*Selected Poetry and Prose*, ed. R. D. Thornton (Boston, 1966).

*Poems and Songs*, ed. James Kinsley (Oxford English Texts, 3 vols, 1968; Oxford Standard Authors, 1 vol., 1969). Vol. III of the Oxford English Texts edition provides an invaluable commentary.

*Biography:*

Hans Hecht, *Robert Burns* (1919; English translation London, 1936, revised 1950).

F. B. Snyder, *The Life of Robert Burns* (New York, 1932).

J. DeLancey Ferguson, *Pride and Passion 1759–1796* (New York, 1939).

R. T. Fitzhugh, *Robert Burns* (Boston, 1971).

*Criticism:*

David Daiches, *Robert Burns* (London, 1952).

Thomas Crawford, *Burns: a Study of the Poems and Songs* (Edinburgh, 1960; reprinted with new introductions 1965 and 1978); *Society and the Lyric* (Edinburgh, 1979), Chapter 10 ('Burns, Love and Liberty').

Donald A. Low, ed., *Robert Burns: the Critical Heritage* (London, 1974); *Critical Essays on Robert Burns* (London, 1975).

James Kinsley, 'Burns and the Peasantry, 1785', *Proceedings of the British Academy*, 60 (1974), 135–53.

A. H. Maclaine, 'Radicalism and Conservatism in Burns's *The Jolly Beggars*', *Studies in Scottish Literature*, 13 (1978), 125–43.

R. D. S. Jack and Andrew Noble, eds, *The Art of Robert Burns* (London and Totowa, 1982).

Carol McGuirk, *Robert Burns and the Sentimental Era* (Athens, Georgia, 1985).

*Cassettes:*

*Poems of Robert Burns*, ed. Thomas Crawford, 3 cassettes (Scotsoun, Glasgow, 1977).

# THE VISION

## DUAN[n] FIRST

The sun had clos'd the winter day,
The curlers quat their roaring play,
An' hunger'd maukin taen her way
To kail-yards green,
While faithless snaws ilk step betray
Where she has been.

The thresher's weary flingin-tree,
The lee-lang day had tir'd me:
And when the day had clos'd his e'e,
Far i' the west,
Ben i' the spence, right pensivelie,
I gaed to rest.

There, lanely, by the ingle-cheek,
I sat and ey'd the spewing reek.
That fill'd, wi' hoast-provoking smeek,
The auld, clay biggin;
An' heard the restless rattons squeak
About the riggin.

All in this mottie, misty clime,
I backward mus'd on wasted time,
How I had spent my youthfu' prime,
An' done nae-thing,
But stringin blethers up in rhyme,
For fools to sing.

Had I to guid advice but harkit,
I might, by this, hae led a market,
Or strutted in a bank and clarkit
My cash-account:
While here, half-mad, half-fed, half-sarkit,
Is a' th' amount.

2 *quat*: left, abandoned
*roaring*: vigorous
3 *maukin*: hare
4 *kail-yards*: kitchen gardens
7 *flingin-tree*: striking part of a flail
8 *lee-lang*: live-long, all through (the day)
11 *ben*: inside
*spence*: parlour, inner room
13 *ingle-cheek*: corner of the fire
14 *reek*: smoke
15 *hoast*: cough
*smeek*: smoke
16 *clay biggin*: cottage of turf, or mud and wattle
17 *rattons*: rats
18 *riggin*: beams or boughs used in the roof
19 *mottie*: full of dust, or specks of soot
25 *harkit*: harkened
29 *sarkit*: shirted

I started, mutt'ring blockhead! coof!
And heav'd on high my waukit loof,
To swear by a' yon starry roof,
Or some rash aith,
That I, henceforth, would be *rhyme-proof*
Till my last breath—

When click! the string the snick did draw;
And jee! the door gaed to the wa';
And by my ingle-lowe I saw,
Now bleezin bright,
A tight, outlandish hizzie, braw,
Come full in sight.

Ye need na doubt, I held my whisht;
The infant aith, half-form'd was crusht;
I glowr'd as eerie's I'd been dusht
In some wild glen;
When sweet, like modest worth, she blusht,
An' stepped ben.

Green, slender, leaf-clad holly-boughs
Were twisted, gracefu', round her brows,
I took her for some Scottish muse,
By that same token;
And come to stop those reckless vows,
Would soon been broken.

A 'hare-brain'd, sentimental trace'
Was strongly marked in her face;
A wildly-witty, rustic grace
Shone full upon her;
Her eye, ev'n turn'd on empty space,
Beam'd keen with honor.

Down flow'd her robe, a tartan[n] sheen,
Till half a leg was scrimply seen;
And such a leg! my bonie Jean[n]
Could only peer it;
Sae straught, sae taper, tight and clean,
Nane else came near it.

31 *coof*: fool
32 *waukit*: rough, horny
*loof*: palm of hand
37 *snick*: latch
39 *ingle-lowe*: firelight
41 *tight*: neat, shapely
*hizzie*: young woman
43 *held . . . whisht*: stayed quiet
*glowr'd*: stared open-mouthed
45 *eerie*: 'frighted, *dreading spirits*' (B)
*dusht*: 'pushed by a ram, ox, etc.' (B)
57 *wildly-witty*: full of imaginative power
62 *scrimply*: barely
64 *peer*: equal
65 *straught*: straight
*taper*: slender
*clean*: shapely

Her mantle[n] large, of greenish hue,
My gazing wonder chiefly drew:
Deep lights and shades, bold-mingling, threw
A lustre grand;
And seem'd, to my astonish'd view,
A well-known land.[n]

Here, rivers in the sea were lost;
There, mountains to the skies were tost:
Here, tumbling billows mark'd the coast
With surging foam;
There, distant shone art's lofty boast,
The lordly dome.

Here,[n] Doon[n] pour'd down his far-fetch'd floods;
There, well-fed Irwine[n] stately thuds:
Auld hermit Ayr[n] staw thro' his woods,
On to the shore;
And many a lesser torrent scuds,
With seeming roar.

Low, in a sandy valley spread,
An ancient borough[n] rear'd her head;
Still, as in Scottish story read,
She boasts a race,
To ev'ry nobler virtue bred,
And polish'd grace.

By stately tow'r or palace fair,
Or ruins pendent on the air,
Bold stems of heroes, here and there,
I could discern;
Some seem'd to muse, some seem'd to dare,
With feature stern.

My heart did glowing transport feel,
To see a race[n] heroic wheel,
And brandish round, the deep-dy'd steel
In sturdy blows;
While back-recoiling seem'd to reel
Their suthron foes.

77 *art*: architectural knowledge and practical skill

78 *dome*: mansion-house or other large building

81 *staw*: stole

His *country's saviour*,[n] mark him well!
Bold Richardton's[n] heroic swell;
The Chief on Sark who glorious fell,[n]
In high command;
And he[n] whom ruthless fates expel
His native land.[n]

There, where a sceptred Pictish shade[n]
Stalk'd round his ashes lowly laid,
I mark'd a martial race[n], pourtray'd
In colours strong;
Bold, soldier-featur'd, undismay'd
They strode along.

Thro' many a wild, romantic grove[n],
Near many a hermit-fancy'd cove
(Fit haunts for friendship or for love,
In musing mood)
An aged judge, I saw him rove
Dispensing good.

With deep-struck, reverential awe,
The learned sire and son[n] I saw,
To nature's God and nature's law
They gave their lore,
This, all its source and end to draw,
That, to adore,

Brydon's brave ward[n] I well could spy,
Beneath old Scotia's smiling eye;
Who call'd on fame, low standing by,
To hand him on,
Where many a patriot-name on high
And hero shone.

## DUAN SECOND

With musing-deep, astonish'd stare,
I view'd the heavenly-seeming fair;
A whisp'ring throb did witness bear
Of kindred sweet,
When with an elder sister's air
She did me greet.

'All hail! my own inspired bard!
In me thy native muse regard!

Nor longer mourn thy fate is hard,
Thus poorly low
I come to give thee such reward
As we bestow.

'Know, the great genius of this land
Has many a light, aerial band[n],
Who, all beneath his high command,
Harmoniously,
As arts or arms they understand,
Their labors ply.

'They Scotia's race among them share;
Some fire the soldier on to dare;
Some rouse the patriot up to bare
Corruption's heart:
Some teach the bard, a darling care,
The tuneful art.

' 'Mong swelling floods of reeking gore,
They ardent, kindling spirits pour;
Or, mid the venal senate's roar,
They, sightless, stand,
To mend the honest patriot-lore,
And grace the hand.

'And when the bard, or hoary sage,
Charm or instruct the future age,
They bind the wild, poetic rage,
In energy,
Or point the inconclusive page
Full on the eye.

'Hence, Fullarton, the brave and young;
Hence, Dempster's[n] zeal-inspired tongue;
Hence, sweet harmonious Beattie[n] sung
His "Minstrel lays,"
Or tore, with noble ardour stung,
The sceptic's bays.

'To lower orders are assign'd
The humbler ranks of human-kind,
The rustic bard, the lab'ring hind,
The artisan;
All chuse, as, various they're inclin'd,
The various man.

'When yellow waves the heavy grain,
The threat'ning storm, some, strongly, rein;
Some teach to meliorate the plain,
With tillage-skill;
And some instruct the shepherd-train,
Blythe o'er the hill.

'Some hint the lover's harmless wile;
Some grace the maiden's artless smile;
Some soothe the lab'rer's weary toil,
For humble gains,
And make his cottage-scenes beguile
His cares and pains.

'Some, bounded to a district-space,
Explore at large man's infant race,
To mark the embryotic trace
Of rustic bard;
And careful note each op'ning grace,
A guide and guard.

'Of these am I — Coila my name;
And this district as mine I claim,
Where once the Campbells, chiefs of fame,
Held ruling pow'r[n]:
I mark'd thy embryo-tuneful flame,
Thy natal hour.

'With future hope, I oft would gaze,
Fond, on thy little, early ways,
Thy rudely-caroll'd chiming phrase,
In uncouth rhymes,
Fir'd at the simple, artless lays
Of other times.

'I saw thee seek the sounding shore,
Delighted with the dashing roar;
Or when the north his fleecy store
Drove thro' the sky,
I saw grim nature's visage hoar,
Struck thy young eye.

'Or when the deep green-mantled earth,
Warm-cherish'd ev'ry flow'ret's birth,
And joy and music pouring forth,
In ev'ry grove,
I saw thee eye the gen'ral mirth
With the boundless love.

'When ripen'd fields, and azure skies,
Call'd forth the reaper's rustling noise,
I saw thee leave their ev'ning joys,
And lonely stalk,
To vent thy bosom's swelling rise,
In pensive walk.

'When youthful love, warm-blushing, strong,
Keen-shivering shot thy nerves along,
Those accents, grateful to thy tongue,
Th' adored name,
I taught thee how to pour in song,
To soothe thy flame.

'I saw thy pulse's maddening play,
Wild-send thee pleasure's devious way,
Misled by fancy's meteor ray,
By passion driven;
But yet the light that led astray
Was light from heaven.

'I taught thy manners-painting[n] strains,
The loves, the ways of simple swains,
Till now, o'er all my wide domains,
Thy fame extends;
And some, the pride of Coila's plains,
Become thy friends.

'Thou canst not learn, nor can I show,
To paint with Thomson's landscape-glow;
Or wake the bosom-melting throe,
With Shenstone's art;
Or pour, with Gray, the moving flow,
Warm on the heart.

'Yet, all beneath th' unrivall'd rose,
The lowly daisy sweetly blows;
Tho' large the forest's monarch throws
His army shade,
Yet green the juicy hawthorn grows,
Adown the glade.

'Then never murmur nor repine;
Strive in thy humble sphere to shine;
And trust me, not Potosi's mine,[n]
Nor king's regard,
Can give a bliss o'ermatching thine,
A rustic bard.

'To give my counsels all in one,
Thy tuneful flame still careful fan;
Preserve the dignity of man,
With soul erect;
And trust, the universal plan
Will all protect.

'And wear thou this' — she solemn said,
And bound the holly round my head:
The polish'd leaves, and berries red,
Did rustling play;
And, like a passing thought, she fled
In light away.

## THE HOLY FAIR

*A robe of seeming truth and trust*
*Hid crafty observation;*
*And secret hung, with poison'd crust,*
*The dirk of defamation:*
*A mask that like the gorget show'd,*
*Dye-varying, on the pigeon;*
*And for a mantle large and broad,*
*He wrapt him in religion.*
HYPOCRISY A-LA-MODE[n]

Upon a simmer Sunday morn,
When nature's face is fair,
I walked forth to view the corn,
An' snuff the callor air.
The rising sun, ower Galston[n] muirs,
Wi' glorious light was glintan;
The hares were hirplan down the furrs,
The lav'rocks they were chantan
Fu' sweet that day.

As lightsomely I glowr'd abroad,
To see a scene sae gay,
Three hizzies, early at the road,
Cam skelpan up the way.

4 *callor*: fresh
7 *hirplan*: limping
*furrs*: furrows, ditches
8 *lav'rocks*: larks
12 *hizzies*: young women
13 *skelpan*: hurrying

Twa had manteeles o' dolefu' black,
  But ane wi' lyart lining;
The third, that gaed a wee aback,
  Was in the fashion shining
        Fu' gay that day.

The twa appear'd like sisters twin,
  In feature, form an' claes;
Their visage wither'd, lang an' thin,
  An' sour as ony slaes:
The third cam up, hap-step-an'-loup,
  As light as ony lambie,
An' wi' a curchie low did stoop,
  As soon as e'er she saw me,
        Fu' kind that day.

Wi' bonnet aff, quoth I, 'Sweet lass,
  I think ye seem to ken me;
I'm sure I've seen that bonie face,
  But yet I canna name ye.'
Quo' she, an' laughan as she spak,
  An' taks me by the han's,
'Ye, for my sake, hae gien the feck
  Of a' the ten comman's
        A screed some day.

'My name is *Fun*[n]— your cronie dear,
  The nearest friend ye hae;
An' this is *Superstition* here,
  An' that's *Hypocrisy*.
I'm gaun to Mauchline holy fair,
  To spend an hour in daffin:
Gin ye'll go there, yon runkl'd pair,
  We will get famous laughin
        At them this day.'

Quoth I, 'Wi' a' my heart, I'll do't;
  I'll get my sunday's sark on,
An' meet you on the holy spot;
  Faith, we'se hae fine remarkin!'

15 *lyart*: grey
25 *curchie*: curtsy
32 *laughan*: laughing
34 *feck*: most, the majority
36 *screed*: tear, gash, slash
37 *cronie*: close friend
42 *daffin*: fun, sport or play (esp. between sexes)
43 *gin*: if
*runkl'd*: wrinkled
47 *sark*: shirt
49 *we'se*: we shall
*remarkin*: spectacle, things to see

Then I gaed hame at crowdie-time,
  An' soon I made me ready;
For roads were clad, frae side to side,
  Wi' monie a wearie bodie,
      In droves that day.

Here, farmers gash, in ridin graith,
  Gaed hoddan by their cotters;
There, swankies young, in braw braid-claith,
  Are springan owre the gutters.
The lasses, skelpan barefit, thrang,
  In silks an' scarlets[n] glitter;
Wi' sweet-milk cheese, in monie a whang,
  An' farls, bak'd wi' butter,
      Fu' crump that day.

When by the plate we set our nose,
  Weel heaped up wi' ha'pence,
A greedy glowr black-bonnet throws,
  An' we maun draw our tippence.
Then in we go to see the show,
  On ev'ry side they're gath'ran;
Some carryan dails, some chairs an' stools,
  An' some are busy bleth'ran
      Right loud that day.

Here, stands a shed to fend the show'rs,
  An' screen our countra gentry;
There, racer Jess, an' twathree whores,
  Are blinkan at the entry.
Here sits a raw o' tittlan jads,
  Wi' heaving breasts an' bare neck;
An' there, a batch o' wabster lads,
  Blackguarding frae Kilmarnock
      For *fun* this day.

50 *crowdie-time*: porridge time, i.e. breakfast
53 *bodie*: person
55 *gash*: smart, well-turned out
*graith*: dress, gear
56 *hoddan*: jogging along on horseback
57 *swankie*: strapping lad
*braid-claith*: broad cloth
59 *thrang*: crowded
61 *whang*: chunk, thick slice
62 *farls*: quarters of an oat bannock
63 *crump*: dry, crisp
64 *plate:* plate for church collection
66 *black-bonnet*: the elder, who wears a Covenanting black bonnet
67 *maun*: must
*tippence*: twopence (a generous offering)
70 *dails*: deal planks
76 *blinkan*: gazing or glancing fondly, leering
77 *tittlan*: chatting emptily
*jads*: jades
*wabster*: weaver

Here, some are thinkan on their sins,
An' some upo' their claes;
Ane curses feet that fyl'd his shins,
Anither sighs an' prays:
On this hand sits a chosen[n] swatch,
Wi' screw'd-up, grace-proud faces;
On that, a set o' chaps, at watch,
Thrang winkan on the lasses
To chairs that day.

O happy is that man, an' blest![n]
Nae wonder that it pride him!
Whase ain dear lass, that he likes best,
Comes clinkan down beside him!
Wi' arm repos'd on the chair-back,
He sweetly does compose him;
Which, by degrees, slips round her neck,
An 's loof upon her bosom
Unkend that day.

Now a' the congregation o'er
Is silent expectation;
For Moodie[n] speels the holy door,
Wi' tidings o' damnation[n].
Should Hornie, as in ancient days,
'Mang sons o' God present him,
The vera sight o' Moodie's face,
To 's ain het hame had sent him
Wi' fright that day.

Hear how he clears the points o' faith
Wi' rattlin an' thumpin!
Now meekly calm, now wild in wrath,
He's stampan, an he's jumpan!
His lengthen'd chin, his turn'd up snout,
His eldritch squeel an' gestures,
O how they fire the heart devout,
Like cantharidian plaisters
On sic a day!

84 *fyl'd*: dirtied
86 *swatch*: sample, typical selection
94 *clinkan*: sitting down suddenly
98 *loof*: palm of hand
99 *unkend*: unnoticed
102 *speels*: climbs
104 *Hornie*: the devil
114 *eldritch*: strange
116 *cantharidian plaisters*: plasters from Spanish fly for medical use, also an aphrodisiac

But hark! the tent has chang'd its voice;
  There's peace an' rest nae langer;
For a' the *real judges* rise,
  They canna sit for anger.
Smith opens out his cauld harangues,
  On practice and on morals;
An' aff the godly pour in thrangs,
  To gie the jars an' barrels
    A lift that day.

What signifies his barren shine,
  Of moral pow'rs an' reason?
His English style, and gesture fine,
  Are a' clean out o' season,
Like Socrates or Antonine,
  Or some auld pagan heathen,
The moral man he does define,
  But ne'er a word o' faith in
    That's right that day.

In guid time comes an antidote
  Against sic poison'd nostrum;
For Peebles, frae the water-fit,
  Ascends the holy rostrum:
See, up he's got the word o' God,
  An' meek an' mim has view'd it,
While common-sense has taen the road,
  An' aff, an' up the Cowgate
    Fast, fast that day.

Wee Miller neist, the guard relieves,
  An' orthodoxy raibles,
Tho' in his heart he weel believes,
  An' thinks it auld wives' fables:
But faith! the birkie wants a manse,
  So, cannilie he hums them;
Altho' his carnal wit an' sense
  Like hafflins-wise o'ercomes him
    At times that day.

118 *tent*: 'a field pulpit' (B.)
131 *Antonine*: Marcus Aurelius Antoninus, Roman emperor (161–8) and stoic philosopher
137 *nostrum*: quack medicine
138 *water-fit*: mouth of river or burn
146 *raibles*: gabbles
149 *birkie*: lively fellow
150 *cannilie*: carefully
*hums*: humbugs
152 *hafflins-wise*: partly, nearly

Now, butt an' ben, the change-house fills,
Wi' yill-caup commentators:
Here's crying out for bakes an' gills,
An' there the pint-stowp clatters;
While thick an' thrang, an' loud an' lang,
Wi' Logic, an' wi' Scripture,
They raise a din, that, in the end,
Is like to breed a rupture
O' wrath that day.

Leeze me on drink! it gies us mair
Than either school or colledge:
It kindles wit, it waukens lear,
It pangs us fou o' knowledge.
Be't whisky-gill or penny-wheep,
Or ony stronger potion,
It never fails, on drinkin deep,
To kittle up our notion,
By night or day.

The lads an' lasses, blythely bent
To mind baith saul an' body,
Sit round the table, weel content,
An' steer about the toddy.
On this ane's dress, an' that ane's leuk,
They're makin observations;
While some are cozie i' the neuk,
An' forming assignations
To meet some day.

But now the Lord's ain trumpet[n] touts,
Till a' the hills are rairan,
An' echos back return the shouts;
Black Russel is na spairan:
His piercin words[n], like highlan swords,
Divide the joints an' marrow;
His talk o' hell, whare devils dwell,
Our vera 'Sauls does harrow'[n]
Wi' fright that day!

154 *butt*: outer room
*ben*: inner room
*change-house*: ale house
155 *yill-caup*: ale cup
156 *bakes*: biscuits
163 *Leeze me on*: literally, dear is to me; i.e. I like, am fond of
165 *waukens*: wakens
*lear*: learning, knowledge
166 *pangs*: fills, crams
167 *penny-wheep*: small beer
170 *kittle up*: rouse up
*notion*: understanding
175 *steer about*: keep circulating
*toddy*: a drink of whisky, hot water, sugar
176 *leuk*: appearance
178 *neuk*: corner
182 *rairan*: crying loudly

A vast, unbottom'd, boundless pit,
  Fill'd fou o' lowan brunstane,
Whase raging flame, an' scorching heat,
  Wad melt the hardest whun-stane!
The half asleep start up wi' fear,
  An' think they hear it roaran,
When presently it does appear,
  'Twas but some neebor snoran
          Asleep that day.

'Twad be owre lang a tale to tell,
  How monie stories past,
An' how they crouded to the yill,
  When they were a' dismist:
How drink gaed round, in cogs an' caups,
  Amang the furms an' benches;
An' cheese an' bread, frae women's laps,
  Was dealt about in lunches,
          An' dawds that day.

In comes a gawsie, gash guidwife,
  An' sits down by the fire,
Syne draws her kebbuck an' her knife;
  The lasses they are shyer.
The auld guidmen, about the grace,
  Frae side to side they bother,
Till some ane by his bonnet lays,
  An' gies them't, like a tether,
          Fu' lang that day.

Waesucks! for him that gets nae lass,
  Or lasses that hae naething!
Sma' need has he to say a grace,
  Or melvie his braw claithing!
O wives be mindfu', ance yoursel,
  How bonie lads ye wanted,
An' dinna, for a kebbuck-heel,
  Let lasses be affronted
          On sic a day!

191 *lowan*: burning, flaming
*brunstane*: brimstone
193 *whun-stane*: whinstone
203 *cogs*: wooden vessels girded with metal bands for drinking
*caups*: wooden bowls
204 *furms*: forms
206 *lunches*: large slices
207 *dawds*: hunks
208 *gawsie*: plump and jovial
210 *kebbuck*: cheese
217 *waesucks*: woe, alas
220 *melvie*: 'to soil with meal' (B.)

Now clinkumbell, wi' rattlan tow,
Begins to jow an' croon;
Some swagger hame, the best they dow,
Some wait the afternoon.
At slaps the billies halt a blink,
Till lasses strip their shoon:
Wi' *faith* an' *hope*, an' *love*[n] an' *drink*,
They're a' in famous tune
For crack that day.

How monie hearts this day converts,
O' sinners and o' lasses!
Their hearts o' stane, gin night, are gane
As saft as ony flesh is.[n]
There's some are fou o' love divine;
There's some are fou o' brandy;
An' monie jobs that day begin,
May end in houghmagandie
Some ither day.

226 *clinkumbell*: town bell
*rattlan*: talking
*tow*: bell-rope
227 *jow*: ring
*croon*: sing as a bell sings
228 *dow*: are able
230 *slaps*: gaps in walls, fences or hedges
*billies*: lads
*blink*: moment
231 *shoon*: shoes
234 *crack*: talk, gossip
242 *houghmagandie*: fornication

## THE TWA DOGS, A TALE

'Twas in that place o' Scotland's isle,
That bears the name o' auld King Coil,[n]
Upon a bonie day in June,
When wearing thro' the afternoon,
Twa dogs, that were na thrang at hame,
Forgather'd ance upon a time.

The first I'll name, they ca'd him *Caesar*,
Was keepet for his honor's pleasure;
His hair, his size, his mouth, his lugs,
Shew'd he was nane o' Scotland's dogs,
But whalpet some place far abroad,
Where sailors gang to fish for cod.

His locked, letter'd, braw brass-collar
Shew'd him the gentleman an' scholar;

1 *that place*: Kyle, a district of Ayrshire
5 *thrang*: busy
9 *lugs*: ears
11 *place . . . abroad*: Newfoundland

But tho' he was o' high degree,
The fient a pride na pride had he,
But wad hae spent an hour caressan,
Ev'n wi' a tinkler-gipsey's messan:
At kirk or market, mill or smiddie,
Nae tawted tyke, tho' e'er sae duddie,
But he wad stan't, as glad to see him,
An' stroan't on stanes an' hillocks wi' him.

The tither was a ploughman's collie,
A rhyming, ranting, raving billie,
Wha for his friend an' comrade had him,
And in his freaks had *Luath* ca'd him,
After some dog in Highland sang,
Was made lang syne, lord knows how lang.

He was a gash an' faithfu' tyke,
As ever lap a sheugh or dyke.
His honest, sonsie, baws'nt face,
Ay gat him friends in ilka place;
His breast was white, his towzie back,
Weel clad wi coat o' glossy black;
His gawsie tail, wi' upward curl,
Hung owre his hurdies wi' a swirl.

Nae doubt but they were fain o' ither,
An' unco pack an' thick thegither;
Wi' social nose whyles snuff'd an' snowket;
Whiles mice and modewurks they howket;
Whiles scour'd awa in lang excursion,
An' worry'd ither in diversion;
Till tir'd at last wi' mony a farce,
They set them down upon their arse,
An' there began a lang digression
About the lords o' the creation.

16 *fient a*: fient is specifically the devil; the phrase is an emphatic negative meaning not a bit.
18 *tinkler-gipsy*: gipsy who mends pots and pans
*messan*: pet (contemptuous) dog, as distinct from one kept for work
19 *smiddie*: blacksmith's
20 *tawted*: shaggy
*tyke*: cur, mongrel
*duddie*: ragged
21 *he wad stan't*: he would have stood
22 *stroan't*: pissed
23 *tither*: the other
24 *ranting*: uproariously merry
*billie*: fellow, lad
26 *freaks*: odd notions
27 *dog . . . sang*: 'Cuchullin's dog in Ossian's *Fingal*' (B.)
29 *gash*: shrewd
30 *lap*: leapt
*sheugh*: ditch
31 *sonsie*: good-natured
*baws'nt*: 'having a white stripe down the face' (B.)
32 *ilka*: each
33 *towzie*: unkempt, shaggy
35 *gawsie*: showy
36 *hurdies*: buttocks
37 *fain o' ither*: fond of each other
38 *pack*: 'intimate, familiar' (B.)
39 *snowket*: smelt about
40 *modewurks*: moles
*howket*: dug, delved
41 *scour'd awa*: ranged about

CAESAR

I've aften wonder'd, honest Luath,
What sort o' life poor dogs like you have;
An' when the gentry's life I saw,
What way poor bodies liv'd ava.

Our Laird gets in his racked rents[n],
His coals, his kane, an' a' his stents:
He rises when he likes himsel;
His flunkies answer at the bell;
He ca's his coach; he ca's his horse;
He draws a bonie, silken purse
As lang's my tail, whare thro' the steeks,
The yellow letter'd geordie keeks.

Frae morn to een it's nought but toiling,
At baking, roasting, frying, boiling;
An' tho' the gentry first are steghan,
Yet ev'n the ha' folk fill their peghan
Wi' sauce, ragouts, an' sic like trashtrie,
That's little short o' downright wastrie.
Our whipper-in, wee, blastet wonner,
Poor, worthless elf, it eats a dinner,
Better than ony tenant-man
His honor has in a' the lan':
An' what poor cot-folk pit their painch in,
I own it's past my comprehension.

LUATH

Trowth, Caesar, whyles they're fash't enough;[n]
A cotter howkan in a sheugh,
Wi' dirty stanes biggan a dyke,
Bairan a quarry, an' sic like,
Himsel, a wife, he thus sustains,
A smytrie o' wee, duddie weans,

50 *ava*: at all
51 *racked*: forced up, extortionate
52 *kane*: payment in kind
*stents*: duties
57 *steeks*: stitches
58 *geordie*: guinea (£1.05)
61 *steghan*: 'stuffing themselves'
62 *ha' folk*: servants, people who live in the 'big' house
*peghan*: stomach
63 *ragouts*: dishes of meat, cut in small pieces, stewed with vegetables and highly seasoned
*trashtrie*: trash, rubbish
64 *wastrie*: wastefulness, extravagance
65 *whipper-in*: orraman, odd-job man
69 *cot-folk*: smallholders who also work for wages
*painch*: stomach
71 *fash't*: bothered, troubled
72 *sheugh*: ditch
73 *biggan*: building
74 *bairan*: clearing

An' nought but his han'-daurk, to keep
Them right an' tight in thack an' raep.

An' when they meet wi' sair disasters,
Like loss o' health or want o' masters,
Ye maist wad think, a wee touch langer,
An' they maun starve o' cauld and hunger:
But how it comes, I never kent yet,
They're maistly wonderfu contented;
An' buirdly chiels, and clever hizzies,
Are bred in sic a way as this is.

CAESAR

But then, to see how ye're negleket,
How huff'd, an' cuff'd, an' disrespeket!
Lord man, our gentry care as little
For delvers, ditchers, an' sic cattle;
They gang as saucy by poor folk,
As I wad by a stinkan brock.

I've notic'd on our laird's court-day,
An' mony a time my heart's been wae,
Poor tenant bodies, scant o' cash,
How they maun thole a factor's snash;
He'll stamp an' threaten, curse an' swear,
He'll apprehend them, poind their gear;
While they maun stan', wi' aspect humble,
An' hear it a', an' fear an' tremble!

I see how folk live that hae riches;
But surely poor-folk maun be wretches!

LUATH

They're no sae wretched's ane wad think;
Tho' constantly on poortith's brink,
They're sae accustom'd wi' the sight,
The view o't gies them little fright.

76 *smytrie*: collection (somewhat contemptuous)
*weans*: wee ones, children
77 *han'daurk*: manual labour
78 *thack*: thatch; *raep*: rope; so the phrase means 'comfortably housed'
82 *maun*: must
85 *buirdly*: stalwart, powerful
*chiels*: young strapping fellows
*hizzies*: young women
86 *sic*: such
88 *huff'd*: scolded
90 *delvers*: diggers, labourers
92 *stinkan*: stinking
*brock*: badger
93 *court-day*: rent-day
95 *bodies*: people
96 *thole*: suffer, put up with
*snash*: abuse
98 *poind:* distrain
*gear*: goods and chattels
104 *poortith*: poverty

Then chance and fortune are sae guided,
They're ay in less or mair provided;
An' tho' fatigu'd wi' close employment,
A blink o' rest's a sweet enjoyment.

The dearest comfort o' their lives,
Their grushie weans an' faithfu' wives;
The prattling things are just their pride,
That sweetens a' their fire side.

An' whyles twalpennie-worth o' nappy
Can mak the bodies unco happy;
They lay aside their private cares,
To mind the kirk and state affairs;
They'll talk o' patronage an' priests,[n]
Wi' kindling fury i' their breasts,
Or tell what new taxation's comin,
An' ferlie at the folk in Lon'on.

As bleak-fac'd Hallowmass returns,
They get the jovial, rantan kirns,
When rural life, of ev'ry station,
Unite in common recreation;
Love blinks, wit slaps, an' social mirth
Forgets there's care upo' the earth.

That merry day the year begins,
They bar the door on frosty win's;
The nappy reeks wi' mantling ream,
An' sheds a heart-inspiring steam;
The luntan pipe, an' sneeshin mill,
Are handed round wi' right guid will;
The cantie, auld folks, crackan crouse,
The young anes rantan thro' the house —
My heart has been sae fain to see them,
That I for joy hae barket wi' them.

Still it's owre true that ye hae said,
Sic game is now owre aften play'd;
There's monie a creditable stock[n]
O' decent, honest, fawsont folk,

112 *grushie*: thriving
115 *twalpennie-worth*: twelve-penny worth
*nappy*: ale
122 *ferlie*: wonder
123 *Hallowmass*: 1 November, i.e. harvest
124 *kirns*: harvest celebrations
127 *blinks*: glances
*slaps*: is sharp
131 *reeks*: smokes
*mantling*: foaming
*ream*: froth
133 *luntan*: smoking
*sneeshin mill*: snuff mill or horn
135 *cantie*: lively
*crackan*: chatting
*crouse*: merrily
142 *fawsont*: 'decent, seemly' (B.)

Are riven out baith root an' branch,
Some rascal's pridefu' greed to quench,
Wha thinks to knit himsel the faster
In favor wi' some gentle master,
Wha aiblins thrang a parliamentin,
For Britain's guid his saul indentin —

CAESAR

Haith lad ye little ken about it;
*For Britain's guid!* — guid faith! I doubt it.
Say rather, gaun as premiers lead him,[n]
An' saying aye or no's they bid him:
At operas an' plays parading,
Mortgaging, gambling, masquerading:
Or maybe, in a frolic daft,
To Hague or Calais takes a waft,
To make a tour[n] an' tak a whirl,
To learn bon ton and see the worl'.

There, at Vienna or Versailles,
He rives his father's auld entails;[n]
Or by Madrid he takes the rout,
To thrum guittars an' fecht wi' nowt;
Or down Italian vista startles,
Whore-hunting amang groves o' myrtles:[n]
Then bowses drumlie German-water,
To mak himsel look fair and fatter,
An' purge the bitter ga's an' cankers,
O' curst Venetian bores an' chancres.

*For Britain's guid!* for her destruction!
Wi' dissipation, feud, an' faction!

LUATH

Hech man! dear sirs! is that the gate,
They waste sae mony a braw estate!
Are we sae foughten and harass'd
For gear to gang that gate at last!

143 *riven*: torn
147 *aiblins*: perhaps
148 *indentin*: binding, pledging
149 *haith*: 'a petty oath' (B.)
151 *gaun*: going
156 *waft*: sea trip
157 *whirl*: rapid trip
160 *rives*: breaks apart
162 *fecht*: fight
*nowt*: cattle
165 *bowses*: booses
*drumlie*: cloudy
168 *bores*: holes
*chancres*: venereal ulcers
171 *gate*: way
173 *foughten*: pa. pple. of fecht, here worn out, harassed

O would they stay aback frae courts,
An' please themsels wi' countra sports,[n]
It wad for ev'ry ane be better,
The laird, the tenant, an' the cotter!
For thae frank, rantan, ramblan billies,
Fient haet o' them 's ill hearted fellows;
Except for breakin o' their timmer,
Or speakin lightly o' their limmer,
Or shootin of a hare or moorcock,
The ne'er-a-bit they're ill to poor folk.

But will ye tell me, master Caesar,
Sure great folk's life's a life o' pleasure?
Nae cauld nor hunger e'er can steer them,
The vera thought o't need na fear them.

CAESAR

Lord man, were ye but whyles where I am,
The gentles ye wad ne'er envy them!

It's true, they need na starve or sweat,
Thro' winter's cauld, or summer's heat;
They've nae sair-wark to craze their banes,
An' fill auld-age wi' grips an' granes;
But human-bodies are sic fools,
For a' their colledges an' schools,
That when nae *real* ills perplex them,
They *mak* enow themsels to vex them;
An' ay the less they hae to sturt them,
In like proportion, less will hurt them.

A country fellow at the pleugh,
His acre's till'd, he's right eneugh;
A country girl at her wheel,
Her dizzen's done, she's unco weel;
But gentlemen, an' ladies warst,
Wi' ev'n down want o' wark are curst.
They loiter, lounging, lank an' lazy;
Tho' deil-haet ails them, yet uneasy;
Their days, insipid, dull an' tasteless,
Their nights, unquiet, lang an' restless.

181 *timmer*: timber
182 *limmer*: mistress, whore
187 *steer*: affect
193 *sair-work*: hard labour
194 *grips*: gripes, sharp pains
199 *sturt*: trouble
204 *dizzen*: a dozen cuts of yarn (each 310 yards) was the standard of a day's spinning
207 *lank*: languid
208 *deil-haet*: damn-all

An' ev'n their sports, their balls an' races,
Their galloping thro' public places,
There's sic parade, sic pomp an' art,
The joy can scarcely reach the heart.[n]

The men cast out in party-matches,
Then sowther a' in deep debauches.
Ae night, they're mad wi' drink an' whoring,
Niest day their life is past enduring.

The ladies arm-in-arm in clusters,
As great an' gracious a' as sisters;
But hear their absent thoughts o' ither,
They're a' run deils an' jads thegither.
Whyles, owre the wee bit cup an' platie,
They sip the scandal-potion pretty;
Or lee-lang nights, wi' crabbit leuks,
Pore owre the devil's pictur'd beuks;
Stake on a chance a farmer's stackyard,
An' cheat like ony unhang'd blackguard.

There's some exceptions, man an' woman;
But this is gentry's life in common.

By this, the sun was out o' sight,
An' darker gloamin brought the night:
The bum-clock humm'd wi' lazy drone,
The kye stood rowtan i' the loan;
When up they gat an' shook their lugs,
Rejoic'd they were na *men* but *dogs*;
An' each took off his several way,
Resolv'd to meet some ither day.

215 *sowther*: solder, settle
216 *ae*: one
217 *niest*: next
222 *run deils*: thorough going devils
*jads*: jades
*thegither*: together
223 *wee bit cup*: tea cup
225 *lee-lang*: whole
*crabbet*: crabbed, ill-natured
*leuks*: looks
226 *devil's . . . beuks*: playing cards
232 *gloamin*: twilight
233 *bum-clock*: 'a humming beetle that flies in the summer evening' (B.)
234 *kye*: cows
*rowtan*: lowing
*loan*: strip of grass in arable land that acts as a path

## THE COTTER'S SATURDAY NIGHT

Inscribed to R. Aiken, Esq.

*Let not ambition mock their useful toil,*
*Their homely joys, and destiny obscure;*
*Nor grandeur hear, with a disdainful smile,*
*The short and simple annals of the poor.*
GRAY.[n]

My lov'd, my honor'd, much respected friend,[n]
No mercenary bard his homage pays;
With honest pride, I scorn each selfish end,
My dearest meed, a friend's esteem and praise:[n]
To you I sing, in simple Scottish lays,
The lowly train in life's sequester'd scene;
The native feelings strong, the guileless ways,
What Aiken in a cottage would have been;
Ah! tho' his worth unknown, far happier there I ween!

November chill blaws loud wi' angry sugh;
The short'ning winter-day is near a close;
The miry beasts retreating frae the pleugh;
The black'ning trains o' craws to their repose:
The toil-worn cotter frae his labor goes,
This night his weekly moil is at an end,
Collects his spades, his mattocks and his hoes,
Hoping the morn in ease and rest to spend,
And weary, o'er the moor, his course does hameward bend.

At length his lonely cot appears in view,
Beneath the shelter of an aged tree;
The expectant wee-things, toddlan, stacher through
To meet their dad, wi' flichterin noise and glee.
His wee-bit ingle, blinkan bonilie,
His clean hearth-stane, his thrifty wifie's smile,
The lisping infant, prattling on his knee,
Does a' his weary kiaugh and care beguile,
An' makes him quite forget his labor and his toil.

4 *meed*: reward
9 *ween*: think, suppose
10 *sugh*: sighing or moaning noise made by wind
12 *pleugh*: plough
14 *cotter*: a smallholder, renting perhaps only two acres
15 *moil*: toil, drudgery
16 *mattocks*: instruments for digging similar to picks, but the blades having one pointed and one broad end.
19 *cot*: cottage
21 *stacher*: totter, walk unsteadily
22 *flichterin*: fluttering 'as young nestlings when their dam approaches' (B.)
23 *wee-bit ingle*: little bit of a fire (burning on hearth)
26 *kiaugh*: 'carking anxiety' (B.)

Belyve, the elder bairns come drapping in,
At service out, amang the farmers roun';
Some ca' the pleugh, some herd, some tentie rin
A cannie errand to a neebor town:
Their eldest hope, their Jenny, woman-grown,
In youthfu' bloom, love sparkling in her e'e,
Comes hame, perhaps, to shew a braw new gown,
Or deposite her sair-won penny-fee,
To help her parents dear, if they in hardship be.

With joy unfeign'd, brothers and sisters meet,
And each for other's weelfare kindly spiers:
The social hours, swift-wing'd, unnotic'd fleet;
Each tells the uncos that he sees or hears.
The parents partial eye their hopeful years;
Anticipation forward points the view;
The mother, wi' her needle an' her sheers,
Gars auld claes look amaist as weel's the new;
The father mixes a' wi' admonition due.

Their master's and their mistress's command,
The youngkers a' are warned to obey;
And mind their labors wi' an eydent hand,
And ne'er, tho' out o' sight, to jauk or play:
'And O! be sure to fear the Lord[n] alway!
And mind your duty, duely, morn and night!
Lest in temptation's path ye gang astray,
Implore his counsel and assisting might:
They never sought in vain that sought the Lord aright.'

But hark! a rap comes gently to the door;
Jenny, wha kens the meaning o' the same,
Tells how a neebor lad came o'er the moor,
To do some errands, and convoy her hame.
The wily mother sees the conscious flame
Sparkle in Jenny's e'e, and flush her cheek,
With heart-struck, anxious care enquires his name,
While Jenny hafflins is afraid to speak;
Weel-pleas'd the mother hears, it's nae wild, worthless rake.

28 *belyve*: quickly
29 *service*: domestic service
30 *ca'*: drive
*tentie*: careful
31 *cannie*: requiring care
*neebor*: neighbouring
*town*: group of farm dwellings
33 e'e: eye
35 *penny-fee*: wages
38 *spiers*: asks
39 *fleet*: hurry
40 *uncos*: strange happenings
43 *sheers*: scissors
44 *gars*: makes
*claes*: clothes
*amaist*: almost
47 *youngkers*: youngsters
48 *mind*: attend to
*eydent*: diligent
49 *jauk*: waste time
62 *hafflins*: nearly

With kindly welcome, Jenny brings him ben;
  A strappan youth; he takes the mother's eye;
Blythe Jenny sees the visit's no ill taen;
  The father cracks of horses, pleughs and kye.
  The youngster's artless heart o'erflows wi' joy,
But blate and laithfu', scarce can weel behave;
  The mother, wi' a woman's wiles, can spy
What makes the youth sae bashfu' and sae grave;
Weel-pleas'd to think her bairn's respected like the lave.

O happy love! where love like this is found!
  O heart-felt raptures! bliss beyond compare!
I've paced much this weary, mortal round,
  And sage experience bids me this declare —
  'If heaven a draught of heavenly pleasure spare,
One cordial in this melancholy vale,
  'Tis when a youthful, loving, modest pair,
In other's arms, breathe out the tender tale,
Beneath the milk-white thorn that scents the ev'ning gale.'

Is there, in human form, that bears a heart —
  A wretch! a villain! lost to love and truth!
That can, with studied, sly, ensnaring art,
  Betray sweet Jenny's unsuspecting youth?
  Curse on his perjur'd arts! dissembling smooth!
Are honor, virtue, conscience, all exil'd?
  Is there no pity, no relenting ruth,
Points to the parents fondling o'er their child?
Then paints the ruin'd maid, and their distraction wild!

But now the supper crowns their simple board,
  The healsome porritch, chief of Scotia's food:
The soupe their only hawkie does afford,
  That 'yont the hallan snugly chows her cood:
  The dame brings forth, in complimental mood,
To grace the lad, her weel-hain'd kebbuck, fell,
  And aft he's prest, and aft he ca's it guid;
The frugal wifie, garrulous, will tell,
How 'twas a towmond auld, sin' lint was i' the bell.

64 *ben*: into the inner room
67 *cracks*: chats
*kye*: cattle
69 *blate*: bashful, diffident
*laithfu'*: 'bashful, sheepish' (B.)
72 *lave*: rest
92 *healsome*: wholesome
93 *soupe*: what they *sup*, i.e. milk
*hawkie*: pet cow
94 *yont*: beyond
*hallan*: partition between living room and byre
*chows*: chews
*cood*: cud
96 *weel-hain'd:* well-preserved
*kebbuck*: cheese
*fell*: strong
97 *prest*: pressed
99 *towmond*: twelve months
*lint . . . bell*: the flax plant was in flower

The chearfu' supper done, wi' serious face,
 They, round the ingle, form a circle wide;
The sire turns o'er, with patriarchal grace,
 The big ha'-bible, ance his father's pride:
 His bonnet rev'rently is laid aside,
His lyart haffets wearing thin and bare;
 Those strains that once did sweet in Zion[n] glide,
He wales a portion with judicious care;
'And let us worship God!'[n] he says with solemn air.

They chant their artless notes in simple guise;
 They tune their hearts, by far the noblest aim:
Perhaps Dundee's[n] wild warbling measures rise,
 Or plaintive Martyrs, worthy of the name;
 Or noble Elgin beets the heaven-ward flame,
The sweetest far of Scotia's holy lays:
 Compar'd with these, Italian trills are tame;
The tickl'd ears no heart-felt raptures raise;
Nae unison hae they, with our creator's praise.

The priest-like father reads the sacred page,
 How Abram was the friend of God on high;
Or, Moses bade eternal warfare wage,
 With Amalek's ungracious progeny;
 Or how the royal bard did groaning lye,
Beneath the stroke of heaven's avenging ire;
 Or Job's pathetic plaint, and wailing cry;
Or rapt Isaiah's wild, seraphic fire;
Or other holy seers that tune the sacred lyre.[n]

Perhaps the christian volume is the theme,
 How guiltless blood for guilty man was shed;
How he, who bore in heaven the second name,
 Had not on earth whereon to lay his head:
 How his first followers and servants sped;
The precepts sage they wrote to many a land:
 How he, who lone in Patmos banished,
Saw in the sun a mighty angel stand;
And heard great Bab'lon's doom pronounc'd by heaven's
 command.

103 *ha'-bible*: hall bible, large bible
105 *lyart haffets*: grey hair on temples
107 *wales*: chooses
122 *royal bard*: King David, described in the Bible as author of the psalms
127 *christian volume*: new testament
129 *he . . . name*: Christ
131 *How . . . sped*: refers to the Acts of the Apostles
132 *precepts sage*: in the epistles
133 *he . . . banished*: John, whose Revelation (the last book of the Bible) describes allegorically the last judgment

Then kneeling down to heaven's eternal king,
The saint, the father, and the husband prays:
Hope 'springs exulting on triumphant wing,'[n]
That thus they all shall meet in future days:
There, ever bask in uncreated rays,[n]
No more to sigh, or shed the bitter tear,
Together hymning their creator's praise,
In such society, yet still more dear;
While circling time moves round in an eternal sphere.

Compar'd with this, how poor religion's pride,
In all the pomp of method, and of art,
When men display to congregations wide,
Devotion's ev'ry grace, except the heart!
The power, incens'd, the pageant will desert,
The pompous strain, the sacredotal stole;
But haply, in some cottage far apart,
May hear, well pleas'd, the language of the soul;
And in his book of life[n] the inmates poor enroll.

Then homeward all take off their sev'ral way;
The youngling cottagers retire to rest:
The parent-pair their secret homage pay,
And proffer up to heaven the warm request,
That he who stills the raven's clam'rous nest,
And decks the lily fair in flow'ry pride,
Would, in the way his wisdom sees the best,
For them and for their little ones provide;
But chiefly, in their hearts with grace divine preside.

From scenes like these, old Scotia's grandeur springs,
That makes her lov'd at home, rever'd abroad:
Princes and lords are but the breath of kings,
'An honest man's the noble work of God:'[n]
And certes, in fair virtue's heavenly road,
The cottage leaves the palace far behind:
What is a lordling's pomp? a cumbrous load,
Disguising oft the wretch of human kind,
Studied in arts of hell, in wickedness refin'd!

O Scotia! my dear, my native soil!
For whom my warmest wish to heaven is sent!
Long may thy hardy sons of rustic toil,
Be blest with health, and peace, and sweet content!
And O may heaven their simple lives prevent
From luxury's[n] contagion, weak and vile!
Then howe'er crowns and coronets be rent,

A virtuous populace may rise the while,
And stand a wall of fire around their much-loved isle.

O thou! who pour'd the patriotic tide,
That stream'd thro' great, unhappy Wallace'[n] heart;
Who dar'd to, nobly, stem tyrannic pride,
Or nobly die, the second glorious part:
(The patriot's God, peculiarly thou art,
His friend, inspirer, guardian, and reward!)
O never, never Scotia's realm desert,
But still the patriot, and the patriot-bard,
In bright succession raise, her ornament and guard!

## HALLOWEEN

The following poem will, by many readers, be well enough understood; but, for the sake of those who are unacquainted with the manners and traditions of the country where the scene is cast, notes are added, to give some account of the principal charms and spells of that night, so big with prophecy to the peasantry in the west of Scotland. The passion of prying into futurity makes a striking part of the history of human-nature, in its rude state, in all ages and nations; and it may be some entertainment to a philosophic mind, if any such should honor the author with a perusal, to see the remains of it, among the more unenlightened in our own.

*Yes! let the rich deride, the proud disdain,*
*The simple pleasures of the lowly train;*
*To me more dear, congenial to my heart,*
*One native charm, than all the gloss of art.*
GOLDSMITH

Upon that night, when fairies light,
On Cassilis Downans[n] dance,
Or owre the lays, in splendid blaze,
On sprightly coursers prance;
Or for Colean,[n] the rout is taen,
Beneath the moon's pale beams;
There, up the Cove,[n] to stray an' rove,
Amang the rocks an' streams
To sport that night.

3 *lays*: (= leas) untilled ground that has been left fallow for some time

5 *rout*: way

Amang the bonie, winding banks,
   Where Doon[n] rins, wimplin', clear,
Where Bruce[n] ance rul'd the martial ranks,
   An' shook his Carrick spear,
Some merry, friendly, countra folks,
   Together did convene,
To burn their nits, an' pou their stocks,
   An' haud their halloween
         Fu' blythe that night.

The lasses feat, an' cleanly neat,
   Mair braw than when they're fine;
Their faces blythe, fu' sweetly kythe,
   Hearts leal, an' warm, an' kin':
The lads sae trig, wi' wooer-babs,
   Weel knotted on their garten,
Some unco blate, an' some wi' gabs,
   Gar lasses' hearts gang startin
         Whyles fast at night.

Then, first an' foremost, thro' the kail,
   Their stocks[n] maun a' be sought ance;
They steek their een, an' grape an' wale,
   For muckle anes, an' straught anes.
Poor hav'rel Will fell aff the drift,
   An' wander'd thro' the bow-kail,
An' pow't, for want o' better shift,
   A runt was like a sow-tail
         Sae bow't that night.

Then, straught or crooked, yird or nane,
   They roar an' cry a' throw'ther;
The vera wee-things, toddlan, rin,
   Wi' stocks out owre their shouther:

11 *wimplin*: twisting
16 *nits*: nuts
*pou*: pull
*stocks*: plants, stems
17 *haud*: hold
19 *feat*: spruce, tidy
21 *kythe*: make known
22 *leal*: loyal, faithful
23 *trig*: neat, smart
*wooer-babs*: double-looped knots (or garters) below the knee, a sign of the wearer's intention to propose marriage
24 *garten*: garter(s)
25 *blate*: shy, retiring
*gabs*: bold chatter
26 *gar*: make
27 *whyles*: at times
30 *steek*: close
*een*: eyes
*grape*: grope, feel for
*wale*: choose
31 *straught*: straight
32 *hav'rel*: simpleton
*fell . . . drift*: fell behind
33 *bow-kail*: cabbage
34 *pow't*: pulled
35 *runt*: cabbage stalk
36 *bow't*: bent
37 *yird*: earth
38 *throw'ther*: through each other, i.e. in confusion
39 *vera*: very
40 *shouther*: shoulders

An' gif the custock's sweet or sour,
Wi' joctelegs they taste them;
Syne coziely, aboon the door,
Wi' cannie care, they've plac'd them
To lye that night.

The lasses staw frae 'mang them a',
To pou their stalks o' corn[n];
But Rab slips out, an' jinks about,
Behint the muckle thorn:
He grippet Nelly hard an' fast;
Loud skirl'd a' the lasses;
But her tap-pickle maist was lost,
When kiutlan in the fause-house[n]
Wi' him that night.

The auld guidwife's weel-hoordet nits[n]
Are round an' round divided,
An' monie lads' an' lasses' fates
Are there that night decided:
Some kindle, couthie, side by side,
An' burn thegither trimly;
Some start awa, wi' saucy pride,
An' jump out owre the chimlie
Fu' high that night.

Jean slips in twa, wi' tentie e'e;
Wha 'twas, she wadna tell;
But this is *Jock*, an' this is *me*,
She says in to hersel:
He bleez'd owre her, an' she owre him,
As they wad never mair part,
Till fuff! he started up the lum,
An' Jean had e'en a sair heart
To see't that night.

Poor Willie, wi' his bow-kail runt,
Was brunt wi' primsie Mallie;
An' Mary, nae doubt, took the drunt,
To be compar'd to Willie:

41 *gif*: if
*custock*: kale or cabbage stalk
42 *joctelegs*: clasp knives
43 *syne*: then
*aboon*: above
46 *staw*: steal away
48 *jinks about*: dodges round
51 *skirl'd*: shouted
52 *tap-pickle*: grain at the end of the stalk (with sexual innuendo)
53 *kiutlan*: 'cuddling, caressing, fondling' (B.)
*fausehouse*: conical wooden frame inside a stack of corn
55 *weel-hoordet*: well hoarded
59 *couthie*: warmly, sociably
60 *thegither*: together
62 *chimlie*: fire place, hearth
64 *tentie*: watchful, careful
68 *bleez'd*: blazed
70 *lum*: chimney
74 *brunt*: burnt
*primsie*: 'demure, precise' (B.)
75 *drunt*: sulks

Mall's nit lap out, wi' pridefu' fling,
An' her ain fit, it brunt it;
While Willie lap, an' swoor by jing,
'Twas just the way he wanted
To be that night.

Nell had the fause-house in her min',
She pits hersel an' Rob in;
In loving bleeze they sweetly join,
Till white in ase they're sobbin:
Nell's heart was dancin at the view;
She whisper'd Rob to leuk for't:
Rob, stownlins, prie'd her bonie mou,
Fu' cozie in the neuk for't,
Unseen that night.

But Merran sat behint their backs,
Her thoughts on Andrew Bell;
She lea'es them gashan at their cracks,
An' slips out by hersel:
She thro' the yard the nearest taks,
An' for the kiln she goes then,
An' darklins grapet for the bauks,
And in the blue-clue[n] throws then,
Right fear't that night.

An' ay she win't, an' ay she swat,
I wat she made nae jaukin;
Till something held within the pat,
Guid Lord! but she was quaukin!
But whether 'twas the deil himsel,
Or whether 'twas a bauk-en',
Or whether it was Andrew Bell,
She did na wait on talkin
To spier that night.

Wee Jenny to her graunie says,
'Will ye go wi' me, graunie?
I'll eat the apple[n] at the glass,
I gat frae uncle Johnie:'

77 *lap*: leaped
78 *fitt*: foot
79 *swoor*: swore
85 *ase*: ash
88 *stownlins*: secretly
*prie'd*: tasted
*mou*: mouth
89 *neuk*: corner
93 *gashan*: chatting
*cracks*: gossip, talk
96 *kiln*: for drying grain
*darklins*: in the dark
*grapet*: groped
*bauks*: balks, cross beams
98 *blue-clue*: ball of blue wool used for divining
99 *fear't*: frightened
100 *win't*: wound
*swat*: sweated
101 *I wat*: I know, I'm sure
*jaukin*: delay
102 *pat*: pot
103 *quaukin*: quaking
108 *spier*: ask
111 *glass*: mirror

She fuff't her pipe wi' sic a lunt,
In wrath she was sae vap'rin,
She notic't na, an aizle brunt
Her braw, new, worset apron
Out thro' that night.

'Ye little skelpie-limmer's-face!
I daur you try sic sportin,
As seek the foul thief onie place,
For him to spae your fortune:
Nae doubt but ye may get a sight!
Great cause ye hae to fear it;
For monie a ane has gotten a fright,
An' liv'd an' di'd deleeret,
On sic a night.

'Ae hairst afore the Sherra-moor,[n]
I mind't as weel's yestreen,
I was a gilpey then, I'm sure,
I was na past fyfteen:
The simmer had been cauld an' wat,
An stuff was unco green;
An' ay a rantan kirn we gat,
An' just on Halloween
It fell that night.

'Our stibble-rig was Rab M'Graen,
A clever, sturdy fallow;
His sin gat Eppie Sim wi' wean,
That liv'd in Achmacalla:
He gat hemp-seed[n], I mind it weel,
An' he made unco light o't;
But monie a day was by himsel,
He was sae sairly frighted
That vera night.'

Then up gat fechtan Jamie Fleck,
An' he swoor by his conscience,
That he could saw hemp-seed a peck;
For it was a' but nonsense:

113 *fuff't*: puffed
*sic*: such
*lunt*: puff of smoke
114 *vap'rin*: fuming
115 *aizle*: ember (from her pipe)
118 *skelpie-limmer*: hussy
119 *daur*: dare
*sportin*: jesting
120 *foul thief*: devil
121 *spae*: divine
125 *deleeret*: delirious
127 *hairst*: harvest
128 *mind*: remember
*yestreen*: yesterday
129 *gilpey*: young girl
132 *stuff*: grain
133 *ay*: always
*kirn*: harvest celebration
136 *stibble-rig*: 'the reaper who takes the lead' (B.)
138 *wean*: child
145 *fechtan*: fighting, argumentative

The auld guidman raught down the pock,
  An' out a handfu' gied him;
Syne bad him slip frae 'mang the folk,
  Sometime when nae ane see'd him,
      An' try't that night.

He marches thro' amang the stacks,
  Tho' he was something sturtan;
The graip he for a harrow taks,
  An' haurls at his curpan:
And ev'ry now an' then, he says,
  'Hemp-seed I saw thee,
An' her that is to be my lass,
  Come after me an' draw thee
      As fast this night.'

He whistled up lord Lenox' march,
  To keep his courage cheary;
Altho' his hair began to arch,
  He was sae fley'd an' eerie:
Till presently he hears a squeak,
  An' then a grane an' gruntle;
He by his showther gae a keek,
  An' tumbl'd wi' a wintle
      Out owre that night.

He roar'd a horrid murder-shout,
  In dreadfu' desperation!
An' young an' auld come rinnan out,
  An' hear the sad narration;
He swoor 'twas hilchan Jean M'Craw,
  Or crouchie Merran Humphie,
Till stop! she trotted thro' them a';
  An' wha was it but Grumphie
      Asteer that night?

Meg fain wad to the barn gaen,
  To winn three wechts o' naething;[n]
But for to meet the deil her lane,
  She pat but little faith in:

149 *raught*: reached
*pock*: poke
155 *sturtan*: afraid
156 *graip*: fork for digging
157 *haurls*: drags
*curpan*: rump
166 *fley'd*: frightened
*eerie*: 'frighted, *dreading spirits*' (B.)
168 *grane*: groan
*gruntle*: grunt
169 *keek*; glance
170 *wintle*: 'a wavering, swinging motion' (B.)
176 *hilchan*: limping
177 *crouchie*: hump-backed
179 *grumphie*: the sow
182 *winn*: winnow
*wechts*: sievefuls
183 *her lane*: alone

She gies the herd a pickle nits,
An' twa red cheeket apples,
To watch, while for the barn she sets,
In hopes to see Tam Kipples
That vera night.

She turns the key, wi' cannie thraw,
An' owre the threshold ventures;
But first on Sawnie gies a ca',
Syne bauldly in she enters:
A ratton rattl'd up the wa',
An' she cry'd, 'Lord preserve her!'
An' ran thro' midden-hole an' a',
An' pray'd wi' zeal and fervour,
Fu' fast that night.

They hoy't out Will, wi' sair advice;
They hecht him some fine braw ane;
It chanc'd the stack he faddom't thrice,[n]
Was timmer-propt for thrawin:
He taks a swirlie, auld moss-oak,
For some black, grousome carlin;
An' loot a winze, an' drew a stroke,
Till skin in blypes cam haurlin
Aff's nieves that night.

A wanton widow Leezie was,
As cantie as a kittlen;
But och! that night, amang the shaws,
She gat a fearfu' settlin!
She thro' the whins, an' by the cairn,
An' owre the hill gaed scrievin,
Whare three lairds' lan's met at a burn,[n]
To dip her left sark-sleeve in,
Was bent that night.

190 *cannie*: careful
*thraw*: turn
192 *Sawnie*: short for Alexander, here the devil
194 *ratton*: rat
199 *hoy't*: summoned
200 *hecht*: promised
201 *faddom't*: measured by the fathom, i.e. with outstretched arms.
202 *timmer . . . thrawin*: propped with timber to keep it straight
203 *swirlie*: 'knaggy, full of knots' (B.)
204 *carlin*: old woman, witch
205 *loot*: let out
*winze*: curse
206 *blypes*: shreds
*haurlin*: peeling
207 *nieves*: fists
209 *cantie*: lively
*kittlen*: kitten
210 *shaws*: 'a small wood in a hollow place' (B.)
211 *settlin*: putting down, reducing to silence
212 *whins*: gorse
213 *scrievin*: gliding swiftly along (B.)
215 *sark*: shirt

Whyles owre a linn the burnie plays,
  As thro' the glen it wimpl't;
Whyles round a rocky scar it strays;
  Whyles in a wiel it dimpl't;
Whyles glitter'd to the nightly rays,
  Wi' bickerin, dancin dazzle;
Whyles cocket underneath the braes,
  Below the spreading hazle
      Unseen that night.

Amang the brachens, on the brae,
  Between her an' the moon,
The deil, or else an outler quey,
  Gat up an' gae a croon:
Poor Leezie's heart maist lap the hool;
  Near lav'rock-height she jumpet,
But mist a fit, an' in the pool,
  Out owre the lugs she plumpet,
      Wi' a plunge that night.

In order, on the clean hearth-stane,
  The luggies[n] three are ranged;
And ev'ry time great care is taen,
  To see them duely changed;
Auld, uncle John, wha wedlock's joys,
  Sin' Mar's-year did desire,
Because he gat the toom dish thrice,
  He heav'd them on the fire,
      In wrath that night.

Wi' merry sangs, an' friendly cracks,
  I wat they did na weary;
And unco tales, an' funnie jokes,
  Their sports were cheap and cheary:
Till butter'd so'ns,[n] wi' fragrant lunt,
  Set a' their gabs a steerin;
Syne, wi' a social glass o' strunt,
  They parted aff careerin
      Fu' blythe that night.

217 *linn*: waterfall
219 *scar*: bank, cliff
220 *wiel*: eddy
222 *bickerin*: scurrying
223 *cooket*: 'appeared and disappeared by fits' (B.)
226 *brachens*: bracken
228 *outler quey*: young cow lying out at night
229 *croon*: low
230 *maist*: almost
*hool*: membrane surrounding the heart
231 *lav'rock*: lark
236 *luggies*: wooden bowls with handles
241 *toom*: empty
246 *unco*: strange
248 *so'ns*: sowens, a kind of porridge
*lunt*: steam
249 *gabs*: mouths
*a steerin*: in motion
250 *strunt*: spirits, esp. whisky or toddy

# LOVE AND LIBERTY ('THE JOLLY BEGGARS')

## A CANTATA

### Recitativo

When lyart leaves bestrow the yird,
Or wavering like the bauckie-bird,
Bedim cauld Boreas' blast;
When hailstanes drive wi' bitter skyte,
And infant frosts begin to bite,
In hoary cranreuch drest;
Ae night at e'en a merry core
O' randie, gangrel bodies,
In Poosie-Nansie's[n] held the splore,
To drink their orra dudies:
Wi' quaffing, and laughing,
They ranted an' they sang;
Wi' jumping, an' thumping,
The vera girdle rang.

First, niest the fire, in auld, red rags,
Ane sat; weel brac'd wi' mealy bags,
And knapsack a' in order;
His doxy lay within his arm;
Wi' usquebae an' blankets warm,
She blinket on her sodger:
An' ay he gies the tozie drab
The tither skelpan kiss,
While she held up her greedy gab,
Just like an aumous dish:
Ilk smack still, did crack still,
Just like a cadger's whip;
Then staggering, an' swaggering,
He roar'd this ditty up —

1 *lyart*: grey, withered
*yird*: ground
2 *bauckie-bird*: bat
3 *Boreas*: north wind
4 *skyte*: 'a smart and sudden blow, so as to make what strikes rebound in a slanting direction' (Jamieson)
6 *cranreuch*: hoar-frost
7 *ae*: one
*core*: company
8 *randie*: riotous
*gangrel*: vagrant
9 *splore*: drinking party
10 *orra dudies*: spare rags
14 *girdle*: griddle, hung over the fire for baking.
15 *niest*: next
*red rags*: tattered scarlet uniform
18 *doxy*: beggar's harlot
19 *usquebae*: whisky
20 *blinket on*: leered at
21 *ay*: constantly
*tozie*: tipsy
22 *tither*: yet another
*skelpan*: smacking
23 *gab*: mouth
25 *ilk*: each
26 *cadger*: pedlar

### Air

Tune, Soldier's joy

I am a son of Mars who have been in many wars,
And show my cuts and scars wherever I come;
This here was for a wench, and that other in a trench,
When welcoming the French at the sound of the drum.
Lal de daudle, &c.

My prenticeship I past where my leader breath'd his last,
When the bloody die was cast on the heights of Abram;[n]
And I served out my trade when the gallant game was play'd,
And the Moro[n] low was laid at the sound of the drum.

I lastly was with Curtis[n] among the floating batt'ries,
And there I left for witness, an arm and a limb;
Yet let my country need me, with Elliot[n] to head me,
I'd clatter on my stumps at the sound of a drum.

And now tho' I must beg, with a wooden arm and leg,
And many a tatter'd rag hanging over my bum,
I'm as happy with my wallet, my bottle and my callet,
As when I us'd in scarlet to follow a drum.

What tho', with hoary locks, I must stand the winter shocks,
Beneath the woods and rocks oftentimes for a home,
When the tother bag I sell and the tother bottle tell,
I could meet a troop of hell at the sound of the drum.

### Recitativo —

He ended; and the kebars sheuk,
Aboon the chorus roar;
While frighted rattons backward leuk,
An' seek the benmost bore;
A fairy fiddler frae the neuk,
He skirl'd out, ENCORE.
But up arose the martial chuck,
An' laid the loud uproar —

43 *callet*: wench
47 *tother*: tither, another
*bag*: of oatmeal
*tell*: both to count the cost of and to drink off
49 *kebars*: rafters
50 *aboon*: above
51 *rattons*: rats
52 *benmost bore*: innermost hole
53 *fairy*: tiny
*neuk*: corner
54 *skirl'd*: yelled
55 *martial chuck*: regimental whore

Air

Tune, Sodger laddie

I once was a maid tho' I cannot tell when,
And still my delight is in proper young men:
Some one of a troop of dragoons was my dadie,
No wonder I'm fond of a sodger laddie.
Sing lal de lal, &c.

The first of my loves was a swaggering blade,
To rattle the thundering drum was his trade;
His leg was so tight and his cheek was so ruddy,
Transported I was with my sodger laddie.

But the godly, old chaplain left him in the lurch,
The sword I forsook for the sake of the church;
He ventur'd the soul, and I risked the body,
'Twas then I prov'd false to my sodger laddie.

Full soon I grew sick of my sanctified sot,
The regiment at large for a husband I got;
From the gilded spontoon to the fife I was ready;
I asked no more but a sodger laddie.

But the Peace it reduc'd me to beg in despair,
Till I met my old boy in a Cunningham fair;
His rags regimental they flutter'd so gaudy,
My heart it rejoic'd at a sodger laddie.

And now I have lived — I know not how long,
And still I can join in a cup and a song;
But whilst with both hands I can hold the glass steady,
Here's to thee, my hero, my sodger laddie.

Recitative

Poor Merry-andrew, in the neuk,
Sat guzzling wi' a tinkler-hizzie;
They mind't na wha the chorus teuk,
Between themsels they were sae busy:

58 *proper*: well-made, handsome
71 *spontoon*: half-pike carried by infantry officers
73 *Peace*: of Versailles (1783)
74 *Cunningham*: district of north Ayrshire
81 *Merry-andrew*: clown, buffoon
82 *tinkler-hizzie*: tinker wench
83 *mind't na*: didn't mind, care

At length wi' drink an' courting dizzy,
   He stoiter'd up an' made a face;
Then turn'd, an' laid a smack on Grizzie,
   Syne tun'd his pipes wi' grave grimace.

Air

Tune, Auld Sir Symon

Sir Wisdom's a fool when he's fou;
   Sir Knave is a fool in a session,
He's there but a prentice, I trow,
   But I am a fool by profession.

My grannie she bought me a beuk,
   An' I held awa' to the school;
I fear I my talent misteuk,
   But what will ye hae of a fool.

For drink I would venture my neck;
   A hizzie's the half of my craft:
But what could ye other expect
   Of ane that's avowedly daft.

I, ance, was ty'd up like a stirk,
   For civilly swearing and quaffing;
I, ance, was abus'd i' the kirk,
   For towsing a lass i' my daffin.

Poor Andrew that tumbles for sport,
   Let nae body name wi' a jeer;
There's even, I'm tauld, i' the court,
   A tumbler ca'd the premier.

Observ'd ye yon reverend lad
   Mak faces to tickle the mob;
He rails at our mountebank squad,
   It's rivalship just i' the job.

And now my conclusion I'll tell,
For faith I'm confoundedly dry:
The chiel that's a fool for himsel,
   Guid Lord, he's far dafter than I.

86 *stoiter'd*: lurched
88 *syne*: then
89 *fou*: drunk
90 *session*: sitting of a law court
101 *stirk*: bullock
104 *towsing*: rumpling
*daffin*: fun
115 *chiel*: fellow

Recitativo —

Then niest outspak a raucle carlin,
Wha kent fu' weel to cleek the sterlin;
For mony a pursie she had hooked,
An' had in mony a well been douked:
Her love had been a Highland laddie,
But weary fa' the waefu' woodie!
Wi' sighs an' sobs she thus began
To wail her braw John Highlandman —

Air

Tune, O an' ye were dead gudeman

A highland lad my love was born,
The lalland laws he held in scorn;
But he still was faithfu' to his clan,
My gallant, braw John Highlandman.

Chorus

Sing hey my braw John Highlandman!
Sing ho my braw John Highlandman!
There's not a lad in a' the lan'
Was match for my John Highlandman.

With his philibeg, an' tartan plaid,
An' guid claymore down by his side,
The ladies' hearts he did trepan,
My gallant, braw John Highlandman.
Sing hey &c.

We ranged a' from Tweed to Spey,
An' liv'd like lords an' ladies gay:
For a lalland face he feared none,
My gallant, braw John Highlandman.
Sing hey &c.

117 *raucle*: coarse and sturdy
*carlin*: old woman
118 *cleek the sterlin*: literally, hook money; i.e. steal cash
120 *well . . . douked*: immersing in water is an old punishment for being a witch; here it is for pilfering
122 *weary . . . woodie*: a plague on the woeful gallows
126 *lalland*: lowland
133 *philibeg*: little kilt, developed from full belted plaid in the early eighteenth century
135 *trepan*: ensnare

They banish'd him beyond the sea,
But ere the bud was on the tree,
Adown my cheeks the pearls ran,
Embracing my John Highlandman.
Sing hey &c.

But och! they catch'd him at the last,
And bound him in a dungeon fast,
My curse upon them every one,
They've hang'd my braw John Highlandman.
Sing hey &c.

And now a widow I must mourn
The pleasures that will ne'er return;
No comfort but a hearty can,
When I think on John Highlandman.
Sing hey &c.

Recitativo —

A pigmy scraper wi' his fiddle,
Wha us'd to trystes an' fairs to driddle,
Her strappan limb an' gausy middle,
(He reach'd nae higher)
Had hol'd his heartie like a riddle,
An' blawn't on fire.

Wi' hand on hainch, and upward e'e,
He croon'd his gamut, one, two, three,
Then in an arioso key,
The wee Apollo
Set off wi' allegretto glee
His giga solo.

Air

Tune, Whistle owre the lave o't

Let me ryke up to dight that tear,
An' go wi' me an' be my dear;
An' then your every care an' fear
May whistle owre the lave o't.

151 *can*: drink
154 *trystes*: markets
*driddle*: saunter idly
155 *gausy*: large, ample
157 *hol'd . . . riddle*: had pierced his heart as though it were a riddle (sieve)
159 *hainch*: hip
161 *arioso*: melodious
164 *giga*: jig
165 *ryke*: reach
*dight*: wipe
168 *lave*: what is left

Chorus

I am a fiddler to my trade,
An' a' the tunes that e'er I play'd,
The sweetest still to wife or maid,
Was whistle owre the lave o't.

At kirns an' weddins we'se be there,
An' O sae nicely's we will fare!
We'll bowse about till Dadie Care
Sing whistle owre the lave o't.
I am &c.

Sae merrily's the banes we'll pyke,
An' sun oursells about the dyke;
An' at our leisure when ye like
We'll whistle owre the lave o't.
I am &c.

But bless me wi' your heav'n o' charms,
An' while I kittle hair on thairms
Hunger, cauld, an' a' sic harms
May whistle owre the lave o't.
I am &c.

Recitativo —

Her charms had struck a sturdy caird,
As weel as poor gutscraper;
He taks the fiddler by the beard,
An' draws a roosty rapier —
He swoor by a' was swearing worth
To speet him like a pliver,
Unless he would from that time forth
Relinquish her for ever:

Wi' ghastly e'e poor tweedledee
Upon his hunkers bended,
An' pray'd for grace wi ruefu' face,
An' so the quarrel ended;

173 *kirns*: harvest celebrations
*we'se*: we shall
177 *pyke*: pick
178 *dyke*: dry-stone wall
182 *kittle . . . thairms*: literally tickle hair on gut; i.e. to play the fiddle; here, the phrase has also sexual overtones
185 *caird*: tinker
190 *speet*: spit
*pliver*: plover
194 *upon . . . bended*: squatted down

But tho' his little heart did grieve,
When round the tinkler prest her,
He feign'd to snirtle in his sleeve
When thus the caird address'd her —

Air

Tune, Clout the Caudron

My bonie lass I work in brass,
A tinkler is my station;
I've travell'd round all Christian ground
In this my occupation;
I've ta'en the gold an' been enroll'd
In many a noble squadron;
But vain they search'd when off I march'd
To go an' clout the caudron.
I've ta'en the gold &c.

Despise that shrimp, that wither'd imp,
With a' his noise an' cap'rin;
An' take a share, with those that bear
The budget and the apron!
And *by* that stowp! my faith an' houpe,
And *by* that dear keilbaigie,
If e'er ye want, or meet with scant,
May I ne'er weet my craigie!
And by that stowp &c.

Recitativo —

The caird prevail'd — th' unblushing fair
In his embraces sunk;
Partly wi' love o'ercome sae sair,
An' partly she was drunk:
Sir Violino with an air,
That show'd a man o' spunk,
Wish'd unison between the pair,
An' made the bottle clunk
To their health that night.

But hurchin Cupid shot a shaft,
That play'd a dame a shavie —
The fiddler rak'd her, fore and aft,
Behint the chicken cavie:

199 *snirtle*: snigger
208 *clout*: patch
212 *budget*: leather bag
213 *stowp*: tankard, ale jug
214 *keilbaigie*: whisky distilled at Kilbagie, Clackmannan
216 *craigie*: throat
224 *clunk*: gurgle
226 *hurchin*: urchin, mischievous child
227 *shavie*: trick
229 *cavie*: coop

Her lord, a wight of Homer's craft,
  Tho' limpan wi' the spavie,
He hirpl'd up an' lap like daft,
  An' shor'd them Dainty Davie
    O' boot that night.

He was a care-defying blade,
  As ever Bacchus listed!
Tho' Fortune sair upon him laid,
  His heart she ever miss'd it.
He had no wish but — to be glad,
  Nor want but — when he thristed;
He hated nought but — to be sad,
  An' thus the Muse suggested
    His sang that night.

Air

Tune, For a' that an' a' that

I am a bard of no regard,
  Wi' gentle folks an' a' that;
But Homer like the glowran byke,
  Frae town to town I draw that.

Chorus

For a' that an' a' that,
  An' twice as muckle's a' that,
I've lost but ane, I've twa behin',
  I've wife eneugh for a' that.

I never drank the Muses' stank,
  Castalia's burn an' a' that,
But there it streams an' richly reams,
  My Helicon I ca' that.
    For a' that &c.

231 *spavie*: spavin, a disease of horses; here rheumatism
232 *hirpl'd*: hobbled
*lap*: leapt (presumably in anger)
233 *shor'd . . . boot*: invited them to continue; *shor'd*: offered; Dainty Davie was a covenanting minister whose name became synonymous with sexual vigour; *o'boot*: without charge
236 *listed*: enlisted
246 *glowran byke*: staring crowd
249 *muckle's*: much as
252 *stank*: pool
253 *Castalia's burn*: fountain on Parnassus, sacred to Apollo and the Muses
254 *reams*: foams
255 *Helicon*: mountain, sacred to the Muses, on which are the springs Hippocrene and Aganippe

Great love I bear to all the fair,
  Their humble slave an' a' that;
But lordly will, I hold it still
  A mortal sin to thraw that.
          For a' that &c.

In raptures sweet this hour we meet,
  Wi' mutual love an' a' that;
But for how lang the flie may stang,
  Let inclination law that.
          For a' that &c.

Their tricks an' craft hae put me daft,
  They've ta'en me in, an' a' that,
But clear the decks an' here's the sex!
  I like the jads for a' that.

For a' that an' a' that
  An' twice as muckle's a' that,
My dearest bluid to do them guid,
  They're welcome till't for a' that.

Recitativo —

So sung the bard — and Nansie's waws
Shook with a thunder of applause
  Re-echo'd from each mouth!
They toom'd their pocks, they pawn'd their duds;
They scarcely left to coor their fuds
  To quench their lowan drouth;
Then owre again the jovial thrang
  The poet did request
To lowse his pack an' wale a sang,
  A ballad o' the best.
    He, rising, rejoicing,
      Between his twa Deborahs,
    Looks round him an' found them
      Impatient for the chorus.

258 *will*: sexual desire, potency
259 *thraw*: thwart
262 *flie . . . stang*: metaphor perhaps suggested by 'Spanish fly' (cantharides), an aphrodisiac
265 *ta'en me in*: an equivocal pun, admitted me sexually
270 *dearest bluid*: with sexual equivocation implying seminal fluid
272 *waws*: walls
275 *toom'd*: emptied
*pocks*: bags
*duds*: clothes
276 *coor*: cover
*fuds*: backsides
277 *lowan drouth*: burning thirst
280 *wale*: choose
283 *Deborahs*: see Judges IV–V, esp. V. 12.

Air

Tune, Jolly mortals, fill your glasses —

See the smoking bowl before us,
Mark our jovial, ragged ring!
Round and round take up the chorus,
And in raptures let us sing —

Chorus —

A fig for those by law protected!
Liberty's a glorious feast!
Courts for cowards were erected,
Churches built to please the priest.

What is title, what is treasure,
What is reputation's care?
If we lead a life of pleasure,
'Tis no matter how or where.
A fig &c.

With the ready trick and fable
Round we wander all the day;
And at night, in barn or stable,
Hug our doxies on the hay.
A fig &c.

Does the train-attended carriage
Thro' the country lighter rove?
Does the sober bed of marriage
Witness brighter scenes of love?
A fig &c.

Life is all a variorum,
We regard not how it goes;
Let them cant about decorum,
Who have character to lose.
A fig &c.

Here's to budgets, bags and wallets!
Here's to all the wandering train!
Here's our ragged brats and callets!
One and all cry out, Amen!
A fig for those by law protected,
Liberty's a glorious feast!
Courts for cowards were erected,
Churches built to please the priest.

306 *variorum*: changing scene

## TAM O' SHANTER. A TALE

*Of brownyis and of bogillis full is this buke.*
GAWIN DOUGLAS

When chapman billies leave the street,
And drouthy neebors, neebors meet,
As market-days are wearing late,
An' folk begin to tak the gate;
While we sit bousing at the nappy,
And getting fou and unco happy,
We think na on the lang Scots miles,[n]
The mosses, waters, slaps, and styles,
That lie between us and our hame,
Whare sits our sulky sullen dame,
Gathering her brows like gathering storm,
Nursing her wrath to keep it warm.

This truth fand honest Tam o' Shanter,
As he frae Ayr ae night did canter,
(Auld Ayr, wham ne'er a town surpasses,
For honest men and bonny lasses.)

O Tam! hadst thou but been sae wise,
As ta'en thy ain wife Kate's advice!
She tauld thee weel thou was a skellum,
A blethering, blustering, drunken blellum;
That frae November till October,
Ae market-day thou was nae sober;
That ilka melder, wi' the miller,
Thou sat as lang as thou had siller;
That every naig was ca'd a shoe on,
The smith and thee gat roaring fou on;
That at the Lord's house,[n] even on Sunday,
Thou drank wi' Kirkton Jean till Monday.

*brownyis*: brownies
1 *chapman*: pedlar
*billies*: fellows
2 *drouthy*: thirsty
*neebors*: neighbours
4 *tak . . . gate*: set off home
5 *nappy*: ale
8 *mosses*: areas of boggy ground
*slaps*: gaps in dykes or hedges
14 *ae*: one
19 *skellum*: rascal, rogue
20 *blellum*: 'an idle talking fellow' (Jamieson)
22 *ae*: each
23 *ilka*: each
*melder*: the occasion on which one's corn is ground
25 *naig*: horse
*ca'd . . . on*: had a shoe hammered on
26 *roarin' fou*: wildly drunk
28 *Kirkton*: a village where the parish church stands

She prophesied that late or soon,
Thou would be found deep drown'd in Doon;
Or catch'd wi' warlocks in the mirk,
By Alloway's auld haunted kirk.[n]

Ah, gentle dames! it gars me greet,
To think how mony counsels sweet,
How mony lengthen'd sage advices,
The husband frae the wife despises!

But to our tale: Ae market-night,
Tam had got planted unco right;
Fast by an ingle, bleezing finely,
Wi' reaming swats, that drank divinely;
And at his elbow, Souter Johnny,
His ancient, trusty, drouthy crony;
Tam lo'ed him like a vera brither;
They had been fou for weeks thegither.
The night drave on wi' sangs and clatter;
And ay the ale was growing better:
The landlady and Tam grew gracious,
Wi' favours, secret, sweet, and precious:
The souter tauld his queerest stories;
The landlord's laugh was ready chorus:
The storm without might rair and rustle,
Tam did na mind the storm a whistle.

Care, mad to see a man sae happy,
E'en drown'd himsel amang the nappy:
As bees flee hame wi' lades o' treasure,
The minutes wing'd their way wi' pleasure:
Kings may be blest, but Tam was glorious,
O'er a' the ills o' life victorious!

But pleasures are like poppies spread,
You seize the flower, its bloom is shed;
Or like the snow falls in the river,
A moment white — then melts for ever;
Or like the borealis race,
That flit ere you can point their place;
Or like the rainbow's lovely form
Evanishing amid the storm. —

31 *warlocks*: wizards
33 *gars*: makes
*greet*: cry, weep
38 *unco*: very
39 *ingle*: fire
40 *reaming*: foaming
*swats*: beer
*drank*: tasted
41 *souter*: shoemaker
45 *clatter*: talk, chatter
51 *rair*: roar
55 *lades*: loads

Nae man can tether time or tide;
The hour approaches Tam maun ride;
That hour, o' night's black arch the key-stane,
That dreary hour he mounts his beast in;
And sic a night he taks the road in,
As ne'er poor sinner was abroad in.

The wind blew as 'twad blawn its last;
The rattling showers rose on the blast;
The speedy gleams the darkness swallow'd;
Loud, deep, and lang, the thunder bellow'd:
That night, a child might understand,
The deil had business on his hand.

Weel mounted on his gray mare, Meg,
A better never lifted leg,
Tam skelpit on thro' dub and mire,
Despising wind, and rain, and fire;
Whiles holding fast his gude blue bonnet;
Whiles crooning o'er some auld Scots sonnet;
Whiles glowring round wi' prudent cares,
Lest bogles catch him unawares:
Kirk-Alloway was drawing nigh,
Whare ghaists and houlets nightly cry. —

By this time he was cross the ford,
Whare, in the snaw, the chapman smoor'd;
And past the birks and meikle stane,
Where drunken Charlie brak's neck-bane;
And thro' the whins, and by the cairn,
Whare hunters fand the murder'd bairn;
And near the thorn, aboon the well,
Where Mungo's mither hang'd hersel. —
Before him Doon pours all his floods;
The doubling storm roars thro' the woods;
The lightnings flash from pole to pole;
Near and more near the thunders roll:
When, glimmering thro' the groaning trees,
Kirk-Alloway seem'd in a bleeze;
Thro' ilka bore the beams were glancing;
And loud resounded mirth and dancing. —

68 *maun*: must
71 *sic*: such
81 *skelpit*: galloped
*dub*: muddy pool
88 *houlets*: owls
90 *smoor'd*: smothered
91 *birks*: birches
*meikle*: muckle, great
95 *aboon*: above
103 *bore*: crack

Inspiring bold John Barleycorn!
What dangers thou canst make us scorn!
Wi' tippenny, we fear nae evil;
Wi' usquebae, we'll face the devil! —
The swats sae ream'd in Tammie's noddle,
Fair play, he car'd na deils a boddle.
But Maggie stood right sair astonish'd,
Till, by the heel and hand admonish'd,
She ventured forward on the light;
And, vow! Tam saw an unco sight!
Warlocks[n] and witches in a dance;
Nae cotillion brent new frae France,
But hornpipes, jigs, strathspeys, and reels,
Put life and mettle in their heels.
A winnock-bunker in the east,
There sat auld Nick,[n] in shape o' beast;
A towzie tyke, black, grim, and large,
To gie them music was his charge:
He screw'd the pipes and gart them skirl,
Till roof and rafters a' did dirl. —
Coffins stood round, like open presses,
That shaw'd the dead in their last dresses;
And by some devilish cantraip slight
Each in its cauld hand held a light. —
By which heroic Tam was able
To note upon the haly table,[n]
A murderer's banes in gibbet airns;
Twa span-lang, wee, unchristen'd bairns;
A thief, new-cutted frae a rape,
Wi' his last gasp his gab did gape;
Five tomahawks, wi' blude red-rusted;
Five scymitars, wi' murder crusted;
A garter, which a babe had strangled;
A knife, a father's throat had mangled,
Whom his ain son o' life bereft,
The gray hairs yet stack to the heft;
Wi' mair o' horrible and awefu',
Which even to name wad be unlawfu'.

107 *tippenny*: twopenny ale
*usquebae*: whisky
110 *fair play*: to be fair
*he . . . boddle*: he didn't care a little bit for devils
*boddle*: copper coin, $\frac{1}{6}$ of an English penny
116 *cotillion*: 18th century French dance
*brent*: brand
119 *winnock-bunker*: window seat
120 *auld Nick*: the devil
*towzie*: unkempt, shaggy, tousled
*tyke*: dog
123 *screw'd*: tuned (by screwing the drones)
*gart*: made
125 *presses*: cupboards
127 *cantraip*: magic
*slight*: trickery
131 *airns*: irons, fetters
132 *span-lang*: small, one hand's span
134 *gab*: mouth

As Tammie glowr'd, amaz'd, and curious,
The mirth and fun grew fast and furious:
The piper loud and louder blew;
The dancers quick and quicker flew;
They reel'd, they set, they cross'd, they cleekit,
Till ilka carlin swat and reekit,
And coost her duddies to the wark,
And linket at it in her sark!

Now, Tam, O Tam! had thae been queans,
A' plump and strapping in their teens,
Their sarks, instead o' creeshie flannen,
Been snaw-white seventeen hunder linnen!
Thir breeks o' mine, my only pair,
That ance were plush, o' gude blue hair,
I wad hae gi'en them off my hurdies,
For ae blink o' the bonie burdies!

But wither'd beldams, auld and droll,
Rigwoodie hags wad spean a foal,
Lowping and flinging on a crummock,
I wonder didna turn thy stomach.

But Tam kend what was what fu' brawlie,
There was ae winsome wench and wawlie,
That night enlisted in the core,
(Lang after kend on Carrick shore;
For mony a beast to dead she shot,[n]
And perish'd mony a bony boat,
And shook baith meikle corn and bear,
And kept the country-side in fear).
Her cutty sark,[n] o' Paisley harn,
That while a lassie she had worn,
In longitude tho' sorely scanty,
It was her best, and she was vauntie. —
Ah! little kend thy reverend grannie,
That sark she coft for her wee Nannie,
Wi' twa pund Scots, ('twas a' her riches),
Wad ever grac'd a dance of witches!

147 *cleekit*: linked arms
148 *carlin*: old woman
*reekit*: steamed
149 *coost*: cast
*duddies*: clothes
150 *linket*: skipped, danced briskly
*sark*: shirt
151 *queans*: girls, young women
153 *creeshie*: greasy
*flannen*: flannel
154 *seventeen hunder*: 1700 threads to the warp
155 *thir*: these
157 *hurdies*: backside
160 *rigwoodie*: wizened and gnarled
*spean a foal*: make a foal go off its milk in disgust
161 *crummock*: crook
164 *wawlie*: handsome
169 *bear*: a grain like barley
171 *cutty:* short
*harn*: coarse linen
174 *vauntie*: vain, proud
176 *coft*: bought
177 *twa . . . Scots*: 3/6 ($17\frac{1}{2}$p) in English money

But here my muse her wing maun cour;
Sic flights are far beyond her pow'r;
To sing how Nannie lap and flang,
(A souple jade she was, and strang),
And how Tam stood, like ane bewitch'd,
And thought his very een enrich'd;
Even Satan glowr'd, and fidg'd fu' fain,
And hotch'd and blew wi' might and main:
Till first ae caper, syne anither,
Tam tint his reason a' thegither,
And roars out, 'Weel done, Cutty-sark!'
And in an instant all was dark:
And scarcely had he Maggie rallied,
When out the hellish legion sallied.

As bees bizz out wi' angry fyke,
When plundering herds assail their byke;
As open pussie's mortal foes,
When, pop! she starts before their nose;
As eager runs the market-crowd,
When 'Catch the thief!' resounds aloud;
So Maggie runs, the witches follow,
Wi' mony an eldritch skreech and hollow.

Ah, Tam! Ah, Tam! thou'll get thy fairin!
In hell they'll roast thee like a herrin!
In vain thy Kate awaits thy comin!
Kate soon will be a woefu' woman!
Now, do thy speedy utmost, Meg,
And win the key-stane[n] of the brig;
There at them thou thy tail may toss,
A running stream they dare na cross.
But ere the key-stane she could make,
The fient a tail she had to shake!
For Nannie, far before the rest,
Hard upon noble Maggie prest,
And flew at Tam wi' furious ettle;
But little wist she Maggie's mettle —

179 *cour*: fold, close
181 *lap*: leaped
185 *fidg'd . . . fain*: wriggled with excitement
186 *hotch'd*: hitched
187 *syne*: then
*tint*: lost
193 *fyke*: commotion
195 *open*: give tongue when following a scent
*pussie*: hare
200 *eldritch*: 'ghastly, frightful' (B)
201 *fairin*: deserts
210 *fient a*: not a blessed bit
213 *ettle*: purpose, aim
214 *wist*: knew

Ae spring brought off her master hale,
But left behind her ain gray tail:
The carlin claught her by the rump,
And left poor Maggie scarce a stump.

Now, wha this tale o' truth shall read,
Ilk man and mother's son, take heed:
Whene'er to drink you are inclin'd,
Or cutty-sarks run in your mind,
Think, ye may buy the joys o'er dear,
Remember Tam o' Shanter's mare.

217 *claught*: clutched

# Walter Scott
## 1771–1832

Where Burns's structures are built out of intense and vigorously presented impressions, often on a relatively small scale, Scott's are of altogether ampler proportions. Of all Scottish writers except perhaps MacDiarmid, this son of a calvinistic Edinburgh lawyer comes closest to the stereotype of the 'Renaissance man'. He is of course best known as the author of the Waverley novels — all twenty-six of them, and the associated short stories. Yet he has many other claims to fame. He was one of the three great ballad editors (the others are Bishop Percy, 1729–1811 and Francis James Child, 1825–96), and if he had done nothing else he would still be remembered as a major literary entrepreneur. His editions of Dryden (18 vols, 1808) and Swift (19 vols, 1814) remained standard until well into the nineteenth century, and their prefatory volumes form outstanding examples both of the 'life and times' school of literary criticism and of the biographical art. His huge *Life of Napoleon Buonaparte* (1827) can still provoke historians to controversy, and his deeply moving *Journal* (edited by W. E. K. Anderson, Oxford, 1972) and other autobiographical writings (*Scott on Himself*, edited by David Hewitt, Edinburgh, 1980) provide a fine revelation of his personality.

Scott's development as a poet began under the influences of popular balladry, of the German poems and plays he translated between 1792 and 1800, and of the ballad imitations in Gregory Lewis's gothic novel *The Monk* (1796). He injected this Germanic and 'Monkish' style into his own compositions, *Glenfinlas* and *The Eve of St John*, both printed in *Minstrelsy of the Scottish Border* (1802–3). But his best poetry from this period is to be found in his rearrangement of lines and stanzas — a sort of controlled collage effect — in some of the border ballads printed in the *Minstrelsy*; particularly in *Jamie Telfer of the fair Dodhead, Kinmont Willie* and *Katherine Janfarie*, rather than in his own imitations. With *The Lay of the Last Minstrel* (1805) he moved on to extended narrative poems drawing sometimes on ballad techniques and sometimes on ballad themes. Always in these ballad epics and ballad romances, as they have been variously called, there are anticipations of the later Waverley novels: in *Marmion* (1808), *The Lady of the Lake* (1810) and above all in *Rokeby* (1813), set in Yorkshire during the English Civil War. The latter is a narrative poem striving to become a historical novel, with its villain, Bertram, sharing many of the features of the Byronic 'hero' a bare year after that type had made his debut in the first two cantos of *Childe Harold's Pilgrimage*.

In the first half of the twentieth century Scott's longer poems were under a critical cloud, and it was widely held that his only good poems were the short lyrics and ballads scattered through his longer works, like *Lochinvar* in *Marmion*

(Canto 5), *Proud Maisie* in *The Heart of Mid-Lothian* (Chapter 40) and Rebecca's hymn in *Ivanhoe* (Chapter 39). Today, however, the balance is being redressed, and many think more highly of them, as can be seen from some of the articles listed below. They are currently valued for the pace of their action, their brilliant contrasts of light and colour, the way in which landscape description is fused with national feeling, their narrative framing devices and multiple time effects. In *The Lay of the Last Minstrel*, for example, J. H. Alexander has recently discerned no fewer than twelve layers of time, which is surely as complicated as anything to be found in the novels. The introductory epistles to the six cantos of *Marmion* have been admired by many for their fluent, informal rendering of the author's personality (two of them are included below), and there have always been those who have liked the robust and sometimes realistically imagined battle scenes (Flodden in *Marmion*, Bannockburn in *The Lord of the Isles*, 1815). New readers may find Scott's versification rather monotonous at first, but after some time with *Marmion*, for example, they will learn to respond to the repeated interpretation of groups of eight-syllabled lines by a six-syllabled line, which will rhyme with another six-syllabled one further down the page, producing an effect which has been likened to the rising and falling of a wave. Scott's grammar works similarly to his versification. He will repeat identical constructions again and again, just as a traditional ballad singer will repeat a word or a short phrase in the device known as 'incremental repetition' ('They hadna gane a league, a league/A league but barely three'). Scott piles up longer phrases and clauses to build up parallel climaxes at the same time as he piles up his lexical units (individual words and phrases considered for their meaning) to create another sort of breaker effect. On that level Scott's is a poetry of order organised through what Donald Davie has called augmentation: rhythmical augmentation, syntactical augmentation and lexical augmentation. To get the most from it, as with all poetry, it must be approached with an open mind and above all with an open ear, on its own terms.

When all is said and done, however, Scott's best poetry is in his novels, particularly in *The Bride of Lammermoor*. The poetry of the novels is not just a matter of interspersed lyrics or even interspersed prose descriptions with a poetic flavour, but has to do with the very structure of the work itself and substance of the action. In the nineteenth century the central British poetic tradition, with Shakespeare as its main figure, entered the novel. It did so in the first instance through Scott, who was followed in very different ways by such later novelists as Emily Brontë, Dickens and Hardy.

*Editions:*

*The Poetical Works of Sir Walter Scott, Bart.*, ed. J. G. Lockhart, 12 vols (Edinburgh 1833–4).

*Poetical Works*, ed. J. Logie Robertson (Oxford, 1904).

*Biography:*

J. G. Lockhart, *Memoirs of the Life of Sir Walter Scott*, 10 vols (Edinburgh, 1839).

John Buchan, *Sir Walter Scott* (London, 1932).

Edgar Johnson, *Sir Walter Scott: the Great Unknown*, 2 vols (London, 1970).
Walter Scott, *Scott on Himself*, ed. David Hewitt (Edinburgh, 1981).

*Criticism:*
Francis Jeffrey, *Contributions to the Edinburgh Review* (London, 1844), vol. 2, 460–519.
H. J. C. Grierson, 'The Man and the Poet', in *Sir Walter Scott Lectures 1940–1948*, ed. W. L. Renwick (Edinburgh, 1950), pp. 3–51.
D. Nichol Smith, 'The Poetry of Sir Walter Scott', *University of Edinburgh Journal*, 15 (1949–51), 63–80.
Donald Davie, 'The Poetry of Sir Walter Scott', *Proceedings of the British Academy*, 47 (1961), 60–75.
Thomas Crawford, *Scott* (Edinburgh, 1965; 1982); 'Scott as a Poet', *Etudes Anglaises*, 24 (1971), 478–91; Introduction to *Sir Walter Scott: Selected Poems* (Oxford, 1972).
John O. Hayden, *Scott: the Critical Heritage* (London, 1970).
J. Pikoulis, 'Scott and *Marmion*: the Discovery of Identity', *Modern Language Review*, 66 (1971), 738–50.
J. D. McClatchy, 'The Ravages of Time: the Function of the *Marmion* Epistles', *Studies in Scottish Literature*, 9 (1972), 256–63.
Ruth Eller, 'Themes of Time and Art in *The Lay of the Last Minstrel*', *Studies in Scottish Literature*, 13 (1978), 43–56.
J. H. Alexander, *'The Lay of the Last Minstrel': Three Essays*, Salzburg Studies in English Literature: Romantic Reassessment, 77 (Salzburg, 1978).
J. H. Alexander, *'Marmion': Studies in Interpretation and Composition*, Salzburg Studies in English Literature: Romantic Reassessment, 30 (Salzburg, 1981).

## THE EVE OF SAINT JOHN

The Baron of Smaylho'me[n] rose with day,
He spurr'd his courser on,
Without stop or stay, down the rocky way,
That leads to Brotherstone.

He went not with the bold Buccleuch,
His banner broad to rear;
He went not 'gainst the English yew,
To lift the Scottish spear.

Yet his plate-jack was braced, and his helmet was laced,
And his vaunt-brace of proof he wore;
At his saddle-gerthe was a good steel sperthe,
Full ten pound weight and more.

The baron returned in three days' space,
And his looks were sad and sour;
And weary was his courser's pace,
As he reached his rocky tower.

He came not from where Ancram Moor[n]
Ran red with English blood;
Where the Douglas true, and the bold Buccleuch,
'Gainst keen Lord Evers stood.

Yet was his helmet hack'd and hew'd,
His acton pierc'd and tore;
His axe and his dagger with blood embrued,
But it was not English gore.

He lighted at the Chapellage,
He held him close and still;
And he whistled thrice for his little foot-page,
His name was English Will.

'Come thou hither, my little foot-page;
Come hither to my knee;
Though thou art young, and tender of age,
I think thou art true to me.

4 *Brotherstone*: a moor near Smailholm Tower
9 *plate-jack*: coat armour
10 *vaunt-brace*: armour for the body
11 *sperthe*: battle axe
22 *acton*: jacket of leather, plated with mail
25 *Chapellage*: a chapel outside the court yard of Smailholm Tower

'Come, tell me all that thou has seen,
And look thou tell me true!
Since I from Smaylho'me tower have been,
What did thy lady do?'

'My lady, each night, sought the lonely light,
That burns on the wild Watchfold;
For, from height to height, the beacons bright
Of the English foemen told.

'The bittern clamour'd from the moss,
The wind blew loud and shrill;
Yet the craggy pathway she did cross,
To the eiry beacon hill.

'I watched her steps, and silent came
Where she sat her on a stone;
No watchman stood by the dreary flame;
It burned all alone.

'The second night I kept her in sight,
Till to the fire she came,
And, by Mary's might! an armed knight
Stood by the lonely flame.

'And many a word that warlike lord
Did speak to my lady there;
But the rain fell fast, and loud blew the blast,
And I heard not what they were.

'The third night there the sky was fair,
And the mountain-blast was still,
As again I watched the secret pair,
On the lonesome beacon hill.

'And I heard her name the midnight hour,
And name this holy eve;
And say, "Come this night to thy lady's bower;
Ask no bold baron's leave.

' "He lifts his spear with the bold Buccleuch;
His lady is all alone;
The door she'll undo, to her knight so true,
On the eve of good St John."

38 *Watchfold*: one of the higher crags around the tower, where a beacon was lit in times of war with England.

'"I cannot come; I must not come;
I dare not come to thee;
On the eve of St John I must wander alone:
In thy bower I may not be."

'"Now, out on thee, faint-hearted knight!
Thou should'st not say me nay;
For the eve is sweet, and when lovers meet,
Is worth the whole summer's day.

'"And I'll chain the blood-hound, and the warder shall not sound,
And rushes shall be strewed on the stair;
So, by the black rood-stone[n], and by holy St John,
I conjure thee, my love, to be there!"

'"Though the blood-hound be mute, and the rush beneath my foot,
And the warder his bugle should not blow,
Yet there sleepeth a priest in the chamber to the east,
And my foot-step he would know."

'"O fear not the priest, who sleepeth to the east!
For to Dryburgh[n] the way he has ta'en;
And there to say mass, till three days do pass,
For the soul of a knight that is slayne."

'He turn'd him around, and grimly he frown'd;
Then he laughed right scornfully —
"He who says the mass-rite for the soul of that knight,
May as well say mass for me.

'"At the lone midnight hour, when bad spirits have power,
In thy chamber will I be."
With that he was gone, and my lady left alone,
And no more did I see.'

Then changed, I trow, was that bold baron's brow,
From the dark to the blood-red high;
'Now, tell me the mien of the knight thou hast seen,
For, by Mary, he shall die!'

'His arms shone full bright, in the beacon's red light;
His plume it was scarlet and blue;
On his shield was a hound, in a silver leash bound,
And his crest was a branch of the yew.'

'Thou liest, thou liest, thou little foot-page,
Loud dost thou lie to me!
For that knight is cold, and low laid in the mould,
All under the Eildon-tree.'[n]

'Yet hear but my word, my noble lord!
For I heard her name his name;
And that lady bright, she called the knight
Sir Richard of Coldinghame.'

The bold baron's brow then chang'd, I trow,
From high blood-red to pale —
'The grave is deep and dark — and the corpse is stiff
and stark —
So I may not trust thy tale.

'Where fair Tweed flows round holy Melrose,
And Eildon slopes to the plain,
Full three nights ago, by some secret foe,
That gay gallant was slain.

'The varying light deceived thy sight,
And the wild winds drown'd the name;
For the Dryburgh bells ring, and the white monks do sing,
For Sir Richard of Coldinghame!'

He pass'd the court-gate, and he oped the tower-gate,
And he mounted the narrow stair,
To the bartizan-seat, where, with maids that on her wait,
He found his lady fair.

That lady sat in mournful mood;
Look'd over hill and vale;
Over Tweed's fair flood, and Mertoun's wood,[n]
And all down Tiviotdale.

'Now hail, now hail, thou lady bright!'
'Now hail, thou baron true!
What news, what news from Ancram fight?
What news from the bold Buccleuch?'

'The Ancram Moor is red with gore,
For many a southern fell;
And Buccleuch has charged us, evermore,
To watch our beacons well.

The lady blush'd red, but nothing she said;
Nor added the baron a word:
Then she stepp'd down the stair to her chamber fair,
And so did her moody lord.

In sleep the lady mourn'd, and the baron toss'd and turn'd,
And oft to himself he said —
'The worms around him creep, and his bloody grave is deep . . .
It cannot give up the dead!'

It was near the ringing of matin-bell,
The night was well nigh done,
When a heavy sleep on that baron fell,
On the eve of good Saint John.

The lady looked through the chamber fair,
By the light of a dying flame;
And she was aware of a knight stood there —
Sir Richard of Coldinghame!

'Alas! away, away!' she cried,
'For the holy Virgin's sake!'
'Lady, I know who sleeps by the side;
But, lady, he will not awake.

'By Eildon-tree, for long nights three,
In bloody grave have I lain;
The mass and the death-prayer are said for me,
But, lady, they are said in vain.

'By the baron's brand, near Tweed's fair strand,
Most foully slain I fell;
And my restless sprite on the beacon's height,
For a space is doom'd to dwell.

'At our trysting-place, for a certain space,
I must wander to and fro;
But I had not had power to come to thy bower,
Had'st thou not conjured me so.'

169 *trysting-place*: 'place of rendezvous' (S.)

Love master'd fear; her bower[n] she crossed;
'How, Richard, hast thou sped?
And art thou saved, or art thou lost?'
The vision shook his head!

'Who spilleth life, shall forfeit life;
So bid thy lord believe:
That lawless love is guilt above,
This awful sign receive.'

He laid his left palm on an oaken beam;
His right upon her hand:
The lady shrunk, and fainting sunk,
For it scorch'd like a fiery brand.

The sable score, of fingers four
Remains on that board impress'd;
And for evermore that lady wore
A covering on her wrist.

There is a nun in Dryburgh bower,
Ne'er looks upon the sun:
There is a monk in Melrose tower,
He speaketh word to none.

That nun, who ne'er beholds the day,
That monk, who speaks to none —
That nun was Smaylho'me's Lady gay,
That monk the bold Baron.

## THE LAY OF THE LAST MINSTREL

The poem now offered to the public is intended to illustrate the customs and manners which anciently prevailed on the Borders of England and Scotland. The inhabitants, living in a state partly pastoral and partly warlike, and combining habits of constant depredation with the influence of a rude spirit of chivalry, were often engaged in scenes highly susceptible of poetical ornament. As the description of scenery and manners was more the object of the author, than a combined and regular narrative, the plan of the ancient metrical romance was adopted, which allows greater latitude in this respect, than would be consistent with the dignity of a regular poem. The same model offered other facilities, as it permits an occasional alteration of measure, which, in some degree, authorises the change of rhythm in the text. The machinery also, adopted from popular belief, would have seemed puerile in a poem which did not partake of the rudeness of the old ballad, or metrical romance.

For these reasons, the poem was put into the mouth of an ancient Minstrel, the last of the race, who, as he is supposed to have survived the Revolution, might have caught somewhat of the refinement of modern poetry, without losing the simplicity of his original model. The date of the tale itself is about the middle of the 16th century, when most of the personages actually flourished. The time occupied by the action is three nights and three days.

## INTRODUCTION

The way was long, the wind was cold,
The Minstrel was infirm and old;
His withered cheek, and tresses gray,
Seemed to have known a better day;
The harp, his sole remaining joy,
Was carried by an orphan boy.
The last of all the bards was he,
Who sung of Border chivalry;
For, well-a-day! their date was fled,
His tuneful brethren all were dead;
And he, neglected and oppressed,
Wished to be with them and at rest.
No more, on prancing palfrey borne,
He carolled, light as lark at morn;
No longer, courted and caressed,
High placed in hall, a welcome guest,
He poured, to lord and lady gay,
The unpremeditated lay;
Old times were changed, old manners gone,
A stranger filled the Stuarts' throne;
The bigots of the iron time
Had called his harmless art a crime.
A wandering harper, scorned and poor,
He begged his bread from door to door;
And tuned, to please a peasant's ear,
The harp, a king[n] had loved to hear.

He passed where Newark's stately tower[n]
Looks out from Yarrow's birchen bower:
The Minstrel gazed with wishful eye —
No humbler resting place was nigh.
With hesitating step, at last,
The embattled portal-arch he passed,

*Revolution*: the revolution of 1688

20 *stranger*: William III (1689–1702)

21 *iron time*: the Commonwealth (1649–1660)

Whose ponderous grate, and massy bar,
Had oft rolled back the tide of war,
But never closed the iron door
Against the desolate and poor.
The Duchess marked his weary pace,
His timid mien, and reverend face,
And bade her page the menials tell,
That they should tend the old man well:
For she had known adversity,
Though born in such a high degree;
In pride of power, in beauty's bloom,
Had wept o'er Monmouth's bloody tomb!

When kindness had his wants supplied,
And the old man was gratified,
Began to rise his minstrel pride:
And he began to talk anon,
Of good Earl Francis, dead and gone,
And of Earl Walter, rest him God!
A braver ne'er to battle rode:
And how full many a tale he knew,
Of the old warriors of Buccleuch;
And, would the noble Duchess deign
To listen to an old man's strain,
Though stiff his hand, his voice though weak,
He thought even yet, the sooth to speak,
That, if she loved the harp to hear,
He could make music to her ear.

The humble boon was soon obtained;
The aged Minstrel audience gained.
But, when he reached the room of state,
Where she, with all her ladies, sate,
Perchance he wished his boon denied;
For, when to tune his harp he tried,
His trembling hand had lost the ease,
Which marks security to please;
And scenes, long past, of joy and pain,
Came wildering o'er his aged brain —
He tried to tune his harp in vain.
The pitying Duchess praised its chime,
And gave him heart, and gave him time,
Till every string's according glee

33 *grate*: door of criss-crossing iron bars

49 *Earl Francis*: the Duchess's father

50 *Earl Walter*: the Duchess's grandfather

67 *security*: confidence

Was blended into harmony.
And then, he said, he would full fain
He could recall an ancient strain,
He never thought to sing again.
It was not framed for village churles,
But for high dames and mighty earls;
He had played it to King Charles the Good,
When he kept court at Holyrood;
And much he wished, yet feared, to try
The long forgotten melody.

Amid the strings his fingers strayed,
And an uncertain warbling made,
And oft he shook his hoary head.
But when he caught the measure wild,
The old man raised his face, and smiled;
And lightened up his faded eye,
With all a poet's extacy!
In varying cadence, soft or strong,
He swept the sounding chords along;
The present scene, the future lot;
His toils, his wants, were all forgot:
Cold diffidence, and age's frost,
In the full tide of song were lost;
Each blank, in faithless memory void,
The poet's glowing thought supplied;
And, while his harp responsive rung,
'Twas thus the LATEST MINSTREL sung.

## CANTO FIRST

### I

The feast was over in Branksome tower,[n]
And the Ladye had gone to her secret bower;
Her bower, that was guarded by word and by spell,
Deadly to hear, and deadly to tell —
Jesu Maria, shield us well!
No living wight, save the Ladye alone,
Had dared to cross the threshold stone.

### 2

The tables were drawn, it was idlesse all;
Knight, and page, and household squire,
Loitered through the lofty hall,
Or crowded round the ample fire.

8 *drawn*: drawn back to the side of the hall

The stag-hounds, weary with the chase,
 Lay stretched upon the rushy floor,
And urged, in dreams, the forest race,
 From Teviot-stone to Eskdale-moor.

3

Nine-and-twenty knights of fame
 Hung their shields in Branksome Hall;[n]
Nine-and-twenty squires of name
 Brought them their steeds from bower to stall;
  Nine-and-twenty yeomen tall
  Waited, duteous, on them all:
  They were all knights of mettle true,
  Kinsmen to the bold Buccleuch.

4

Ten of them were sheathed in steel,
With belted sword, and spur on heel:
They quitted not their harness bright,
Neither by day, nor yet by night:
 They lay down to rest
 With corslet laced,
Pillowed on buckler cold and hard;
 They carved at the meal
 With gloves of steel,
And they drank the red wine through the helmet
 barred.

5

Ten squires, ten yeomen, mail-clad men,
Waited the beck of the warders ten.
Thirty steeds, both fleet and wight,
Stood saddled in stable day and night,
Barbed with frontlet of steel, I trow,
And with Jedwood-axe at saddle bow.
A hundred more fed free in stall —
Such was the custom of Branksome Hall.

17 *hung . . . shields*: i.e. Branksome could call upon 29 knights
30 *buckler*: shield
33 *barred*: through the bars of the helmet
36 *wight*: strong
38 *barbed*: protected (with armour)
39 *Jedwood-axe*: long-handled spear, the blade having one or more lateral projections

6

Why do these steeds stand ready dight?
Why watch these warriors, armed, by night?
They watch, to hear the blood-hound baying;
They watch, to hear the war-horn braying;
To see St George's red cross streaming,
To see the midnight beacon gleaming;
They watch, against southern force and guile,
Lest Scroop, or Howard, or Percy's powers,[n]
Threaten Branksome's lordly towers,
From Warkworth, or Naworth, or merry Carlisle.

7

Such is the custom of Branksome Hall.
Many a valiant knight is here;
But he, the Chieftain of them all,
His sword hangs rusting on the wall,
Beside his broken spear.
Bards long shall tell,
How lord Walter[n] fell!
When startled burghers fled, afar,
The furies of the Border war;
When the streets of high Dunedin
Saw lances gleam, and falchions redden,
And heard the slogan's deadly yell —
Then the Chief of Branksome fell.

8

Can piety the discord[n] heal,
Or staunch the death-feud's enmity?
Can Christian lore, can patriot zeal,
Can love of blessed charity?
No! vainly to each holy shrine,
In mutual pilgrimage,[n] they drew;
Implored, in vain, the grace divine
For chiefs, their own red falchions slew:
While Cessford[n] owns the rule of Car,
While Ettrick[n] boast the line of Scott,
The slaughtered chiefs, the mortal jar,
The havoc of the feudal war,
Shall never, never be forgot!

42 *dight*: dressed

47 *beacon*: beacons on hill tops were the usual way of warning of an English incursion

61 *Dunedin*: Edinburgh

62 *falchions*: swords

63 *slogan*: war or rallying cry

9

In sorrow, o'er lord Walter's bier
The warlike foresters had bent;
And many a flower, and many a tear,
Old Teviot's maids and matrons lent:
But o'er her warrior's bloody bier
The Ladye dropped nor flower nor tear!
Vengeance, deep-brooding o'er the slain,
Had locked the source of softer woe;
And burning pride, and high disdain,
Forbade the rising tear to flow;
Until, amid his sorrowing clan,
Her son lisped from the nurse's knee —
'And, if I live to be a man,
My father's death revenged shall be!'
Then fast the mother's tears did seek
To dew the infant's kindling cheek.

10

All loose her negligent attire,
All loose her golden hair,
Hung Margaret o'er her slaughtered sire,
And wept in wild despair.
But not alone the bitter tear
Had filial grief supplied;
For hopeless love, and anxious fear,
Had lent their mingled tide:
Nor in her mother's altered eye
Dared she to look for sympathy.
Her lover, 'gainst her father's clan,
With Car in arms had stood,
When Mathouse burn to Melrose ran,
All purple with their blood.
And well she knew, her mother dread,
Before lord Cranstoun[n] she should wed,
Would see her on her dying bed.

11

Of noble race the Lady came;
Her father was a clerk of fame,
Of Bethune's line[n] of Picardie:

He learned the art, that none may name,
In Padua, far beyond the sea.
Men said, he changed his mortal frame
By feat of magic mystery;
For when, in studious mood, he paced
St Andrew's cloistered hall,
His form no darkening shadow traced
Upon the sunny wall![n]

12

And, of his skill, as bards avow,
He taught that Ladye fair,
Till to her bidding she could bow
The viewless forms of air.[n]
And now she sits in secret bower,
In old lord David's[n] western tower,
And listens to a heavy sound,
That moans the mossy turrets round.
Is it the roar of Teviot's tide,
That chafes against the scaur's red side?
Is it the wind, that swings the oaks?
Is it the echo from the rocks?
What may it be, the heavy sound,
That moans old Branksome's turrets round?

13

At the sullen, moaning sound,
The ban-dogs bay and howl;
And, from the turrets round,
Loud whoops the startled owl.
In the hall, both squire and knight
Swore that a storm was near,
And looked forth to view the night;
But the night was still and clear!

14

From the sound of Teviot's tide,
Chafing with the mountain's side,
From the groan of the wind-swung oak,
From the sullen echo of the rock,

115 *Padua*: 'the principal school of necromancy' (S)

119 *St Andrew's . . . hall*: St Andrews University

134 *scaur*: 'a precipitous bank of earth' (S)

137 *ban-dogs*: dogs held in bands (chains)

From the voice of the coming storm,
  The Ladye knew it well!
It was the Spirit of the Flood that spoke,
  And he called on the Spirit of the Fell.

15

RIVER SPIRIT

'Sleepest thou, brother?'

MOUNTAIN SPIRIT

———'Brother, nay —
On my hills the moon-beams play.
From the Craik-cross to Skelfhill-pen,[n]
By every rill, in every glen,
  Merry elves, their morrice pacing,
    To aerial minstrelsy,
  Emerald rings on brown heath tracing,
    Trip it deft and merrily.
Up, and mark their nimble feet!
Up, and list their music sweet!'

16

RIVER SPIRIT

'Tears of an imprisoned maiden
  Mix with my polluted stream;
Margaret of Branksome, sorrow-laden,
  Mourns beneath the moon's pale beam.
Tell me, thou, who viewest the stars,
When shall cease these feudal jars?
What shall be the maiden's fate?
Who shall be the maiden's mate?'

17

MOUNTAIN SPIRIT

'Arthur's slow wain his course doth roll,
In utter darkness, round the pole;
The Northern Bear lowers black and grim;
Orion's studded belt is dim;

151 *Fell*: hillside

158 *emerald rings*: supposedly made by fairy feet

171 *utter*: outer; cf. *Paradise Lost* I, 72.

Twinkling faint, and distant far,
Shimmers through mist each planet star;
   Ill may I read their high decree:
But no kind influence deign they shower
On Teviot's tide, and Branksome's tower,
   Till pride be quelled, and love be free.'

18

The unearthly voices ceast,
   And the heavy sound was still;
It died on the river's breast,
   It died on the side of the hill. —
But round lord David's tower
   The sound still floated near;
For it rung in the Ladye's bower,
   And it rung in the Ladye's ear.
She raised her stately head,
   And her heart throbbed high with pride:
'Your mountains shall bend,
And your streams ascend,
   Ere Margaret be our foeman's bride!'

19

The Ladye sought the lofty hall,
   Where many a bold retainer lay,
And, with jocund din, among them all,
   Her son pursued his infant play.
A fancied moss-trooper,[n] the boy
   The truncheon of a spear bestrode,
And round the hall, right merrily,
   In mimic foray rode.
Even bearded knights, in arms grown old,
   Share in his frolic gambols bore,
Albeit their hearts, of rugged mould,
   Were stubborn as the steel they wore.
For the gay warriors prophesied,
   How the brave boy, in future war,
Should tame the Unicorn's[n] pride,
   Exalt the Crescents and the Star.

20

The Ladye forgot her purpose high,
   One moment, and no more;
One moment gazed with a mother's eye,
   As she paused at the arched door.

Then, from amid the armed train,
She called to her William of Deloraine.[n]

21

A stark moss-trooping Scott was he,
As e'er couched Border lance by knee:
Through Solway sands, through Tarras moss,[n]
Blindfold, he knew the paths to cross;
By wily turns, by desperate bounds,
Had baffled Percy's best blood-hounds;
In Eske, or Liddel,[n] fords were none,
But he would ride them one by one;
Alike to him was time, or tide,
December's snow, or July's pride;
Alike to him was tide, or time,
Moonless midnight, or mattin prime.
Steady of heart, and stout of hand,
As ever drove prey from Cumberland;
Five times outlawed had he been,
By England's king and Scotland's queen.[n]

22

'Sir William of Deloraine, good at need,
Mount thee on the wightest steed;
Spare not to spur, nor stint to ride,
Until thou come to fair Tweedside;
And in Melrose's holy pile
Seek thou the Monk of St Mary's aisle:
  Greet the father well from me;
    Say, that the fated hour is come,
  And to night he shall watch with thee,
    To win the treasure of the tomb:[n]
For this will be St Michael's night,
And though stars be dim the moon is bright;
And the cross of bloody red
Will point to the grave of the mighty dead.

23

'What he gives thee, see thou keep;
Stay not thou for food or sleep.

226 *mattin prime*: best of the morning

241 *St . . . night*: Michaelmas (29 Sept.)

Be it scroll, or be it book,
Into it, knight, thou must not look;
If thou readest thou art lorn!
Better hadst thou ne'er been born.'

24

'O swiftly can speed my dapple-gray steed,
Which drinks of the Teviot clear;
Ere break of day,' the warrior 'gan say,
'Again will I be here:
And safer by none may thy errand be done,
Than, noble dame, by me;
Letter nor line know I never a one,
Wer't my neck-verse at Hairibee.'[n]

25

Soon in his saddle sate he fast,[n]
And soon the steep descent he past;
Soon crossed the sounding barbican,
And soon the Teviot side he won.
Eastward the wooded path he rode;
Green hazels o'er his basnet nod:
He passed the Peel of Goldiland,
And crossed old Borthwick's roaring strand;
Dimly he viewed the Moat-hill's mound,
Where Druid shades still flitted round:
In Hawick twinkled many a light;
Behind him soon they set in night;
And soon he spurred his courser keen
Beneath the tower of Hazeldean.

26

The clattering hoofs the watchmen mark;
'Stand, ho! thou courier of the dark.'
'For Branksome, ho!' the knight rejoined,
And left the friendly tower behind.
He turned him now from Teviotside,
And, guided by the tinkling rill,
Northward the dark ascent did ride,
And gained the moor at Horsliehill;

249 *lorn*: lost
261 *barbican*: double tower over a castle's outer gate or bridge
264 *basnet*: light globular steel headpiece closed in front with a visor
265 *Peel*: border tower

Broad on the left before him lay,
For many a mile, the Roman way.

27

A moment now he slackened his speed,
A moment breathed his panting steed;
Drew saddle-girth and corslet-band,
And loosened in the sheath his brand.
On Minto-crags the moon-beams glint,
Where Barnhill hewed his bed of flint;
Who flung his outlawed limbs to rest,
Where falcons hang their giddy nest,
Mid cliffs, from whence his eagle eye
For many a league his prey could spy;
Cliffs doubling, on their echoes borne,
The terrors of the robber's horn;
Cliffs, which, for many a later year,
The warbling Doric reed shall hear,
When some sad swain shall teach the grove,
Ambition is no cure for love.

28

Unchallenged, thence past Deloraine
To ancient Riddell's fair domain,
   Where Aill, from mountains freed,
Down from the lakes did raving come;
Each wave was crested with tawny foam,
   Like the mane of a chesnut steed.
In vain! no torrent, deep or broad,
Might bar the bold moss-trooper's road.

29

At the first plunge the horse sunk low,
And the water broke o'er the saddle-bow;
Above the foaming tide, I ween,
Scarce half the charger's neck was seen;
For he was barded from counter to tail,
And the rider was armed complete in mail;
Never heavier man and horse
Stemmed a midnight torrent's force;

285 *drew*: i.e. tighter, against possible attack

311 *barded*: from Fr. *barde*, horse armour

The warrior's very plume, I say,
Was daggled by the dashing spray;
Yet, through good heart, and our Ladye's grace,
At length he gained the landing place.

30

Now Bowden Moor the march-man won,
   And sternly shook his plumed head,
As glanced his eye o'er Halidon;
   For on his soul the slaughter red
Of that unhallowed morn arose,
When first the Scott and Car were foes;
When royal James beheld the fray,
Prize to the victor of the day;
When Home and Douglas, in the van,
Bore down Buccleuch's retiring clan,
Till gallant Cessford's heart-blood dear
Reeked on dark Elliot's Border spear.

31

In bitter mood he spurred fast,
And soon the hated heath was past;
And far beneath, in lustre wan,
Old Melros' rose, and fair Tweed ran:
Like some tall rock, with lichens gray,
Seemed, dimly huge, the dark Abbaye.
When Hawick he passed, had curfew rung,
Now midnight lauds were in Melrose sung.
The sound upon the fitful gale,
In solemn wise, did rise and fail,
Like that wild harp, whose magic tone
Is wakened by the winds alone:
But when Melrose he reached, 'twas silence all;
He meetly stabled his steed in stall,
And sought the convent's lonely wall.

---

Here paused the harp; and with its swell
The Master's fire and courage fell:

316 *daggled*: wet
319 *march-man*: borderer
337 *curfew*: about 8 or 9 p.m.
338 *lauds*: part of the first of the daily offices, ending with Psalms 148–150
341 *harp*: Aeolian harp, a stringed instrument designed to sound in wind

Dejectedly, and low, he bowed,
And, gazing timid on the crowd,
He seemed to seek, in every eye,
If they approved his minstrelsy;
And, diffident of present praise,
Somewhat he spoke of former days,
And how old age, and wandering long,
Had done his hand and harp some wrong.

The Duchess, and her daughters fair,
And every gentle ladye there,
Each after each, in due degree,
Gave praises to his melody;
His hand was true, his voice was clear,
And much they longed the rest to hear.
Encouraged thus, the Aged Man,
After meet rest, again began.

In the cantos that follow William of Deloraine obtains Michael Scott's book of magic from his tomb, and sets off for Branksome. On the way he meets Lord Cranstoun, Margaret of Branksome's secret lover, fights him and is badly wounded. Cranstoun's goblin page glances into the magic book, returns William of Deloraine and the book to Lady Scott, absconds with the Scott heir and allows him to be captured by English invaders. The borderers rise to oppose them; Lord Howard and the English appear before Branksome, demanding that Deloraine suffer 'march-treason pain' because of his depredations and the murder of Richard Musgrave's brother. Howard obtains word that they are about to be cut off by superior forces and proposes that Deloraine and Musgrave should decide the issue in single combat: the Buccleuch heir should be released if Deloraine wins, but kept as a hostage if Musgrave wins. The proposal is accepted. Cranstoun substitutes himself for the wounded Deloraine and kills Musgrave. *The Lay* ends with Scots and English coming together to celebrate the marriage of Margaret and Cranstoun.

# MARMION

TO

WILLIAM ERSKINE, ESQ.

*Ashestiel, Ettricke Forest.*

Like April morning clouds, that pass,
With varying shadow, o'er the grass,
And imitate, on field and furrow,
Life's chequered scene of joy and sorrow;
Like streamlet of the mountain north,
Now in a torrent racing forth,
Now winding slow its silver train,
And almost slumbering on the plain;
Like breezes of the autumn day,
Whose voice inconstant dies away,
And ever swells again as fast,
When the ear deems its murmur past;
Thus various my romantic theme
Flits, winds, or sinks, a morning dream.
Yet pleased, our eye pursues the trace
Of light and shade's inconstant race;
Pleased, views the rivulet afar,
Weaving its maze irregular;
And pleased, we listen as the breeze
Heaves its wild sigh through autumn trees.
Then wild as cloud, or stream, or gale,
Flow on, flow unconfined, my tale.

Need I to thee, dear Erskine,[n] tell
I love the license all too well,
In sound now lowly, and now strong,
To raise the desultory song.
Oft, when mid such capricious chime,
Some transient fit of loftier rhime,
To thy kind judgment seemed excuse
For many an error of the muse;
Oft hast thou said, 'If still mis-spent,
Thine hours to poetry are lent;
Go, and to tame thy wandering course,
Quaff from the fountain at the source;
Approach those masters, o'er whose tomb,
Immortal laurels ever bloom:
Instructive of the feebler bard,
Still from the grave their voice is heard;

From them, and from the paths they shew'd,
Chuse honoured guide and practised road;
Nor ramble on through brake and maze,
With harpers rude of barbarous days.[n]

'Or deem'st thou not our later time
Yields topic meet for classic rhime?
Hast thou no elegiac verse
For Brunswick's venerable hearse?[n]
What! not a line, a tear, a sigh,
When valour bleeds for liberty?
Oh, hero of that glorious time,
When with unrivalled light sublime, —
Though martial Austria, and though all
The might of Russia, and the Gaul,
Though banded Europe stood her foes —
The star of Brandenburgh[n] arose!
Thou couldst not live to see her beam
For ever quenched in Jena's stream.
Lamented chief! — it was not given,
To thee to change the doom of heaven,
And crash that dragon[n] in its birth,
Predestined scourge of guilty earth.
Lamented chief! — not thine the power,
To save in that presumptuous hour,[n]
When Prussia hurried to the field,
And snatched the spear, but left the shield;
Valour and skill 'twas thine to try,
And, tried in vain, 'twas thine to die.
Ill had it seemed thy silver hair
The last, the bitterest pang to share,
For princedoms reft, and scutcheons riven,
And birthrights to usurpers given;[n]
Thy land's, thy children's wrongs to feel,
And witness woes thou could'st not heal;
On thee relenting heaven bestows
For honoured life an honoured close;
And when revolves, in time's sure change,
The hour of Germany's revenge,
When, breathing fury for her sake,
Some new Arminius[n] shall awake,
Her champion, ere he strike, shall come
To whet his sword on Brunswick's tomb.

'Or of the Red-Cross hero[n] teach,
Dauntless in dungeon as on breach:

Alike to him the sea, the shore,
The brand, the bridle, or the oar;
Alike to him the war that calls
Its votaries to the shattered walls,
Which the grim Turk besmeared with blood,
Against the Invincible made good;
Or that whose thundering voice could wake
The silence of the polar lake,
When stubborn Russ, and metal'd Swede,
On the warped wave their death-game played;
Or that where vengeance and affright
Howl'd round the father of the fight,[n]
Who snatched on Alexandria's sand
The conqueror's wreath with dying hand.

'Or if to touch such chord be thine,
Restore the ancient tragic line,
And emulate the notes that rung
From the wild harp which silent hung,
By silver Avon's holy shore,
Till twice an hundred years rolled o'er;
When she, the bold Enchantress,[n] came,
With fearless hand and heart on flame,
From the pale willow snatched the treasure,
And swept it with a kindred measure,
Till Avon's swans, while rung the grove
With Monfort's hate and Basil's love,
Awakening at the inspired strain,
Deemed their own Shakespeare lived again.'

Thy friendship thus thy judgment wronging,
With praises not to me belonging,
In task more meet for mightiest powers,
Would'st thou engage my thriftless hours.
But say, my Erskine, hast thou weighed
That secret power by all obeyed,
Which warps not less the passive mind,
Its source concealed or undefined;
Whether an impulse, that has birth
Soon as the infant wakes on earth,
One with our feelings and our powers,
And rather part of us than ours;
Or whether fitlier termed the sway
Of habit formed in early day?
Howe'er derived, its force confessed
Rules with despotic sway the breast,

And drags us on by viewless chain,
While taste and reason plead in vain.
Look east, and ask the Belgian why,
Beneath Batavia's[n] sultry sky,
He seeks not eager to inhale
The freshness of the mountain gale,
Content to rear his whitened wall
Beside the dank and dull canal?
He'll say, from youth he loved to see
The white sail gliding by the tree.
Or see yon weather-beaten hind,
Whose sluggish herds before him wind,
Whose tattered plaid and rugged cheek
His northern clime and kindred speak;
Through England's laughing meads he goes,
And England's wealth around him flows;
Ask, if it would content him well,
At ease in these gay plains to dwell,
Where hedge-rows spread a verdant screen,
And spires and forests intervene,
And the neat cottage peeps between?
No, not for these will he exchange
His dark Lochaber's[n] boundless range,
Nor for fair Devon's meads forsake
Bennevis grey and Garry's lake.

Thus, while I ape the measure wild
Of tales that charmed me yet a child,
Rude though they be, still with the chime
Return the thoughts of early time;
And feelings roused in life's first day,
Glow in the line, and prompt the lay.
Then rise those crags, that mountain tower,
Which charmed my fancy's wakening hour:
Though no broad river swept along
To claim perchance heroic song;
Though sighed no groves in summer gale
To prompt of love a softer tale;
Though scarce a puny streamlet's speed
Claimed homage from a shepherd's reed;
Yet was poetic impulse given,
By the green hill and clear blue heaven.
It was a barren scene,[n] and wild,
Where naked cliffs were rudely piled;
But ever and anon between
Lay velvet tufts of loveliest green;

And well the lonely infant knew
Recesses where the wall-flower grew,
And honey-suckle loved to crawl
Up the low crag and ruined wall.
I deemed such nooks the sweetest shade
The sun in all his round surveyed;
And still I thought that shattered tower
The mightiest work of human power;
And marvelled, as the aged hind[n]
With some strange tale bewitched my mind,
Of forayers, who, with headlong force,
Down from that strength had spurred their horse,
Their southern rapine to renew,
Far in the distant Cheviots blue,
And, home returning, filled the hall
With revel, wassell-rout, and brawl —
Methought that still with tramp and clang
The gate-way's broken arches rang;
Methought grim features, seamed with scars,
Glared through the window's rusty bars.
And ever by the winter hearth,
Old tales I heard of woe or mirth,
Of lovers' sleights, of ladies' charms,
Of witches' spells, of warriors' arms;
Of patriot battles, won of old
By Wallace wight and Bruce the bold;
Of later fields of feud and fight,
When, pouring from their Highland height,
The Scottish clans, in headlong sway,
Had swept the scarlet ranks away.
While stretched at length upon the floor,
Again I fought each combat o'er,
Pebbles and shells, in order laid,
The mimic ranks of war displayed;
And onward still the Scottish Lion[n] bore,
And still the scattered Southron fled before.

Still with vain fondness could I trace,
Anew, each kind familiar face,
That brightened at our evening fire;
From the thatched mansion's grey-haired sire,[n]
Wise without learning, plain and good,
And sprung of Scotland's gentler blood
Whose eye in age, quick, clear and keen,
Shewed what in youth its glance had been;
Whose doom discording neighbours sought,
Content with equity unbought;

To him the venerable priest,[n]
Our frequent and familiar guest,
Whose life and manners well could paint
Alike the student and the saint;
Alas! whose speech too oft I broke
With gambol rude and timeless joke;
For I was wayward, bold, and wild,
A self-will'd imp, a grandame's child;
But half a plague, and half a jest,
Was still endured, beloved, carest.

From me, thus nurtured, dost thou ask
The classic poet's well-conned task?
Nay, Erskine, nay — on the wild hill
Let the wild heathbell flourish still;
Cherish the tulip, prune the vine,
But freely let the woodbine twine,
And leave untrimmed the eglantine:
Nay, my friend, nay — since oft thy praise
Hath given fresh vigour to my lays,
Since oft thy judgment could refine
My flattened thought, or cumbrous line,
Still kind, as is thy wont, attend,
And in the minstrel spare the friend.
Though wild as cloud, as stream, as gale,
Flow forth, flow unrestrained, my tale.

## TO

## JAMES SKENE, ESQ.

*Ashestiel, Ettricke Forest.*

An ancient minstrel sagely said,
'Where is the life which late we led?'
That motley clown,[n] in Arden wood,
Whom humorous Jaques with envy viewed,
Not even that clown could amplify,
On this trite text, so long as I.
Eleven years we now may tell,
Since we have known each other well;
Since, riding side by side, our hand
First drew the voluntary brand;[n]
And sure, through many a varied scene,
Unkindness never came between.
Away these winged years have flown,
To join the mass of ages gone;

And though deep marked, like all below,
With chequered shades of joy and woe;
Though thou o'er realms and seas hast ranged,
Marked cities lost, and empires changed,
While here, at home, my narrower ken
Somewhat of manners saw, and men;
Though varying wishes, hopes, and fears,
Fevered the progress of these years,
Yet now, days, weeks, and months, but seem
The recollection of a dream,
So still we glide down to the sea
Of fathomless eternity.

Even now, it scarcely seems a day,
Since first I tuned this idle lay;
A task so often thrown aside,
When leisure graver cares denied,
That now, November's dreary gale,[n]
Whose voice inspired my opening tale,
That same November gale once more
Whirls the dry leaves on Yarrow[n] shore;
Their vex'd boughs streaming to the sky,
Once more our naked birches sigh;
And Blackhouse heights, and Ettricke Pen,
Have donned their wintry shrouds again;
And mountain dark, and flooded mead,
Bid us forsake the banks of Tweed,
Earlier than wont along the sky,
Mixed with the rack, the snow-mists fly:
The shepherd, who, in summer sun,
Has something of our envy won,
As thou with pencil, I with pen,
The features traced of hill and glen;[n]
He who, outstretched, the livelong day,
At ease among the heath-flower lay,
Viewed the light clouds with vacant look,
Or slumbered o'er his tattered book,
Or idly busied him to guide
His angle o'er the lessen'd tide; —
At midnight now, the snowy plain
Finds sterner labour for the swain.

When red hath set the beamless sun,[n]
Through heavy vapours dank and dun;
When the tired ploughman, dry and warm,
Hears, half asleep, the rising storm

52 *angle*: fishing rod

Hurling the hail, and sleeted rain,
Against the casement's tinkling pane;
The sounds that drive wild deer, and fox,
To shelter in the brake and rocks,
Are warnings which the shepherd ask,
To dismal, and to dangerous task.
Oft he looks forth, and hopes, in vain,
The blast may sink in mellowing rain,
Till, dark above, and white below,
Decided drives the flaky snow,
And forth the hardy swain must go.
Long, with dejected look and whine,
To leave the hearth his dogs repine;
Whistling, and cheering them to aid,
Around his back he wreathes the plaid:
His flock he gathers, and he guides
To open downs, and mountain sides,
Where, fiercest though the tempest blow,
Least deeply lies the drift below.
The blast, that whistles o'er the fells,
Stiffens his locks to icicles;
Oft he looks back, while, streaming far,
His cottage window seems a star,
Loses its feeble gleam, and then
Turns patient to the blast again,
And, facing to the tempest's sweep,
Drives through the gloom his lagging sheep:
If fails his heart, if his limbs fail,
Benumbing death is in the gale;
His paths, his landmarks, all unknown,
Close to the hut, no more his own,
Close to the aid he sought in vain,
The morn may find the stiffen'd swain:
His widow sees, at dawning pale,
His orphans raise their feeble wail;
And, close beside him, in his snow,
Poor Yarrow, partner of their woe,
Couches upon his master's breast,
And licks his cheek, to break his rest.

Who envies now the shepherd's lot,
His healthy fare, his rural cot,
His summer couch by greenwood tree,
His rustic kirn's loud revelry,

101 *kirn*: harvest home

His native hill-notes, tuned on high,
To Marion of the blithesome eye;
His crook, his scrip, his oaten reed,
And all Arcadia's golden creed.

Changes not so with us, my Skene,
Of human life the varying scene?
Our youthful summer oft we see
Dance by on wings of game and glee,
While the dark storm reserves its rage,
Against the winter of our age:
As he, the ancient chief of Troy,
His manhood spent in peace and joy;
But Grecian fires, and loud alarms,
Called ancient Priam forth to arms.
Then happy those, — since each must drain
His share of pleasure, share of pain, —
Then happy those, beloved of heaven,
To whom the mingled cup is given;
Whose lenient sorrows find relief,
Whose joys are chastened by their grief.
And such a lot, my Skene, was thine,
When thou of late wert doomed to twine, —
Just when thy bridal hour was by, —
The cypress with the myrtle tie;
Just on thy bride her Sire had smiled,
And blessed the union of his child,
When love must change its joyous cheer,
And wipe affection's filial tear.
Nor did the actions next his end,
Speak more the father than the friend:
Scarce had lamented Forbes[n] paid
The tribute to his minstrel's shade;
The tale of friendship scarce was told,
Ere the narrator's heart was cold.
Far may we search, before we find
A heart so manly and so kind.
But not around his honoured urn,
Shall friends alone, and kindred mourn;
The thousand eyes his care had dried,
Pour at his name a bitter tide;
And frequent falls the grateful dew,
For benefits the world ne'er knew.
If mortal charity dare claim
The Almighty's attributed name,
Inscribe above his mouldering clay,
'The widow's shield, the orphan's stay.'[n]

Nor, though it wake thy sorrow, deem
My verse intrudes on this sad theme;
For sacred was the pen that wrote,
'Thy father's friend forget thou not:'
And grateful title may I plead,
For many a kindly word and deed,
To bring my tribute to his grave:—
'Tis little — but 'tis all I have.

To thee, perchance, this rambling strain
Recalls our summer walks again;
When doing nought, — and, to speak true,
Not anxious to find ought to do, —
The wild unbounded hills we ranged;
While oft our talk its topic changed,
And desultory, as our way,
Ranged unconfined from grave to gay.
Even when it flagged, as oft will chance,
No effort made to break its trance,
We could right pleasantly pursue
Our sports, in social silence too.
Thou gravely labouring to pourtray
The blighted oak's fantastic spray;
I spelling o'er, with much delight,
The legend of that antique knight,
Tirante by name, ycleped the White.[n]
At either's feet a trusty squire,
Pandour and Camp,[n] with eyes of fire,
Jealous, each other's motions viewed,
And scarce suppressed their ancient feud.
The laverock whistled from the cloud;
The stream was lively, but not loud;
From the white-thorn the may-flower shed
Its dewy fragrance round our head:
Not Ariel[n] lived more merrily
Under the blossom'd bough, than we.

And blithsome nights, too, have been ours,
When winter stript the summer's bowers;
Careless we heard, what now I hear,
The wild blast sighing deep and drear,
When fires were bright, and lamps beamed gay,
And ladies tuned the lovely lay;
And he was held a laggard soul,
Who shunn'd to quaff the sparkling bowl.

177 *laverock*: lark

Then he, whose absence we deplore,[n]
Who breathes the gales of Devon's shore,
The longer missed, bewailed the more;
And thou, and I, and dear-loved Rae[n],
And one[n] whose name I may not say, —
For not Mimosa's tender tree
Shrinks sooner from the touch than he, —
In merry chorus, well combined,
With laughter drowned the whistling wind.
Mirth was within; and Care without
Might gnaw her nails to hear our shout.
Not but amid the buxom scene
Some grave discourse might intervene —
Of the good horse that bore him best,
His shoulder, hoof, and arching crest:
For like mad Tom's,[n] our chiefest care,
Was horse to ride, and weapon wear.
Such nights we've had, and though the game
Of manhood be more sober tame,
And though the field-day, or the drill
Seem less important now — yet still
Such may we hope to share again.
The sprightly thought inspires my strain;
And mark, how like a horseman true,
Lord Marmion's march I thus renew.

## MARMION

### CANTO SIXTH

*The Battle*

Lord Marmion is Henry VIII's ambassador to the court of James IV of Scotland. The date is 1513, shortly before the battle of Flodden. The poem opens at Norham, an English castle on the southern bank of Tweed, with Marmion *en route* to Scotland. He is guided on his journey through the Borders of Scotland by a palmer (his enemy, de Wilton, in disguise). He stays at an inn at Gifford, East Lothian, where he fights and is defeated by a ghostly knight. He inspects the Scottish army on the boroughmuir of Edinburgh and is received at court. When this canto begins he is at Tantallon Castle where he has been sent by James who had refused to negotiate until the Scottish herald sent to defy Henry returns.

The sub-plot is considerably more complicated and much of what is most important happens before *Marmion* opens, with different parts of the history being reported by different characters as the poem unfolds. Lord Marmion had a mistress Constance de Beverley, a renegade nun, but his attentions turned elsewhere towards Clare de Clare who was rich and well-descended and also betrothed to de Wilton. Marmion persuaded the king to approve his match, and got Constance, who was desperate to win him back, to forge a correspondence showing de Wilton guilty of treason. Marmion challenged de Wilton, who was defeated but survived (although none realised this). Clare fled to the monastery of St Hilda at Whitby to escape Marmion, yet the king vowed that Marmion should have her nonetheless. Constance plotted with an accomplice to murder her, but was betrayed to the church, and tried and executed on Holy Isle off the coast of Northumberland. One of her judges was the Abbess of Whitby who had been accompanied by Clare to Holy Isle. On their departure, they were captured by the Scots and taken to Edinburgh. The Abbess was later sent back by sea, and Clare, at Henry's request, was to be taken south by Marmion, to be handed over to her guardian. She too is now at Tantallon.

1

While great events were on the gale,
And each hour brought a varying tale,
And the demeanour, changed and cold,
Of Douglas,[n] fretted Marmion bold,
And, like the impatient steed of war,
He snuffed the battle from afar;
And hopes were none, that back again
Herald should come from Terouenne,[n]
Where England's king in leaguer lay,
Before decisive battle-day; —
While these things were, the mournful Clare
Did in the Dame's[n] devotions share:
For the good Countess ceaseless prayed,
To heaven and saints, her sons to aid,
And, with short interval, did pass
From prayer to book, from book to mass,
And all in high baronial pride, —
A life both dull and dignified; —
Yet as Lord Marmion nothing pressed
Upon her intervals of rest,
Dejected Clara well could bear
The formal state, the lengthened prayer,
Though dearest to her wounded heart
The hours that she might spend apart.

2

I said, Tantallon's dizzy steep[n]
Hung o'er the margin of the deep.
Many a rude tower and rampart there
Repelled the insult of the air,

Which, when the tempest vexed the sky,
Half breeze, half spray, came whistling by.
Above the rest, a turret square
Did o'er its gothic entrance bear,
Of sculpture rude, a stony shield;
The Bloody Heart was in the field,
And in the chief three mullets stood,
The cognizance of Douglas blood.
The turret held a narrow stair,
Which, mounted, gave you access where
A parapet's embattled row
Did seaward round the castle go;
Sometimes in dizzy steps descending,
Sometimes in narrow circuit bending,
Sometimes in platform broad extending,
Its varying circuit did combine
Bulwark, and bartisan, and line,
And bastion, tower, and the vantage-coign;
Above the booming ocean leant
The far-projecting battlement;
The billows burst, in ceaseless flow,
Upon the precipice below.
Where'er Tantallon faced the land,
Gate-works, and walls, were strongly manned;
No need upon the sea-girt side;
The steepy rock, and frantic tide,
Approach of human step denied;
And thus these lines, and ramparts rude,
Were left in deepest solitude.

3

And, for they were so lonely, Clare
Would to these battlements repair,
And muse upon her sorrows there,
  And list the sea-bird's cry;
Or slow, like noon-tide ghost, would glide
Along the dark-gray bulwark's side,
And ever on the heaving tide
  Look down with weary eye.
Oft did the cliff, and swelling main,
Recal the thoughts of Whitby's fane, —
A home she ne'er might see again;
  For she had laid adown,

45 *bartisan*: battlemented parapet or turret

67 *fane*: temple

So Douglas bade, the hood and veil,
And frontlet of the cloister pale,
  And Benedictine[n] gown:
It were unseemly sight, he said,
A novice out of convent shade. —
Now her bright locks, with sunny glow,
Again adorned her brow of snow;
Her mantle rich, whose borders, round,
A deep and fretted broidery bound,
In golden foldings sought the ground;
Of holy ornament, alone
Remained a cross with ruby stone;
  And often did she look
On that which in her hand she bore,
With velvet bound, and broidered o'er,
  Her breviary book.
In such a place, so lone, so grim,
At dawning pale, or twilight dim,
  It fearful would have been,
To meet a form so richly dressed,
With book in hand, and cross on breast,
  And such a woeful mien.
Fitz-Eustace,[n] loitering with his bow,
To practise on the gull and crow,
Saw her, at distance, gliding slow,
  And did by Mary swear, —
Some love-lorn fay she might have been,
Or, in romance, some spell-bound queen;
For ne'er, in work-day world, was seen
  A form so witching fair.

4

Once walking thus, at evening tide,
It chanced a gliding sail she spied,
And, sighing, thought, — 'The Abbess there,
Perchance, does to her home repair;
Her peaceful rule, where duty, free,
Walks hand in hand with charity;
Where oft devotion's tranced glow
Can such a glimpse of heaven bestow,
That the enraptured sisters see
High vision, and deep mystery;
The very form of Hilda fair,[n]
Hovering upon the sunny air,
And smiling on her votaries' prayer.

O! wherefore, to my duller eye,
Did still the Saint her form deny!
Was it, that, seared by sinful scorn,
My heart could neither melt nor burn?
Or lie my warm affections low,
With him, that taught them first to glow? —
Yet, gentle Abbess, well I knew,
To pay thy kindness grateful due,
And well could brook the mild command,
That ruled thy simple maiden band. —
How different now! condemned to bide
My doom from this dark tyrant's pride. —
But Marmion has to learn, ere long,
That constant mind, and hate of wrong,
Descended to a feeble girl,
From Red De Clare, stout Gloster's Earl.
Of such a stem a sapling weak,
He ne'er shall bend, although he break.

5

'But see! — what makes this armour here?'
   For in her path there lay
Targe, corslet, helm; — she viewed them near. —
'The breast-plate pierced! — Aye, much I fear,
Weak fence wert thou 'gainst foeman's spear,
That hath made fatal entrance here,
   As these dark blood-gouts say. —
Thus Wilton! — Oh! not corslet's ward,
Not truth, as diamond pure and hard,
Could be thy manly bosom's guard,
   On yon disastrous day!'—
She raised her eyes in mournful mood, —
*Wilton* himself before her stood!
It might have seemed his passing ghost;
For every youthful grace was lost,
And joy unwonted, and surprise,
Gave their strange wildness to his eyes. —
Expect not, noble dames and lords,
That I can tell such scene in words:
What skilful limner e'er would chuse
To paint the rainbow's varying hues,
Unless to mortal it were given
To dip his brush in dyes of heaven?
   Far less can my weak line declare
      Each changing passion's shade;

Brightening to rapture from despair,
Sorrow, surprise, and pity there,
And joy, with her angelic air,
And hope, that paints the future fair,
Their varying hues displayed:
Each o'er its rival's ground extending,
Alternate conquering, shifting, blending,
Till all, fatigued, the conflict yield,
And mighty love retains the field.
Shortly I tell what then he said,
By many a tender word delayed,
And modest blush and bursting sigh,
And question kind, and fond reply.

6

*De Wilton's History*

'Forget we that disastrous day,
When senseless in the lists I lay.
Thence dragged, — but how I cannot know,
For sense and recollection fled, —
I found me on a pallet low,
Within my ancient beadsman's shed.
Austin, — remember'st thou, my Clare,
How thou didst blush, when the old man,
When first our infant love began,
Said we would make a matchless pair? —
Menials, and friends, and kinsmen fled
From the degraded traitor's bed, —
He only held my burning head,
And tended me for many a day,
While wounds and fever held their sway.
But far more needful was his care,
When sense returned, to wake despair;
For I did tear the closing wound,
And dash me frantic on the ground,
If e'er I heard the name of Clare.
At length, to calmer reason brought,
Much by his kind attendance wrought,
With him I left my native strand,
And, in a palmer's weeds arrayed,
My hated name and form to shade,
I journeyed many a land;
No more a lord of rank and birth,
But mingled with the dregs of earth.
Oft, Austin for my reason feared,

When I would sit, and deeply brood
On dark revenge, and deeds of blood,
Or wild mad schemes upreared.
My friend at length fell sick, and said,
God would remove him soon;
And while upon his dying bed,
He begged of me a boon —
If ere my deadliest enemy
Beneath my brand should conquered lie,
Even then my mercy should awake,
And spare his life for Austin's sake.

7

'Still restless as a second Cain,
To Scotland next my route was ta'en,
Full well the paths I knew;
Fame of my fate made various sound,
That death in pilgrimage I found,
That I had perished of my wound, —
None cared which tale was true:
And living eye could never guess
De Wilton in his palmer's dress;
For now that sable slough is shed,
And trimmed my shaggy beard and head.
I scarcely know me in the glass.
A chance most wond'rous did provide,
That I should be that baron's guide —
I will not name his name! —
Vengeance to God alone belongs;[n]
But, when I think on all my wrongs,
My blood is liquid flame!
And ne'er the time shall I forget,
When, in a Scottish hostel set,
Dark looks we did exchange:
What were his thoughts I cannot tell;
But in my bosom mustered hell
Its plans of dark revenge.

8

'A word of vulgar augury,
That broke from me I scarce knew why,
Brought on a village tale;
Which wrought upon his moody sprite,
And sent him armed forth by night.
I borrowed steed and mail,

And weapons, from his sleeping band;
   And, passing from a postern door,
We met, and 'countered, hand to hand, —
   He fell on Gifford-moor.
For the death-stroke my brand I drew,
(O then my helmed head he knew,
   The palmer's cowl was gone,)
Then had three inches of my blade
The heavy debt of vengeance paid, —
My hand the thought of Austin staid;
   I left him there alone. —
O good old man! even from the grave,
Thy spirit could thy master save:
If I had slain my foeman,[n] ne'er
Had Whitby's Abbess, in her fear,
Given to my hand this packet dear,
Of power to clear my injured fame,
And vindicate De Wilton's name. —
Perchance you heard the Abbess tell
Of the strange pageantry of hell
   That broke our secret speech —
It rose from the infernal shade,
Or featly was some juggle played,
   A tale of peace to teach.
Appeal to heaven I judged was best,
When my name came among the rest.

9

'Now here, within Tantallon Hold,
To Douglas late my tale I told,
To whom my house was known of old.
Won by my proofs, his faulchion bright
This eve anew shall dub me knight.
These were the arms that once did turn
The tide of fight on Otterburne,[n]
And Harry Hotspur forced to yield,
When the dead Douglas won the field.
These Angus gave — his armourer's care,
Ere morn, shall every breach repair;
For nought, he said, was in his halls,
But ancient armour on the walls,
And aged chargers in the stalls,
And women, priests, and gray-haired men;
The rest were all in Twisell[n] glen.

268 *faulchion*: sword

And now I watch my armour here,
By law of arms, till midnight's near;
Then, once again a belted knight,
Seek Surrey's[n] camp with dawn of light.

10

'There soon again we meet, my Clare!
This baron means to guide thee there.
Douglas reveres his king's command,
Else would he take thee from his band.
And there thy kinsman Surrey, too,
Will give De Wilton justice due.
Now meeter far for martial broil,
Firmer my limbs, and strung by toil,
Once more' —— 'O, Wilton! must we then
Risque new-found happiness again,
Trust fate of arms once more?
And is there not a humble glen,
Where we, content and poor,
Might build a cottage in the shade,
A shepherd thou, and I to aid
Thy task on dale and moor? —
That reddening brow! — too well I know,
Not even thy Clare can peace bestow,
While falsehood stains thy name:
Go then to fight! Clare bids thee go!
Clare can a warrior's feelings know,
And weep a warrior's shame;
Can Red Earl Gilbert's spirit feel,
Buckle the spurs upon thy heel,
And belt thee with thy brand of steel,
And send thee forth to fame!' —

11

That night, upon the rocks and bay,
The midnight moon-beam slumbering lay,
And poured its silver light, and pure,
Through loop-hole, and through embrazure,
Upon Tantallon tower and hall;
But chief where arched windows wide
Illuminate the chapel's pride,
The sober glances fall.
Much was there need; though, seamed with scars,
Two veterans of the Douglas' wars,

Though two gray priests were there,
And each a blazing torch held high,
You could not by their blaze descry
The chapel's carving fair.
Amid that dim and smoky light,
Chequering the silvery moon-shine bright,
A bishop[n] by the altar stood,
A noble lord of Douglas blood,
With mitre sheen, and rocquet white;
Yet shewed his meek and thoughtful eye
But little pride of prelacy:
More pleased that, in a barbarous age,
He gave rude Scotland Virgil's page,
Than that beneath his rule he held
The bishopric of fair Dunkeld.
Beside him ancient Angus stood,
Doffed his furred gown, and sable hood;
O'er his huge form, and visage pale,
He wore a cap and shirt of mail,
And lean'd his large and wrinkled hand
Upon the huge and sweeping brand,
Which wont, of yore, in battle-fray,
His foeman's limbs to shred away,
As wood-knife lops the sapling spray.
He seemed as, from the tombs around
Rising at judgment-day,
Some giant Douglas may be found
In all his old array;
So pale his face, so huge his limb,
So old his arms, his look so grim.

12

Then at the altar Wilton kneels,
And Clare the spurs bound on his heels;
And think what next he must have felt,
At buckling of the faulchion belt!
And judge how Clara changed her hue,
While fastening to her lover's side
A friend, which, though in danger tried,
He once had found untrue!
Then Douglas struck him with his blade:
'Saint Michael, and Saint Andrew aid,
I dub thee knight.

329 *rocquet*: rochet, type of surplice

Arise Sir Ralph, De Wilton's heir!
For king, for church, for lady fair,
See that thou fight.' —
And Bishop Gawain, as he rose,
Said, — 'Wilton! grieve not for thy woes,
Disgrace, and trouble,
For He, who honour best bestows,
May give thee double.' —
De Wilton sobbed, for sob he must —
'Where'er I meet a Douglas, trust
That Douglas is my brother!'
'Nay, nay,' old Angus said, 'not so;
To Surrey's camp thou now must go,
Thy wrongs no longer smother.
I have two sons in yonder field;
And, if thou meet'st them under shield,
Upon them bravely — do thy worst;
And foul fall him that blenches first!' —

13

Not far advanced was morning day,
When Marmion did his troop array
To Surrey's camp to ride;
He had safe-conduct for his band,
Beneath the royal seal and hand,
And Douglas gave a guide:
The ancient Earl, with stately grace,
Would Clara on her palfrey place,
And whispered, in an under tone,
'Let the hawk stoop, his prey is flown.'
The train from out the castle drew;
But Marmion stopp'd to bid adieu: —
'Though something I might plain,' he said,
'Of cold respect to stranger guest,
Sent hither by your king's behest,
While in Tantallon's towers I staid,
Part we in friendship from your land,
And, noble Earl, receive my hand.' —
But Douglas round him drew his cloak,
Folded his arms, and thus he spoke: —
'My manors, halls, and bowers, shall still
Be open, at my sovereign's will,
To each one whom he lists, howe'er
Unmeet to be the owner's peer.
My castles are my king's alone,
From turret to foundation-stone —

The hand of Douglas is his own;
And never shall in friendly grasp
The hand of such as Marmion clasp.' —

14

Burned Marmion's swarthy cheek like fire,
And shook his very frame for ire,
And — 'This to me!' he said, —
'An 'twere not for thy hoary beard,
Such hand as Marmion's had not spared
To cleave the Douglas' head!
And, first, I tell thee, haughty peer,
He, who does England's message here,
Although the meanest in her state,
May well, proud Angus, be thy mate:
And, Douglas, more I tell thee here,
Even in thy pitch of pride,
Here in thy hold, thy vassals near,
(Nay, never look upon your lord,
And lay your hands upon your sword,)
I tell thee, thou'rt defied!
And if thou said'st, I am not peer
To any lord in Scotland here,
Lowland or Highland, far or near,
Lord Angus, thou hast lied!' —
On the Earl's cheek the flush of rage
O'ercame the ashen hue of age:
Fierce he broke forth: 'And dar'st thou then
To beard the lion in his den,
The Douglas in his hall?
And hop'st thou hence unscathed to go? —
No, by Saint Bryde of Bothwell, no! —
Up drawbridge, grooms — what, warder, ho!
Let the portcullis fall.' —
Lord Marmion turned, — well was his need!
And dashed the rowels in his steed,
Like arrow through the arch-way sprung,
The ponderous grate behind him rung:
To pass there was such scanty room,
The bars, descending, razed his plume.

15

The steed along the drawbridge flies,
Just as it trembled on the rise;

Not lighter does the swallow skim
Along the smooth lake's level brim.
And when Lord Marmion reached his band,
He halts, and turns with clenched hand,
And shout of loud defiance pours,
And shook his gauntlet at the towers.
'Horse! horse!' the Douglas cried, 'and chase!'
But soon he reined his fury's pace:
'A royal messenger he came,
Though most unworthy of the name. —
A letter forged! Saint Jude to speed!
Did ever knight so foul a deed!
At first in heart it liked me ill,
When the King praised his clerkly skill.
Thanks to Saint Bothan, son of mine,
Save Gawain, ne'er could pen a line:
So swore I, and I swear it still,
Let my boy-bishop fret his fill. —
Saint Mary mend my fiery mood!
Old age ne'er cools the Douglas blood,
I thought to slay him where he stood. —
'Tis pity of him, too,' he cried;
'Bold can he speak, and fairly ride,
I warrant him a warrior tried.' —
With this his mandate he recals,
And slowly seeks his castle halls.

16

The day in Marmion's journey wore;
Yet, ere his passion's gust was o'er,
They crossed the heights of Stanrigg-moor.
His troop more closely there he scann'd,
And missed the Palmer from the band. —
'Palmer or not,' young Blount did say,
'He parted at the peep of day;
Good sooth it was in strange array.' —
'In what array?' said Marmion, quick.
'My lord, I ill can spell the trick;
But all night long, with clink and bang,
Close to my couch did hammers clang;
At dawn the falling drawbridge rang,
And from a loop-hole while I peep,
Old Bell-the-Cat came from the keep,
Wrapped in a gown of sables fair,
As fearful of the morning air;

Beneath, when that was blown aside,
A rusty shirt of mail I spied,
By Archibald won in bloody work,
Against the Saracen and Turk;
Last night it hung not in the hall;
I thought some marvel would befal.
And next I saw them saddled lead
Old Cheviot forth, the Earl's best steed;
A matchless horse, though something old,
Prompt to his paces, cool and bold.
I heard the Sheriff Sholto say,
The Earl did much the Master[n] pray
To use him on the battle-day;
But he preferred' — 'Nay, Henry, cease!
Thou sworn horse-courser, hold thy peace. —
Eustace, thou bear'st a brain — I pray,
What did Blount see at break of day?' —

## 17

'In brief, my lord, we both descried
(For I then stood by Henry's side)
The Palmer mount, and outwards ride,
Upon the Earl's own favourite steed;
All sheathed he was in armour bright,
And much resembled that same knight,
Subdued by you in Cotswold fight:
Lord Angus wished him speed.' —
The instant that Fitz Eustace spoke,
A sudden light on Marmion broke; —
'Ah! dastard fool, to reason lost!'
He muttered; ' 'Twas nor fay nor ghost,
I met upon the moonlight wold,
But living man of earthly mould. —
O dotage blind and gross!
Had I but fought as wont, one thrust
Had laid De Wilton in the dust,
My path no more to cross. —
How stand we now? — he told his tale
To Douglas; and with some avail;
'Twas therefore gloomed his rugged brow. —
Will Surrey dare to entertain,
'Gainst Marmion, charge disproved and vain?
Small risque of that, I trow. —
Yet Clare's sharp questions must I shun;
Must separate Constance from the Nun —

O what a tangled web we weave,
When first we practice to deceive! —
A Palmer too ! — no wonder why
I felt rebuked beneath his eye:
I might have known there was but one,
Whose look could quell Lord Marmion.' —

18

Stung with these thoughts, he urged to speed
His troop, and reached, at eve, the Tweed,
Where Lennel's convent[n] closed their march.
(There now is left but one frail arch,
   Yet mourn thou not its cells;
Our time a fair exchange has made;
Hard by, in hospitable shade,
   A reverend pilgrim[n] dwells,
Well worth the whole Bernardine[n] brood,
That e'er wore sandal, frock, or hood.)
Yet did Saint Bernard's Abbot there
Give Marmion entertainment fair,
And lodging for his train, and Clare.
Next morn the Baron climbed the tower,
To view afar the Scottish power,
   Encamped on Flodden edge:
The white pavilions made a show,
Like remnants of the winter snow,
   Along the dusky ridge.
Long Marmion looked: — at length his eye
Unusual movement might descry,
   Amid the shifting lines:
The Scottish host drawn out appears,
For, flashing on the hedge of spears
   The eastern sun-beam shines.
Their front now deepening, now extending;
Their flank inclining, wheeling, bending,
Now drawing back, and now descending,
The skilful Marmion well could know,
They watched the motions of some foe,
Who traversed on the plain below.

19

Even so it was;— from Flodden ridge
   The Scots beheld the English host
   Leave Barmore-wood,[n] their evening post,
   And heedful watched them as they crossed
The Till by Twisel Bridge.

High sight it is, and haughty, while
They dive into the deep defile;
Beneath the caverned cliff they fall,
Beneath the castle's airy wall.
By rock, by oak, by hawthorn tree,
Troop after troop is disappearing;
Troop after troop their banners rearing,
Upon the eastern bank you see.
Still pouring down the rocky den,
Where flows the sullen Till,
And rising from the dim-wood glen,
Standards on standards, men on men,
In slow succession still,
And bending o'er the Gothic arch,
And pressing on, in ceaseless march,
To gain the opposing hill.
That morn, to many a trumpet-clang,
Twisel! thy rock's deep echo rang;
And many a chief of birth and rank,
Saint Helen! at thy fountain drank.
Thy hawthorn glade, which now we see
In spring-tide bloom so lavishly,
Had then from many an axe its doom,
To give the marching columns room.

20

And why stands Scotland idly now,
Dark Flodden! on thy airy brow,
Since England gains the pass the while,
And struggles through the deep defile?
What checks the fiery soul of James?
Why sits that champion of the dames
Inactive on his steed,
And sees, between him and his land,
Between him and Tweed's southern strand,
His host Lord Surrey lead?
What vails the vain knight-errant's brand? —
O, Douglas,[n] for thy leading wand!
Fierce Randolph, for thy speed!
O for one hour of Wallace[n] wight,
Or well-skilled Bruce, to rule the fight,
And cry — 'Saint Andrew and our right!'
Another sight had seen that morn,
From fate's dark book a leaf been torn,
And Flodden had been Bannock-bourne! —

The precious hour has passed in vain,
And England's host has gained the plain;
Wheeling their march, and circling still,
Around the base of Flodden-hill.

21

Ere yet the bands met Marmion's eye,
Fitz-Eustace shouted loud and high, —
'Hark! hark! my lord, an English drum!
And see ascending squadrons come
Between Tweed's river and the hill,
Foot, horse, and cannon: — hap what hap,
My basnet to a prentice cap,
Lord Surrey's o'er the Till! —
Yet more! yet more! — how fair arrayed
They file from out the hawthorn shade,
And sweep so gallant by!
With all their banners bravely spread,
And all their armour flashing high,
Saint George might waken from the dead,
To see fair England's banners fly.' —
'Stint in thy prate,' quoth Blount; 'thou'dst best,
And listen to our lord's behest.' —
With kindling brow Lord Marmion said, —
'This instant be our band arrayed;
The river must be quickly crossed,
That we may join Lord Surrey's host.
If fight King James, — as well I trust,
That fight he will, and fight he must, —
The Lady Clare behind our lines
Shall tarry, while the battle joins.' —

22

Himself he swift on horseback threw,
Scarce to the Abbot bade adieu;
Far less would listen to his prayer,
To leave behind the helpless Clare.
Down to the Tweed his band he drew,
And muttered, as the flood they view,
'The pheasant in the falcon's claw,
He scarce will yield to please a daw:

627 *basnet*: light globular steel headpiece closed in front with a visor

Lord Angus may the Abbot awe,
So Clare shall bide with me.'
Then on that dangerous ford, and deep,
Where to the Tweed Leat's eddies creep,
He ventured desperately;
And not a moment will he bide,
Till squire, or groom, before him ride;
Headmost of all he stems the tide,
And stems it gallantly.
Eustace held Clare upon her horse,
Old Hubert led her rein,
Stoutly they braved the current's course,
And, though far downward driven per force,
The southern bank they gain;
Behind them, straggling, came to shore;
As best they might, the train:
Each o'er his head his yew-bow bore,
A caution not in vain;
Deep need that day that every string,
By wet unharmed, should sharply ring.
A moment then Lord Marmion staid,
And breathed his steed, his men arrayed,
Then forward moved his band,
Until, Lord Surrey's rear-guard won,
He halted by a cross of stone,
That, on a hillock standing lone,
Did all the field command.

23

Hence might they see the full array
Of either host, for deadly fray;
Their marshalled lines stretched east and west,
And fronted north and south,
And distant salutation past
From the loud cannon mouth;
Not in the close successive rattle,
That breathes the voice of modern battle,
But slow and far between. —
The hillock gained, Lord Marmion staid:
'Here, by this cross,' he gently said,
'You well may view the scene.
Here shalt thou tarry, lovely Clare:
O! think of Marmion in thy prayer! —
Thou wilt not? — well, — no less my care
Shall, watchful, for thy weal prepare. —

You, Blount and Eustace, are her guard,
With ten picked archers of my train;
With England if the day go hard,
To Berwick speed amain. —
But, if we conquer, cruel maid!
My spoils shall at your feet be laid,
When here we meet again.' —
He waited not for answer there,
And would not mark the maid's despair,
Nor heed the discontented look
From either squire; but spurred amain,
And, dashing through the battle-plain,
His way to Surrey took.

24

'—— The good Lord Marmion, by my life!
Welcome to danger's hour! —
Short greeting serves in time of strife: —
Thus have I ranged my power:
Myself will rule this central host,
Stout Stanley fronts their[n] right,
My sons command the vaward post,
With Brian Tunstall, stainless knight;
Lord Dacre, with his horsemen light,
Shall be in rear-ward of the fight,
And succour those that need it most.
Now, gallant Marmion, well I know,
Would gladly to the vanguard go;
Edmund, the Admiral, Tunstall there,
With thee their charge will blithely share;
There fight thine own retainers too,
Beneath De Burg, thy steward true.' —
'Thanks, noble Surrey!' Marmion said,
Nor further greeting there he paid;
But, parting like a thunder-bolt,
First in the vanguard made a halt,
Where such a shout there rose
Of 'Marmion! Marmion!' that the cry
Up Flodden mountain shrilling high,
Startled the Scottish foes.

25

Blount and Fitz-Eustace rested still
With Lady Clare upon the hill;

716 *vaward*: reduced form of vanguard

On which, (for far the day was spent,)
The western sun-beams now were bent.
The cry they heard, its meaning knew,
Could plain their distant comrades view:
Sadly to Blount did Eustace say,
'Unworthy office here to stay!
No hope of gilded spurs to-day. —
But, see! look up — on Flodden bent,
The Scottish foe has fired his tent.'
  And sudden, as he spoke,
From the sharp ridges of the hill,
All downward to the banks of Till,
  Was wreathed in sable smoke;
Volumed and vast, and rolling far,
The cloud enveloped Scotland's war,
  As down the hill they broke;
Nor martial shout, nor minstrel tone,
Announced their march; their tread alone,
At times one warning trumpet blown,
  At times a stifled hum,
Told England, from his mountain-throne
  King James did rushing come. —
Scarce could they hear, or see their foes,
Until at weapon-point they close. —
They close, in clouds of smoke and dust,
With sword-sway, and with lance's thrust;
  And such a yell was there,
Of sudden and portentous birth,
As if men fought upon the earth,
  And fiends in upper air.[n]
Long looked the anxious squires; their eye
Could in the darkness nought descry.

26

At length the freshening western blast
Aside the shroud of battle cast;
And, first, the ridge of mingled spears
Above the brightening cloud appears;
And in the smoke the pennons flew,
As in the storm the white sea-mew.
Then marked they dashing broad and far,
The broken billows of the war,
And plumed crests of chieftains brave,
Floating like foam upon the wave;
  But nought distinct they see:
Wide raged the battle on the plain;

Spears shook, and faulchions flashed amain;
Fell England's arrow-flight like rain;
Crests rose, and stooped, and rose again,
Wild and disorderly.
Amid the scene of tumult, high
They saw Lord Marmion's falcon fly:
And stainless Tunstall's banner white,
And Edmund Howard's lion bright,
Still bear them bravely in the fight;
Although against them come,
Of gallant Gordons many a one,
And many a stubborn Highlandman,
And many a rugged Border clan,
With Huntley, and with Home.

27

Far on the left, unseen the while,
Stanley broke Lennox and Argyle;
Though there the western mountaineer
Rushed with bare bosom on the spear,
And flung the feeble targe aside,
And with both hands the broad-sword plied:
'Twas vain. — But Fortune, on the right,
With fickle smile, cheered Scotland's fight.
Then fell that spotless banner white,
The Howard's lion fell;
Yet still Lord Marmion's falcon flew
With wavering flight, while fiercer grew
Around the battle yell.
The Border slogan rent the sky:
A Home! a Gordon! was the cry;
Loud were the clanging blows;
Advanced, — forced back, — now low, now high,
The pennon sunk and rose;
As bends the bark's mast in the gale,
When rent are rigging, shrouds, and sail,
It wavered mid the foes.
No longer Blount the view could bear: —
'By heaven, and all its saints!' I swear,
I will not see it lost!
Fitz-Eustace, you with Lady Clare
May bid your beads, and patter prayer, —
I gallop to the host.'
And to the fray he rode amain,
Followed by all the archer train.

The fiery youth, with desperate charge,
Made, for a space, an opening large, —
The rescued banner rose, —
But darkly closed the war around,
Like pine-tree, rooted from the ground,
It sunk among the foes.
Then Eustace mounted too; — yet staid,
As loth to leave the helpless maid,
When, fast as shaft can fly,
Blood-shot his eyes, his nostrils spread,
The loose rein dangling from his head,
Housing and saddle bloody red,
Lord Marmion's steed rushed by;
And Eustace, maddening at the sight,
A look and sign to Clara cast,
To mark he would return in haste,
Then plunged into the fight.

28

Ask me not what the maiden feels,
Left in that dreadful hour alone:
Perchance her reason stoops, or reels;
Perchance a courage, not her own,
Braces her mind to desperate tone. —
The scattered van of England wheels; —
She only said, as loud in air
The tumult roared, 'Is Wilton there?' —
They fly, or, maddened by despair,
Fight but to die. — 'Is Wilton there?' —
With that, straight up the hill there rode
Two horsemen drenched with gore,
And in their arms, a helpless load,
A wounded knight they bore.
His hand still strained the broken brand;
His arms were smeared with blood, and sand.
Dragged from among the horses' feet,
With dinted shield, and helmet beat,
The falcon-crest and plumage gone,
Can that be haughty Marmion! . . . .
Young Blount his armour did unlace,
And, gazing on his ghastly face,
Said — 'By Saint George, he's gone!
That spear-wound has our master sped;
And see the deep cut on his head!
Good night to Marmion.' —

'Unnurtured Blount! thy brawling cease:
He opes his eyes,' said Eustace; 'peace!' —

29

When, doffed his casque, he felt free air,
Around gan Marmion wildly stare: —
'Where's Harry Blount? Fitz-Eustace where?
Linger ye here, ye hearts of hare!
Redeem my pennon, — charge again!
Cry — "Marmion to the rescue!" — Vain!
Last of my race, on battle-plain
That shout shall ne'er be heard again! —
Yet my last thought is England's: — fly,
  To Dacre bear my signet-ring;
  Tell him his squadrons up to bring. —
Fitz-Eustace, to Lord Surrey hie:
  Tunstall lies dead upon the field;
  His life-blood stains the spotless shield:
  Edmund is down; — my life is reft; —
  The Admiral alone is left.
  Let Stanley charge with spur of fire, —
  With Chester charge, and Lancashire,
  Full upon Scotland's central host,
  Or victory and England's lost. —
  Must I bid twice? — hence, varlets! fly!
  Leave Marmion here alone — to die.' —
  They parted, and alone he lay;
  Clare drew her from the sight away,
  Till pain wrung forth a lowly moan,
  And half he murmured, — 'Is there none,
  Of all my halls have nurst,
Page, squire, or groom, one cup to bring
Of blessed water, from the spring,
  To slake my dying thirst!' —

30

O, woman! in our hours of ease,
Uncertain, coy, and hard to please,
And variable as the shade
By the light quivering aspen made;
When pain and anguish wring the brow,
A ministering angel thou! —
Scarce were the piteous accents said,
When, with the Baron's casque, the maid
  To the nigh streamlet ran:

Forgot were hatred, wrongs, and fears;
The plaintive voice alone she hears,
   Sees but the dying man.
She stooped her by the runnel's side,
   But in abhorrence backward drew,
For, oozing from the mountain's side,
Where raged the war, a dark red tide
   Was curdling in the streamlet blue.
Where shall she turn! — behold her mark
   A little fountain-cell,
Where water, clear as diamond-spark,
   In a stone bason fell.
Above, some half-worn letters say,
'*Drink · weary · pilgrim · drink · and · pray ·*
*For · the · kind · soul · of · Sybil · Grey ·*
   *Who · built · this · cross · and · well.*'
She filled the helm, and back she hied,
And with surprise and joy espied
   A monk supporting Marmion's head;
A pious man, whom duty brought
To dubious verge of battle fought,
   To shrieve the dying, bless the dead.

31

Deep drank Lord Marmion of the wave,
And, as she stooped his brow to lave —
'Is it the hand of Clare,' he said,
'Or injured Constance, bathes my head?'
   Then, as remembrance rose, —
'Speak not to me of shrift or prayer!
   I must redress her woes.
Short space, few words, are mine to spare;
Forgive and listen, gentle Clare!' —
   'Alas!' she said, 'the while, —
O think of your immortal weal!
In vain for Constance is your zeal;
   She died at Holy Isle.' —
Lord Marmion started from the ground,
As light as if he felt no wound;
Though in the action burst the tide,
In torrents, from his wounded side.
'Then it was truth!' — he said — 'I knew
That the dark presage must be true. —
   I would the fiend, to whom belongs
   The vengeance due to all her wrongs,
      Would spare me but a day!

For wasting fire, and dying groan,
And priests slain on the altar stone,
Might bribe him for delay.
It may not be! — this dizzy trance —
Curse on yon base marauder's lance,
And doubly cursed my failing brand!
A sinful heart makes feeble hand.' —
Then, fainting, down on earth he sunk,
Supported by the trembling monk.

32

With fruitless labour, Clara bound,
And strove to staunch, the gushing wound:
The monk, with unavailing cares,
Exhausted all the church's prayers;
Ever, he said, that, close and near,
A lady's voice was in his ear,
And that the priest he could not hear,
For that she ever sung,
*'In the lost battle, borne down by the flying,*
*Where mingles war's rattle with groans of the dying!'*
So the notes rung;
'Avoid thee, fiend! — with cruel hand,
Shake not the dying sinner's sand! —
O look, my son, upon yon sign
Of the Redeemer's grace divine;
O think on faith and bliss! —
By many a death-bed I have been,
And many a sinner's parting seen,
But never aught like this.' —
The war, that for a space did fail,
Now trebly thundering swelled the gale,
And — *Stanley!* was the cry; —
A light on Marmion's visage spread,
And fired his glazing eye:
With dying hand, above his head
He shook the fragment of his blade,
And shouted 'Victory! —
Charge, Chester, charge! On, Stanley, on!' . . . .
Were the last words of Marmion.

33

By this, though deep the evening fell,
Still rose the battle's deadly swell,
For still the Scots, around their king,
Unbroken, fought in desperate ring.

Where's now their victor vaward wing,
Where Huntley, and where Home? —
O for a blast of that dread horn,
On Fontarabian echoes borne,
That to King Charles did come,
When Rowland brave, and Olivier,[n]
And every paladin and peer,
On Roncesvalles died!
Such blast might warn them, not in vain,
To quit the plunder of the slain,
And turn the doubtful day again,
While yet on Flodden side,
Afar, the royal standard flies,
And round it toils and bleeds and dies,
Our Caledonian pride!
In vain the wish — for far away,
While spoil and havoc mark their way,
Near Sybil's Cross the plunderers stray. —
'O Lady,' cried the monk, 'away!' —
And placed her on her steed;
And led her to the chapel fair,
Of Tilmouth upon Tweed.
There all the night they spent in prayer,
And, at the dawn of morning, there
She met her kinsman, Lord Fitz-Clare.

34

But as they left the dark'ning heath,
More desperate grew the strife of death.
The English shafts in vollies hailed,
In headlong charge their horse assailed;
Front, flank, and rear, the squadrons sweep,
To break the Scottish circle deep,
That fought around their king.
But yet, though thick the shafts as snow,
Though charging knights like whirlwinds go,
Though bill-men deal the ghastly blow,
Unbroken was the ring;
The stubborn spear-men still made good
Their dark impenetrable wood,
Each stepping where his comrade stood,
The instant that he fell.
No thought was there of dastard flight; —
Linked in the serried phalanx tight,
Groom fought like noble, squire like knight,
As fearlessly and well,

Till utter darkness closed her wing
O'er their thin host and wounded king.
Then skilful Surrey's sage commands
Led back from strife his shatter'd bands;
And from the charge they drew,
As mountain-waves, from wasted lands,
Sweep back to ocean blue.
Then did their loss his foemen know;
Their king, their lords, their mightiest low,
They melted from the field as snow,
When streams are swoln, and south winds blow,
Dissolves in silent dew.
Tweed's echoes heard the ceaseless plash,
While many a broken band,
Disordered, through her currents dash,
To gain the Scottish land;
To town and tower, to down and dale,
To tell red Flodden's dismal tale,
And raise the universal wail.
Tradition, legend, tune, and song,
Shall many an age that wail prolong:
Still from the sire the son shall hear
Of the stern strife, and carnage drear,
Of Flodden's fatal field,
Where shivered was fair Scotland's spear,
And broken was her shield!

35

Day dawns upon the mountain's side: —
There, Scotland! lay thy bravest pride,
Chiefs, knights, and nobles, many a one;
The sad survivors all are gone. —
View not that corpse mistrustfully,
Defaced and mangled though it be;
Nor to yon Border castle high[n]
Look northward with upbraiding eye;
Nor cherish hope in vain,
That, journeying far on foreign strand,
The royal pilgrim to his land
May yet return again.
He saw the wreck his rashness wrought;
Reckless of life, he desperate fought,
And fell on Flodden plain:
And well in death his trusty brand,
Firm clenched within his manly hand,

  Beseemed the monarch slain.
But, O! how changed since yon blithe night! —
Gladly I turn me from the sight,
  Unto my tale again.

36

Short is my tale: — Fitz-Eustace' care
A pierced and mangled body bare
To moated Lichfield's lofty pile;
And there, beneath the southern aisle,
A tomb, with gothic sculpture fair,
Did long Lord Marmion's image bear.
(Now vainly for its site you look;
'Twas levelled, when fanatic Brook[n]
The fair cathedral stormed and took;
But, thanks to heaven, and good Saint Chad,
A guerdon meet the spoiler had!)
There erst was martial Marmion found,
His feet upon a couchant hound,
  His hands to heaven upraised;
And all around, on scutcheon rich,
And tablet carved, and fretted niche,
  His arms and feats were blazed.
And yet, though all was carved so fair,
And priests for Marmion breathed the prayer,
The last Lord Marmion lay not there.
From Ettrick woods, a peasant swain
Followed his lord to Flodden plain, —
One of those flowers, whom plaintive lay
In Scotland mourns as 'wede away:'[n]
Sore wounded, Sybil's Cross he spied,
And dragged him to its foot, and died,
Close by the noble Marmion's side.
The spoilers stripped and gashed the slain,
And thus their corpses were mista'en;
And thus, in the proud Baron's tomb,
The lowly woodsman took the room.

37

Less easy task it were, to shew
Lord Marmion's nameless grave, and low:
  They dug his grave e'en where he lay,
    But every mark is gone;
  Time's wasting hand has done away

The simple Cross of Sybil Grey,
And broke her font of stone:
But yet from out the little hill
Oozes the slender springlet still.
Oft halts the stranger there,
For thence may best his curious eye
The memorable field descry;
And shepherd boys repair
To seek the water-flag and rush,
And rest them by the hazel bush,
And plait their garlands fair;
Nor dream they sit upon the grave,
That holds the bones of Marmion brave. —
When thou shalt find the little hill,
With thy heart commune, and be still.
If ever, in temptation strong,
Thou left'st the right path for the wrong;
If every devious step, thus trode,
Still led thee farther from the road;
Dread thou to speak presumptuous doom,
On noble Marmion's lowly tomb;
But say, 'He died a gallant knight,
With sword in hand, for England's right.'

38

I do not rhyme to that dull elf,
Who cannot image to himself,
That all through Flodden's dismal night,
Wilton was foremost in the fight;
That, when brave Surrey's steed was slain,
'Twas Wilton mounted him again;
'Twas Wilton's brand that deepest hewed,
Amid the spearmen's stubborn wood;
Unnamed by Hollinshed or Hall,[n]
He was the living soul of all;
That, after fight, his faith made plain,
He won his rank and lands again;
And charged his old paternal shield
With bearings won on Flodden field. —
Nor sing I to that simple maid,
To whom it must in terms be said,
That king and kinsmen did agree,
To bless fair Clara's constancy;
Who cannot, unless I relate,
Paint to her mind the bridal's state,
That Wolsey's[n] voice the blessing spoke,

More, Sands, and Denny,[n] passed the joke;
That bluff King Hal the curtain drew,
And Catherine's hand the stocking threw;
And afterwards, for many a day,
That it was held enough to say,
In blessing to a wedded pair,
'Love they like Wilton and like Clare!' —

# James Hogg
## 1770–1835

James Hogg, 'the Ettrick Shepherd', was born in Ettrick in Selkirkshire and received there a scanty schooling. His father, a shepherd and later tenant of a small farm, failed, and the lad went to work herding at the age of seven. His formal education, though supplemented in later years, was never extensive, but by sheer application he taught himself to read, write and play the fiddle. His mother possessed a great store of ballads, traditional songs and stories and from her and her relatives, the Laidlaws of Willenslee, Hogg got to know not only the old popular literature of Scotland but also Hary's *Wallace*, in Hamilton of Gilbertfield's version, and Allan Ramsay's *The Gentle Shepherd*. In 1790 Hogg became a shepherd for another relative, Laidlaw of Blackhouse, and with his encouragement began to write songs and ballads which gained him a local reputation as 'Jamie the poeter'. His first volume of verse, *Scottish Pastorals*, appeared in 1801 but it was the publication of *Minstrelsy of the Scottish Border* in 1802 that inspired him to a literary career and led to his lifelong friendship with Scott. However he was, in his own words, 'much dissatisfied with the imitations of the ancient ballads contained in it, and immediately set about imitating the ancient ballads myself' (*Memoirs of the Author's Life*, ed. Douglas S. Mack, p. 16). These imitations, first published periodically in *The Scots Magazine*, were collected as *The Mountain Bard* in 1807.

Hogg wrote voluminously in verse and prose, and his works included songs and collections of tales, novels, and much journalism. The famous conversations of 'Christopher North' and his friends in the series *Noctes Ambrosianae* in *Blackwood's Magazine*, in which he was caricatured as 'The Shepherd', made him known all over Britain. This exaggerated picture, which Hogg sometimes resented, made him a national figure; yet he also much enjoyed his celebrity, in a simple, vain, way. Patronised by Scott and often made a butt by his more cultured friends, Hogg was not truly appreciated until the present century, when *The Private Memoirs and Confessions of a Justified Sinner* was acclaimed as a profound study of moral evil and cultural schizophrenia, and *The Three Perils of Man* recognised as a unique blend of romance, comedy and fantasy.

His literary output was large, miscellaneous, and of uneven quality. His songs are in the tradition of Ramsay and Burns: the best of them, such as *When the Kye Comes Hame*, and *A Boy's Song*, are simple and memorable, but many others pander to popular sentiment in the manner of the later 'kailyard' school. *Kilmeny* and *The Witch of Fife* are narrative inserts in a longer poem, *The Queen's Wake* (1813), structured around a festival of poetry to celebrate the arrival in Scotland of Mary, Queen of Scots. Both poems have links with the older ballads, *Kilmeny* with *Thomas the Rhymer* and *Tam Lin*, and *The Witch of Fife* with the folklore of witchcraft and with the popular comic tradition.

Although the opening and ending of *Kilmeny* are amongst the finest passages in Scottish poetry, some may feel that the middle section sinks to a rather pedestrian level and that its historical allegory is inappropriate in a poem whose visionary content invites comparison with Blake's *The Little Girl Lost* and *The Little Girl Found* ('In futurity/I prophetic see' and 'All the night in woe/Lyca's parents go'). Yet that very allegory is profoundly Scottish, in the tradition of Ramsay's *The Vision*.

Like Ramsay too, and so many other Scottish writers (including Scott), Hogg delights in antiquarian embellishments and mystification. Hogg was a master of humorous effect and a parodist of genius: it is only space that makes us exclude one of his two brilliant parodies of Wordsworth, *James Rigg* and *The Flying Taylor* from *The Poetic Mirror* (1816), a volume in which Hogg 'took off' most of his contemporaries. It may be argued that this aspect of his genius found its best vehicle in his pieces in *Blackwood's Magazine*, a compendium of prose and verse, of serious political commentary, inventive literary criticism, satire, fiction and fantasy, whose brilliance is only now beginning to win recognition again. *May of the Moril Glen* was first published in *Blackwood's* in August 1827 (vol. 22, pp. 214–221) under the title *The Perilis of Wemyng*. Although nominally a parody of a supernatural ballad, it is a rollicking and exuberant satire, directed at male sexuality, that deflates by inflation.

*Editions:*

*The Works of the Ettrick Shepherd*, ed. Thomas Thomson, 2 vols (London, Edinburgh and Glasgow, 1865).

*Selected Poems*, ed. Douglas S. Mack (Oxford, 1970).

*Biography:*

Edith C. Batho, *The Ettrick Shepherd* (Cambridge, 1927).

James Hogg, *Memoirs of the Author's Life, and Familiar Anecdotes of Sir Walter Scott*, ed. Douglas S. Mack (Edinburgh, 1972).

*Criticism:*

Douglas Gifford, *James Hogg* (Edinburgh, 1976).

Louis Simpson, *James Hogg: a Critical Study* (Edinburgh and London, 1962).

Douglas S. Mack, 'Hogg's *Kilmeny*: an Interpretation', *Studies in Scottish Literature* 4 (1966–67), 42–45; 'The Development of Hogg's Poetry', *Scottish Literary News* 3(1) (1973), 1–8.

Alexander Scott, 'Hogg's *May of the Moril Glen*', *Scottish Literary News* 3(1) (1973), 9–16.

John R. Mair, 'A Note on Hogg's *Kilmeny*', *Scottish Literary News* 3(1) (1973), 17–20.

*Scottish Literary Journal* 10(1) (May, 1983): James Hogg Number.

## THE WITCH OF FIFE

'Quhare haif ye been, ye ill womyne,
These three lang nightis fra hame?
Quhat garris the sweit drap fra yer brow,
Like clotis of the saut sea faem?

'It fearis me muckil ye haif seen
Quhat good man never knew;
It fearis me muckil ye haif been
Quhare the gray cock never crew.

'But the spell may crack, and the brydel breck,
Then sherpe yer werde will be;
Ye had better sleipe in yer bed at hame,
Wi' yer deire littil bairnis and me' —

'Sit dune, sit dune, my leil auld man,
Sit dune, and listin to me;
I'll gar the hayre stand on yer crown,
And the cauld sweit blind yer e'e.

'But tell nae wordis, my gude auld man,
Tell never word again;
Or deire shall be yer courtisye,
And driche and sair yer pain.

'The first leet night, quhan the new moon set,
Quhan all was douffe and mirk,
We saddled ouir naigis wi' the moon-fern leif,
And rode fra Kilmerrin kirk.

'Some horses ware of the brume-cow framit,
And some of the greine bay tree;
But mine was made of ane humloke schaw,
And a stout stallion was he.

'We raide the tod doune on the hill,
The martin on the law;
And we huntyd the hoolet out of brethe,
And forcit him doune to fa.' —

1 *Quhare*: where
3 *Quhat*: what
*garris*: makes
5 *muckil*: much
10 *werde*: fate
13 *leil*: loyal
20 *driche*: dreary
21 *leet*: chosen
22 *douffe*: gloomy, dull
*mirk*: dark
23 *moon-fern*: ox-eye daisy
25 *brume-cow*: besom of broom twigs
27 *humloke*: hemlock
*schaw*: bush
29 *tod*: fox
30 *law*: hill
31 *hoolet*: owl

'Quhat guid was that, ye ill womyne?
  Quhat guid was that to thee?
Ye wald better haif been in yer bed at hame,
  Wi' yer deire littil bairnis and me.' —

'And aye we raide, and se merrily we raide,
  Throw the merkist gloffis of the night;
And we swam the floode, and we darnit the woode,
  Till we cam to the Lommond height.[n]

'And quhen we cam to the Lommond height,
  Se lythlye we lychtid doune;
And we drank fra the hornis that never grew,
  The beer that was never browin.

'Then up there raise ane wee wee man,
  Franethe the moss-gray stane;
His face was wan like the collifloure,
  For he nouthir had blude nor bane.

'He set ane reid-pipe till his muthe,
  And he playit se bonnilye,
Till the gray curlew, and the black-cock, flew
  To listen his melodye.

'It rang se sweet through the grein Lommond,
  That the nycht-winde lowner blew;
And it soupit alang the Loch Leven,
  And wakinit the white sea-mew.

'It rang se sweet through the grein Lommond,
  Se sweitly butt and se shill,
That the wezilis laup out of their mouldy holis,
  And dancit on the mydnycht hill.

'The corby craw cam gledgin near,
  The ern gede veeryng bye;
And the troutis laup out of the Leven Loch,
  Charmit with the melodye.

38 *merkist*: darkest
*gloffis*: fears
39 *darnit*: passed secretly through
44 *browin*: brewed
46 *Franethe*: from underneath
51 *black-cock*: black grouse
54 *lowner*: milder
55 *soupit*: swept
58 *butt*: certainly
59 *mouldy*: in the earth
61 *corby craw*: carrion crow
*gledgin*: glancing
62 *ern*: eagle

'And aye we dancit on the grein Lommond,
Till the dawn on the ocean grew:
Ne wonder I was a weary wycht
Quhan I cam hame to you.'—

'Quhat guid, quhat guid, my weird weird wyfe,
Quhat guid was that to thee?
Ye wald better haif bein in yer bed at hame,
Wi yer deire littil bairnis and me.'

'The second nycht, quhan the new moon set,
O'er the roaryng sea we flew;
The cockle-shell owr trusty bark,
Our sailis of the grein sea-rue.

'And the bauld windis blew, and the fire-flauchtis flew,
And the sea ran to the skie;
And the thunner it growlit, and the sea-dogs howlit,
And we gaed scouryng bye.

'And aye we mountit the sea-green hillis,
Quhill we brushit thro' the cludis of the hevin;
Than sousit dounright like the stern-shot light,
Fra the liftis blue casement driven.

'But our taickil stood, and our bark was good,
And se pang was our pearily prowe;
Quhan we culdna speil the brow of the wavis,
We needilit them throu belowe.

'As fast as the hail, as fast as the gale,
As fast as the midnycht leme,
We borit the breiste of the burstyng swale,
Or fluffit i' the flotyng faem.

'And quhan to the Norraway shore we wan,
We muntyd our steedis of the wynd,
And we splashit the floode, and we darnit the woode,
And we left the shouir behynde.

'Fleet is the roe on the grein Lommond,
And swift is the couryng grew;
The rein-deer dun can eithly run,
Quhan the houndis and the hornis pursue.

67 *wycht*: person
77 *fire-flauchtis*: lightning
82 *quhill*: till
83 *sousit*: swooped down
*stern-shot*: meteor
84 *liftis*: sky's
86 *pang*: tough
*pearily*: pearly, shell-like
87 *speil*: climb
90 *leme*: gleam
91 *swale*: swell
92 *fluffit*: shot past
96 *shouir*: shore
98 *couryng*: ?coursing
*grew*: greyhound
99 *eithly*: easily

'But nowther the roe, nor the rein-deer dun,
  The hinde nor the couryng grew,
Culd fly owr muntaine, muir, and dale,
  As owr braw steedis they flew.

'The dales war deep, and the Doffrinis[n] steep,
  And we rase to the skyis e'e-bree;
Quhite, quhite was ouir rode, that was never trode,
  Owr the snawis of eternity!

'And quhan we cam to the Lapland lone,
  The fairies war all in array;
For all the genii of the north
  War keepyng their holeday.

'The warlock men and the weird wemyng,
  And the fays of the wood and the steep,
And the phantom hunteris[n] all war there,
  And the mermaidis of the deep.

'And they washit us all with the witch-water,
  Distillit fra the moorland dew,
Quhill our beauty blumit like the Lapland rose,
  That wylde in the foreste grew.' —

'Ye lee, ye lee, ye ill womyne,
  Se loud as I heir ye lee!
For the warst-faurd wyfe on the shoris of Fyfe
  Is cumlye comparet wi' thee.' —

'Then the mer-maidis sang and the woodlandis rang,
  Se sweetly swellit the quire;
On every cliff a herpe they hang,
  On every tree a lyre.

'And aye they sang, and the woodlandis rang,
  And we drank, and we drank se deep;
Then soft in the armis of the warlock men,
  We laid us dune to sleep.' —

'Away, away, ye ill womyne,
  An ill deide met ye dee!
Quhan ye hae pruvit se false to yer God,
  Ye can never pruve trew to me.' —

122 *se*: so 123 *faurd*: favoured

'And there we lernit fra the fairy foke,
And fra our master true,
The wordis that can beire us throu the air,
And lokkis and baris undo.

'Last nycht we met at Maisry's cot;
Richt weil the wordis we knew;
And we set a foot on the black cruik-shell,
And out at the lum we flew.

'And we flew owr hill, and we flew owr dale,
And we flew owr firth and sea,
Until we cam to merry Carlisle,
Quhar we lightit on the lea.

'We gaed to the vault beyound the towir,
Quhar we enterit free as ayr;
And we drank, and we drank of the bishopis wine
Quhill we culde drynk ne mair.' —

'Gin that be trew, my gude auld wyfe,
Whilk thou hast tauld to me,
Betide my death, betide my lyfe,
I'll beire thee companye.

'Neist tyme ye gaung to merry Carlisle
To drynk of the blude-reid wine,
Beshrew my heart, I'll fly with thee,
If the diel should fly behynde.'

'Ah! little do ye ken, my silly auld man,
The daingeris we maun dree;
Last nichte we drank of the bishopis wyne,
Quhill near near taen war we.

'Afore we wan to the sandy ford,
The gor-cockis nichering flew;
The lofty crest of Ettrick Pen[n]
Was wavit about with blew,
And, flichtering throu the air, we fand
The chill chill mornyng dew.

143 *cruik-shell*: chain and hook for a pot over a fire
144 *lum*: chimney
153 *gin*: if
157 *neist*: next
162 *dree*: endure
166 *gor-cockis*: moorcocks
166 *nichering*: whinnying, like a horse
169 *flichtering*: fluttering

'As we flew owr the hillis of Braid,[n]
The sun rase fair and clear;
There gurly James[n], and his baronis braw,
War out to hunt the deere.

'Their bowis they drew, their arrowis flew,
And peircit the ayr with speede,
Quhill purpil fell the mornyng dew
With witch-blude rank and reide.

'Littil do ye ken, my silly auld man,
The dangeris we maun dree;
Ne wonder I am a weary wycht
Quhan I come hame to thee.' —

'But tell me the *word*, my gude auld wyfe,
Come tell it me speedilye:
For I lang to drink of the gude reide wyne,
And to wyng the ayr with thee.

'Yer hellish horse I wilna ryde,
Nor sail the seas in the wynd;
But I can flee as well as thee,
And I'll drynk quhile ye be blynd.' —

'O fy! O fy! my leil auld man,
That word I darena tell;
It wald turn this warld all upside down,
And make it warse than hell.

'For all the lasses in the land
Wald munt the wynd and fly;
And the men wald doff their doublets syde,
And after them wald ply.' —

But the auld gudeman was ane cunnyng auld man,
And ane cynnyng auld man was he;
And he watchit, and he watchit for mony a nychte,
The witches' flychte to see.

Ane nychte he darnit in Maisry's cot;
The fearless haggs came in;
And he heard the word of awsome weird,
And he saw their deedis of synn.

173 *gurly*: surly
189 *flee*: fly
197 *syde*: long
203 *darnit*: hid

Then ane by ane, they said that word,
As fast to the fire they drew;
Then set a foot on the black cruik-shell,
And out at the lum they flew.

The auld gudeman cam fra his hole
With feire and muckil dreide,
But yet he culdna think to rue,
For the wyne came in his head.

He set his foot in the black cruik-shell,
With ane fixit and ane wawlyng e'e;
And he said the word that I darena say,
And out at the lum flew he.

The witches skalit the moon-beam pale;
Deep groanit the trembling wynde;
But they never wist till our auld gudeman
Was hoveryng them behynde.

They flew to the vaultis of merry Carlisle,
Quhair they enterit free as ayr;
And they drank and they drank of the bishopis wyne
Quhill they culde drynk ne mair.

The auld gudeman he grew se crouse,
He dancit on the mouldy ground,
And he sang the bonniest sangs of Fife,
And he tuzzlit the kerlyngs round.

And aye he peircit the tither butt,
And he suckit, and he suckit se lang,
Quhill his e'en they closit, and his voice grew low,
And his tongue wald hardly gang.

The kerlyngs drank of the bishopis wyne
Quhill they scentit the mornyng wynde;
Then clove again the yeilding ayr,
And left the auld man behynde.

And aye he slepit on the damp damp floor,
He slepit and he snorit amain;
He never dreamit he was far fra hame,
Or that the auld wyvis war gane.

213 *rue*: repent (of his decision)
216 *wawlyng*: rolling
221 *wist till*: knew that
227 *crouse*: merry
230 *tuzzlit*: fondled roughly
*kerlyngs*: old women
231 *tither*: other

And aye he slepit on the damp damp floor,
  Quhill past the mid-day highte,
Quhan wakenit by five rough Englishmen,
  That trailit him to the lychte.

'Now quha are ye, ye silly auld man,
  That sleepis se sound and se weil?
Or how gat ye into the bishopis vault
  Throu lokkis and barris of steel?'

The auld gudeman he tryit to speak,
  But ane word he culdna fynde;
He tryit to think, but his head whirlit round,
  And ane thing he culdna mynde:—
'I cam fra Fyfe,' the auld man cryit,
  'And I cam on the midnight wynde.'

They nickit the auld man, and they prickit the auld man,
  And they yerkit his limbis with twine,
Quhill the reide blude ran in his hose and shoon,
  But some cryit it was wyne.

They lickit the auld man, and they prickit the auld man,
  And they tyit him till ane stone;
And they set ane bele-fire him about,
  To burn him skin and bone.

'O wae to me!' said the puir auld man,
  'That ever I saw the day!
And wae be to all the ill wemyng
  That lead puir men astray!

'Let nevir ane auld man after this
  To lawless greide inclyne;
Let nevir ane auld man after this
  Rin post to the deil for wyne.'

The reike flew up in the auld manis face,
  And choukit him bitterlye;
And the lowe cam up with ane angry blese,
  And it syngit his auld breek-nee.

254 *ane thing*: a single thing
258 *yerkit*: bound
261 *lickit*: beat
263 *bele-fire*: bonfire
273 *reike*: smoke
275 *lowe*: fire
276 *breek-nee*: the knees of his breeches

He lukit to the land fra whence he came,
For lukis he culde get ne mae;
And he thochte of his deire littil bairnis at hame,
And O the auld man was wae!

But they turnit their facis to the sun,
With gloffe and wonderous glair,
For they saw ane thing beth lairge and dun,
Comin swaipin down the aire.

That burd it cam fra the landis o' Fife,
And it cam rycht tymeouslye,
For quha was it but the auld manis wife,
Just comit his dethe to see.

Scho pat ane reide cap on his heide,
And the auld gudeman lookit fain,
Then whisperit ane word intil his lug,
And tovit to the aire again.

The auld gudeman he gae ane bob
I' the mids o' the burnyng lowe;
And the sheklis that band him to the ring,
They fell fra his armis like towe.

He drew his breath, and he said the word,
And he said it with muckle glee,
Then set his fit on the burnyng pile,
And away to the aire flew he.

Till aince he cleirit the swirlyng reike,
He lukit beth ferit and sad;
But whan he wan to the lycht blue aire,
He lauchit as he'd been mad.

His armis war spred, and his heide was hiche,
And his feite stack out behynde;
And the laibies of the auld manis cote
War wauffyng in the wynde.

And aye he neicherit, and aye he flew,
For he thochte the ploy se raire;
It was like the voice of the gainder blue,
Whan he flees throu the aire.

282 *gloffe*: sudden
286 *tymeouslye*: in time
289 *scho*: she
291 *lug*: ear
292 *tovit*: flew
302 *ferit*: afraid
307 *laibies*: skirts
308 *wauffyng*: waving
309 *neicherit*: chortled uproariously

He lukit back to the Carlisle men
As he borit the norlan sky;
He noddit his heide, and gae ane girn,
But he nevir said gude-bye.

They vanisht far i' the liftis blue wale,
Ne maire the English saw,
But the auld manis lauche cam on the gale,
With a lang and a loud gaffa.

May everilke man in the land of Fife
Read what the drinkeris dree;
And nevir curse his puir auld wife,
Rychte wicked altho scho be.

315 *girn*: grin, grimace
317 *wale*: veil

## KILMENY

Bonny Kilmeny gaed up the glen;
But it wasna to meet Duneira's[n] men,
Nor the rosy monk of the isle to see,
For Kilmeny was pure as pure could be.
It was only to hear the yorlin sing,
And pu' the cress-flower round the spring;
The scarlet hypp and the hindberrye,
And the nut that hang frae the hazel tree;
For Kilmeny was pure as pure could be.
But lang may her minny look o'er the wa',
And lang may she seek i' the green-wood shaw;
Lang the laird of Duneira blame,
And lang, lang greet or Kilmeny come hame!

When many a day had come and fled,
When grief grew calm, and hope was dead,
When mess for Kilmeny's soul had been sung,
When the bedes-man had prayed, and the dead-bell rung,
Late, late in a gloamin when all was still,
When the fringe was red on the westlin hill,
The wood was sere, the moon i' the wane,
The reek o' the cot hung over the plain,

5 *yorlin*: yellow-hammer
7 *hindberrye*: raspberry
10 *minny*: mother
11 *shaw*: grove, covert
13 *greet*: weep
*or*: before
19 *westlin*: westward
20 *sere*: withered
21 *reek*: smoke

Like a little wee cloud in the world its lane;
When the ingle lowed with an eiry leme,
Late, late in the gloamin Kilmeny came hame!

'Kilmeny, Kilmeny, where have you been?
Lang hae we sought baith holt and den;
By linn, by ford, and green-wood tree,
Yet you are halesome and fair to see.
Where gat you that joup o' the lilly scheen?
That bonny snood of the birk sae green?
And these roses, the fairest that ever were seen?
Kilmeny, Kilmeny, where have you been?'

Kilmeny looked up with a lovely grace,
But nae smile was seen on Kilmeny's face;
As still was her look, and as still was her ee,
As the stillness that lay on the emerant lea,
Or the mist that sleeps on a waveless sea.
For Kilmeny had been she knew not where,
And Kilmeny had seen what she could not declare;
Kilmeny had been where the cock never crew,
Where the rain never fell, and the wind never blew,
But it seemed as the harp of the sky had rung,
And the airs of heaven[n] played round her tongue,
When she spake of the lovely forms she had seen,
And a land where sin had never been;
A land of love, and a land of light,
Withouten sun, or moon, or night:
Where the river swa'd a living stream,
And the light a pure celestial beam:
The land of vision it would seem,
A still, an everlasting dream.

In yon green-wood there is a waik,
And in that waik there is a wene,
And in that wene there is a maike,
That neither has flesh, blood, nor bane;
And down in yon green-wood he walks his lane.

In that green wene Kilmeny lay,
Her bosom happed wi' the flowerits gay;

22 *its lane*: by itself
23 *ingle*: fire
*lowed*: glowed
*leme*: gleam, light
26 *holt*: high ground
*den*: dingle, dell
27 *linn*: waterfall
29 *joup*: woman's mantle
30 *snood*: girl's hair-band
36 *emerant*: emerald
48 *swa'd*: rolled
52 *waik*: walk, area
53 *wene*: dwelling
*maike*: fellow
58 *happed*: covered, screened

But the air was soft and the silence deep,
And bonny Kilmeny fell sound asleep.
She kend nae mair, nor opened her ee,
Till waked by the hymns of a far countrye.

She 'wakened on couch of the silk sae slim,
All striped wi' the bars of the rainbow's rim;
And lovely beings round were rife,
Who erst had travelled mortal life;
And aye they smiled, and 'gan to speer,
'What spirit has brought this mortal here?' —

'Lang have I journeyed the world wide,'
A meek and reverend fere replied;
'Baith night and day I have watched the fair,
Eident a thousand years and mair.
Yes, I have watched o'er ilk degree,
Wherever blooms femenitye;
But sinless virgin, free of stain
In mind and body, fand I nane.
Never, since the banquet of time,
Found I a virgin in her prime,
Till late this bonny maiden I saw
As spotless as the morning snaw:
Full twenty years she has lived as free
As the spirits that sojourn this countrye.
I have brought her away frae the snares of men,
That sin or death she never may ken.' —

They clasped her waiste and her hands sae fair,
They kissed her cheek, and they kemed her hair,
And round came many a blooming fere,
Saying, 'Bonny Kilmeny, ye're welcome here!
Women are freed of the littand scorn:
O, blessed be the day Kilmeny was born!
Now shall the land of the spirits see,
Now shall it ken what a woman may be!
Many a lang year in sorrow and pain,
Many a lang year through the world we've gane,
Commissioned to watch fair womankind,
For its they who nurice th'immortal mind.
We have watched their steps as the dawning shone,
And deep in the green-wood walks alone;

67 *speer*: ask
70 *fere*: companion
72 *Eident*: diligent
80 *snaw*: snow
89 *littand*: staining, disgracing

By lilly bower and silken bed,
The viewless tears have o'er them shed;
Have soothed their ardent minds to sleep,
Or left the couch of love to weep.
We have seen! we have seen! but the time must come,
And the angels will weep at the day of doom!

'O, would the fairest of mortal kind
Aye keep the holy truths in mind,
That kindred spirits their motions see,
Who watch their ways with anxious ee,
And grieve for the guilt of humanitye!
O, sweet to Heaven the maiden's prayer,
And the sigh that heaves a bosom sae fair!
And dear to Heaven the words of truth,
And the praise of virtue frae beauty's mouth!
And dear to the viewless forms of air,
The minds that kyth as the body fair!

'O, bonny Kilmeny! free frae stain,
If ever you seek the world again,
That world of sin, of sorrow and fear,
O, tell of the joys that are waiting here;
And tell of the signs you shall shortly see;
Of the times that are now, and the times that shall be.' —

They lifted Kilmeny, they led her away,
And she walked in the light of a sunless day:
The sky was a dome of crystal bright,
The fountain of vision, and fountain of light:
The emerald fields were of dazzling glow,
And the flowers of everlasting blow.
Then deep in the stream her body they laid,
That her youth and beauty never might fade;
And they smiled on heaven, when they saw her lie
In the stream of life that wandered bye.
And she heard a song, she heard it sung,
She kend not where; but sae sweetly it rung,
It fell on her ear like a dream of the morn:
'O! blest be the day Kilmeny was born!
Now shall the land of the spirits see,
Now shall it ken what a woman may be!
The sun that shines on the world sae bright,
A borrowed gleid frae the fountain of light;

115 *kyth*: appear 127 *blow*: bloom 139 *gleid*: fire

And the moon that sleeks the sky sae dun,
Like a gouden bow, or a beamless sun,
Shall wear away, and be seen nae mair,
And the angels shall miss them travelling the air.
But lang, lang after baith night and day,
When the sun and the world have elyed away;
When the sinner has gane to his waesome doom,
Kilmeny shall smile in eternal bloom!' —

They bore her away she wist not how,
For she felt not arm nor rest below;
But so swift they wained her through the light,
'Twas like the motion of sound or sight;
They seemed to split the gales of air,
And yet nor gale nor breeze was there.
Unnumbered groves below them grew,
They came, they past, and backward flew,
Like floods of blossoms gliding on,
In moment seen, in moment gone.
O, never vales to mortal view
Appeared like those o'er which they flew!
That land to human spirits given,
The lowermost vales of the storied heaven;
From thence they can view the world below,
And heaven's blue gates with sapphires glow,
More glory yet unmeet to know.

They bore her far to a mountain green,
To see what mortal never had seen;
And they seated her high on a purple sward,
And bade her heed what she saw and heard,
And note the changes the spirits wrought,
For now she lived in the land of thought.
She looked, and she saw nor sun nor skies,
But a crystal dome of a thousand dies.
She looked, and she saw nae land aright,
But an endless whirl of glory and light.
And radiant beings went and came
Far swifter than wind, or the linked flame.
She hid her een frae the dazzling view;
She looked again and the scene was new.

She saw a sun on a summer sky,
And clouds of amber sailing bye;

145 *elyed*: vanished

150 *wained*: carried

161 *storied*: we have heard in stories

A lovely land[n] beneath her lay,
And that land had glens and mountains gray;
And that land had vallies and hoary piles,
And marled seas, and a thousand isles;
Its fields were speckled, its forests green,
And its lakes were all of the dazzling sheen,
Like magic mirrors, where slumbering lay
The sun and the sky and the cloudlet gray;
Which heaved and trembled and gently swung,
On every shore they seemed to be hung;
For there they were seen on their downward plain
A thousand times and a thousand again;
In winding lake and placid firth,
Little peaceful heavens in the bosom of earth.

Kilmeny sighed and seemed to grieve,
For she found her heart to that land did cleave;
She saw the corn wave on the vale,
She saw the deer run down the dale;
She saw the plaid and the broad claymore,
And the brows that the badge of freedom bore;
And she thought she had seen the land before.

She saw a lady sit on a throne,[n]
The fairest that ever the sun shone on!
A lion[n] licked her hand of milk,
And she held him in a leish of silk;
And a leifu' maiden stood at her knee,
With a silver wand and melting ee;
Her sovereign shield till love stole in,
And poisoned all the fount within.

Then a gruff untoward bedeman[n] came,
And hundit the lion on his dame:
And the guardian maid wi' the dauntless ee,
She dropped a tear, and left her knee;
And she saw till the queen frae the lion fled,
Till the bonniest flower of the world lay dead.
A coffin was set on a distant plain,
And she saw the red blood fall like rain:
Then bonny Kilmeny's heart grew sair,
And she turned away, and could look nae mair.

Then the gruff grim carle girned amain,[n]
And they trampled him down, but he rose again;

206 *leifu'*: lovely    211 *hundit*: hounded

And he baited the lion to deeds of weir,
Till he lapped the blood to the kingdom dear;
And weening his head was danger-preef,
When crowned with the rose and clover leaf,[n]
He gowled at the carle, and chased him away
To feed wi' the deer on the mountain gray.
He gowled at the carle, and he gecked at heaven,
But his mark was set, and his arles given.
Kilmeny a while her een withdrew;
She looked again, and the scene was new.

She saw below her fair unfurled
One half of all the glowing world,
Where oceans rolled, and rivers ran,
To bound the aims of sinful man.
She saw a people, fierce and fell,
Burst frae their bounds like fiends of hell;
There lilies grew, and the eagle[n] flew,
And she herked on her ravening crew,
Till the cities and towers were wrapt in a blaze,
And the thunder it roared o'er the lands and the seas.
The widows they wailed, and the red blood ran,
And she threatened an end to the race of man:
She never lened, nor stood in awe,
Till claught by the lion's[n] deadly paw.
Oh! then the eagle swinked for life,
And brainzelled up a mortal strife;
But flew she north, or flew she south,
She met wi' the gowl of the lion's mouth.

With a mooted wing and waefu' maen,
The eagle sought her eiry again;
But lang may she cour in her bloody nest,
And lang, lang sleek her wounded breast,
Before she sey another flight,
To play wi' the norland lion's might.

But to sing the sights Kilmeny saw,
So far surpassing nature's law,
The singer's voice wad sink away,
And the string of his harp wad cease to play.
But she saw till the sorrows of man were bye,
And all was love and harmony;

228 *gowled*: howled
*gecked*: gazed
229 *arles*: money confirming a bargain
239 *herked*: urged
244 *lened*: rested
246 *swinked*: struggled
247 *brainzelled*: threatened
250 *mooted*: muted, drooping
*waefu' maen*: woeful moan
254 *sey*: try

Till the stars of heaven fell calmly away,
Like the flakes of snaw on a winter day.

Then Kilmeny begged again to see
The friends she had left in her own country,
To tell of the place where she had been,
And the glories that lay in the land unseen;
To warn the living maidens fair,
The loved of Heaven, the spirits' care,
That all whose minds unmeled remain
Shall bloom in beauty when time is gane.

With distant music, soft and deep,
They lulled Kilmeny sound asleep;
And when she awakened, she lay her lane,
All happed with flowers in the green-wood wene.
When seven lang years had come and fled;
When grief was calm, and hope was dead;
When scarce was remembered Kilmeny's name,
Late, late in a gloamin Kilmeny came hame!
And O, her beauty was fair to see,
But still and stedfast was her ee!
Such beauty bard many never declare,
For there was no pride nor passion there;
And the soft desire of maidens een
In that mild face could never be seen.
Her seymar was the lilly flower,
And her cheek the moss-rose in the shower;
And her voice like the distant melodye,
That floats along the twilight sea.
But she loved to raike the lanely glen,
And keeped afar frae the haunts of men;
Her holy hymns unheard to sing,
To suck the flowers, and drink the spring.
But wherever her peaceful form appeared,
The wild beasts[n] of the hill were cheered;
The wolf played blythly round the field,
The lordly byson lowed and kneeled;
The dun deer wooed with manner bland,
And cowered aneath her lilly hand.
And when at even the woodlands rung,
When hymns of other worlds she sung,
In ecstacy of sweet devotion,
O, then the glen was all in motion.

270 *unmeled*: pure
274 *her lane*: by herself
286 *seymar*: loose coat
290 *raike*: roam

The wild beasts of the forest came,
Broke from their bughts and faulds the tame,
And goved around, charmed and amazed;
Even the dull cattle crooned and gazed,
And murmured and looked with anxious pain
For something the mystery to explain.
The buzzard came with the throstle-cock;
The corby left her houf in the rock;
The blackbird alang wi' th eagle flew;
The hind came tripping o'er the dew;
The wolf and the kid their raike began,
And the tod, and the lamb, and the leveret ran;
The hawk and the hern attour them hung,
And the merl and the mavis forhooyed their young;
And all in a peaceful ring were hurled:
It was like an eve in a sinless world!

When a month and a day had come and gane,
Kilmeny sought the greenwood wene;
There laid her down on the leaves sae green,
And Kilmeny on earth was never mair seen.
But O, the words that fell from her mouth,
Were words of wonder, and words of truth!
But all the land were in fear and dread,
For they kendna whether she was living or dead.
It wasna her hame, and she couldna remain;
She left this world of sorrow and pain,
And returned to the land of thought again.

305 *bughts*: shelters
*faulds*: folds
306 *goved*: stared
310 *throstle*: thrush
311 *corby*: raven
*houf*: haunt, shelter
314 *raike*: stroll
315 *tod*: fox
*leveret*: young hare
*attour*: above
317 *merl*: blackbird
*mavis*: song-thrush
*forhooyed*: abandoned
318 *hurled*: drawn round

## MAY OF THE MORIL GLEN

OR

## THE PERILIS OF WEMYNG

### ANE MOSTE WOEFUL TRAGEDYE

I will tell you of ane wonderous taille
Als euir was tolde be manne,
Or euir wals sung by mynstrel meete
Sin' this baisse worild beganne: —

3 *wals*: was

It is of ane May, and ane lovelye May,
That dwallit in the Moril Glenne,
The fayrest flower of mortyl fraime,
But ane deuil amangis the menne;

For nine of them styckit themsellis for lofe,
And tenne louped in the maine,
And seuin-and-threttye brakke their hertis,
And neuir lofit womyn againe;

For ilk ane trowit sho wals in lofe,
And ranne wodde for ane whyle —
There wals sickan language in every looke,
And ane speire in every smyle.

And sho had seuinty skoris of yowis,
That blette o'er daille and downe,
On the bonny braide landes of the Moril Glenne,
And these beine all hir owne;

And sho had stottis and sturdy steris,
And blythsome kyddis enewe,
That dancit als lychte als glomyng fleeis
Out through the fallyng dewe;

And this May sho hald ane snow-whytte bulle,
The dreidde of the haille countrye,
And three-and-threttye goode mylke kie,
To beire him companye;

And sho had geese and gezlyngis too,
And gainderis of muckil dynne,
And peacokkis, with their gawdye trainis,
And hertis of prydde withinne;

And sho had cokkis with curlit kaimis,
And hennis full crousse and gladde,
That chanted in her own stacke-yairde,
And cockillit and laidde lyke madde;

8 *amangis*: amongst
9 *styckit*: disabled
*lofe*: love
13 *ilk*: each
*trowit*: believed
14 *wodde*: mad
15 *sickan*: such
17 *skoris*: scores
*yowis*: ewes
21 *stottis*: bullocks
23 *glomyng*: dusk
29 *gezlyngis*: goslings
34 *crousse*: attractive, lively
36 *cockillit*: clucked

But qhuaire hir minnye gat all that geare,
And all that lordlye trimme,
The Lorde in heuin he kennit full weille,
But naebodye kennit but himme;

For sho neuir yeildit to mortyl manne,
To prynce, nor yet to kynge —
Sho neuir wals given in holye churche,
Nor wedded with ane rynge.

So all men wiste, and all men sayde;
But the taille wals in sor mistyme,
For ane mayden sho colde hardly bee,
With ane doughter in beautye's pryme.

But this bonnye May, sho never knewe
Ane faderis kindlye claime;
She nevir wals blessit in holye churche,
Nor chrystenit in holye naime.

But there sho leevit ane yirdlye flowir
Of beautye so supreme,
Some fearit sho wals of the mermaidis broode,
Comit out of the sault sea-faeme.

Some sayit she wals founde in ane fairye rynge,[n]
And born of the fairye queene;
For there wals ane rainbowe ahynde the mone
That nychte sho first wals seene.

Some sayit her moder wals ane wytche,
Comit from a farre countrye;
Or ane princesse lofit be ane weirde warlocke
In a lande beyond the se!

Och, there are doyngis here belowe
That mortyl nefer sholde kenne;
For ther are thyngis in this fayre worlde
Beyond the reche of menne.

Ane thinge moste sure and certainne wals —
For the bedisman tolde it mee —
That the knychte who coft the Moril Glenne
Nefer spok ane worde but three.

37 *quhaire*: where
*minnye*: mother
45 *wiste*: knew
46 *mistyme*: mixed-up farrago
50 *faderis*: father's
53 *yirdlye*: earthly
63 *lofit*: loved
65 *doyngis*: doings
71 *coft*: bought

And the maisonis who biggit that wylde ha' housse
   Nefer spoke worde goode nor ill;
They came lyke ane dreime, and passit awaye
   Lyke shaddowis ower the hill.

They came lyke ane dreime, and passit awaye
   Whidder no manne colde telle;
But they eated their brede lyke Chrystyan menne,
   And dranke of the krystil welle.

And whenever manne sayit worde to them,
   They stayit their speche full sone;
For they shoke their hedis, and raisit their handis,
   And lokit to Hefen abone.

And the ladye came — and there she baide
   For mony a lanelye daye;
But whedder she bred hir bairn to Gode —
   To reade but and to praye —

There wals no man wist, thof all men guessit,
   And guessit with feire and dreide;
But O sho grewe ane vyrgin roz,
   To seimlye womanheide:

And no manne colde loke on hir face,
   And eyne, that bemit so cleire;
But feelit ane stang gang throu his herte,
   Far sharper than ane speire.

It wals not lyke ane prodde or pang
   That strength colde overwinne,
But lyke ane reide hett gaad of erne
   Reekyng his herte withinne.

So that arounde the Moril Glenne
   Our braife yong menne did lye,
With limbis als lydder, and als lythe,
   Als duddis hung oute to drye.

And aye the teris ranne down in streim
   Ower chekis rychte woe-begone;
And aye they gaspit, and they gratte,
   And thus maide pyteous moane: —

73 *biggit*: built
84 *abone*: above
89 *thof*: though
94 *eyne*: eyes
95 *stang*: acute pain
99 *gaad*: goad
*erne*: iron
103 *lydder*: sluggish
104 *duddis*: clothes

'Alake that I had ever beene borne,
Or dandelit on the knee;
Or rockit in ane creddil-bedde,
Benethe ane moderis ee!

'Och! had I dyit before myne cheike
To woman's breste had layne,
Then had I ne'er for womanis lofe
Endurit this burning payne!

'For lofe is lyke the fyerie flaime
That quiveris thru the rayne,
And lofe is lyke the pawng of dethe
That spletis the herte in twayne.

'If I had lovit yirdlye thyng,
Of yirdlye blithesomnesse,
I mochte haif bene belovit agayne,
And bathit in yirdlye blisse.

'But I haif lovit ane frekyshe faye
Of frowardnesse and synne,
With hefenlye beautye on the faice,
And herte of ston withynne.

'O, for the glomyng calme of dethe
To close my mortyl daye —
The last benightyng heave of brethe,
That rendis the soule awaye!'

But wordis gone eiste, and wordis gone weste,
'Mong high and low degre,
Quhille it wente to the Kynge upon the thronne,
And ane wrothfulle manne wals hee. —

'What!' said the Kynge, 'and shall wee sitte
In sackclothe murnyng sadde,
Quhille all myne leigis of the londe
For ane yong queine run madde?

'Go saddil mee myne mylke-whyte stede,
Of true Megaira brode;
I will goe and se this wonderous daime,
And prof hir by the Rode.

119 *pawng*: pang
135 *Quhille*: while
138 *murnyng*: mourning
140 *queine*: girl
142 *brode*: breed

'And gif I finde hir elfyne queine,
Or thynge of fairye kynde,
I will byrne hir into ashes smalle,
And syfte them on the wynde!'

The Kynge hethe chosen four-score knychtis,
All buskit gallantlye,
And hee is awaye to the Moril Glenne,
Als faste als hee can dre.

And quhan hee came to the Moril Glenne,
Ane mornynge fayre and cleire,
This lovely May on horsebakke rode,
To hunte the fallowe deire.

Her palfrey wals of snawye hue,
Ane paille wanyirdlye thynge,
That revellit ower hille and daille
Lyke birde upon the wynge.

Hir skrene wals lyke ane nette of golde,
That dazzlit als it flew;
Hir mantil wals of the raynbowis reide,
Hir raille of its bonnye blue.

Ane goldene kembe with dymindis brychte,
Hir semelye vyrgin crowne,
Shone lyke the newe monis laidye lychte
Ower cludde of awmber browne.

The lychtening that shotte from hir eyne,
Flyckerit lyke elfin brande;
It wals sherper nor the sherpest speire
In all North Humber Lande.

The hawke that on hir brydel arme
Outspredde his pinyans blue,
To keipe him steddye on the perche
Als his lovit mystresse flewe,

Although his eyne shone lyke the gleime
Upon ane saible se,
Yet to the twaine that ower them bemit,
Comparit they colde not be.

152 *dre*: endure
158 *wanyirdlye*: unearthly
161 *skrene*: veil
164 *raille*: bodice
165 *kembe*: comb
*dymindis*: diamonds
168 *cludde*: cloud
169 *lychtening*: lightning
171 *nor*: than
176 *Als*: as

Lyke carrye ower the mornyng sone
That shymmeris to the wynde,
So flewe her lockis upon the gaille,
And stremit afar behynde.

The Kynge hee whelit him rounde aboute,
And calleth to his menne,
'Yonder sho comis, this weirdlye wytche,
This spyrit of the glenne!

'Come ranke your mayster up behynde,
This serpente to belaye;
I'll let you heire me put her downe
In grand polemyck waye.'

Swyfte came the mayde ower strath and stron —
Ne dantonit dame wals shee —
Until the Kynge hir pathe withstode,
In mychte and maijestye.

The vyrgin caste on him ane loke,
With gaye and gracefulle ayre,
Als on some thynge belowe hir notte,
That oughte not to haif bene there.

The Kynge, whose belte wals lyke to byrste
With spechis most dyvine,
Now felit ane throbbyng of the herte,
And quaikyng of the spyne.

And aye he gasped for his brethe,
And gaped in dyre dismaye,
And wavit his airm, and smotte his breste,
But worde hee colde not saye.

The spankye grewis they scowrit the daille,
The dunne deire to restrayne;
The vyrgin gaif hir stede the reyne,
And followit, mychte and mayne.

'Go brynge hir backe,' the Kynge he cryit;
'This reiferye moste not bee.
Though you sholde bynde hir handis and feite,
Go brynge hir backe to mee.'

181 *carrye*: cloud driven by wind

193 *strath*: valley
*stron*: hill

209 *spankye*: dashing
*grewis*: greyhounds

214 *reifery*: robbery

The deire sho flewe, the garf and grewe
They followit harde behynde;
The mylk-whyte palfreye brushit the dewe
Far fleeter nor the wynde.

But woe betyde the lordis and knychtis,
That taiglit in the delle!
For thof with whip and spurre theye plyit,
Full far behynde theye felle.

They lokit outowre their left shoulderis,
To se quhat they mocht se,
And there the Kynge, in fitte of lofe,
Lay spurrying on the le.

And aye he batterit with his feite,
And rowted with dispayre,
And pullit the gerse up be the rotis,
And flang it on the ayre.

'Quhat ailis, quhat ailis myne royale liege?
Soche grieffe I doo deplore.'
'Och I'm bewytchit,' the Kynge replyit,
'And gone for evermore!

'Go brynge hir backe — go brynge hir backe —
Go brynge hir backe to mee;
For I moste either die of lofe,
Or owne that deire ladye!

'That godde of lofe out through myne soule
Hathe shotte his arrowes keine;
And I am enchanted through the herte,
The lyvir, and the spleine.'

The deire wals slayne; the royale trayne
Then closit the vyrgin rounde,
And then hir fayre and lyllie handis
Behynde hir backe were bounde.

But who sholde bynde hir wynsome feite?
That bredde soche stryffe and payne,
That sixteen braif and belted knychtis
Lay gaspyng on the playne.

217 *garf*: meaning uncertain
*grewe*: greyhound
222 *taiglit*: tarried
228 *spurrying*: spurring
230 *rowted*: turned up soil
231 *gerse*: grass
*rotis*: roots

And quhan sho came before the Kynge,
Ane yreful caryl wals hee:
Saythe hee, 'Dame, you moste be myne lofe,
Or byrne benethe ane tre.

'For I am so sore in lofe with thee,
I cannot goe nor stande;
And thinks thou nothynge to put downe
The Kynge of fayre Scotlande?'

'No, I can ne'er be lofe to thee,
Nor any lorde thou haste;
For you are married menne eche one,
And I ane mayden chaste.

'But here I promiss, and I vow
By Scotlandis Kynge and Crowne,
Who first a widower shall profe,
Shall clayme mee als his owne.'

The Kynge hath mounted his mylk-whyte stede, —
One worde he sayde not more, —
And he is awaye from the Moril Glenne,
Als ne'er rode kynge before.

He sanke his rowillis to the naife,
And scourit the muire and daille,
He helde his bonnette to his heide,
And louted to the gale,

Till wifis ranne skreighynge to the door,
Holdynge their handis on highe;
Theye nefer saw kynge in lofe before,
In soche extreimitye.

And everye lorde and everye knychte
Maide off his several waye,
All gallopynge als they had bene madde,
Withoutten stop or staie.

But there wals nefer soche dole and payne
In any lande befelle;
For there is wyckednesse in manne,
That griefeth mee to telle.

256 *byrne*: burn 273 *naife*: navel 276 *louted*: bowed

There wals one eye, and one alone,
   Behelde the dedis were done;
But the lovelye Queene of fayre Scotlande
   Ne'er sawe the mornyng sone;

And seuintye-seuin wedded demis,
   Als fayre as e'er were borne,
The very pryde of all the lande,
   Were corpis befor the morne.

Then there wals noughte but murnynge wedis,
   And sorrowe, and dismaye;
While buryal met with buryal stille,
   And jostled by the waye.

And graffis were howkyt in grene kyrkyardis,
   And howkyt deipe and wyde;
Quhille bedlaris swairfit for verye toyle,
   The cumlye corpis to hyde.

The graffis, with their unseimlye jawis,
   Stode gaipyng daye and nychte
To swallye up the fayre and yonge; —
   It wals ane grefous sychte!

And the bonny May of the Moril Glenne
   Is weipynge in dispayre,
For sho saw the hillis of fayre Scotlande
   Colde bee hir home no mayre.

Then there wals chariotis came owernychte,
   Als sylente and als sone
As shaddowe of ane littil cludde
   In the wan lychte of the mone.

Some sayde theye came out of the rocke,
   And some out of the se;
And some sayde theye were sent from helle,
   To bryng that fayre ladye.

When the day skye beganne to fraime
   The grizelye eistren felle,
And the littil wee batte wals bounde to seike
   His darke and eirye celle,

301 *graffis*: graves
*howkyt*:dug

303 *bedlaris*: sextons
*swairfit*: fainted

313 *owernychte*: overnight

The fayrest flowir of mortal fraime
Passit from the Moril Glenne;
And ne'er maye soche ane deidlie eye
Shyne amongis Chrystyan menne!

In seuin chariotis gildit brychte,
The trayne went owre the felle,
All wrappit withynne ane shower of haille;
Whidder no manne colde telle;

But there was ane shippe in the Firthe of Forthe,
The lyke ne'er sailit the faeme,
For no manne of hir country knew,
Hir coloris, or hir naime.

Hir maste wals maide of beaten golde,
Hir sailis of the sylken twyne,
And a thousande pennonis streimyt behynde,
And tremblit owre the bryne.

Als sho laye mirrorit in the mayne,
It wals ane comelye viewe,
So manye raynbowis rounde hir playit,
With euery breeze that blewe.

And the hailstone shroude it rattled loude,
Rychte over forde and fenne,
And swathit the flower of the Moril Glenne
From eyes of sinfulle menne.

And the hailstone shroude it quhelit and rowed,
Als wan as dethe unshriven,
Lyke deidclothe of ane angelle grymme,
Or wynding sheete of hevin.

It wals ane feirsome sychte to se
Toylle through the mornyng graye,
And whenever it reachit the comelye shippe,
Sho set saille and awaye.

Sho set hir saille before the gaille,
Als it beganne to syng,
And sho hevit and rockit doune the tyde,
Unlyke ane yirthlye thyng.

The dolfinis fledde oute of hir waye
   Into the crekis of Fyffe,
And the blackgaird seelis they yowlit for dredde,
   And swamme for dethe and lyfe.

And the pellochis snyfterit, puffit, and rowed,
   In dreddour sadde to se,
And lyke the rain-drop from the cloudde,
   Theye shotte alangis the sea;

And they bullerrit into the bayis of Fyffe,
   Als if through terrour blynde,
And tossit and tombilit on the strande,
   In greate dismaye of mynde.

But ay the shyppe, the bonnye shyppe,
   Outowre the greene waive flewe,
Swyffte als the solan on the wyng,
   Or terrifyit sea-mewe.

No billowe breisted on her prowe,
   Nor levellit on the lee;
Sho semit to sayle upon the ayre,
   And neuer touche the sea.

And awaye, and awaye went the bonnye shyppe,
   Whiche manne never more did se;
But whedder sho went to hefen or helle,
   Wals nefer maide knowne to mee.

365 *pellochis*: porpoises    369 *bullerrit*: dashed

# William Tennant
## 1784–1848

William Tennant, the son of a small farmer and merchant, was born in Easter Anstruther, Fife. He was lame from infancy and used crutches all his life. He received his early training at the burgh school, where one of his older contemporaries was Thomas Chalmers, later to be famous as leader of the 'Disruption' of the Church of Scotland in 1843, which led to the formation of the Free Church of Scotland. Tennant proceeded to St Andrews University but had to leave after two years because of financial difficulties at home. He spent a few years assisting his brother in a corn-factor's business in Glasgow and Anstruther, but all the while retained and developed his interest in the classics and in poetry. He published *Anster Fair* anonymously in 1812. It was praised by, among others, Lord Woodhouselee, and a second edition, still anonymous, appeared in 1814; the third edition of 1815 (Edinburgh) bore Tennant's name. Meanwhile he had become schoolmaster of Dunino, not far from his old university and its library, where he continued to study the classics and oriental languages. He became schoolmaster at Lasswade in 1816, which brought him more easily in touch with the Edinburgh literary world. In 1819 he became a master in what was to become Dollar Academy in Clackmannanshire. He gained a reputation as a fine linguist in the classics and in Persian, Syriac and Arabic and was eventually appointed Professor of Oriental Languages at St Mary's College, St Andrews, in 1835. His career is a remarkable example of courage and determination in the face of poverty in youth and the lifelong handicap of lameness. His mock epic *Papistry Storm'd* is due for revival.

*Anster Fair* is based on the song *Maggie Lauder*, attributed to Francis Sempill of Beltrees and dated about 1642. The first two verses are:

Wha wadna be in love
   Wi' bonnie Maggie Lauder?
A piper met her gaun to Fife,
   And speir'd what was't they ca'd her,
Right scornfully she answer'd him,
   'Be gone ye hallanshaker!
Jog on your gate, ye bladderskate,
   My name is Maggie Lauder!'

'Maggie', quo he, 'an by my bags,
   I'm fidgin' fain to see thee;

4 *speir'd*: asked
6 *hallanshaker*: disorderly vagabond
7 *gate*: way
*bladderskate*: vain babbler
9 *bags*: i.e. of the pipes (with sexual innuendo)
10 *fidgin' fain*: itching

Sit down by me, my bonnie bird,
In troth I winna steer thee:
For I'm a piper to my trade,
My name is Rob the Ranter,
The lasses loup as they were daft,
When I blaw up my chanter.'

After Maggie has danced to his playing she says:

'There's nane in Scotland plays sae weel,
Since we lost Habbie Simson.[n]
I've lived in Fife, baith maid and wife,
These ten years and a quarter,
Gin ye should come to Anster Fair,
Speir ye for Maggie Lauder.'

Tennant sets the story of his poem in the Fair held three times a year in his native Anstruther. (Anstruther is locally pronounced 'Anster'.) The idea is that games and sports would be held to find the finest athlete in Scotland, one fit to marry Maggie Lauder. Shakespeare's Puck, Scotticised as Tommy Puck and turned into a mustard-pot by the wiles of Michael Scott the wizard (see above, *Lay of the Last Minstrel*) comes into Maggie's possession, and is allowed by Oberon to advise her on her choice. The games are described with comic elaboration in six cantos, at the end of which the victor, none other than Rob the Ranter, gains the hand of the beautiful Maggie Lauder.

Of the stanza he chose, Tennant wrote: 'The poem is written in stanzas of octave rhime, or the *ottava rima* of the Italians; a measure . . . transferred into English poetry by Fairfax, in his translation of *Jerusalem Delivered*, but since his days, has been by our poets, perhaps, too little cultivated. The stanza of Fairfax is here shut with the Alexandrine of Spenser, that its close may be more full and sounding.' At the same time as Tennant's experiment, Byron was writing in both *ottava rima* and Spenserian stanza.

We reproduce the first of the six cantos.

*Edition:*

M. F. Conolly, *Memoirs of the life and writings of William Tennant* (1861). This volume also contains biographical and critical matters.

*Biography:*

*Dictionary of National Biography*

12 *steer*: harm    15 *loup*: leap    20 *gin*: if

## ANSTER FAIR

### CANTO I

While some of Troy and pettish heroes[n] sing,
And some of Rome and chiefs of pious fame,
And some of men that thought it harmless thing
To smite off heads in Mars's[n] bloody game,
And some of Eden's garden[n] gay with spring,
And Hell's dominions terrible to name,—
I sing a theme far livelier, happier, gladder,
I sing of Anster Fair and bonny Maggie Lauder.

What time from east, from west, from south, from north,
From every hamlet, town, and smoky city,
Laird, clown, and beau, to Anster Fair came forth,
The young, the gay, the handsome, and the witty,
To try in various sport and game their worth,
Whilst prize before them Maggie sat, the pretty,
And after many a feat, and joke, and banter,
Fair Maggies's hand was won by mighty Rob the Ranter.

Muse, that from top of thine old Greekish hill,[n]
Didst the harp-fing'ring Theban younker[n] view,
And on his lips bid bees their sweets distil,[n]
And gav'st the chariot that the white swans drew,
O let me scoop, from thine ethereal rill,
Some little palmfuls of the blessed dew,
And lend the swan-drawn car, that safely I,
Like him, may scorn the earth, and burst into the sky.

Our themes are like; for he the games extoll'd
Held in the chariot-shaken Grecian plains,
Where the vain victor, arrogant and bold,
A pickle parsley got for all his pains;[n]
I sing of sports more worthy to be told,
Where better prize the Scottish victor gains;
What were the crowns of Greece but wind and bladder
Compared with marriage-bed of bonnie Maggie Lauder?

And O that king Apollo[n] would but grant
A little spark of that transcendant flame,
That fir'd the Chian rhapsodist[n] to chant
How vied the bowmen for Ulysses' dame,

And him of Rome to sing how Atalant[n]
Plied, dart in hand, the suitor-slaught'ring game,
Till the bright gold, bowl'd forth along the grass,
Betray'd her to a spouse, and stopp'd the bounding lass.

But lo! from bosom of yon southern cloud,
I see the chariot come which Pindar bore;
I see the swans, whose white necks, arching proud,
Glitter with golden yoke, approach my shore;
For me they come — O Phoebus, potent god!
Spare, spare me now — Enough, good king — no more —
A little spark I ask'd in moderation,
Why scorch me ev'n to death with fiery inspiration?

My pulse beats fire — my pericranium glows,
Like baker's oven, with poetic heat;
A thousand bright ideas, spurning prose,
Are in a twinkling hatch'd in fancy's seat;
Zounds! they will fly, out at my ears and nose,
If through my mouth they find not passage fleet;
I hear them buzzing deep within my noddle,
Like bees that in their hives confus'dly hum and huddle.

How now? — what's this? — my very eyes, I trow,
Drop on my hands their base prosaic scales;
My visual orbs are purg'd from film, and lo!
Instead of Anster's turnip-bearing vales
I see old Fairyland's mirac'lous show,
Her trees of tinsel kiss'd by freakish gales,
Her ouphes, that cloak'd in leaf-gold skim the breeze,
And fairies swarming thick as mites in rotten cheese.

I see the puny fair-chinn'd goblin rise
Suddenly glorious from his mustard pot;
I see him wave his hand in seemly wise,
And button round him tight his fulgent coat;
While Maggie Lauder, in a great surprise,
Sits startled on her chair, yet fearing not;
I see him ope his dewy lips; I hear
The strange and strict command address'd to Maggie's ear.

63 *ouphes*: elves' children (Spenserian)

I see the Ranter with bagpipe on back,
  As to the fair he rides jocundly on;
I see the crowds that press with speed not slack
  Along each road that leads to Anster loan;
I see the suitors, that, deep-sheath'd in sack,
  Hobble and tumble, bawl and swear, and groan;
I see — but fie, thou brainish muse! what mean
These vapourings and brags of what by thee is seen?

Go to — be cooler, and in order tell
  To all my good co-townsmen list'ning round,
How every merry incident befel,
  Whereby our loan shall ever be renown'd;
Say first, what elf or fairy could impel
  Fair Mag, with wit, and wealth, and beauty
    crown'd,
To put her suitors to such waggish test,
And give her happy bed to him that jumped best?

'Twas on a keen December night, John Frost
  Drove through mid air his chariot, icy-wheel'd,
And from the sky's crisp ceiling star-embost,
  Whiff'd off the clouds that the pure blue conceal'd;
The hornless moon amid her brilliant host
  Shone, and with silver sheeted lake and field;
'Twas cutting cold; I'm sure, each trav'ler's nose
Was pinch'd right red that night, and numb'd were
    all his toes.

Not so were Maggie Lauder's toes, as she
  In her warm chamber at her supper sate,
(For 'twas that hour when burgesses agree
  To eat their suppers ere the night grows late).
Alone she sat, and pensive as may be
  A young fair lady, wishful of a mate;
Yet with her teeth held now and then a picking,
Her stomach to refresh, the breast-bone of a chicken:

She thought upon her suitors, that with love
  Besiege her chamber all the livelong day,
Aspiring each her virgin heart to move,
  With courtship's every troublesome essay;
Calling her, angel, sweeting, fondling, dove,
  And other nicknames in love's friv'lous way;

84 *loan*: common pasture land

While she, though their addresses still she heard,
Held back from all her heart, and still no beau
preferr'd.

'What, what,' quo' Mag, 'must thus it be my doom
To spend my prime in maidhood's joyless state,
And waste away my sprightly body's bloom
In spouseless solitude without a mate,
Still toying with my suitors, as they come
Cringing in lowly courtship to my gate?
Fool that I am, to live unwed so long!
More fool, since I am woo'd by such a clam'rous throng!

'For was e'er heiress with much gold in chest
And dow'rd with acres of wheat-bearing land,
By such a pack of men, in am'rous quest,
Fawningly spaniel'd to bestow her hand?
Where'er I walk, the air that feeds my breast
Is by the gusty sighs of lovers fann'd;
Each wind that blows wafts love-cards to my lap;
Whilst I — ah stupid Mag! — avoid each am'rous trap!

'Then come, let me my suitors' merits weigh,
And in the worthiest lad my spouse select: —
First, there's our Anster merchant, Norman Ray,
A powder'd wight with golden buttons deck'd,
That stinks with scent, and chats like popinjay,
And struts with phiz tremendously erect:
Four brigs has he, that on the broad sea swim; —
He is a pompous fool — I cannot think of him:

'Next is the maltster Andrew Strang, that takes
His seat i' th' bailies' loft[n] on sabbath-day,
With paltry visage white as oaten cakes,
As if no blood runs gurgling in his clay;
Heav'ns! what an awkward hunch the fellow makes,
As to the priest he does the bow repay!
Yet he is rich — a very wealthy man, true —
But, by the holy rood, I will have none of Andrew.

'Then for the Lairds — there's Melvil of Carnbee,[n]
A handsome gallant, and a beau of spirit;
Who can go down the dance so well as he?
And who can fiddle with such manly merit?

134 *phiz*: face, head

135 *brigs*: two-masted trading vessels

141 *hunch*: act of 'hunching' his back

— Ay, but he is too much the debauchee —
His cheeks seem sponges oozing port and claret;
In marrying him I should bestow myself ill,
And so, I'll not have you, thou fuddler, Harry Melvil!

'There's Cunningham of Barns,[n] that still assails
With verse and billet-doux my gentle heart,
A bookish squire, and good at telling tales,
That rhimes and whines of Cupid, flame, and dart;
But, oh! his mouth a sorry smell exhales,
And on his nose sprouts horribly the wart;
What though there be a fund of lore and fun in him?
He has a rotten breath — I cannot think of
Cunningham.

'Why then, there's Allardyce, that plies his suit
And battery of courtship more and more;
Spruce Lochmalonie,[n] that with booted foot
Each morning wears the threshold of my door;
Auchmoutie[n] too, and Bruce that persecute
My tender heart with am'rous buffets sore: —
— Whom to my hand and bed should I promote? —
— Eh-la! what sight is this? — what ails my
mustard-pot?'

Here broke the lady her soliloquy,
For in a twink her pot of mustard, lo!
Self-mov'd, like Jove's wheel'd stool that rolls on high,
'Gan caper on her table to and fro,
And hopp'd and fidgeted before her eye,
Spontaneous, here and there, a wondrous show;
As leaps, instinct with mercury, a bladder,
So leaps the mustard-pot of bonnie Maggie
Lauder.

Soon stopp'd its dance th' ignoble utensil,
When from its round and small recess there came
Thin curling wreaths of paly smoke, that still,
Fed by some magic unapparent flame,
Mount to the chamber's stucco'd roof, and fill
Each nook with fragrance, and refresh the dame:
Ne'er smelt a phoenix-nest[n] so sweet, I wot,
As smelt the luscious fumes of Maggie's mustard-pot.

152 *fuddler*: fiddler

It reeked censer-like; then, (strange to tell)!
Forth from the smoke, that thick and thicker grows,
A fairy of the height of half an ell,[n]
In dwarfish pomp, majestically rose:
His feet, upon the table 'stablish'd well,
Stood trim and splendid in their snake-skin hose;
Gleam'd, topaz-like, the breeches he had on,
Whose waistband like the bend of summer rainbow
shone.

His coat seem'd fashion'd of the threads of gold,
That intertwine the clouds at sun-set hour,
And, certes, Iris[n] with her shuttle bold
Wove the rich garment in her lofty bower;
To form its buttons were the Pleiads[n] old
Pluck'd from their sockets, sure by genie-power,
And sew'd upon the coat's resplendent hem;
Its neck was lovely green; each cuff a sapphire gem.

As when the churlish spirit of the Cape
To Gama,[n] voyaging to Mozambique,
Up-popp'd from sea, a tangle-tassel'd[n] shape,
With mussels sticking inch-thick on his cheek,
And 'gan with tortoise-shell his limbs to scrape,
And yawn'd his monstrous blobberlips to speak;
Brave Gama's hairs stood bristled at the sight,
And on the tarry deck sunk down his men with
fright.

So sudden (not so huge and grimly dire)
Uprose to Maggie's stounded eyne, the sprite,
As fair a fairy as you could desire,
With ruddy cheek, and chin and temples white;
His eyes seem'd little points of sparkling fire,
That, as he look'd, charm'd with inviting light;
He was, indeed as bonny a fay and brisk,
As e'er on long moon-beam was seen to ride and frisk.

Around his bosom, by a silken zone,
A little bagpipe gracefully was bound,
Whose pipes like hollow stalks of silver shone,
The glist'ring tiny avenues of sound;
Beneath his arm the windy bag, full-blown,
Heav'd up its purple like an orange round,
And only waited orders to discharge
Its blasts with charming groan into the sky at large.

He wav'd his hand to Maggie, as she sat
Amaz'd and startled on her carved chair;
Then took his petty feather-garnish'd hat
In honour to the lady, from his hair,
And made a bow so dignifiedly flat,
That Mag was witched with his beauish air:
At last he spoke, with voice so soft, so kind,
So sweet, as if his throat with fiddle-strings was lin'd.

'Lady! be not offended that I dare,
Thus forward and impertinently rude,
Emerge, uncall'd, into the upper air,
Intruding on a maiden's solitude;
Nay, do not be alarm'd, thou lady fair!
Why startle so? — I am a fairy good;
Not one of those that, envying beauteous maids,
Speckle their skins with moles, and fill with spleens their heads.

'For, as conceal'd in this clay-house of mine,
I overheard thee, in a lowly voice,
Weighing thy lovers' merits, with design
Now on the worthiest lad to fix thy choice,
I have up-bolted from my paltry shrine,
To give thee, sweet-ey'd lass, my best advice;
For by the life of Oberon[n] my king!
To pick good husband out is, sure, a ticklish thing:

'And never shall good Tommy Puck permit
Such an assemblage of unwonted charms
To cool some lecher's lewd licentious fit,
And sleep imbounded by his boisterous arms;
What though his fields by twenty ploughs be split,
And golden wheat wave riches on his farms?
His house is shame — it cannot, shall not be;
A greater, happier doom, O Mag, awaiteth thee.

'Strange are indeed the steps, by which thou must
Thy glory's happy eminence attain,
But fate hath fix'd them, and 'tis fate's t' adjust
The mighty links that ends to means enchain,
Nor may poor Puck his little fingers thrust
Into the links to break Jove's steel in twain:

240 *spleens*: moods of capricious irritability

Then, Maggie, hear, and let my words descend
Into thy soul, for much it boots thee to attend.

'To-morrow, when o'er th' Isle of May[n] the sun
Lifts up his forehead bright with golden crown,
Call to thine house the light-heel'd men, that run
Afar on messages for Anster Town,
Fellows of sp'rit, by none in speed out-done,
Of lofty voice, enough a drum to drown,
And bid them hie, post-haste, through all the nation,
And publish, far and near, this famous proclama-
tion:

'Let them proclaim, with voice's loudest tone,
That on your next approaching market-day,
Shall merry sports be held in Anster loan,
With celebration notable and gay:
And that a prize, than gold or costly stone
More precious, shall the victor's toils repay,
Ev'n thy own form with beauties so replete,
— Nay Maggie, start not thus! — thy marriage-
bed, my sweet.

'First, on the loan shall ride full many an ass,
With stout whip-wielding rider on his back,
Intent with twinkling hoof to pelt the grass,
And pricking up his long ears at the crack;
Next o'er the ground the daring men shall pass,
Half-coffin'd in their cumbrances of sack,
With heads just peeping from their shrines of bag,
Horribly hobbling round and straining hard for Mag;

'Then shall the pipers groaningly begin
In squeaking rivalry their merry strain,
Till Billyness[n] shall echo back the din,
And Innergelly[n] woods shall ring again;
Last, let each man that hopes thy hand to win
By witty product of prolific brain,
Approach, and, confident of Pallas'[n] aid,
Claim by an hum'rous tale possession of thy bed.

'Such are the wondrous tests, by which, my love!
The merits of thy husband must be try'd,
And he that shall in these superior prove,
(One proper husband shall the Fates provide)
Shall from the loan with thee triumphant move
Homeward, the jolly bridegroom and the bride,

And at thy house shall eat the marriage-feast,
When I'll pop up again:' — Here Tommy Puck
surceast.

He ceas'd, and to his wee mouth dewy-wet,
His bagpipe's tube of silver up he held,
And, underneath his down-press'd arm he set
His purple bag that with a tempest swell'd;
He play'd and pip'd so sweet, that never yet
Mag had a piper heard that Puck excell'd;
Had Midas[n] heard a tune so exquisite,
By heav'n! his long base ears had quiver'd with
delight.

Tingle the fire-ir'ns, poker, tongs, and grate,
Responsive to the blithesome melody;
The tables and the chairs inanimate
Wish they had muscles now to trip it high;
Wave back and forwards at a wondrous rate,
The window-curtains, touch'd with sympathy;
Fork, knife, and trencher, almost break their sloth,
And caper on their ends upon the table-cloth.

How then could Maggie, sprightly, smart and young,
Withstand that bagpipe's blithe awak'ning air?
She, as her ear-drum caught the sounds, up-sprung
Like lightning, and despis'd her idle chair,
And into all the dance's graces flung
The bounding members of her body fair;
From nook to nook through all her room she tript,
And whirl'd like whirligig, and reel'd, and bobb'd,
and skipt.

At last the little piper ceas'd to play,
And deftly bow'd and said, 'My dear, goodnight;'
Then in a smoke evanish'd clean away,
With all his gaudy apparatus bright;
As breaks soap-bubble, which a boy in play
Blows from his short tobacco-pipe aright,
So broke poor Puck from view, and on the spot
Y-smoking aloes-reek he left his mustard-pot.

Whereat the furious lady's wriggling feet
Forgot to patter in such pelting wise,
And down she gladly sunk upon her seat,
Fatigu'd and panting from her exercise;

304 *surceast*: stopped

She sat, and mus'd a while, as it was meet,
On what so late had occupy'd her eyes;
Then to her bed-room went and doff'd her gown,
And laid upon her couch her charming person down.

Some say that Maggie slept so sound that night,
As never she had slept since she was born;
But sure am I, that, thoughtful of the sprite,
She twenty times upon her bed did turn;
For still appear'd to stand before her sight
The gaudy goblin, glorious from his urn,
And still, within the cavern of her ear,
Th' injunction echoing rung, so strict and strange
to hear.

But when the silver-harness'd steeds, that draw
The car of morning up th' empyreal height,
Had snorted day upon North-Berwick Law,[n]
And from their glist'ring loose manes toss'd
the light,
Immediately from bed she rose, (such awe
Of Tommy press'd her soul with anxious weight)
And donn'd her tissued fragrant morning vest,
And to fulfil his charge her earliest care addrest.

Straight to her house she tarried not to call
Her messengers and heralds swift of foot,
Men skill'd to hop o'er dikes and ditches; all
Gifted with sturdy brazen lungs to boot;
She bade them halt at every town, and bawl
Her proclamation outwith mighty bruit,
Inviting loud, to Anster loan and Fair,
The Scottish beaux to jump for her sweet person
there.

They took each man his staff into his hand;
They button'd round their bellies close their coats;
They flew divided through the frozen land;
Were never seen such swiftly-trav'lling Scots!
Nor ford, slough, mountain, could their speed with-
stand;
Such fleetness have the men that feed on oats!
They skirr'd, they flounder'd through the sleets
and snows
And puff'd against the winds, that bit in spite each
nose.

375 *skirr'd*: ran at speed

They halted at each wall-fenc'd town renown'd,
And ev'ry lesser borough of the nation;
And with the trumpet's welkin-rifting sound,
And tuck of drum of loud reverberation,
Tow'rds the four wings of heav'n, they, round and round,
Proclaim'd in Stentor-like[n] vociferation,
That, on th' approaching day of Anster market,
Should merry sports be held: — Hush! listen now and hark it! —

'Ho! beaux and pipers, wits and jumpers, ho!
Ye buxom blades that like to kiss the lasses;
Ye that are skill'd sew'd up in sacks to go;
Ye that excel in horsemanship of asses;
Ye that are smart at telling tales, and know
On rhime's two stilts to crutch it up Parnassus;[n]
Ho! lads, your sacks, pipes, asses, tales, prepare
To jump, play, ride, and rhime, at Anster loan and Fair!

'First, on the green turf shall each ass draw nigh,
Caparison'd or clouted for the race,
With mounted rider, sedulous to ply
Cudgel or whip, and win the foremost place;
Next, shall th' adventurous men, that dare to try
Their bodies' springiness in hempen case,
Put on their bags, and, with ridic'lous bound,
And sweat and huge turmoil, pass lab'ring o'er the ground.

'Then shall the pipers, gentlemen o' th' drone,
Their pipes in gleesome competition screw,
And grace, with loud solemnity of groan,
Each his invented tune to th' audience new;
Last shall each witty bard, to whom is known
The craft of Helicon's rhime-jingling crew,
His story tell in good poetic strains,
And make his learned tongue the midwife to his brains.

'And he whose tongue the wittiest tale shall tell,
Whose bagpipe shall the sweetest tune resound,
Whose heels, tho' clogg'd with sack, shall jump it well,
Whose ass shall foot with fleetest hoof the ground,
He who from all the rest shall bear the bell,
With victory in every trial crown'd,

He (mark it, lads!) to Maggie Lauder's house
That self-same night shall go, and take her for his spouse.'

Here ceas'd the criers of the sturdy lungs;
 But here the gossip Fame, (whose body's pores
Are nought but open ears and babbling tongues,
 That gape and wriggle on her hide in scores),
Began to jabber o'er each city's throngs,
 Blaz'ning the news through all the Scottish shores;
Nor had she blabb'd, methinks, so stoutly, since
Queen Dido's peace was broke by Troy's love-truant prince.[n]

In every Lowland vale and Highland glen,
 She nois'd th' approaching fun of Anster Fair;
Ev'n when in sleep were laid the sons of men,
 Snoring away on good chaff beds their care,
You might have heard her faintly murm'ring then,
 For lack of audience, to the midnight air,
That from Fife's East Nook up to farthest Stornoway,
Fair Maggie's loud report most rapidly was borne away.

And soon the mortals, that design to strive
 By meritorious jumping for the prize,
Train up their bodies, ere the day arrive,
 To th' lumpish sack-encumber'd exercise;
You might have seen no less than four or five
 Hobbling in each town-loan in awkward guise;
E'en little boys, when from the school let out,
Mimick'd the bigger beaux, and leap'd in pokes about.

Through cots and granges with industrious foot,
 By laird and knight were light-heel'd asses sought,
So that no ass of any great repute,
 For twenty Scots marks could have then been
  bought;
Nor e'er, before or since, the long-ear'd brute,
 Was such a goodly acquisition thought.
The pipers vex'd their ears and pipes, t' invent
Some tune that might the taste of Anster Mag
  content.

Each poet, too, whose lore-manured brain
 Is hot of soil, and sprouts up mushroom wit,
Ponder'd his noddle into extreme pain
 T' excogitate some story nice and fit:
When rack'd had been his scull some hours in vain,
 He, to relax his mind a little bit,

Plung'd deep into a sack his precious body,
And school'd it for the race, and hopp'd around his study.

Such was the sore preparatory care
  Of all th' ambitious that for April sigh:
Nor sigh the young alone for Anster Fair:
  Old men and wives, erewhile content to die,
Who hardly can forsake their easy-chair
  To take, abroad, farewell of sun and sky,
With new desire of life now glowing, pray,
That they may just o'erlive our famous market-day.

# Notes

Cleland, *Hallow my Fancie, whither wilt thou go?*

10 *Hallow*: is used in the sense of an exclamation, as 'Hail', or even 'Hello'.

69 *Erra Pater*: the supposed author of an almanac, first published in 1535, containing astrological tables, rules of health, etc.

74 *Phalaris*: the tyrant of Agrigentum, for whom Perillos, an Athenian brass-founder, proposed to make a bull of brass with a hole in the side, through which victims could be pushed and then roasted alive. Phalaris ordered that Perillus should be the first to try it out.

79 *Cynthia*: the moon. The moon goddess Artemis, or Diana, was said to have been born on Mount Cynthus in Delos.

81 *Phaëton*: the son of Phoebus, the sun-god. He was allowed by his father to drive the sun's horses for one day, but could not hold them in, and the world would have been destroyed if Zeus, or Jupiter, king of the gods, had not stepped in and killed him with a thunderbolt.

92 It was an ancient belief that pelicans feed their young with blood from their own breasts.

99 The ancients believed that the swan sang beautifully just before it died.

106 Influenced by the wording of Isaiah, chapter XI, verse 6: 'The wolf also shall dwell with the lamb . . .'.

107 *nature's alchymists*: scientists capable of working wonders, i.e. the ants, endlessly hard-working, and disliking sloth. See Proverbs, VI, 6: 'Go to the ant, thou sluggard; consider her ways, and be wise'.

127 In the old cosmogony, the moon, sun, planets and fixed stars were thought to be carried round the earth (the centre of the universe) by the concentric hollow globes called spheres, turned by spirits or angels.

146 *adamantick*: probably does not have the transferred sense of 'magnetic' (from *adamant*: loadstone), but means rather 'pertaining to adamant', a legendary and fabulously hard mineral. Cp. Milton, 'gates of burning adamant' (*Paradise Lost*, II. 436).

Ramsay, *Christ's Kirk on the Green*

Ramsay added his own notes to this poem, most of which, marked (R), are given below. He introduced his own Canto II with the following reference to the original, supposedly by King James I.

> The King having painted the rustick squabble with an uncommon spirit, in a most ludicrous manner, in a stanza of verse the most difficult to keep the sense complete, as he has done, without being forced to bring in words for crambo's sake [i.e. for the sake of the rhyme], where they return so frequently: ambitious to imitate so great an original, I put a stop to the war; called a congress, and made them sign a peace, that the world might have their picture in the more agreeable hours of drinking, dancing, and singing. The following cantos were wrote, one in 1715, the other in 1718, about 300 years after the first. Let no worthy poet despair of immortality; good sense will always be the same in spite of the revolution of words.

Ramsay assumes that the Christ's Kirk was that of Leslie, in Fife.

*Canto II*

7 *Came bellyflaught*: 'came in great haste, as it were flying full upon them with her arms spread, as a falcon with expanded wings comes soussing upon her prey' (R.).

15 *Let's . . . rows*: 'a bowling-green phrase, commonly used when people would examine any affair that's a little ravel'd' (R.).

56 *Did . . . birle*: 'contributed for fresh bottles' (R.).

68 *He lap bawk-hight*: 'so high as his head could strike the loft, or joining of the couples [principal rafters]' (R.).

75 *Falkland bred*: 'been a journeyman to the King's taylor, and had seen court dancing' (R.). Falkland is the site of a royal palace: the reference is a jibe from the neighbouring village of Leslie.

92 *glowming hous'd them*: 'twilight brought them into the house' (R.).

107 *Cuttymun . . .*: 'a tune that goes very quick' (R.).

132 *His face . . . moon*: 'When one is staring full of drink, he's said to have a face like a full moon' (R.).

136 *latter-gae of haly rhime*: 'the reader or church precenter, who *lets go*, i.e. gives out the tune to be sung by the rest of the congregation' (R.).

141 *baith write and read*: 'a rarity in those days' (R.).

143 *keek on a bead*: 'pray after the Roman Catholick manner, which was the religion then in fashion' (R.).

147 *cowping o' the creels*: 'from turning topsy turvy' (R.).

152 *rix-dollar*: 'a silver coin and money of account, current c. 1600–1850 in various European countries and in their commerce with the East' (O.E.D.).

161 *To Brownies*: 'Many whimsical stories are handed down to us by old women of these brownies: they tell us they were a kind of good

drudging spirits, who appeared in shape of rough men, would have lyen familiarly by the fire all night, threshen in the barn, brought a midwife at a time, and done many such kind offices. But none of them has been seen in Scotland since the Reformation . . .' (R.).

178–9 *A kebbuck . . . sheaf*: 'A cheese full of crawling mites crown'd the feast' (R.).

182 *Her . . . flung*: 'The practice of throwing the bridegroom or the bride's stocking when they are going to bed, is well known: the person who it lights on is to be next married of the company' (R.).

*Canto III*

Ramsay introduces Canto III as follows: 'Curious to know how my bridal folks would look next day after the marriage, I attempted this third canto, which opens with a description of the morning. Then the friends come and present their gifts to the new married couple. A view is taken of one girl (Kirsh) who had come fairly off, and of Mause who had stumbled with the laird. Next a new scene of drinking is represented, and the young good-man is creel'd. Then the character of the smith's ill-natured shrew is drawn, which leads in the description of riding the stang. Next Magy Murdy has an exemplary character of a good wise wife. Deep drinking and bloodless quarrels makes an end of an old tale' (R.).

13 *their groat*: 'Payment of the drunken groat is very peremptorily demanded by the common people next morning; but if they frankly confess the debt due, they are passed for two-pence' (R.). The 'drunken groat' was the fine of fourpence levied by the kirk session. See also the note to Fergusson's *Hallow-Fair*, l. 98.

16 *rake their een*: 'rub open their eyes' (R.).

19 *fair foor days*: 'broad day light' (R.) Foor or fure days means late afternoon.

23 *aboon the claiths*: 'They commonly throw their gifts of household furniture [i.e. furnishings] above the bed-cloaths where the young folks are lying' (R.).

42 *Word . . . kanny*: 'It was reported she was a witch' (R.).

69 *mount the creepy*: 'the stool of repentance' (R.), on which those guilty of fornication sat publicly in church.

75 *coost a legen-girth*: 'like a tub that loses one of its bottom hoops' (R.), i.e. to bear an illegitimate child.

94 *fill young Roger fou*: ' 'Tis a custom for the friends to endeavour the next day after the wedding to make the new married man as drunk as possible' (R.).

100 *A creel*: 'for merryment, a creel or basket is bound, full of stones upon his back; and if he has acted a manly part, his young wife with all imaginable speed cuts the cords, and relieves him from the burthen . . .' (R.).

128 *skin and birn*: 'the marks of a sheep; the burn on the nose, and the tar

on the skin i.e. she was sure it was him, with all the marks of her drunken husband about him' (R.).

134 *wind ye a pirn*: 'is a threatening expression, when one designs to contrive some malicious thing to vex you' (R.). A pirn is the reel or bobbin of a spinning wheel. See also the note to l. 94 of Fergusson's *The Election*.

161 *stang*: 'a rough pole or tree trunk on which an offender against the laws or conventions of a community, as by wife-beating, adultery, etc. was mounted astride and carried about as an object of public opprobrium' (S.N.D.).

177 *tane the sturdy*: 'a disease amongst sheep that makes them giddy, and run off from the rest of the herd' (R.), i.e. vertigo caused by tapeworm in the brain.

## Ramsay, *The Vision*

The subject of the poem is Scottish independence, and its ostensible author is supposed to be a contemporary of Wallace and Bruce in the late thirteenth and early fourteenth centuries. In the words of Ramsay's own footnote, 'the history of the Scots sufferings, by the unworthy condescension of Baliol to Edward I of England, till they recovered their independence by the conduct and valour of the great Bruce, is so universally known, that any argument to this antique poem seems useless'. Actually, Ramsay had in mind the more recent loss of independence by the Union of Parliaments of 1707. He did not publish the poem under his own name, but passed it off as the work of 'Ar. Scot': the letters 'Ar.' are an abbreviation of Alexander as well as being Ramsay's own initials — 'A. R. Scot[sman]'. The poem is a fine example of militant nationalist antiquarianism. Its language is deliberately archaic, employing the middle Scots ending 'and' for the present participle, as well as one rather irritating feature — the spelling 'z' for the obsolete letter 'ȝ' [yogh], pronounced like modern 'y' at the beginning of words and sometimes like 'g' when it occurs in the middle. We have substituted 'y' or 'g' where appropriate, but retained 'quh' in such words as 'quhilk' [whilk] 'quhase' [whase], 'oir' in words like 'befoir', 'sch' in words like 'schaking' — i.e. sufficient to retain something of the old-fashioned artifice of Ramsay's antiquarian hoax.

1 *Banquo brae*: no known location is indicated, but Banquo was the legendary ancestor of the Stewart kings, as mentioned in Shakespeare's *Macbeth*.

5 *stane frae Scone*: 'the old chair (now in Westminster Abbey) in which the Scots kings were always crown'd, wherein there is a piece of marble with this inscription;

> Ni fallat fatum, Scoti, quocunque locatum
> Invenient lapidem, regnare tenentur ibidem.' (R.)

The *lia fail*, or stone of destiny, is of sandstone. There is no trace of the Latin verse quoted by Ramsay, which was first mentioned in

John Bellenden's translation of Boece's *Chronicles of Scotland* (1533). A translation in the *Official Guide* (1966) is:

If Fates go right, where'er this stone is found,
The Scots shall monarch of that realm be crowned.

16 *Boreas*: the north wind.

43 *Somnus*: the god of sleep.

47–8 *quha . . . rare*: who rarely find [peace] in their waking hours.

74 *Nemo . . . lacesset*: motto of the Scottish kings, and popularly translated 'wha daur meddle wi' me'.

86 *Warden*: there is a suggestion here of the title of Guardian of Scotland, given to Wallace after the battle of Stirling Bridge (1297).

103 *Langshanks*: Edward I, King of England.

107 *Baliol*: John Baliol, King of Scotland (1292–96).

177 Allegations of bribery were made at the time of Edward I's intervention in Scottish affairs, and also at the time of the Union of the Parliaments (1707).

201 *feild neir Forthe*: battle of Bannockburn (24 June, 1314).

250 *Roman gods*: Ramsay lists both Greek and Latin names for the gods. Jove, or Jupiter, was chief of the gods; Mars, god of war; Bacchus, god of wine; Phoebus Apollo, god of the sun; Neptune, god of the sea; Vulcan, god of fire; Pluto, ruler of the underworld; Cupid, son of Venus, goddess of love; Pan, Greek god of music; Hermes, the Greek messenger of the gods.

281 *Gothus and Vandall &c.*: the European states did not exist in these forms in 1300, but may be identified as follows: Gothus, Sweden; Vandall, Russia; Gallus, France; Allmane, Germany or the Holy Roman Empire: Latinus, Naples; Batavius, Holland, the Netherlands; Iberius, Spain; Heptarchus, the Papal States; 'she of the seven hills', Rome.

296 *Hogan*: Hogen Mogen, the Netherlands.

337 *Bruce*: Robert the Bruce was crowned King of Scots at Scone in 1306.

379 *Flora*: goddess of flowers and springtime.

393 *Quod Ar. Scot*: quoth, or said. This form of words was used in the Bannatyne Manuscript, from which Ramsay gathered poems for *The Ever Green*. *The Vision* comes between a poem described as 'Quod Dunbar' and one 'Quod Kennedy'.

## Ramsay, *The Gentle Shepherd*

The action of *The Gentle Shepherd* takes place on the southern slopes of the Pentland Hills about the year 1660, after the restoration of King Charles II. The laird, Sir William Worthy, had been exiled, but had left his son and heir, Patie, in the charge of a shepherd, Symon. Patie, unaware of his identity, has become a shepherd. At the same time, Mause, a nurse in the family of Sir William's sister, had rescued the sister's daughter Peggy from being killed by jealous relatives, and had placed her as a baby at Glaud's door; he is a contemporary of Symon, and a shepherd too. In this opening scene, Patie, now a young man, has fallen in love with Peggy, and talks of his love to his friend Roger, a wealthy shepherd. Roger, for his part, is gloomy because Jenny, Glaud's daughter, does not seem to return his love.

In the course of the play that follows Sir William returns and the future of the young lovers is threatened when Patie's identity is revealed. After various episodes, some of them comic, the true history of Peggy's birth is told, and the play ends happily with rural festivities to celebrate the marriages of Patie and Peggy, Roger and Jenny. Finally, Peggy sings the song 'My Patie is a lover gay' to the old tune 'Corn rigs are bonny'.

42 *elf-shot*: 'Bewitch'd, shot by fairies, country people tell odd tales of this distemper amongst cows. When elf-shot, the cow falls down suddenly dead, no part of the skin is pierced, but often a little triangular flat stone is found near the beast, as they report, which is called the elf's arrow' (R.).

56 *West-port*: 'the sheep market place of Edinburgh' (R.); a gate in the city wall at the west end of the Grassmarket.

78 *shelly coat*: 'One of those frightful spectres the ignorant people are terrified at, and tell us strange stories of; that they are clothed with a coat of shells, which make a horrid rattling . . .' (R.).

89 *stock and horn*: 'a reed or whistle, with a horn fixed to it by the smaller end' (R.). It was a primitive instrument compared with Patie's flute.

123 *gather dew*: it is presumably May Day, when girls rose early for this purpose.

154 *red up*: 'is a metaphorical phrase from the putting in order, or winding up yarn that has been ravel'd' (R.).

169 *the grace-drink*: 'The King's health, begun first by the religious Margaret Queen of Scots, known by the name of St Margaret. The piety of her design was to oblige the courtiers not to rise from table till the thanksgiving grace was said, well judging, that tho some folks have little regard for religion, yet they will be mannerly to their prince' (R.).

Ramsay, *The Monk and the Miller's Wife*

24 *Ceres*: the Roman goddess associated with corn and the spring. The 'schools' are the universities, which in Scotland broke up in spring for a vacation, and the time must be the vernal equinox.

26 *Saint Andro's Alma Mater*: the University of St Andrews, Scotland's oldest, founded in 1411.

218 *Rosiecrucian*: the 'brethren of the Rosy Cross' were members of a

secret society based on the ideas in some pamphlets published in Germany in the early seventeenth century. They sought to change the world by magic and alchemy: their ideas were held to be subversive to society and were much feared.

223 *Albumazor*: a wizard in a play of the same name performed before James VI and I in 1615. The original Albumazor was an Arabian astronomer of the ninth century.

230 *Pacolet*: a dwarf who journeys speedily on a magic winged wooden horse, in the French romance *Valentine and Orson*.

251–2 *Radamanthus . . . Jingo*: conjurer's rubbish. Radamanthus is Rhadamanthus, judge of the underworld in classical mythology; the horner of 'monk-horner' suggests cuckoldry, and 'hipock' the fashionable hypochondria, while 'Jingo' may be a Basque word for God, but the lines' main function is just to sound impressive.

Thomson, *Winter. A Poem*

44 *Philomel*: in the myth, she was sad because she had been raped by her brother-in-law Tereus, king of Thrace, who cut out her tongue and hid her in a lonely spot. After further violence she was changed into a nightingale, her sister Procne into a swallow.

126 *feathery people*: an expression for domestic poultry which reflects the linguistic conventions of eighteenth-century science, differentiating species according to their habitat or covering. Compare Hugh MacDiarmid's fondness for scientific terms in the twentieth century.

160 *circle*: in folk meteorology, a ring around the moon portends floods and storms.

162 *air*: the air is thought of as a structure supported by pillars, and 'fabric' is the total building rather than the substance of which it is composed.

242–52 One of the specifically Scottish scenes in the poem. These are Border shepherds; 'wreath' is a Scots word for snowdrift. Compare Matthew Bramble's remarks on the sheep of Tweeddale and Nithsdale, in Smollett's *Humphry Clinker* (1771): 'their fleeces are much damaged by the tar, with which they are smeared to preserve them from the rot in winter, during which they run wild night and day, and thousands are lost under huge wreaths of snow' (Everyman edn., p. 257).

268 *Solon*: (c. 640–558 B.C.) Athenian poet, statesman, and lawgiver.

269 *Lycurgus*: the traditional and possibly legendary founder of Spartan laws and institutions.

271 *Numa*: Numa Pompilius (715–673 B.C.) second king of Rome and traditionally the founder of many Roman festivals, sacrifices and other religious rituals. His long and peaceful reign was regarded as a kind of golden age.

272 *Cimon*: (c. 512–449 B.C.) all-powerful ruler of Athens, who perhaps hardly merits the adjective 'sweet-soul'd', on account of his vigorous expansionist policy. He was a follower of Aristides (c. 530–468 B.C.).

273 *Cato*: Marcus Porcius Cato (95–46 B.C.), Roman patriot and stoic who committed suicide rather than surrender to Caesar. One of the culture-heroes of the eighteenth century, he is the protagonist in Addison's tragedy *Cato*, popular in Thomson's day both in England and Scotland.

274 *attemper'd heroe*: Timoleon (died c. 337 B.C.) Greek general and statesman 'who, despite — or because of — his temperate character, had his brother killed when he sought to become tyrant of Corinth. He is said to have covered his head and wept while his companions carried out the assassination' (Thomson).

276 *Scipio*: Scipio Africanus Major (236–184 B.C.), the Roman general who defeated Hannibal.

279 *Theban*: either Pelopidas (c. 410–364 B.C.) or Epaminondas (d. 362 B.C.), both of whom campaigned against Sparta. In his 1746 revision Thomson runs the two together as 'the Theban pair' (l. 476).

288 *Maro*: Publius Vergilius Maro (i.e. Virgil).

291 *The British Muse*: Milton, who, like Homer, was blind.

298 *Lycidas*: this proper name, from the title of Milton's pastoral elegy on Edward King (1638), had by Thomson's period become synonymous with the type of the cultured friend.

302 *aetherial nitre*: an alleged nitrous element in the air or in plants, which was supposed to cause freezing.

311 *influence*: 'the supposed flowing from the stars of an ethereal fluid acting upon the character and destiny of men, and affecting sublunary things generally' (O.E.D.). Here it causes water to freeze.

Hamilton, *The Braes of Yarrow*

Text: *Poems on Several Occasions by William Hamilton of Bangour, Esquire* (Edinburgh, 1760), edited in accordance with the principles of the anthology.

8 *birks*: cutting down branches of birch, a folk custom with, originally, magical significance. F. Marian McNeill (*The Silver Bough*, 4 vols., Glasgow, 1957–68, II, 89) notes that on Midsummer Day, 'branches of birch were cut down and hung over doors and archways', and that 'birken boughs are still a feature of the Lanimer Day procession in Lanark'. Lanimer day ('landmarch' or beating the bounds) is celebrated with pageantry and processions through the town in the first week of June. See the note to l. 30 of Hogg's *Kilmeny*.

Ross, *Helenore*

The text is that established by Margaret Wattie in *The Scottish Works of Alexander Ross, M.A.* (Scottish Text Society, third series, 9, 1938). It has been collated with the first edition of 1768 on which it is based and a few minor corrections to her transcription have been incorporated. A few other minor alterations in the punctuation have been made for the sake of comprehensibility. The punctuation of the first edition is so chaotic that Miss Wattie properly abandoned it and supplied her own, but the orthography is largely Ross's (or his printer's).

3065 *A band of kettrin*: it was a traditional occupation for Highlanders, or rather a class of Highlanders known as caterans, to lift cattle from their lowland neighbours. In his 'Report, etc., relating to the Highlands, 1724' General Wade says:

> They go out in parties from ten to thirty men traverse large tracts of mountains till they arrive at the lowlands where they design to commit depradations which they chuse to do in places distant from the clans where they inhabit; they drive the stolen cattle in the night time, and in the day remain on the tops of the mountains or in the woods (with which the Highlands abound) and take the first occasion to sell them at the fairs or markets that are annually held in many parts of the country. (in *Papers Relating to the Jacobite Period 1699–1750*, ed. James Allardyce, 1895, vol. 1, p. 134).

Such activities were endemic in the highland–lowland border area where Ross lived. The Farquharsons, who belonged to the Braemar district, were particularly troublesome in the late seventeenth and early eighteenth centuries and Lord Forbes, to a branch of whose family Ross was a tutor for a while in Craigievar, had a particular role in trying to contain them. The school and school-house at Lochlee were only a mile west of Invermark Castle which guarded the drove road over the shoulder of Mount Keen to Ballater. In other words Ross lived in excellent reiving country. (See 'Glenesk' in Duncan Fraser, *Discovering Angus and Mearns*, 1972, pp. 31–45 and David Buchan, *The Ballad and the Folk*, 1972, pp. 28–34).

1 *Scota*: Ross's use of Scota suggested to Burns the name of his muse in *The Vision*.

25 *Habbi*: Habbie Simson, piper of Kilbarchan. See the general introduction to this volume.

30 *Pate*: in *The Gentle Shepherd* Patie, the hero, turns out not to be an orphan shepherd but the son of the laird who returns from exile at the restoration in 1660.

40 *Kairn*: Cairn o Mount, an eastern road over the Mounth, which is the line of hills to the south of the Dee. Scota asks Ross if he really thinks he can write like someone from the lowlands.

94 *care and tut'ry*: the steps taken for the care and protection of the child are examples of sympathetic magic. They are also positive magic in that the women are trying to establish a favourable pattern of events in the life of the child. In Scotland, rowan is the most powerful specific against evil and witches. While it is obviously hygienic to wash Jean's paps 'wi' sa't and water' both have connotations of prosperity and fertility. In addition, salt, as an emblem of eternity, is inimical to fairies who might otherwise sour the milk. Throwing the first nappy on the green also has fertility implications. 'Unko words' are charms. Fire and iron ward off fairies; and the fiery coal is taken in the tongs and dropped down through the open shirt so that the fairies will be unable to steal the child of earth and substitute one of their own (before its christening a child was in particular danger of being stolen). Next, Nory is the subject of Christian prayer. Finally, it is significant that all this should be called 'Craft' that is known by 'auld grandys'.

403–21 The agricultural system suggested here is the primitive one gradually supplanted in the course of the eighteenth century. The lines 'no property these honest shepherds pled; / All kept alike, an' all in common fed', which might seem to imply pastoral idealism, in fact reflect an agricultural regime that once really existed. The chief industry of the uplands of Scotland was the raising of livestock and in Flaviana conditions are favourable: the green (the level valley floor) which provides pasture for the cows is 'even, gowanny and fair' and the sides of the valley provide good grazing for sheep and goats ('on every side the braes / To a good height, wi' scatter'd busses raise'). Wealth is measured by the number of beasts owned — 'The fowks were wealthy, store was a' their stock; / With this, but little siller, did they trock'. The grazing land was common and the community's flocks and herds wandered promiscuously at will. There would be no fences marking off different holdings or separating cultivated land from pasture. There would therefore be none of the marks of private property. But the stock is not communally owned — each peasant has his own — and the land is owned by a laird to whom the people pay rent in kind: 'Frae mang the stock his honour gat his fa' '.

1775–7 *sick . . . wark*: in case you will one day be bare of possessions; so good luck to you, or if you miss what is marked down for you one thing I see — you will meet real difficulty.

1818 This description of the fairies gives them traditional attributes. They indulge in dancing and feasting. They meddle in earthly affairs: it was believed to be a common practice that they should steal an earthly woman to be nurse to the children of the fairy king, and that they should play tricks (compare Puck in *A Midsummer Night's Dream*). Ross's fairy lore is correct. The fairies are seen by Bydby because she is a Highlander (in spite of speaking Scots), and Celts see fairies more readily than others. She sees them because she plants herself within the space they are occupying for the moment, and is threatened with transportation as a result. She finds their food insubstantial. See Robert Kirk, *The Secret Commonwealth of Elves, Fauns and Fairies*, ed. R. B. Cunninghame Graham (1933), a 1691 work by the minister of Aberfoyle; also Sir Walter Scott, *Letters on Demonology and Witchcraft* (1830), letter 4.

Skirving, *Tranent Muir*

Text: A. Campbell, *The Poetry of Scotland* (Edinburgh, 1798). The metre of this poem, with its internal rhyme and the repetition of 'man', was associated with the tune *Killiecrankie*; it was used by other Jacobite writers, and by Burns in such political pieces as *When Guilford good* and *The Tree of Liberty*.

1 *The Chevalier*: Prince Charles Edward, who won the Battle of Prestonpans, to the discomfiture of General Sir John Cope, on 21 September, 1745.

2 *Brisle brae*: Birsley brae is on the way from Musselburgh to Tranent.

6 *loud huzza*: On 20 September the Prince's army on its way to Tranent came in sight of Cope's army at Prestonpans: they greeted one another with loud shouts and yells. There is a good account of the battle in Scott's *Tales of a Grandfather*, and it is also featured in *Waverley*, chapters 46–7.

9 *brave*: copy text reads 'brae-lochaber'. As Skirving's syntax is simple, he probably does not mean 'Lochaber men came up the brae'; either an 'e' has been substituted for a 'w', or a 'v' has been omitted.

*Lochaber men*: MacDonalds whose chief was Keppoch.

17 *Lochiel*: Chief of Clan Cameron.

23 *Seaton-Crafts*: crofts of the village of Seton.

41 *Menteith*: the Rev. Robert Monteith, minister of Longformacus, who had volunteered to serve in Cope's army. Laing notes: 'Having accidentally surprised a Highlander, in the act of easing nature, the night previous to the battle, he pushed him over, seized his musket, and bore it off in triumph to Cope's camp.'

45 *Soutra Hill*: on the westerly ridge of the Lammermuir Hills.

49 *Simpson*: the Rev. Patrick Simson, minister of Fala, 'another reverend volunteer, who boasted, that he would soon bring the rebels to their senses by the dint of his pistols; having a brace of them in his pockets, another in his holsters, and one in his belt. On approaching the enemy, however, his courage failed him, and he fled in confusion and terror along with the rest' (Laing in *SMM* IV).

59 *Campbell*: George Campbell, wright (carpenter) in Edinburgh.

*Myrie staid*: 'a student of physic from Jamaica, and entered as a volunteer in the royal army, but was dreadfully mangled in the battle with the Highland claymores' (Laing).

60 *paid the kain*: suffered severely. 'Kain' was a duty paid in kind by tenant to landlord.

65 *Gard'ner*: Colonel Gardiner of Bankton. The ruins of his house and an obelisk to his memory still stand near the site of the battle. Scott quotes a moving contemporary account of his death in *Waverley*, note 19.

111 *her nainsell*: she, but meaning 'he' in comic Gaelic lingo.

125 *On Seaton sands*: Port Seton, where Skirving was robbed by rejoicing Highlanders. The story goes that some years later he recognised the thief at a feeing market, and when he demanded his watch back was told: 'Oh! she (the watch) dee'd that same night, and I gied her till a neighbour, and he's gane far o'er the hills, an', be Got, ye'll never see her again!'

Skinner, *The Christmass Bawing of Monimusk*

As there is no extant MS, the text is based on the first printing, that in the *Caledonian Magazine*, September, 1788. Typographical errors have been corrected and the whole regularised in accordance with the general principles adopted for the anthology.

Nearly every district in Scotland had its annual bawing at Christmas, New Year or Fastern's eve (Shrove Tuesday). The custom still continues in Jedburgh. Sometimes one part of a parish played another; sometimes whole parishes opposed each other. The rules were various but it was standard that in football no handling was permitted and in handball no kicking. In Monymusk, the game was football. It appears that the pitch is the churchyard and one of the goals is in the park, i.e. in the grounds of Monymusk House. It is permissible to trip, kick, fell and otherwise incapacitate opponents. There are spectators but it is part of the game to 'involve' them from time to time and to lower the dignity of the schoolmaster and his like by tackling or by inducing falls in the mud. One goal constitutes a win in this game, but it might have continued had there been light enough.

82 *inset dominie*: as Skinner was assistant schoolmaster in Monymusk in 1739 when the bawing takes place, it is possible that stanza 10 is autobiographical.

Beattie, *To Alexander Ross*

The text is based on the first edition of 1768.

8 *Habby*: Habbie Simson, piper of Kilbarchan.

75 Gawin Douglas: (1475?–1522) bishop of Dunkeld and translator of Virgil's *Æneid*.

77 *first King James*: James Stewart (1394–1437), King James I of Scotland. Author of *The Kingis Quair* and reputed author of *Peblis*

*to the Play* and *Christis Kirk on the Green*. In the 1768 edition Beattie has *fifth* but this is altered in 1778 to *first*.

79 *Montgomery*: Alexander Montgomerie (1545?–1598?). Author of *The Cherrie and the Slae*, and of songs and sonnets, and translator of the Psalms.

80 *Dunbar*: William Dunbar (1460?–1513?). One of the great Scottish medieval poets.

*Scot*: Alexander Scott (1525?–1583?), the finest of the Scots poets of the second half of the sixteenth century.

*Hawthornden*: William Drummond of Hawthornden (1585–1649). A man of wide intellectual interests, a fine poet and a friend of Ben Jonson. He wrote in English, though his rhymes indicate a Scottish pronunciation.

93 *Cairn-a-mounth*: Cairn o Mount, the summit of the road between Banchory and Fettercairn on the hills dividing Aberdeen and its hinterland from the south.

96 *Drousty*: an ale house at Lochlee. In 1803 the site was used for the manse, now the House of Mark.

## Beattie, *The Minstrel*

The text reproduced here is based on the eighth edition of 1784, the last to be corrected by Beattie in his lifetime.

1 Stanzas 1 and 2 were obviously inspired by Gray's *Elegy Written in a Country Churchyard*.

21 *minstrel*: In his original 'Advertisement' to *The Minstrel* Beattie says: 'The first hint of this performance was suggested by Mr Percy's ingenious "Essay on the English Minstrels" ', prefixed to the first volume of his *Reliques of Ancient English Poetry* (1765). Percy's essay, and his anthology, might be considered a part of the primitivist 'movement' whose greatest European exponent was Rousseau.

66 *luxury*: to many philosophers of the eighteenth century the use of the term *luxury* (a passion for riches and physical comfort as well as sensual indulgence) indicates disapproval; for example in Adam Ferguson's *An Essay on the History of Civil Society* (1767) luxury is morally and socially corrupting for it destroys disinterestedness and civic zeal.

91 *gothick days*: vaguely, the middle ages.

93 *fairyland, Sicilian groves, Arcady*: poetry and song were associated with fairyland (see the ballad *Thomas the Rhymer*); Sicily was the home of the pastoral poet Theocritus; Arcady is the perfect never-never land of pastoral poetry.

95 *north countrie*: 'There is hardly an ancient ballad, or romance, wherein a minstrel or harper appears, but he is characterised, by

way of eminence, to have been "*of the north countrie*". It is probable, that under this appellation were formerly comprehended all the provinces to the north of the Trent. See Percy's "Essay on the English Minstrels"' (B.).

109 *From labour health . . .*: compare a similar view in Fergusson's *The Farmer's Ingle* and Burns's development of the theme in *The Cotter's Saturday Night*.

152 *Phoebus*: the sun. Beattie refers poetically to sunset; in the poetic diction of the period, he is concretely visualising the glancing beam, not the sun-god himself.

153 *team*: team of oxen or horses.

163–70 This stanza must have suggested the shape of Wordsworth's *The Simplon Pass* (in *The Prelude*, 1805, VI, 553–572).

181–9 Compare this stanza with Wordsworth's description of looking down on mist from the top of Snowdon (*The Prelude*, 1805, XIII, 10–65).

191 In other words, when Edwin contemplates nature he experiences both sublime and pathetic emotions.

284 Interest in such 'horrors' is part of the taste of the age. Horace Walpole's *The Castle of Otranto*, the prototype gothic novel, appeared first in 1764.

294 *vision*: the advice given by Edwin's father (ll. 248–9) echoes Pope's couplet in *An Essay on Man* (epistle 2, 1–2):

> Know then thyself, presume not God to scan;
> The proper study of mankind is man.

By implication, Edwin rejects his father's view of life as moral obligation. At line 263 he is 'the visionary boy'. He now has a vision of a minstrel. In other words poetic inspiration, rather than ethical commentary as in Pope, is to be the source of his effusions. Wind and light (ll. 295–8) are symbols of inspiration.

357 *Pyrrho's maze*: Pyrrho of Elis (c. 365–275 B.C.), the founder of the sceptical school of Greek philosophers.

*Epicurus' sty*: Epicurus was (falsely) believed to advocate sensual pleasure as the only good. Thus he is associated with pigs. His ethical position is rather that pleasure (or the absence of pain) is the only good known to the senses.

366 *Error*: the Red Crosse Knight defeats Errour in book 1 canto 1 of Spenser's *The Faerie Queene*, but not before she defiles everything with her vomit, which contains all kinds of 'deformed monsters', i.e. particular errors.

370 *masters of the lay*: minstrels, or the authors of ballads and romances.

391 *nut-brown maid*: the heroine of a medieval ballad, admired by the English Augustans, for Matthew Prior (1664–1721) imitated it in his *Henry and Emma*.

406 'See the fine old ballad, called, *The Children in the Wood*' (B.). The line is a paraphrase from the ballad as published by Percy.

523 *Lapponian's dreary land*: Lapland.

534 *Montagu*: Elizabeth Montagu (1720–1800), authoress and blue-stocking, to whom later editions of the poem were dedicated. She was on the outskirts of the Johnson circle and toured Scotland in 1766 with Dr John Gregory, perhaps Beattie's closest friend.

## Fergusson, *Hallow-fair*

The poem, first printed in Ruddiman's *Weekly Magazine*, 12 November, 1772, was the earliest in which Fergusson used the *Christ's Kirk* stanza. It employs the bob-wheel as simplified by Ramsay and Skinner, but makes one innovation — four instead of two rhymes in the octave, viz. abab / cdcd / e.

1 *Hallowmas*: this fair was held in early November, in fields about half a mile west of the Grassmarket, on the Falkirk road. It was mainly a horse and cattle market.

37 *Sawny*: Aberdeen was famous for the making of stockings, a considerable domestic industry in the town and its surrounding country. The Aberdeen accent that Fergusson reproduces is pretty much what can be heard today — *fa, protty, weyr, leem,* for *wha, pretty, wire*, and *loom*.

56 *The serjeant*: the recruiting sergeant, offering what was known in later, and more economical, days as the King's Shilling, paid to the recruit who signed on.

73 *Phoebus . . . Thetis lap*: sunset. Phoebus was god of the sun, and Thetis one of the sea-goddesses.

79 *Lochaber aix*: the halbert carried by the City Guard, a long staff with axe and hook at the end.

93 *Highland aith*: Fergusson pokes fun at the Gaelic accents of the old soldiers from Highland regiments who made up the City Guard. 'She maun pe see' is a Gaelic locution for 'he must be seen by', and 'pring' and 'ta' represent 'bring' and 'the'.

98 *drunken groat*: fine for drunkenness. See also Ramsay's *Christ's Kirk on the Green*, Canto III, note to l. 13.

## Fergusson, *Auld Reikie*

In his *Old and New Edinburgh* (1882), James Grant claimed that the term Auld Reikie has been used affectionately for Edinburgh since the seventeenth century. Its relevance is obvious to any one who pictures the smoke rising from that impressive ridge of houses from the Castle to the Palace of Holyroodhouse. The poem was first printed as a pamphlet in 1773, where it was described as 'Canto I' and ended at l. 328. The remaining 40 lines were printed in *Poems on various subjects by Robert Fergusson*, Part II (1779). The poem, then, is incomplete — the 'brilliant first Act of what was intended to become a full-length comedy of Edinburgh life' (*The Poems of Robert Fergusson*, ed. M. P. McDiarmid, I. 40). Though modelled on John Gay's *Trivia, or the art of walking the streets of London* (1716), *Auld Reikie* is no mere mechanical adaptation into Scots of its Augustan original; it is far more sympathetic and humane than Gay's amusing but objective satire.

19 *Boreas*: the north wind. The high tenement buildings of Edinburgh's High Street, and the narrow closes between them give some protection from the cold winds of winter.

24 *St Giles*: the high kirk of St Giles, in the High Street.

29 *turnpike stair*: the spiral staircase connecting the floors of the high tenements, or lands.

38 *Nore Loch brig*: the Nor' Loch lay in the valley where Princes Street Gardens now are. It was drained gradually in the eighteenth century, and a bridge over the valley, the North Bridge, was started in 1763 but collapsed, with loss of life, in 1769. It was finally opened in 1772.

39 *Edina's roses*: household slops and soil thrown on the street, often from a height, satirically called 'the flowers of Edinburgh' by its inhabitants.

53 *Luckenbooths*: a tall tenement building in the middle of the High Street, which housed many shops and small booths. See also *Plainstanes and Causey*, l. 106.

59 *Phoebus*: the sun, from Apollo, whose epithet 'Phoebus' means 'the bright'.

63 *lawyers*: the Court of Session, the supreme court in Scotland, is near St Giles and the Market Cross. Advocates and their agents, the solicitors, met for business in that neighbourhood.

71 *usefu' cadie*: the cadies were men licensed to run errands, carry messages and attend strangers as servants. They could on occasions supply useful information to the agents of justice.

77 *lazy chairman*: the men who carried the sedan-chairs were often highlanders. See below, *Plainstanes and Causey*, l. 44.

104 *macaronies*: young dandies who affected continental tastes in food and fashions. They had a reputation for vice and insolence.

133 *ten-hours drum*: the town drummer made his rounds at ten o'clock at night, warning sober citizens to be on their way home. Many of the social clubs continued long after that hour.

143 *Pandemonium*: a social club devoted to good eating. *Salamanders* (l. 151) may refer to a similar club.

148 *Epicurus*: See above, Beattie's *Minstrel*, note to l. 357.

153 *Cape*: the Cape Club, of which Fergusson became a member in 1772. The members, called Knights, were given pseudonyms, and Fergusson was known as Sir Precenter, presumably because of his fine singing voice.

168 *saulie*: the hired mourner at a funeral.

191 *sybil*: as told in Virgil's *Aeneid*, Aeneas, led by the sybil of Cumae, a

prophetess, descended to the underworld of Pluto's kingdom and there met many of the shades of the dead.

219 *Gillespie's snuff*: John and James Gillespie were snuff dealers in the High Street. James left his money to found a hospital for old people and a school. The school is now James Gillespie's High School. An Edinburgh saying about Gillespie's generosity was 'Wha wad hae thocht it, that noses had bocht it?'.

253–5 *Comely-Garden . . . Canon-mills*: various places in and around Edinburgh are mentioned here. Comely Garden was a public park east of Holyroodhouse. The Park was Hope Park, now the Meadows, on the south side of Edinburgh. Newhaven is a fishing village on the Forth, west of the port of Leith. Canonmills in the eighteenth century was a little village north of Edinburgh.

263 *Arthur's Seat*: the volcanic hill in Holyrood Park.

273 *Holyrood-house*: the royal palace, neglected in Fergusson's day, of which the Duke of Hamilton was hereditary keeper.

285 *Blest place*: Holyrood Abbey, adjoining the palace, was a debtors' sanctuary. Debtors were free from legal action as long as they were resident within the Abbey bounds, and they were allowed out freely on Sundays.

291 *St Anthon's grassy hight*: the ruined chapel of St Anthony, on the slopes of Arthur's Seat.

300 *Simon Fraser*: keeper of the Tolbooth, the city prison, known as the Heart of Midlothian.

314 *Drummond*: George Drummond (1687–1766), six times Lord Provost, and the most distinguished holder of that office. He was responsible for many building projects, including the Royal Infirmary and the planning of the New Town.

325 *Glasgow*: before the industrial age, Glasgow had the reputation of being a beautiful university and cathedral city.

329 *provosts*: the chief magistrate of Edinburgh is styled Lord Provost. The Town Council in Fergusson's day was largely self-elected (see *The Election*), and allegations of corruption in local politics were frequently made.

361 *Fifan coast*: Fergusson had been at school in Dundee and at university in St Andrews: the journey through Fife, back to his home in Edinburgh, must have been familiar to him.

Fergusson, *Mutual Complaint of Plainstanes and Causey*

The poem was first printed in Ruddiman's *Weekly Magazine*, 4 March 1773.

1 *Merlin*: according to tradition the first causeway in Edinburgh was laid by a Frenchman called Marlin (Walter Merlion, a French mason, appears in records of the late fifteenth and early sixteenth century).

6 *Fraser's ulie*: Fraser was the contractor for the city's oil lamps.

7 *Highland sentries*: the city guard, largely composed of Highlanders. See *Hallow-fair*, l. 79, n.

11 *cadie*: see above, *Auld Reikie*, note to l. 71.

16 *ass of Balaam*: it spoke the truth, as described in Numbers XXII, 28ff.

35 *uncanny nicksticks*: outlandish tallies. Exchequer tally-sticks were about eight inches long. Fergusson is exaggerating for comic effect; the tallies were probably tied by lengths of string to the baskets carried on the porters' backs.

44 *Gallic chairman*: one of the Highlanders who carried sedan-chairs.

67 *whin-stanes*: 'whinstone, a popular name in Scotland for a hard or compact kind of stone, as distinguished from sandstone or freestone or rocks of slaty structure' (Chambers).

101 *libel*: the statement of a plaintiff's grounds of complaint against a defendant, and in Scots law the form of complaint on which a prosecution takes place.

102 *magnum damnum datum*: legal Latin for 'I shall win my case, get damages, and see you fined'.

103 *Arthur's seat*: see *Auld Reikie*, l. 263, n. Quarrying took place from time to time there until the visit to Edinburgh of George IV in 1822, when crown rights over the area were reasserted.

106 *Luckenbooths*: see note to *Auld Reikie*, l. 53.

107 *the Cross*: the Cross of Edinburgh was removed by order of the magistrates in 1756.

108 *the Guard*: the town guard-house, headquarters of the City Guard, Fergusson's 'black banditti'. It was 'a huge misshapen hulk' in the middle of the High Street, until its removal in 1785.

116 *Charlie's Statue*: the equestrian statue of Charles II in Parliament Square.

*Exchange*: the Royal Exchange, built by John and Robert Adam, and finished in 1761, is now the City Chambers. The old Exchange was in Parliament Square.

130 *Robinhood*: a debating society, later called the Pantheon, of which Fergusson was a member.

133 *provost*: see note on *Auld Reikie*, l. 329

*baillies*: municipal officers and magistrates (compare English aldermen).

138 *Thetis*: see *Hallow-fair*, l. 73, note.

Fergusson, *The Farmer's Ingle*

First printed in Ruddiman's *Weekly Magazine*, 13 May 1773.

2 *Batie*: 'a name for a dog, without any particular respect to species; generally given, however, to those of a larger size' (Jamieson).

16 'That every detail is exactly as he would wish it'.

43 *Denmark's daring sons*: the battle of Luncarty, on the Tay five miles north of Perth, where, according to tradition, the Scots defeated Danish invaders in the tenth century. The story goes that a Dane cried out in anguish when he trod on a thistle, and thus gave away his army's position. A natural rock formation on the Tay north of the alleged battle site is still called Thistle Brig.

53 *the cutty stool*: the stool of repentance in the kirk, where those guilty of fornication had to sit, and, in the presence of the congregation, be publicly rebuked by the minister. See also Ramsay's *Christ's Kirk on the Green*, Canto III, l. 69.

54 *Mess John*: here used for the parish minister, but an old pre-Reformation name for the mass priest.

94 *thirling mill*: the grinding mill which a tenant was obliged to use, under the terms of his lease.

102 *leaden god*: Morpheus, god of sleep.

Fergusson, *The Ghaists: A Kirkyard Eclogue*

First printed in Ruddiman's *Weekly Magazine*, 27 May 1773.

5 *Twa sheeted ghaists*: George Heriot, goldsmith and money-lender to James VI, left money to found a hospital for the sons of Edinburgh citizens in difficult circumstances. The beautiful building that bears his name was opened in 1659: it is now George Heriot's School, and must be the oldest school building still in use in Scotland. George Watson was accountant to the Bank of Scotland: he left money to the Merchant Company of Edinburgh for a hospital on the Heriot model, for the sons of merchants. It was opened in 1734, and continues today as George Watson's College. In 1773, a Bill — the Mortmain Bill — was brought forward in Parliament to encourage the trustees of these and similar charities to put all their resources into government stocks, but the Town Council and Merchant Company objected on financial as well as patriotic grounds, and the Bill was withdrawn. Fergusson imagines the ghosts of Heriot and Watson haunting Greyfriars churchyard, where Watson lies buried, adjoining Heriot's Hospital. (Heriot was, in fact, buried in London where he died.) Geordie Girdwood was the gravedigger in Greyfriars.

37 *Danish Jones*: the famous architect, Inigo Jones (1573–1652), was called 'Danish' because he was at one time employed by the King of Denmark. The story that he had anything at all to do with the building of Heriot's Hospital is completely unfounded.

40 *Brawly to busk*: the custom of decorating with flowers the statue of George Heriot above the entrance to the quadrangle of the hospital on his birthday early in June.

43 *Major Weir*: by his own confession Major Weir, who lived in the West Bow off Edinburgh's High Street, was a wizard; he and his

sister were executed in 1670. Their ghosts, it was said, continued to haunt their house in the West Bow, and for many years no one would live in it. The house was demolished in 1878.

49 *Adam's tomb*: the tomb of William Adam (1689–1748), the distinguished architect and father of Robert Adam.

66 *grassum gift*: a fee paid to a landlord by an incoming tenant.

87 *Netherbow*: this street no longer exists but was near the eastern end of the High Street, at the head of the Canongate. 'Bow' was the curve or bending of a street; the old Netherbow Port, one of the city gates, was demolished in 1764.

125 *Mackenzie*: Sir George Mackenzie (1636–91), called 'Bluidy Mackenzie' for his dealings with the Covenanters, but a patriotic Scotsman, founder of what is now the National Library of Scotland.

Fergusson, *Leith Races*

First printed in Ruddiman's *Weekly Magazine*, 22 July 1773

1 *July month*: Leith Races, officially patronised by the Town Council, were held on or about July 20th. There was a grand procession from the Council Chambers in the High Street down to Leith Sands, a purse presented by the Council being borne by officials and protected by the city guard.

11 *musand*: the middle Scots present participle creates a deliberately archaic effect.

25 *Hebe*: daughter of Zeus, and symbol of perpetual youth.

29 *Land o' Cakes*: Scotland, famous for its oatcakes.

31 *late-wakes*: at funerals, mourning for the dead was mingled with dancing, drinking, and mirth, by way of relief after strain.

39 *screw the cheery pegs*: tune the fiddle.

52 *craw kniefly in his crap*: he will find it impossible to forget her; her nagging presence will always be with him.

73 *hafe a care*: here and in the following lines Fergusson is poking fun at the Gaelic accents of the guard — *hafe*, for *have*, *marsh* for *march* and the phrase *her nanesel* (her ain self) for *we*.

80 *birth-day wars*: the celebrations of King's Birthday (June 4th) in Edinburgh often ended in attacks on the city guard.

84 *baxter lads*: young bakers, or apprentices. This refers to an incident reported in the press when one of the city guards was convicted for assaulting and killing a baker. The bakers vowed revenge.

88 *pay the kane*: duty paid in kind by tenant to landlord. See also *Plainstanes and Causey* l. 52, and Skirving, *Tranent Muir* l. 60. The meaning here is 'to suffer'.

89 *tails weel sautit*: to put salt on one's tail is to catch or restrain someone. Here the phrase means 'to be properly punished'.

91 *Bow*: the West Bow, the steep way from Lawnmarket to Grassmarket, where tinsmiths and other craftsmen in metals had their shops.

95 *Leith Walk*: the beginning of the road from Edinburgh to Leith on the Calton side.

115 *toutit aff the horn*: drank off the contents of a drinking cup, with an onomatopoeic pun on the musical instrument.

118 *Buchan bodies*: from the north-eastern corner of Aberdeenshire. They say *gueed* for *good*, and *fa* for *wha*.

119 *Findrums cry*: advertise by means of the appropriate street-cry their small peat-smoked haddocks, called speldings. These were first produced at Findon, Kincardineshire.

127 *rowly powl*: a game played at fairs, in which a stick was thrown at pegs carrying penny cakes of gingerbread.

142 *Dian*: Diana, the virgin goddess and symbol of chastity.

145 *Lyon*: Lord Lyon King of Arms, who can prosecute those who display unrecorded coats of arms.

149 *Jamie's laws*: a statute of 1592, in the reign of James VI, authorising the punishment of those bearing false arms.

152 *Whigs*: the jacobitical Fergusson associates social climbing and spurious armorial bearings with the whigs and the Hanoverians.

163 *Robinhood*: a debating society. See *Plainstanes and Causey*, note to l. 130.

172 *hale the dools*: a dool was a goal in football, and to hale the dools was to be victorious in the game. The phrase here means to celebrate with enthusiasm.

Fergusson, *The Election*

First printed in Ruddiman's *Weekly Magazine*, 16 September 1773. The town council of Edinburgh in the eighteenth century consisted of twenty-five members, seventeen being merchants and eight tradesmen, the latter called deacons. Deacons were elected annually by the fourteen incorporated trades, and the process took place in stages. First, each trade put forward six candidates, called the 'lang leet', and the town council reduced that number to three, the 'short leet', or list. From the 'short leet' each trade chose one to be its deacon. The fourteen incorporations then dined together, a gathering known as the 'showing of faces', and the town council then selected six from the fourteen deacons to be council deacons along with two deacons from the existing council. At another dinner, one of the council deacons was elected convener of trades, and took formal charge of Blue Blanket, the banner presented to the Edinburgh Trades by James III, and, according to tradition, carried by them at Flodden.

The macaronic Latin verse may be rendered as: 'Now is the time for drinking and draining the bowl, but beware of the City Guard, especially Dougal Ged and Dugald Campbell'.

17 *affidavit o' faith*: the oath of loyalty to the king and the established religion, required of all public servants.

43 *Walker's*: a tavern near the Royal Exchange (now the City Chambers), on the north side of the High Street.

67 *handsel-Teysday*: the first Tuesday of the New Year.

74 *lamps*: until the reorganisation of local government in 1975, the bailies, or magistrates, of Edinburgh had special decorated lamp posts placed before their houses.

94 *reel my pirny*: the sense of this metaphor from spinning is 'if you attack me, then look out for the consequences'. See Ramsay, *Christ's Kirk on the Green*, Canto III, l. 120 and note.

111 There were many allegations of corruption, even with debased coins (gold guineas short-weighted, 'inlaked', by as much as an eighth — i.e. to the value of half a crown).

123 *protests*: formal objections raised as a result of the complicated procedure.

124 *Sandy Fife*: ? the town bell-ringer.

125 *Clout the caudron*: a traditional folk tune, played on the bells of St Giles.

134 *lang leet*: the long list of death: the phrase recalls the election procedure.

Mayne, *The Siller Gun*

Text: the Glocester [*sic*] edition of 1808.

4 *The sev'n trades*: there were seven incorporated trades in Dumfries, namely hammermen (or blacksmiths), squaremen (or carpenters), tailors, weavers, shoemakers, skinners, and fleshers (or butchers). A deacon was chosen yearly for each trade, and one of the deacons was elected convener of trades. Convener and deacons became members of the town council. For the different organisation in Edinburgh, see the notes to Fergusson's *The Election*.

5 *siller gun*: Mayne's note (1808) is as follows:

'The following poem is founded on an ancient custom in Dumfries, called *Shooting for the Siller Gun*.

'The Gun is a small silver tube, like the barrel of a pistol, but derives great importance from its being the gift of James VI, that monarch having ordained it as a prize to the best marksman among the Corporations of Dumfries.

'The contest was, by royal authority, licensed to take place every year; but, in consequence of the trouble and expence attending it, the custom has not been so frequently observed. Whenever the festival is appointed, the birth-day of the reigning sovereign is invariably chosen for that purpose.'

According to W. McDowall, *History of Dumfries* (Edinburgh, 1867), King James VI presented the siller gun to Dumfries in 1617.

39 *James M'Noe*: the town drummer.

94 *Geordy Smith*: one of the town officers, an old soldier, formerly a sergeant in the Black Watch.

96 *Nith*: the river on which Dumfries stands, about seven miles from its mouth.

100 *side coats . . . dockit*: a contrast here, between a greatcoat (O.E.D.), and the shorter coat, down to the hips, worn by working people. D. Allan's illustrations to *The Gentle Shepherd* (1788) show Bauldy in such an abbreviated coat. See S. Maxwell and R. Hutchison, *Scottish Costume* (London, 1958), p. 102.

123 *Prestonpans*: the battle fought on 21 September 1745, when General Cope was defeated by the forces of Prince Charles Edward. See Skirving's *Tranent Muir*, above.

147 *the Craigs*: site of the competition, beside the Nith, about a mile from the middle of Dumfries.

156 *Robin Tamson*: deacon of the blacksmiths, and convener.

216 *the stocking*: Mayne's note is as follows: 'When a newly-married couple are bedded, as it is called in Scotland, their wedding-friends of both sexes are present at the ceremony. The bride's left stocking is then thrown promiscuously among them; and the person on whom it falls, or who first catches it, is generally considered as the next to be married of the company.' See also *Christ's Kirk on the Green*, Canto II, l. 182, above.

Keith, *Farmer's Ha'*

The text reproduced here is from the edition published by Chalmers (Aberdeen, 1776). We have omitted thirty-one stanzas: these deal with the visit of a gauger, and of beggars, some talk of the troubles in the American colonies, and the preparations for a wedding.

10 *lang hame*: the grave ('Man goeth to his long home', Ecclesiastes XII, 5).

24 *To mend their shoon*: Dr Thomas Somerville (*My Own Life and Times*, Edinburgh, 1861, p. 341) writes of farm servants: 'The shoes of the men, called *brogues*, were made of leather tanned from horse hides, and, as purchased, had only a single sole (they hence went by the name of *single-soled shoes*)'. James E. Handley (*Scottish Farming in the Eighteenth Century*, London, 1953, p. 87) says the shoes supplied as a bounty to ploughmen 'were called "single soles", for

it was expected that the wearers would double or treble the soles with their own hands in the evening hours'.

35 *chamber cage*: either a separate part of the servants' hall, or, as is more likely, a room of his own in the family's part of the house.

67 *The taylor lad*: James E. Handley (op. cit.) notes that ploughmen received in addition to their wages 'a measure of black kelt or finer grey material for clothes, a couple of harn (coarse linen) shirts, two pairs of shoes and stockings', and the hired women, 'a serge or drugget gown, harn skirts, an apron, and two pairs of shoes and stockings'. He adds 'The cloth was made into clothes at the master's expense by the travelling tailor who spent a few days in each house'. *lang fam'd for fleas*: a contemptuous Scots term for a tailor is prick-the-louse.

82 *needle speed*: all the tailor's metaphors are from his own trade — clippings, the speed of a flying needle, flaws. Compare Burns's more exuberant use of trade jargon in *Death and Dr Hornbook*.

112–13 *rain . . . on-ding*: compare the superstition of the grandmother in *The Farmer's Ingle*, ll. 60–7, above.

131 *swain / of Yarrow*: the farmer's family and their servants are part of a ballad-singing community, and 'Rare Willie's droun'd in Yarrow' (Child 215) is in their repertoire. For ballad communities in N.E. Scotland see David Buchan, *The Ballad and the Folk* (London, 1972).

143 *cutty stool*: see *The Farmer's Ingle*, l. 53 and note.

168 The thirty-one stanzas that follow have been omitted.

Burns, *The Vision*

The text follows the 1787 Edinburgh edition ('skinking' impression) and is modernised in accordance with the general principles of the anthology.

In his commonplace book Burns writes: 'However I am pleased with the works of our Scotch poets, particularly the excellent Ramsay, and the still more excellent Ferguson, yet I am hurt to see other places of Scotland, their towns, rivers, woods, haughs, &c. immortalized in such celebrated performances, whilst my dear native country, the ancient Bailieries of Carrick, Kyle, & Cunningham, famous both in ancient & modern times for a gallant, and warlike race of inhabitants; a country where civil, & particularly religious liberty have ever found their first support, & their last asylum; a country, the birth place of many famous philosophers, soldiers, & statesmen, and the scene of many important events recorded in Scottish history, particularly a great many of the actions of the *glorious Wallace*, the *saviour* of his country; yet, we have never had one Scottish poet of any eminence, to make the fertile banks of Irvine, the romantic woodlands & sequestered scenes on Aire, and the heathy, mountainous source, & winding sweep of Doon emulate Tay, Forth, Ettrick, Tweed &c. this is a complaint I would gladly remedy.' (*Robert Burns's*

*Commonplace Book 1783–1785*, ed. J. C. Ewing and Davidson Cook, 1938; entry for August 1785.)

*Duan*: 'a term of Ossian's for the different divisions of a digressive poem' (B.).

61 *tartan*: tartan is a symbol of Scottish independence. It is seen as such in Ramsay's *The Vision*, lines 63–4, and in his *Tartana*. The wearing of tartan was proscribed after the 1745 rebellion.

63 *Jean*: Jean Armour, Burns's mistress from late 1785, and later his wife.

67 *mantle*: a woman's best cloak.

72–8 In a private letter Dr John Strawhorn writes that 'this reads like a general view of Scotland — rivers, mountains, coast, and "distant" here and there an unidentifiable "lordly dome" as a sign of human habitation. Then (if this is not too modern a concept) we zoom in to a larger scale view of Kyle, with persons and places particularised.' A. and M. Armstrong's map of Ayrshire (1775) has at its head a view with mountains in the background, a river tumbling down to the sea, the coast in the middle distance, and prominently within a wood, the ruin of Kilwinning Abbey. Dr Strawhorn thinks Armstrong's illustration may have inspired these lines.

79–133 Burns now sees a relief map on Coila's mantle, but *not* from a viewpoint near Mauchline.

79 *Doon*: this river flows north-west to enter the sea south of Ayr.

80 *Irwine*: this river flows west to enter the sea at Irvine.

81 *Ayr*: this river flows west to enter the sea at Ayr.

86 *an ancient borough*: Ayr.

98 *a race*: 'the Wallaces' (B.).

103 *country's saviour*: see below, *The Cotter's Saturday Night*, l. 182, note.

104 *Richardton*: 'Adam Wallace of Richardton, cousin to the immortal preserver of Scottish independence' (B.).

105 *chief . . . fell*: 'Wallace laird of Craigie [the estate near Ayr, not the parish further north], who was second in command, under Douglas Earl of Ormond, at the famous battle on the banks of Sark [a river which enters the Solway near Gretna], fought *anno* 1448. That glorious victory was principally owning to the judicious conduct and intrepid valour of the gallant laird of Craigie, who died of his wounds after the action' (B.).

107 *And he . . . land*: James Kinsley suggests that this refers to Mrs Dunlop's oldest son, Sir Thomas Wallace Dunlop, who succeeded to the Craigie estate in 1771 but who sold it to pay his debts in 1783; he went to live in England where he died in 1786.

108 At various points between here and the end of the Duan, the Stair MS inserts fourteen additional stanzas, which Burns never printed. When these extra stanzas are taken into consideration, 'there is a logical progression around seventeen places situated in the most

important part of Kyle' (Strawhorn). These seventeen estates in fact dominate Armstrong's map.

109 *a sceptred Pictish shade*: 'Coilus, king of the Picts, from whom the district of Kyle is said to take its name, lies buried, as tradition says, near the family seat of the Montgomeries of Coilsfield, where his burial place is still shown' (B.).

111 *martial race*: the Montgomeries, Earls of Eglinton, a family with a long line of military achievement. For instance the earl of Eglinton in Burns's day raised the 77th regiment in 1757, commanded the 51st and was appointed governor of Edinburgh Castle in 1782.

115 *wild, romantic grove*: 'Barskimming, the seat of the Lord Justice Clark [Sir Thomas Miller]' (B.).

122 *learned sire and son*: Matthew Stewart (1717–85), professor of mathematics at Edinburgh from 1747; and Dugald Stewart, his son, professor of moral philosophy at Edinburgh from 1785. Their home was at Catrine, near Mauchline.

127 *Brydon's . . . ward*: Colonel William Fullarton, of Fullarton, Dundonald near Kilmarnock. He was a soldier, diplomat, M.P., improver and a friend of Burns.

146 *light aerial band*: spirits similar to Pope's sylphs in *The Rape of the Lock*.

170 *Dempster*: George Dempster, M.P. for Forfar Burghs (1761–1790) with an interest in agriculture and fisheries, and a friend of James Boswell.

171 *Beattie*: the poet and philosopher.

201–2 *Where . . . pow'r*: the Loudoun estate at Galston, east of Kilmarnock.

241 *manners-painting*: i.e. depicting the real circumstances of life, particularly humble life.

261 *Potosi's mine*: silver, gold and copper mines in Bolivia.

Burns, *The Holy Fair*

The text follows the Kilmarnock edition of 1786, except that certain later corrections have been admitted. See below.

A holy fair was an annual gathering in the open air in which several parishes joined together to receive communion, and hear the word as preached by a succession of ministers. As is clear from Burns's description it was as much a holiday as a religious festival. The poem belongs to a genre represented in this book by Ramsay's *Christ's Kirk on the Green*, Fergusson's *Hallow-Fair* and *Leith Races*, and Skinner's *Christmass Bawing of Monimusk*.

*Epigraph* from Tom Brown's *The Stage Beaux toss'd in a Blanket; or Hypocrisie Alamode* (1704).

5 *Galston*: a village close to Kilmarnock and some six miles north of Mauchline.

37 *fun*: Dr Johnson calls fun 'a low cant word' which serves to establish

its tone as used here. Fun is modelled on Fergusson's 'Mirth' in *Leith Races*.

60 *scarlets*: scarlet was the usual colour of a woman's finest cloak. This, together with the food of lines 61–2, indicates that the holy fair was very much a special occasion. Indeed, the popular name for it was 'the occasion'.

86 *chosen*: in the Kilmarnock edition Burns has 'elect', which is more precise, but less euphonious. Article XVII of the Articles of Religion (1562) of the Church of England begins: 'Predestination to life is the everlasting purpose of God, whereby (before the foundations of the world were laid) he hath constantly decreed by his counsel secret to us, to deliver from curse and damnation those whom he hath chosen in Christ out of mankind, and to bring them by Christ to everlasting salvation, as vessels made to honour.' Those chosen are the elect. In spite of God's counsel being 'secret to us' — there was no difference of opinion in this between the Church of England and the Church of Scotland — the doctrine was liable to corruption, and belonging to a particular sect, or being prosperous, were taken, quite wrongly, as signs of election.

91 *O happy . . . blest*: Psalm CXLVI, 5 (metrical version) begins 'O happy is that man and blest, / whom Jacob's God doth aid'. Burns's parody is deliberately blasphemous for he here provides an alternative philosophy of life.

102 *Moodie*: the clergy represent the two dominant parties in the Church of Scotland at the time. They were divided by their attitude to patronage (the right of landlords to appoint qualified clergy to charges), the moderates accepting it because it was the law of the land and the evangelicals rejecting it. This difference in view, however, is only symptomatic of wider divergences. The moderates were responsible for the diffusion of thought about improvement (a term applicable to both the physical environment and the moral man), whereas the evangelicals tended to be fundamentalist, and to be theologically conservative. Burns is equally contemptuous of both.

103 *damnation*: in the Kilmarnock edition (1786) Burns had 'salvation', but in 1787 changed it to 'damnation' on the suggestion of Dr Hugh Blair, minister of the High Kirk (St Giles) in Edinburgh and Professor of Rhetoric and Belles Lettres in the University of Edinburgh.

181 *trumpet*: the instrument that, traditionally, will herald the last judgment.

185 *piercin words*: 'the word of God is quick, and powerful, and sharper than any two-edged sword, piercing even to the dividing asunder of soul and spirit, and of the joints and marrow' (Hebrews IV, 12).

188 *Sauls . . . harrow*: see *Hamlet* I, 5, 154.

232 *faith . . . love*: see I Corinthians XIII, which concludes: 'And now abideth faith, hope, charity, these three; but the greatest of these is

charity'. Burns is delighted to set these two conceptions of love side by side — the young folk's, and that of the 'yill-caup commentators'.

237–8 *Their . . . is*: a further sexual/theological play on ideas.

Burns, *The Twa Dogs*

The text is that of the Kilmarnock edition of 1786, modernised in accordance with the general principles of the anthology.

2 *Coil*: Burns associates the fictitious King Coil with Kyle, the central district of Ayrshire. Coil is the King Cole of the nursery rhyme and in Scotland was thought to be the father of the legendary giant Finn McCoul; see Iona and Peter Opie, *The Oxford Dictionary of Nursery Rhymes* (Oxford, 1952), pp. 134–5.

51–2 *racked . . . stents*: the late eighteenth century saw steep rises in land rents; this was due in part to inflation, but also to the need to obtain a return on the capital investment involved in enclosing, draining and liming land. Further, money rents were gradually substituted for payment in kind and in service, but in the system Burns envisages here such payments have not been entirely superseded. See James E. Handley, *Scottish Farming in the Eighteenth Century* (London, 1953), chapters 2, 9 and 11.

71ff This description of cotters' lives is amplified in Handley, cited above, and in T. C. Smout, *A History of the Scottish People 1560–1830* (London, 1969), pp. 302–31.

119 *patronage . . . priests*: the patronage act of 1712 allowed lay patrons (in effect the more substantial landowners) to nominate properly qualified ministers to vacant charges. This was highly offensive to most members of the Church of Scotland, was the cause of several minor schisms in the course of the eighteenth century and culminated in the Disruption of 1843 in which the greater part of the ministers, elders and people of the Church broke away.

141–4 Many cotters in lowland Scotland were displaced by the reorganisation of land holdings in the course of the agrarian revolution, though not so dramatically as in the Highland Clearances. Burns, like Goldsmith in *The Deserted Village*, blames the greed of individual stewards and bailiffs.

151 *gaun . . . him*: for a good description of the operation of patronage in the unreformed House of Commons, see John Galt's novel *The Member* (Edinburgh and London, 1975), first published in 1832.

157 *tour*: the grand tour of Europe was considered requisite to finish a gentleman's education.

160 *entails*: an entail was a legal device whereby the owner of land could restrict the class of person by whom it was inherited and prevent any successor from alienating the land or any part of it. Riving an

entail (which could be done by finding some legal flaw in it) implies here a violation of the respect due to ancestors and thus one's own history.

164 *groves o' myrtles* were sacred to Venus.

176 *countra sports*: these kept lairds at home and meant that they paid more attention to their estates and people. In addition, country sports such as hunting were felt to create habits which would be of use in time of war.

214 *joy . . . heart*: like all the main thinkers of the Scottish Enlightenment, including Hume, Burns held that both ethics and art were essentially emotional: that values were a matter of feeling. Compare *Epistle to Davie*, ll. 69–70:

> The heart ay's the part ay,
> That makes us right or wrang.

Burns, *The Cotter's Saturday Night*

The text is that of the Kilmarnock (1786) edition of Burns's poems, modernised in accordance with the general principles of the anthology.

*The Cotter's Saturday Night* is a deliberately literary poem. It is not intended to be simple and criticism of its artificiality only shows a lack of awareness of the eighteenth-century genre to which it belongs. In the course of the century the peasantry came to be regarded as an ideal class, uncorrupted by luxury, whose way of life could serve as an example to the more sophisticated and better off. In essence, *The Cotter's Saturday Night* argues this case. For a discussion of the literary antecedents and parallels see the commentary on the poem in *The Poems and Songs of Robert Burns*, ed. James Kinsley (Oxford, 1968), III, pp. 1111–18. Epigraph: from Gray's *Elegy Written in a Country Churchyard.*

1 *My . . . friend*: Robert Aiken (1739–1807), solicitor and surveyor of taxes in Ayr. His early patronage of Burns is acknowledged in the letters.

2–4 *No . . . praise*: Burns repudiates aristocratic patronage. In the seventeenth and in much of the eighteenth century a fulsome, even servile dedication was the price of obtaining financial backing from a peer or similar person, or of ensuring a significant subscription list. (Subscribers paid in advance and thus provided the capital required for publishing a book and in return their names were listed in the publication.) Patronage was almost dead in Burns's day as Samuel Johnson's remarks on Lord Chesterfield's failure to assist him when compiling his dictionary testify. Burns's repudiation of patronage, then, reflects the rise of writing as a profession as well as his own strong sense of independence.

50 *fear the Lord*: many biblical texts enjoin this; e.g. Deuteronomy X, 12–13: 'what doth the Lord thy God require of thee, but to fear the

Lord thy God, to walk in all his ways, and to love him, and to serve the Lord thy God with all thy heart and with all thy soul, to keep the commandments of the Lord, and his statutes.'

82–90 *Is . . . wild*: James Kinsley comments: 'An eighteenth-century set piece. Cf. Burns, *A Winter Night*, ll. 62–72; Johnson, *The Vanity of Human Wishes*, ll. 319–42; Goldsmith, *The Citizen of the World*, cxvii, and *The Deserted Village*, ll. 325ff.' (*Poems and Songs of Robert Burns*, p. 1115.)

106 *Zion*: has three associations — with David, since it was on Mount Zion that he built his city; then, by extension, with Israel, and, by further extension with heaven. The first association links with the next stanza in which the family sings the Psalms of David; and the third from the readings from scripture since the words of the Bible were thought to be the words of God himself and thus were heard in Zion, i.e. heaven.

108 *And . . . God*: family worship was once practised in every household and the form of the cotter's worship is standard and traditional.

111–14 *Dundee . . . Martyrs . . . Elgin*: tunes of Scottish composition from the *Scottish Psalter* of 1635, used when singing the metrical version of the psalms.

126 *other . . . lyre*: other prophets; the authorised version of the Bible gives the impression that the prophets wrote prose, but in fact most of Isaiah, Jeremiah, Ezekiel and the minor prophets is in verse. Burns correctly makes them out to be poets when he says they 'tune the sacred lyre'.

138 *'springs . . . wing'*: 'Pope's *Windsor Forest*' (B.). Line 112. Pope's line describes pheasants.

140 *uncreated rays*: heaven. The phrase comes from Milton (*Paradise Lost* III, 3–6) *via* James Thomson *Summer*, 176–7. Light is an attribute of God, is a metaphor for God, and expresses God. It therefore partakes of the nature of God. The Nicene creed states a belief in 'one Lord Jesus Christ, the only begotten Son of God, begotten of his father before all worlds, God of God, light of light, very God of very God, begotten, not made, being of one substance with the father, by whom all things were made.'

153 *book of life*: the book in which Christ names those who are to be saved, i.e. who are to go to heaven. The book of life is mentioned several times in the *Revelation of St John*. See, for instance, III, 5 and XXI, 27.

166 'An honest man . . .': see Pope, *Essay on Man*, iv. 228, '. . . the noblest work of God.'

177 *luxury*: a taste for physical possessions and comfort as well as those things themselves, condemned in the past by puritans and pastoralists, and now also by contemporary moralists. See *Minstrel*, l. 66, note.

182 *Wallace*: Sir William Wallace, Scottish patriot, beheaded in London by Edward I in 1305 for fighting for Scottish independence.

## Burns, *Halloween*

The text is from the Kilmarnock edition of 1786, modernised in accordance with the general principles of the anthology. Halloween 'is thought to be a night when witches, devils, and other mischief-making beings, are all abroad on their baneful, midnight errands: particularly, those aerial people, the fairies, are said, on that night, to hold a grand anniversary' (B.). Halloween is the eve of Hallowmass or All Saints Day, which is 1st November. It stands in an antithetical relationship to All Saints Day itself, for on Halloween witches held one of their quarterly covens, or meetings, which were a parody of Christian rites. In addition, it was a night when fairies convened. As is obvious in the poem, many harvest and fertility rites were involved in the celebration of Halloween, and Burns's country-folk were not more than half-believers in what they did. The occasion was one for social glee, though the high jinks were more awesome than party games.

2 *Cassilis Downans*: 'Certain little, romantic, rocky, green hills, in the neighbourhood of the ancient seat of the Earls of Cassilis' (B.). They are near Kirkmichael, some eight miles south of Ayr.

5 *Colean*: Culzean Castle, a superb Adam building now in the ownership of the National Trust for Scotland, is on the Ayrshire coast ten miles south of Ayr.

7 *Cove*: 'A noted cavern near Colean-house, called the Cove of Colean; which, as well as Cassillis Downans, is famed, in country story, for being a favourite haunt of Fairies' (B.).

11 *Doon*: a river that runs N.W. to reach the sea just south of Ayr.

12 *Bruce*: 'The famous family of that name, the ancestors of Robert the great deliverer of his country, were Earls of Carrick' (B.). Carrick is the southern part of Ayrshire through which the Doon runs.

29 *stocks*: 'The first ceremony of Halloween, is, pulling each a *stock*, or plant of kail. They must go out, hand in hand, with eyes shut, and pull the first they meet with: its being big or little, straight or crooked, is prophetic of the size and shape of the grand object of all their spells — the husband or wife. If any *yird*, or earth, stick to the root, that is *tocher*, or fortune; and the taste of the *custoc*, that is, the heart of the stem, is indicative of the natural temper and disposition. Lastly, the stems, or to give them their ordinary appellation, the *runts*, are placed somewhere above the head of the door; and the christian names of the people whom chance brings into the house, are, according to the priority of placing the *runts*, the names in question' (B.).

47 *stalks o' corn*: 'They go to the barn-yard, and pull each, at three several times, a stalk of oats. If the third stalk wants the *top-pickle*, that is, the grain at the top of the stock, the party in question will want the maidenhead' (B.).

53 *fause-house*: 'When the corn is in a doubtful state, by being too

green, or wet, the stack builder, by means of old timber, &c. makes a large apartment in his stack, with an opening in the side which is fairest exposed to the wind: this he calls a *fause-house*' (B.).

55 *weel-hoordet nits*: 'Burning the nuts is a favourite charm. They name the lad and lass to each particular nut, as they lay them in the fire; and according as they burn quietly together, or start from beside one another, the course and issue of the courtship will be' (B.).

98 *blue-clue*: 'Whoever would, with success, try this spell, must strictly observe these directions. Steal out, all alone, to the kiln, and, darkling, throw into the pot, a clew of blue yarn: wind it in a new clew off the old one; and towards the latter end, something will hold the thread: demand, *wha hauds*? i.e. who holds? and answer will be returned from the kiln-pot, by naming the christian and sirname of your future spouse' (B.).

111 *eat the apple*: 'Take a candle, and go, alone, to a looking glass: eat an apple before it, and some traditions say you should comb your hair all the time: the face of your conjugal companion, *to be*, will be seen in the glass, as if peeping over your shoulder' (B.).

127 *the Sherra-moor*: the battle of Sheriffmuir, fought near Dunblane, Perthshire, in 1715 between the Jacobites under the Earl of Mar and the Hanoverians under the Duke of Argyll.

140 *hemp-seed*: 'Steal out, unperceived, and sow a handful of hemp seed; harrowing it with any thing you can conveniently draw after you. Repeat, now and then, "Hemp seed I saw thee, Hemp seed I saw thee; and him (or her) that is to be my true-love, come after me and pou thee". Look over your left shoulder, and you will see the appearance of the person invoked, in the attitude of pulling hemp. Some traditions say, "come after me and shaw thee," that is, show thyself; in which case it simply appears. Other omit the harrowing, and say, "come after me and harrow thee"' (B.).

182 *three . . . naething*: 'This charm must likewise be performed, unperceived and alone. You go to the barn, and open both doors; taking them off the hinges, if possible; for there is danger, that the Being, about to appear, may shut the doors, and do you some mischief. Then take that instrument used in winnowing the corn, which, in our country-dialect, we call a *wecht*; and go thro' all the attitudes of letting down corn against the wind. Repeat it three times; and the third time, an apparition will pass thro' the barn, in at the windy door, and out at the other, having both the figure in question and the appearance or retinue, marking the employment or station in life' (B.).

201 *stack . . . thrice*: 'Take an opportunity of going, unnoticed, to a bear-stack, and fathom it three times round. The last fathom of the last time, you will catch in your arms, the appearance of your future conjugal yoke-fellow' (B.).

214 *three . . . burn*: 'You go out, one or more, for this is a social spell, to a south-running spring or rivulet, where "three lairds' lands meet,"

and dip your left shirt-sleeve. Go to bed in sight of a fire, and hang your wet sleeve before it to dry. Ly awake; and sometime near midnight, an apparition, having the exact figure of the grand object in question, will come and turn the sleeve, as if to dry the other side of it' (B.).

236 *luggies*: 'Take three dishes; put clean water in one, foul water in another, and leave the third empty: blindfold a person, and lead him to the hearth where the dishes are ranged; he (or she) dips the left hand: if by chance in the clean water, the future husband or wife will come to the bar of matrimony, a maid; if in the foul, a widow; if in the empty dish, it foretells, with equal certainty, no marriage at all. It is repeated three times; and every time the arrangement of the dishes is altered' (B.).

248 *butter'd so'ns*: 'Sowens, with butter instead of milk to them, is always the Halloween supper' (B.).

Burns, *Love and Liberty: A Cantata*

The text is based upon the MS in Burns's Cottage, Alloway.

9 *Poosie-Nansie*: Agnes Gibson, keeper of a low tavern and lodging house in Mauchline. As early as 1773 she was charged by the kirk session with habitual drunkenness, declared her intention 'to continue in her disorderly way' and was excluded from the privileges of the church. Poosie = pussy, and has sexual implications.

34 *heights of Abram*: the site of Wolfe's victory over the French near Quebec in 1759.

36 *the Moro*: fortress defending the harbour of Santiago in Cuba, stormed by the British in 1762.

37 *Curtis*: Admiral Sir Roger Curtis (1746–1816) who led the force that raised the siege of Gibraltar in 1782.

39 *Elliot*: General George Elliot, the defender of Gibraltar during the siege by French and Spanish forces 1779–83. *Love and Liberty* was written in 1785. It follows that the soldier has been a tramp for two years.

Burns, *Tam o'Shanter*

The text is that of the 1793 edition of Burns's poems modernised in accordance with the general principles of the anthology.

7 *lang Scots miles*: a Scots mile was a variable measurement, but was longer than an English mile of 1760 yards.

27 *Lord's house*: this surely must be an inn, but is also another name

for a church. Burns's deliberate ambiguity, extended by 'Sunday' and 'Kirkton Jean' (a kirkton was a village in which a parish church stood) emphasises Tam's commitment to drink and prefigures, before it is made explicit, the gist of the following 4 lines.

32 *Alloway's . . . kirk* was a ruin in Burns's day.

115 *Warlocks . . .*: it is part of a (traditional) parody of religious ceremony that witches should meet in a church, that they should present offerings, and that the devil should sit in the east.

120 *auld Nick*: throughout European tradition the devil takes beast shapes and is associated (frequently comically as in gargoyles) with piping. See, for instance, the conclusion of William Dunbar's poem *The Dance of the Sevin Deidly Synnis.*

130–42 *upon the haly table . . .*: the witches' offerings are emblems of diabolic power. Unbaptised children were the property of the devil, as were murderers, which explains why the witches should offer murder instruments to their master. The whole description mocks the literary taste for 'horrors' — see James Beattie, *The Minstrel*, lines 284–8.

167–70 Witches were often blamed for dead beasts, damaged property and natural calamities.

171 *cutty sark*: though short, the garment was of superior quality, for it was bought, not woven and made at home.

206 *keystane*: 'It is a well known fact that witches, or any evil spirits, have no power to follow a poor wight any farther than the middle of the next running stream. — It may be proper likewise to mention to the benighted traveller, that when he falls in with *bogles*, whatever danger may be in his going forward, there is much more hazard in turning back' (B.).

## Scott, *The Eve of St John*

The text is taken from the second edition of *Minstrelsy of the Scottish Border.* Accidentals change but no later edition incorporates substantive emendations.

The feast of St John the Baptist (24 June) became linked with various of the customs of the summer solstice.

1 *Smaylho'me*: see Scott, *Marmion: Epistle to William Erskine*, l. 168, note.

17 *Ancram Moor*: in the battle of Ancrum Moor (1545) Lord Evers and Sir Brian Latoun, who had ravaged the Borders of Scotland in two successive years, were decisively defeated, and both killed, by a Scottish army under Archibald Douglas, seventh earl of Angus, and Sir Walter Scott of Buccleuch.

79 *blackrood-stone*: 'The black-rood of Melrose was a crucifix of black marble, and of superior sanctity' (S.).

86 *Dryburgh*: a Premonstratensian abbey on the Tweed in Berwickshire, a little west of Smailholm Tower.

108 *Eildon-tree*: 'Eildon is a high hill, terminating in three conical summits, immediately above the town of Melrose, where are the admired ruins of a magnificent monastery. Eildon-tree is said to be the spot where Thomas the Rhymer uttered his prophecies' (S.).

131 *Mertoun*: Mertoun House is on the Tweed, south of Smailholm. It was owned by one of Scott's relations, Hugh Scott of Harden, as was Smailholm.

173 *bower*: other editions read 'brow' but the 'bower' of this edition seems better sense.

## Scott, *The Lay of the Last Minstrel*

The text is that of the second edition, published in 1805. Earlier editions of *The Lay* accord better with modern conventions of punctuation and spelling than later, but the second edition contains the one substantive correction Scott made to this canto after it first appeared — the replacement at line 119 of 'St Kentigern's hall' with 'St Andrew's cloistered hall.' Some inconsistencies in spelling and capitalisation have been silently corrected.

Scott states his objectives in his preface. In addition the poem is an elaborate compliment to the Scotts of Buccleuch. The main action concerns them, and the minstrel recites his poem to Anne Scott, first Duchess of Buccleuch. The work is dedicated to Charles Scott, Earl of Dalkeith, the eldest son of the fourth Duke of Buccleuch, to which title he succeeded in 1812.

### *Introduction*

26 *a king*: Charles I visited Scotland and held court in Holyrood Palace, Edinburgh, in 1633. We are told at line 80 that the minstrel played to the king on that occasion.

27 *Newark*: Newark Castle, on the banks of the Yarrow, a river in Selkirkshire, is in the grounds of Bowhill, one of the residences of the Dukes of Buccleuch and thus of the man to whom the poem is dedicated. Anne, Duchess of Monmouth and Buccleuch, to whom the minstrel sings, had been brought up there. She was the descendant of the Lords of Buccleuch, hereditary chiefs of the Scott family, and widow of the Duke of Monmouth, the illegitimate son of Charles II, beheaded in 1685, after his rebellion against James II (ll. 41–4).

### *Canto First*

1 *Branksome Tower*: on the Teviot, some three miles south of Hawick, Roxburghshire. It was the principal dwelling of the Buccleuchs in the 16th century. The usual spelling is Branxholme but Scott altered it for poetic reasons.

16–17 *Nine . . . Hall*: 'The ancient barons of Buccleuch, both from feudal splendour, and from their frontier situation, retained in their household, at Branksome, a number of gentlemen of their own name, who held lands from their chief for the military service of watching and warding his castle' (S.).

49 *Scroop, Howard, Percy*: these were the leading families on the English side of the border, who resided in the fortresses of Carlisle, Naworth and Warkworth respectively.

58 *lord Walter*: Sir Walter Scott of Buccleuch was killed by his enemies the Cars (or Kerrs) in the streets of Edinburgh in 1552. The action of *The Lay* takes place shortly after this event.

65 *discord*: the quarrel between the Kerrs and the Scotts of Buccleuch began with an attempt by the latter to free the young king James V (at his request) from the power of the Douglases in 1526. The attempt failed at the battle of Melrose, but in the ensuing flight and pursuit Kerr of Cessford, a supporter of the Douglases, was killed by Elliot of Stobs, an ally of the Scotts.

70 *mutual pilgrimage*: 'Among other expedients resorted to for staunching the feud betwixt the Scotts and Kerrs, there was a bond executed, in 1529, between the heads of each clan, binding themselves to perform reciprocally the four principal pilgrimages of Scotland, for the benefit of the souls of those of the opposite name who had fallen in the quarrel.... But either it never took effect, or else the feud was renewed shortly afterward' (S.).

73 *Cessford*: Cessford castle is between Morebattle and Jedburgh, in the Cheviot hills in Roxburghshire. It was the seat of that part of the family of Cars, or Kerrs, who later became Dukes of Roxburghe.

74 *Ettrick*: Ettrick forest was approximately equivalent to modern Selkirkshire. It was, at the time the events of *The Lay* take place, largely owned by the Scotts; the property descended to the first Duchess of Buccleuch and her heirs.

109 *Cranstoun*: 'The Cranstouns ... are an ancient Border family, whose chief seat was at Crailing in Teviotdale. They were at this time at feud with the clan of Scott; for it appears that the Lady of Buccleuch, in 1557, beset the laird of Cranstoun, seeking his life. Nevertheless the same Cranstoun, or perhaps his son, was married to a daughter of the same lady' (S.). There was, therefore, some basis in fact for Scott's Romeo and Juliet plot.

113 'The Bethunes were of French origin, and derived their name from a small town in Artois.... Of this family was descended Dame Janet Beaton, Lady Buccleuch, widow of Sir Walter Scott of Branksome. She was a woman of masculine spirit, as appeared from her riding at the head of her son's clan, after her husband's murder. She also possessed the hereditary abilities of her family in such a degree, that the superstition of the vulgar imputed them to supernatural knowledge' (S.).

120–1 'The vulgar conceive, that when a class of students have made a certain progress in their mystic studies, they are obliged to run through a subterraneous hall, where the devil literally catches the hindmost in the race, unless he crosses the hall so speedily, that the arch enemy can only apprehend his shadow. In the latter case, the person of the sage never after throws any shade; and those, who have thus *lost their shadow*, always prove the best magicians' (S.).

125 Scott justified his River Spirit and Mountain Spirit by noting that 'the Scottish vulgar . . . believe in the existence of an intermediate class of spirits residing in the air, or in the waters; to whose agency they ascribe floods, storms, and all such phenomena as their own philosophy cannot readily explain'.

127 *lord David*: Sir David Scott enlarged and strengthened the castle prior to his death in 1492.

154 *Craik-cross, Skelfhill-pen*: hills to the west and east of Teviot's catchment area.

197 *moss-trooper*: 'This was the usual appellation of the marauders upon the Border; a profession diligently pursued by the inhabitants on both sides, and by none more actively and successfully than by Buccleuch's clan' (S.).

207 *Unicorn*: the unicorn represents the Cars of Cessford and the crescents and star the Scotts. Unicorn was pronounced with a rolled 'r' by Scott so that the terminal 'n' becomes a syllable in its own right.

214 *Deloraine*: 'The lands of Deloraine are adjoining to those of Buccleuch, in Ettricke Forest. They were immemorially possessed by the Buccleuch family under the strong title of occupancy. . . . Like other possessions, the lands of Deloraine were occasionally granted by them to vassals, or kinsmen, for Border-service' (S.).

217 *Solway . . . moss*: the Solway firth has substantial areas of quicksand and is subject to a particularly fast tide. Tarras moss is an area of boggy wilderness, on Tarras Water, north east of Langholm, Dumfriesshire.

221 *Eske, or Liddel*: rivers of Dumfriesshire and Roxburghshire respectively; both mark part of the national boundary with England.

230 *England's . . . queen*: Henry VIII (1509–47), Edward VI (1547–53) and Mary Queen of Scots (1542–67).

240 *treasure . . . tomb*: the book of magic of Michael Scott, one of the most learned men of the 13th century, and accounted a skilful magician. He was buried with his books in Melrose Abbey, but when in need the chiefs of Branksome had the right to consult them.

258 *Hairibee*: 'the place of executing the Border marauders at Carlisle. The *neck-verse* is the beginning of the 51st psalm, *Miserere me*, &c. anciently read by criminals claiming benefit of clergy' (S.).

259 William of Deloraine's ride is not a precise itinerary, although the general directions are clear enough. Scott uses the journey to compliment further the Scotts and their allies the Elliots, and he

invests the landscape with a rudimentary history of the area. Deloraine proceeds along the western bank of Teviot from Branksome, past the 'Peel of Goldiland', an Elliot seat (265); he fords Borthwick water, a western tributary of Teviot (266), passes the Hawick mott (which Scott believed was a place of assembly in prehistoric times — hence the Druids) and Hawick itself on the other side of the river (267–70). Hazeldean (modern Hassendean) was held by Scotts. Remnants of Roman road lay well to the west (282) while to the east, as he crosses the moor at Horsleyhill (280), lie Minto Crags. Scott describes these as 'a romantic assemblage of cliffs, which rise suddenly above the vale of Teviot, in the immediate vicinity of the family-seat, from which Lord Minto [an Elliot] takes his title'. He continues — 'A small platform, on a projecting crag, commanding a most beautiful prospect, is termed *Barnhills' Bed.* This Barnhills is said to have been a robber or outlaw. There are remains of a strong tower beneath the rocks, where he is supposed to have dwelt, and from which he derived his name.' At ll. 296–8 Scott alludes to Sir Gilbert Elliot and his song 'My sheep I neglected, I lost my sheep-hook'. Deloraine proceeds towards Lilliesleaf in the barony of Riddell, granted by a charter of David I in the 12th century to Walter Rydale (hence 'ancient Riddell's fair domain', 300). He fords Aill (or Ale) Water (301–18), gains Bowden Moor, south-west of the Eildon Hills, contemplates Halidon (or Holydean), the site of the battle of Melrose where the quarrel between the Scotts and the Kerrs began (319–30; and see note on line 65). From the western shoulder of the Eildon hills he looks down to Melrose and its abbey.

Scott, *Marmion*

The text is that of the first edition of 1808, chosen as copy text because it is less heavily punctuated than the final 1833–37 edition (edited by J. G. Lockhart) on which later editions are usually based. It is printed in accordance with the general principles of the anthology. Three minor errors in punctuation have been silently corrected.

In *Marmion*, Scott first establishes the strategy that characterises his fictional treatment of history, namely examining the issues of an epoch by seeing how they impinge on private lives. The poem thus marks a decided intellectual advance on *The Lay of the Last Minstrel.* Scott links past with present by introducing a contemporary social context; each of the six cantos is introduced by long epistles to personal friends, in which he discusses both personal matters and current affairs. Two of these epistles are presented here.

*To William Erskine, Esq.*

23 *Erskine*: William Erskine (1779–1822) was Scott's most intimate friend, his literary adviser and confidant.

42 *harpers . . . days*: Erskine, who was a good classicist, is represented as advising Scott to model his work on great, established poetry rather than popular verse, such as *Minstrelsy of the Scottish Border* (1802–3).

46 *Brunswick*: the Duke of Brunswick (1735–1806) was commander in chief of the Prussian forces defeated by Napoleon at Jena (1806), where he was mortally wounded. His daughter was the Princess of Wales with whom Scott was friendly.

54 *Brandenburgh*: the Prussian royal house.

59 *dragon*: Napoleon was frequently thought to be a devil sent to scourge the earth for its sins.

62 *presumptuous hour*: Prussia entered into war with France with no coherent plan and without proper preparation.

67–72 Brunswick, an old man in 1806 (l. 67), wrote to Napoleon asking for moderation and clemency to be shown to his principality. Napoleon rejected this advance, saying it was his right as the victor of Jena to destroy the town of Brunswick and that it was his purpose to deprive the dying prince and his family of their hereditary sovereignty (69–70).

78 *Arminius*: Arminius led the Cherusci who inhabited the country to the north of the Harz mountains in Germany in a successful revolt against Roman domination (A.D. 9–17).

81 *Red-Cross hero*: Admiral Sir Sidney Smith (1764–1840) was captured by the French and imprisoned in the Temple in Paris (1796) from which he escaped with the help of French royalists. He became directly involved in defending Acre against Napoleon (1799) and led British seamen armed with pikes in close fighting.

94 *father . . . fight*: General Sir Ralph Abercromby (1734–1801) undoubtedly the best British general in the war against revolutionary France, led the British expedition to Egypt in 1801. He defeated the French near Alexandria but was himself killed. The French were outmanoeuvred and forced to surrender and leave Egypt.

103 *Enchantress*: Joanna Baillie (1762–1851), a friend of Scott. Her *Plays on the Passions* (3 vols, 1798, 1802 and 1812) which include *De Monfort* (on hatred) and *Basil* (on love) echo Shakespeare and the Elizabethans, but tend to be literary rather than dramatic.

130 *Batavia*: roughly the area between the estuaries of the Rhine and Maas in the present-day Netherlands.

149 *Lochaber*: a large area of the western Highlands of Scotland round Fort William which contains Loch Garry and some of Britain's highest mountains, including Ben Nevis.

168 *barren scene*: in this paragraph Scott is talking of Smailholm Tower in the north of Roxburghshire. It was close to his grandfather's farm of Sandyknowe, where Scott spent much of his boyhood. A more detailed account of his time here is contained in Scott's autobiography (*Scott on Himself* pp. 1–44) and in chapter two of Lockhart's *Life of Scott*.

180 *aged hind*: Sandy Ormistoun, the cow-bailie.

206 *Scottish Lion*: heraldic emblem of Scotland.

211 *grey-haired sire*: Scott's paternal grandfather, Robert Scott, who died in 1775.

218 *priest*: Dr Alexander Duncan. See introduction to *Hardyknute*.

Scott, *To James Skene, Esq.*

3 *motley clown*: Touchstone, whom Jaques reports as moralising upon time in Shakespeare's *As You Like It*, II, 7, 11.

10 *voluntary brand*: James Skene of Rubislaw, Aberdeen (1775–1864), was one of Scott's closest friends. They first met in 1795 or 1796 when the German-mad Scott sought him out because he knew he had brought back a collection of German books from Saxony. In 1797 Scott, Skene and others formed a volunteer cavalry regiment, the Royal Edinburgh Light Dragoons, to help defend the country in the event of a French invasion. Scott was elected quartermaster and Skene cornet.

31 *November's . . . gale*: the first epistle in *Marmion, to William Stewart Rose, Esq.* begins:

> November's sky is chill and drear,
> November's leaf is red and sear.

Scott began *Marmion* in November 1806 and it was published in February 1808.

34 *Yarrow*: a river in Selkirkshire. Scott is writing this epistle at his house at Ashestiel, on the Tweed (l. 40). Yarrow is to the south, and Blackhouse heights and Ettrick Pen (l. 37) are two of the higher hills to the west of him.

45–6 *As . . . glen*: Skene was a regular visitor at Ashestiel and the two men walked or rode over much of the Ettrick and Yarrow valleys. In his *Memories of Sir Walter Scott* (London, 1909), Skene remarks: 'The beauty of the scenery gave full employment to my pencil, with . . . which he never seemed to feel impatient, for he was ready and willing at all times to alight . . . and set himself down beside me on the braeside to con over some appropriate ballad, or narrate the traditions of the glen, and sometimes, but rarely, to note in his book some passing ideas' (pp. 30–1).

55 The passage that follows is Scott's version of the death of a labourer in a snowstorm in James Thomson's *Winter*, 4th ed. 1746, ll. 276–321. Lockhart remarks in his edition of Scott's poems that a man died in this way near Ashestiel on the night Scott wrote these lines.

132 *Forbes*: Sir William Forbes of Pitsligo (1739–1806) died shortly after Skene married his daughter. Forbes was friend, patron and biographer of James Beattie, author of *The Minstrel*.

147 *widow's . . . stay*: Adapted from metrical psalm CXLVI, 9.

172 *Tirante*: Tirante the White was one of the more redoubtable knights of medieval romance.

174 *Camp*: a bull terrier, one of Scott's favourite dogs.

181 *Ariel*: see *The Tempest*, V, 1, 93–4.

191 *he . . . deplore*: Colin Mackenzie of Portmore, friend, comrade in the Edinburgh Light Dragoons, and, as one of the principal clerks to the Court of Session, a colleague of Scott's.

194 *Rae*: Sir William Rae (1769–1842), captain in the volunteer dragoons. He was Lord Advocate 1819–1830.

195 *one . . . say*: Sir William Forbes (1773–1838), banker, son of the Forbes mentioned in line 132 above. He married Scott's love Williamina Belsches and was brother-in-law of James Skene.

206 *mad Tom's*: Edgar in *King Lear* who, as poor Tom, says that he has *had* 'Horse to ride, and weapon to wear' (III, 4, 134).

Scott, *Marmion Canto VI*

4 *Douglas*: Earl of Angus, owner of Tantallon Castle and known as Bell-the-Cat for his part in the execution of James III's favourites. Douglas has been told of Marmion's treachery by de Wilton.

8 *Herald . . . Terouénne*: Henry VIII was at war with France and was besieging Terouenne (Therouanne) near St Omer in the north of France. The herald was sent here to complain of English provocation, but he did not return until after the battle of Flodden and James's death.

12 *Dame*: i.e. the Countess of Angus.

25 *Tantallon*: just east of North Berwick on a spectacular site on the East Lothian coast. The castle was probably built by William, first Earl of Douglas, c. 1370.

72 *Benedictine*: Whitby Abbey on the coast of Yorkshire was a Benedictine foundation. Members of the order wore black gowns.

92 *Fitz-Eustace*: he and Blount are Marmion's squires.

110 *form . . . Hilda*: Whitby Abbey was founded by St Hilda (d. 680), whose shrouded figure was supposed to appear at certain times during the summer in one of the highest windows.

224 *Vengeance . . . belongs*: See Romans XII, 19: 'Dearly beloved, avenge not yourselves, but rather give place unto wrath: for it is written, Vengeance is mine; I will repay, saith the Lord.'

252–64 The events referred to here take place in Canto V. There the abbess has an interview with the palmer (she does not know that he is de Wilton) and gives him the documentary evidence of Marmion's crime which she herself got from Constance, and which de Wilton as a member of Marmion's party can take back to Henry VIII. She wants to keep Marmion from marrying Clare, so that Clare will remain a nun and bequeath her extensive property to the Abbey. Their interview is interrupted by a ghostly pageant at the Edinburgh market cross prophesying Flodden.

271 *Otterburne*: The Earl of Douglas defeated an English army under Sir Henry Percy ('Hotspur') at Otterburn, Northumberland, in 1388 but was killed in the battle.

280 *Twisell*: where James camped prior to Flodden.

284 *Surrey*: the English commander.

327 *Bishop*: Gavin Douglas (1475?–1522), son of the Earl of Angus. He completed his translation of Virgil's *Aeneid* into Scots in 1513. He did not become Bishop of Dunkeld till 1515, two years after Flodden.

500 *Master*: the Earl's oldest son, the Master of Angus.

540 *Lennel's convent*: A Cistercian religious house near Coldstream and very close to the battlefield.

545 *reverend pilgrim*: presumably Scott's friend Patrick Brydone.

546 *Bernardine*: The Abbey of Cîteaux was founded in 1098. St Bernard joined the community in 1112, founded his own monastery of Clairvaux in 1115, and such was the impact of his personality that by his death there were more than 300 daughter houses of Cîteaux and the whole order was associated with his name.

571 *Barmore-wood*: 'On the evening previous to the memorable battle of Flodden, Surrey's head-quarters were at Barmoor-wood, and King James held an inaccessible position on the ridge of Flodden-hills, one of the last and lowest eminences detached from the ridge of Cheviot. The Till, a deep and slow river, winded between the armies. On the morning of the 9th September, 1513, Surrey marched in a north-westerly direction, and, turning eastward, crossed the Till, with his van and artillery, at Twisell-bridge, nigh where that river joins the Tweed, his rear-guard column passing about a mile higher, by a ford. This movement had the double effect of placing his army between King James and his supplies from Scotland, and of striking the Scottish monarch with surprise, as he seems to have relied on the depth of the river in his front. But as the passage, both over the bridge and through the ford, was difficult and slow, it seems possible that the English might have been attacked to great advantage while struggling with natural obstacles. I know not if we are to impute James's forbearance to want of military skill, or to the romantic declaration which Pitscottie puts in his mouth, "that he was determined to have his enemies before him on a plain field," and therefore would suffer no interruption to be given, even by artillery, to their passing the river' (S.).

609 *Douglas*: Lord James of Douglas and Sir Thomas Randolph fought for King Robert I (the Bruce) in the early fourteenth century. Unlike James IV, they showed decided tactical and strategic intelligence. The war culminated in the Battle of Bannockburn (1314).

611 *Wallace*: see note on *The Cotter's Saturday Night*, l. 182.

715 *fronts . . . right*: corrected from 'Stout Stanley has the right' in the list of corrigenda in the first edition.

766 In later editions three lines are added between ll. 766 and 767:

> O, life and death were in the shout,
> Recoil and rally, charge and rout,
> And triumph and despair.

999 *Rowland . . . Olivier*: In the *Chanson de Roland*, two of Charlemagne's paladins, or knights, who, when conducting the rearguard of his army through a Pyrenean pass at Roncevalles in 778 were ambushed by the Saracens. When only fifty of Roland's men were left he blew his magic horn to summon Charlemagne. The climax of the battle was commonly said to have taken place at Fontarabia.

1070 Scott alludes to the false stories that Lord Home rescued, then murdered James IV and that James, feeling the disgrace of defeat, went on a pilgrimage. Home Castle was near Coldstream, on the Scottish side of Tweed, just north of Flodden.

1092 *Brook*: in the course of the civil war Lord Brook with parliamentary troops stormed Lichfield Cathedral. He was killed in the process. 'The royalists remarked, that he was killed by a shot fired from St Chad's Cathedral, and upon St Chad's day' (S.).

1108 '*wede away*': a reference to the refrain line of Jean Elliot's (1727–1805) song on Flodden (itself a reworking of an older one), 'The flowers of the forest are a' wede away'.

1152 *Hollinshed . . . Hall*: English chroniclers of the sixteenth century.

1164 *Wolsey*: Scott is giving an impression of a wedding of social and political significance, at the expense of historical probability. Thomas Wolsey, who became Archbishop of York in 1514, Henry VIII and Queen Catherine were, of course, established figures, but Thomas More had neither a political nor a religious reputation by this date. William Sandys (d. 1540) was well to the fore, but Sir Anthony Denny (d. 1549) was only thirteen at this time.

## Hogg, *The Witch of Fife*

Text: fifth edition, representing Hogg's final intentions. In the first edition the poem ended at line 272, with the old man actually 'burnit . . . skin and bone', but Scott induced Hogg to write a new ending more in keeping with 'the most happy and splendid piece of humorous ballad poetry which I ever wrote' (Hogg, *Familiar Anecdotes of Sir Walter Scott*, ed. Douglas S. Mack, Edinburgh, 1972, p. 123). It is sung by the eighth bard at the Queen's Wake, who hails from Leven in Fife:

> Of mountain ash his harp was framed,
> The brazen chords all trembling flamed,
> As in a rugged northern tongue,
> This mad unearthly song he sung.

The archaic spelling is a method of conveying this 'rugged' quality.

Hogg's language is pseudo-antique, although he correctly uses the middle Scots 'quh' for 'wh', 'is' where modern English just uses 's' for the plural, and 'it' in place of the past-participle ending 'ed'. But most words, if uttered aloud, are understandable.

40 *the Lommond height*: the Lomond Hills in Fife, overlooking Loch Leven, the home of the eighth bard to sing in the poetry festival in honour of Mary Queen of Scots.
105 *Doffrinis*: The Dovre Fjeld range in Norway.
115 *phantom hunteris*: the traditions concerning supernatural hunters are ancient and persistent. See 'the Wild Hunt' in Katherine Briggs, *A Dictionary of Fairies* (London, 1976).
167 *Ettrick Pen*: hill in the valley of the river Ettrick, near Hogg's birthplace.
171 *hillis of Braid*: low hills on the southern outskirts of Edinburgh.
173 *James*: presumably James V, the father of Mary Queen of Scots.

Hogg, *Kilmeny*

Text: fifth edition (1819), repesenting Hogg's final intentions. In 1819 Hogg left only a few obsolete forms like 'emerant' and 'littand', whereas his original spelling was consistently archaic, as in lines 14–17:

Quhan mony lang day had comit and fledde,
Quhan grief grew caulm, and hope was deade,
Quhan mes for Kilmeny's soul had beine sung,
Quhan the bedis-man had prayit, and the deide-bell rung.

The poem is sung by the thirteenth bard at the wake who hails from west Perthshire, where all the places mentioned are situated.

2 *Duneira*: Dunira is an estate to the east of Loch Earn, owned in 1813 by Lord Melville.
30 *the birk*: the birch tree was supposed to have magical qualities, e.g. *The Wife of Usher's Well*:

It fell about the Martinmass,
   When nights are lang and mirk,
The carlin wife's three sons came hame,
   And their hats were o' the birk.

It neither grew in syke nor ditch,
   Not yet in ony sheugh;
But at the gates o' paradise,
   That birk grew fair eneugh.

43 *airs of heaven*: the 'harp of the sky' is deliberately ambiguous, with a suggestion of that standard romantic property, the aeolian harp

(symbol of spontaneity and inspiration), while 'heaven' has undertones of the divine as well as of the open air.

181 *A lovely land*: Scotland.

202 *a lady sit on a throne*: Mary, Queen of Scots.

204 *A lion*: the heraldic emblem of Scotland.

210 *a gruff untoward bedeman*: someone representing the reformed Kirk of Scotland, such as John Knox.

220 *the gruff grim carle girned amain*: the quarrels of Charles I with the Kirk.

225 *the rose and clover leaf*: i.e. when king of England and Ireland, as well as Scotland.

238 *lilies and eagle*: symbols of France and of the Napoleonic empire.

245 *lion's*: Britain's.

295 *The wild beasts*: The whole passage suggests Isaiah XI, 6: 'The wolf also shall dwell with the lamb, and the leopard shall lie down with the kid; and the calf and the young lion and the fatling together; and a little child shall lead them.'

Hogg, *May of the Moril Glen*

Text: as first published in *Blackwood's Magazine*, 22 (July–Dec. 1827), pp. 214–21. It was only once republished in Hogg's lifetime, in *A Queer Book* (Edinburgh, 1832). In this edition, the antique language was modernised; but although the poem was easier to read, Hogg's broad Scottish accent was obscured and the original flavour of *Blackwood's* learned buffoonery was lost. Readers who find difficulty with Hogg's spelling are advised to read the poem aloud.

56 *fairye ringe*: place where fairies convene and where they can be seen by mortals.

Tennant, *Anster Fair*

Text: second edition of 1814, which has some slight alterations by the author on his first attempt, modernised according to the general principles of the anthology.

Introduction: 'Maggie Lauder'

18 *Habbie Simson*: hero of Robert Sempill of Beltrees' *The Life and Death of Habbie Simson, Piper of Kilbarchan.*

*Anster Fair*

1 *Troy and pettish heroes*: in Homer's *Iliad*, Achilles, the Greek warrior, quarrelled with his leader Agamemnon, and sulked in his tent, refusing to take a further part in the war with Troy.

4 *Mars*: god of war.

5 *Eden's garden*: Milton's epic poem *Paradise Lost* treats of the fall of men and 'loss of Eden'.

17 *Greekish hill*: Mount Parnassus, on which the Castalian spring, sacred to the Muses, was situated.

18 *Theban younker*: Pindar, the Greek poet, many of whose odes celebrated the victors in various Greek games and festivals.

19 The ancient Greeks believed that honey, if given to infants, would impart wisdom or eloquence.

27 *parsley*: the prizes in the Greek games were wreaths of wild olive, wild parsley, or laurel.

33 *Apollo*: the Greek god who was patron of poetry and music, associated with Mount Parnassus. Also called Phoebus.

35 *Chian rhapsodist*: Homer, whose *Odyssey* tells the story of the return of Odysseus (Ulysses) after nineteen years absence at the siege of Troy, and how he slew the suitors who had hoped to marry his wife Penelope.

37 *Atalant*: Atalanta refused to marry any man who could not defeat her in a race and those vanquished were put to death. Hippomanes, guided by Aphrodite (goddess of love), dropped one at a time the golden apples of the Hesperides ('daughters of evening') and Atalanta stopped to pick them up and so lost the race.

138 *th' bailies' loft*: In town churches special seats were often set aside for the town council, whose senior members were bailies, or magistrates.

145–65 *Carnbee . . . Barns . . . Lochmalonie . . . Auchmoutie*: all small estates or large farms in Fife.

171 *Jove's wheel'd stool*: Jove, as god of the heavens, drove his chariot across the sky each day.

183 *phoenix-nest*: a legend about this fabulous bird says that when it knows its life has to end, it makes a nest of spices, sings a song, sets fire to itself, and rises from its own ashes.

187 *ell*: the Scots ell was 37.2 inches, the English 45 inches.

195 *Iris*: goddess of the rainbow.

197 *Pleiads*: the seven stars of the constellation Pleiades.

202 *Gama*: Vasco da Gama (c. 1460–1524), the Portuguese sailor who discovered the sea-route to India in 1498. This episode occurs in *The Lusiad* by Luis de Camoens, Book V. A translation by W. J. Mickle had appeared in 1776. Camoens' model here was the phantom of Fame in *Aeneid* Book IV.

203 *tangle-tassel'd*: 'hung round with tangle (sea-weed) as with tassels.

I observe tangle in Bailey's Dict. though not in Johnson's' (Tennant).

247 *Oberon*: king of the fairies in Shakespeare's *A Midsummer Night's Dream*.

265 *Isle of May*: a small island at the mouth of the Firth of Forth, about five miles from Crail and eleven miles from North Berwick.

291 *Billyness*: the west headland of Anstruther Bay.

292 *Innergelly*: house near Anstruther.

295 *Pallas*: Pallas Athene, daughter of Zeus, supreme among the Greek gods.

311 *Midas*: one of the many indiscretions of the legendary King Midas was his judgment that Pan played the flute better than Apollo. For this tactless decision he had his ears changed into asses' ears by Apollo.

355 *North-Berwick Law*: the conical hill at North Berwick, across the Firth of Forth and visible from Anstruther.

382 *Stentor*: a Greek with a very loud voice, mentioned in Homer's *Iliad*.

390 *Parnassus*: the mountain north of Delphi in Greece, associated with the worship of Apollo and the nine Muses. It is particularly connected with poetry.

424 *Queen Dido*: Dido, Queen of Carthage, fell in love with Aeneas who arrived in her kingdom fleeing from the sack of Troy. The story of their love affair, and how Aeneas deserted her, and she as a result committed suicide, is told by Virgil in the *Aeneid*, Book IV.